# HOW THEY DID IT

Some drifted, it's true: "It just happened!" exclaims one woman with over a hundred stores around the world. Others planned their business concepts with the plodding organization of a Steven Spielberg, sketching out every scene on storyboards before shooting. But all of them have managed to build quite respectable, and often miraculously successful businesses.

Few, if any, of these Canadian entrepreneurs were original in their business concepts—"I plagiarize from only the *best* sources," cracked one—but they each saw a need, a niche in the marketplace, a chance to go for it, and they did.

Canada is overflowing with very impressive entrepreneurs, many of them exporting into the United States and around the world with as much gall and drive as any Yankee carpetbagger. Here are 80 of them, for your edification; they might well make you want to be number 81.

"This book is worth reading. Those not ignited by the entrepreneurial spirit will at least be assured that Canadian verve and imagination are creating a lot of jobs for fellow citizens."

—*The Calgary Herald*

*The*
# NEW
# ENTREPRENEURS

**80 Canadian Success Stories**

New and Revised Through 1987

**Allan Gould**

SEAL BOOKS
MCCLELLAND-BANTAM, INC.
TORONTO

THE NEW ENTREPRENEURS

*A Seal Book*

*Seal hardcover / October 1986*
*2 printings through November 1986*
*Seal paperback / December 1987*

*Original concept: Margaret Lindsay Holton*
*MLH Productions*
*Toronto, Canada*

*Canadian Cataloguing in Publication Data*

Gould, Allan, 1944–
  The new entrepreneurs

Includes index.
ISBN 0-7704-2186-5

1. Businessmen—Canada—Biography.
2. Entrepreneur—Biography. I. Title.

HC112.5.A2G68   1986       339'.092'2       C86-093502-7

*Seal Books are published by McClelland-Bantam Inc. Its trademark, consisting of the words*
*"Seal Books" and the portrayal of a seal, is the property of McClelland-Bantam Inc., 60*
*St. Clair Avenue East, Suite 601, Toronto, Ontario M4T 1N5 Canada. This trademark has*
*been duly registered in the Trademarks Office of Canada. The trademark, consisting of the*
*words "Bantam Books" and the portrayal of a rooster, is the property of and is used with*
*the consent of Bantam Books, Inc., 666 Fifth Avenue, New York, New York 10103. This*
*trademark has been duly registered in the Trademarks Office of Canada and elsewhere.*

PRINTED IN CANADA

COVER PRINTED IN U.S.A.

U    0 9 8 7 6 5 4 3 2 1

# CONTENTS

Racine, Bill Bartels, George Yui, Ernie Butler, Gerald J. Yaffe, Steve Chepa, Leslie Hulicsko, Sandy Archibald.

Barbara Crompton, Michael Levy, Sylvia Rempel, Mike Dyon, Alex Tilley, the Kent family, Harry Bondar, Dave Steele.

Andrew Alexander, John Pozer, Ian Fitzwilliam, Ann Millyard and Rick Wilks, Don McQuaig, Milds Nadal.

Steven Duffy, Sheldon Pollack, Barclay Isherwood, Sheldon Fulton, Alan Krofchick, Lois Warren, Dan Potter, Abe Schwartz.

# ACKNOWLEDGEMENTS

A person cannot write a book about nearly seven dozen business people from across this very large country of ours without some very large assistance. On a personal note, my thanks to Tom Gillman of Winnipeg, Dr. Sheldon Krakofsky of London, and Paul Grescoe of Vancouver, all of whom were more than generous with names of people and their businesses. The last, especially—one of Canada's finest journalists, and the coauthor of 1985's excellent *Money Rustlers*— was exceedingly helpful, showing a kindness with time and ideas which suggested Mother Teresa, in a field—business writing—which can often be more like Muammar el-Qaddafi.

Some of my greatest help in discovering Who Was Doing Interesting Things in the World of Business came from business writers on newspapers across Canada. I called many dozens of these men and women, who were, in nearly every single case, amazingly generous in sharing the most exciting, fascinating people in their respective towns and cities. To all of them, a very hearty, sincere thank you. And thanks, as well, to Brian K. Stanford at Pannell Kerr Forster Management Consultants, John Skeleton at Statistics Canada in Ottawa, and Anthony Carlson at the Canadian Federation of Independent Businesses.

A handful of these profiles, often in quite different form, has appeared in *Canadian Business*, *The Financial Post Magazine*, *Executive*, *Influence*, and *Kudos*. My appreciation to all the fine editors of those excellent publications, especially Margaret Wente, Chuck Davies, Helen Keeler, Patricia Anderson, Carla Micheli, Jim Cormier, and Bonnie Buxton.

Thank you, as well, to Lindsay Holton, who thought up the original concept of this book, and to my delightful, inspired publisher, Janet Turnbull, for her superb advice and guidance, including her fine choice of Margaret Woollard as initial editor. And to my beloved wife, Merle, and our beautiful children, Judah and Elisheva—I'm back now.

Allan Gould
Toronto, February 1987

In the first few weeks of 1987, I telephoned every single one of the entrepreneurs profiled in this book, to bring it up to date, even providing projections through December 1987. I spoke to all but a tiny handful and made hundreds of changes, many of them major. How promising and hopeful that over 90% were thriving, expanding, even rocketing in sales, stores, and/or services, in less than two years since they were originally visited. Congratulations to them all—and thank you.

# INTRODUCTION

Four out of five new businesses fold in their first three years of life. It is a statistic which is repeated again and again in numerous business books. Yet tens of thousands of small businesses are begun every year in Canada. Even in 1982, the peak—or was it the depth?—of that dreadful recessionary period, 84,000 out of 785,000 small businesses closed, and 10,765 went bankrupt. Yet 87,000 firms were *born* in that awful year of astronomical interest rates and flat economic growth!

Why? Why should men and women across Canada quit their old jobs, or set out and begin new ones? What is there in so many of us that chooses to risk all, work 60 to 90 hour weeks, brave the mockery of others, Take the Big Step?

Most would think that it's the hope for wealth and material possessions, but that is simply not so, if one believes the stories of 80 men and women profiled in this book. "I'm money-conscious," says one of them, since "that's what society keeps score on." But less than a half dozen of these dozens and dozens of Canadian entrepreneurs gave "money" as a major reason for why they have done what they've done.

No, it's a hundred other things, but rarely money alone. "The excitement of building something" is what one businessman stated, and it was echoed by dozens of others. "My heart was in business," says another, whose father had been pushing him toward a career in medicine. "If you help enough other people to do well, they'll help you," says a third. "I'm never content with the status quo," says a woman entrepreneur from the west. "There's almost nothing I can't do."

And there isn't, for nearly everyone in this book. Some drifted, it's true: "It just happened!" exclaims one woman with over a hundred stores around the world. Others planned their business concepts with the plodding organization of a Steven Spielberg, sketching out every scene on story-boards before shooting. But all of them have managed to build quite respectable, and often miraculously successful, businesses.

Early in this project, I decided *not* to limit the ways someone could be included in this book. If a man borrowed $30,000 from a parent to start his business, so what? If he ended up as a success, should the family assistance—or help from a bank, or a government grant, for that matter—deny his business acumen? Similarly, if a woman received financial assistance from a father or spouse, I refused to let this deny her the chance to have her story told.

There is a real cross section of Canadian entrepreneurs here, and that's what I think we need to get a sense of just how impressive and creative our business minds can be. There are men and women from small towns (Moose Jaw and North Battleford in the west, Moncton and Bridgetown in the east), as well as from the major cities across Canada. They come from every province in this country, as well as from the United States, England, West and East Germany, Bulgaria, Yugoslavia, Hungary, South Africa, Israel, Japan, Korea, even Manchuria. They are black, white, Oriental, Quebecois, Acadian, Protestant, Catholic, Jew.

There are men and women who did it on their own, as well as several brother teams, sister teams, complete families, and husband/wife combinations. There are many others who hooked up with a partner who has been invaluable (although I usually wrote about only one). Some needed banks to get started, and federal or provincial grants to keep going, while others were either refused the loan or grant, or refused to take it when it was offered. Some were satisfied with one store; others spun them off into dozens and even hundreds—some totally company-owned, others franchised. (And since there are other statistics which say that four out of five franchisees are *still* in business after the first three years, it is good to see so many of the men and women in this book creating *safer* small businesses for future entrepreneurs to enter in the years to come.)

Was it environmental factors which drove these people to become entrepreneurial? In some cases, yes, whether pushed by recollections of poverty, or by their parents, or (by the classic immigrant's desire to prove himself in a new society.) Ethnicity? In many cases. A dissatisfaction with an earlier job? Occasionally. A high need for self-esteem? Often. A sense that "I'm smarter than these other guys"? Frequently.

Most of all, you will find a strong sense of *innovation* in each of these entrepreneurs. A creativity. A longing to start something. One could even say a refusal ever to be satisfied, even with fortune. One millionaire (with three dozen stores) exclaimed, "I don't feel successful; you're only successful if you've done everything that you want to do."

Which means that many of these men and women will move on to other business concepts in the future, whether in spite of, or because of, what they have created so far. (Indeed, a number of these entrepreneurs had started businesses which either succeeded or failed before they hit upon the one which led to their being included here.)

It was a struggle to decide how to divide so many business profiles, and I finally chose to list them under the fields in which they created their businesses: food, shelter, beauty and fashion, service, manufacturing, and so on. I felt that this would have more meaning to the reader than to bunch them under educational background, or sex, or partners, or families. This way, you can follow the various, widely diverse tales of success in a single industry, regardless of how they did it, all in a single section. (Even this proved to be a problem, as you might well imagine; some Food entries could have been listed under Stores or Service; the same with a few Beauty and Fashion profiles, which could have been gathered in the Manufacturing chapter.)

Perhaps most important, I should note that I refused to limit this book only to wildly successful stories or rags-to-riches tales, or only to new millionaires or heads of firms that have sales above $25 million annually. To do this, I felt, would be to keep so many fascinating business stories, and lives, from being shared. And, in fact, many of the smaller firms at the time of this writing could well be large ones by the end of this decade. And some others, alas, could conceivably die. So while a number of the men and women in this book have created businesses which have gone from zero to $10, $50, even $250 *million* in annual sales, others have struggled, or are still struggling, to crack their first million. I found the latter just as interesting and as informative as the former. And Lord knows, they are more typical!

*In Search of Excellence*, that runaway best seller about "America's Best-Run Companies," spoke of eight attributes which tended to characterize the finest corporations studied: a bias for action ("getting on with it"); closeness to the customer (quality, service, reliability); autonomy and entrepreneurship; productivity through people (respecting the workers); hands-on, value-driven policy; a tendency to stick to the knitting (staying close to what you know); simple form, lean staff; and simultaneous loose-tight properties (core values, but often chaotic in their decentralization). Although these attributes refer, by and large, to gigantic American companies of up to hundreds of thousands of employees, they are astonishingly reflective of the values which have made these Canadian entrepreneurs so successful. Nearly every one of the business people in this book spoke of at least a half dozen of these eight aspects of success, usually without knowledge of the Peters and Waterman book: Quotations about "just go ahead and do the jump," the importance of quality and service, need for innovation, "we motivate all our people," corporate culture and values, doing what they do best, being "lean and mean," "controlled growth": It is as if almost every successful entrepreneur comes to these decisions by near-instinct—or they will just not survive.

Few, if any, of these Canadian entrepreneurs were original in their business concepts—"I plagiarize from only the *best* sources," cracked one—but they each saw a need, a niche in the marketplace, a chance to go for it, and they did.

Canada, in spite of the lousy press it gets about its people—living in the shadow of a Giant is never, ever easy—is overflowing with very impressive entrepreneurs, many of them exporting into the United States and around the world with as much gall and drive as any Yankee carpetbagger. Here are 80 of them, for your edification; they might well make you want to be number 81.

# 1.
# THE FOOD INDUSTRY

### *Eats, Drinks, and Be Merry*

The *one* thing that the baker's dozen in this chapter have in common—besides many of them baking—is that they all provide *some* form of nourishment to Canadians and North Americans, and have been doing this, often with explosive success, over the past number of years.

Mark Henderson brought his Labrador Spring Water to millions of thirsty Quebecois; North Americans everywhere are enjoying breakfast, lunch, dinner, and snacks at Michael Bregman's Michel's Baguettes and mmmuffins, Inc.; sisters Tara and Gayle Hallgren offer Cookies by George to Canadians in the west (and, as of 1987, moving into the east as well), while Earl Barish of Winnipeg sells his Dickie Dee treats across the continent; Maritimers enjoy pizza, and more, because of Bernard Cyr of Moncton; many dozens of Cultures Fresh Food Restaurants (fathered by London, Ontario's Hal Gould) and Druxy's Delis (mothered by Winnipeg/Toronto's Bruce Druxerman) provide many thousands of lunches and dinners every day across our country; dinners can be purchased and enjoyed at the many stores across North America run and even created by Winnipeg's Oscar Grubert (Kentucky Fried Chicken and Mother Tucker's Food Experience, among others), as well as the rapidly multiplying O'Toole's Roadhouse Restaurants, and others, of Toronto's Gord Metcalfe; and Edmontonians have grown dependent upon the culinary/ business genius of Saul Reichert. And for those of you who consider their taste buds gourmet as well as gourmand, do not pass up the millions of pounds of fresh lobster sold by John Risley of Halifax, savor the classy meals and cookbooks of Vancouver's Susan Mendelson, and top it all off with some wine and spirits from Anthony von Mandl's vineyards and distilleries on the west coast.

Beyond the food and beverage hook, what do these men and women have in common? Not much. Mark Henderson of Labrador Spring Water flunked out of first-year university, while Michael Bregman of mmmuffins, Inc., has probably the best business education one can receive in the world today: Pennsylvania's Wharton School of Finance, and a Harvard M.B.A. Mother Tucker's Oscar Grubert is a Winnipeg lawyer, while John Risley hated every minute of his three "wasted" years at Halifax's Dalhousie. Gord Metcalfe taught geography in suburban Toronto, and Susan Mendelson did social work with disturbed teens in Vancouver. Some are the children of millionaires; others are the offspring of immigrants or impoverished families, even orphans. I could go on and on, except that I'm getting hungry.

Which is, perhaps, the point. For Canadians have never before been so hungry to eat out, drink pure water or good wine, enjoy a cookie, muffin, ice cream, or lobster, or have something catered for them. Some statistics: Under the headline "Bright Future Predicted for Canadian Bottled Industry," the *Canadian Beverage Review* of March/April 1984 reported that "the industry as a whole recorded sales of $36.4 million in 1983—an increase of more than $10 million from the year previous."

*Advertising Age* noted in early 1986 the "huge growth in the breakfast segment"—the customer count in the A.M. leapt 46% between 1978 and 1984, with a large potential for growth, since the average soul—still not listening to mother—continues to skip 22% of morning meals. Ethnic foods remain hugely popular in North America, and "grazing" has become extremely common, with light, casual meals and snacks throughout the day, in lieu of three major meals—primarily finger foods, such as vegetables, dips, pasta salads, and minipizzas.

In a sentence: Consumers spend well over 30% of their food budget on meals away from home (single Canadians, 37.7%) and *eat* 19% of their meals away from home. True, statistics sometimes seem unpromising, such as the fact that Canada's per capita annual consumption of wine is below that of almost every Western nation, even most Common Bloc countries (France, 96 litres; Italy, 93 L; Portugal, 70 L; Spain, 65 L; Hungary, 35 L; Yugoslavia, 27.33 L; Czechoslovakia, 15.5 L; Soviet Union, 14.4 L; East Germany, 9.5 L; and Canada, a sobering 8.8 L: *Foodservice & Hospitality*, April 1984). Yet in spite/because of this lack of interest in having on their tables Château Canuck 1975 instead of Classic Coke 1986 ("a bit pretentious, but with a sparkling aftertaste and a traditional effervescence"), our countrymen have made Anthony von Mandl's Mark Anthony Group one of the great success stories of the past decade.

For all the extraordinary growth in eating-out patterns across North America, opening a restaurant has traditionally been the fastest way of going belly-up, pun intended, with the exception of playing penny stocks on the VSE. "There is nothing faddier than food fads," says Michael Bregman. But these men and women have done it, whether with one store or one hundred, wholesale or retail, a few dozen employees or a few thousand. Why?

We *could* look at the childhoods of these entrepreneurs for some clues: Mark Henderson was given no allowance by his businessman father, and was ordered to "work hard"; Michael Bregman had a (wealthy) father and (poor) grandfather in the baking business; Earl Barish was selling ice cream from a bike at 14, and had purchased his first eight bikes (and a business) only two years later; poverty-stricken Acadian Bernard Cyr, the second of ten children, sold cod tongues as a child to earn money to purchase a bicycle; Saul Reichert starved in Poland and in the death camps of Hitler ("I want to succeed and *do* something" he says); John Risley made (and lost) a fortune in the stock market and in real estate as a young man; Susan Mendelson was obsessed with cooking from her childhood; Anthony von Mandl was fascinated by wine and food since his youth. But that hardly explains the first quarter century of drifting of the sisters Hallgren before they finally began Cookies by George in Vancouver, or the upper-class upbringing of Hal Gould and Bruce Druxerman before they began to open their Cultures and Druxy's places in neighbouring locations across Canada, or Oscar Grubert's lack of knowledge of restaurants—he was kosher, for God's sake—before he "got in on the ground floor of the fast-food trend" in Winnipeg, or Gord Metcalfe's background in teaching before building an empire of three dozen-plus stores, 2,000 employees, and over $50 million in sales, all in the first 36 months (!).

No, what we have in this chapter is a collection of Canadians who latched onto brilliant, often inspired, food and beverage concepts at a time when North American families were fragmenting, becoming richer, with women joining the job market (and, ergo, less anxious to cook after a hard day at the office). And, it must be noted, none of the profiles that follow is of people with original ideas: What could be less original than Mark Henderson bottling spring water? Or Michael Bregman actually stealing the idea of giant, high-priced, high-quality muffins from a man who brought them into the Loblaw's store where he was working? Or Tara and Gayle Hallgren ripping off the idea of fresh-baked cookies after seeing successful stores offering the product in New York? Or Earl Barish buying out someone else's ice cream bike business? Or Bernard Cyr joining Pizza Delight when it was a small firm? Or Hal Gould listening to his mamma, who tasted frozen yoghurt being sold in New York and liked it?

You get the idea. There *is* nothing new under the sun in eating and drinking, to paraphrase Ecclesiastes, with his kind permission. But these men and women *saw a need*. In some cases, it was sparked by a highly personal matter, such as Gord Metcalfe's situation: He needed a place for the employees at the craft kit business which he ran, where they could grab a fast bite and return to work, and it was such a runaway success, he heard gold tinkling in the cash registers. In Oscar Grubert's case, it was a simple observation: In his Winnipeg neighbourhood, there was a lot of traffic and no drive-in eatery to satisfy the people. John Risley of Halifax felt the Maritime "affinity to the sea," bought and sold lobster, and then "saw an opportunity in Europe," which led to $30 million in sales and 350 employees when I wrote this book in 1985/86 and $115 million and more than 2,100 employees by 1987! Anthony von Mandl "anticipated the white wine boom" and, like everyone in this chapter, was "aggressive" as all get-out.

Henderson of Labrador Spring Water calls it "timing and luck," but that's too modest and almost self-deprecating. Writing thank-you notes to former clients, insisting on "polite delivery men," flooding his staff with gifts, free trips, and wine, manoeuvring his product into grocery stores across Quebec—these are hardly "timing and luck." Nor is there "timing and luck" in the tradition of the Hallgren sisters to pay their employees for "bright ideas" to sell their cookies. Nor is Earl Barish's hiring large numbers of disabled to sell his frozen treats; Hal Gould's and Bruce Druxerman's personally designing better plastic containers for their food; Oscar Grubert's continual tryouts of new restaurant concepts in Winnipeg. "I'm commited to whatever I do," says von Mandl of the Mark Anthony Group, and he speaks for them all: an insistence on quality—whether the stores are franchised or company-owned; a refusal to take much money home until long after the firms are well established; and insistence on driving themselves and their businesses; a frequent risk-taking; a sense of fun, tempered by determination.

Sure, Canadians (and Americans) have to eat and drink, but they didn't have to eat and drink at *these* people's tables, and nibble and sip *their* products. But they have, by the tens of millions, and it is a cause for celebration. And like their multitude of satisfied customers, these entrepreneurs will never, ever starve.

# MAKING MONEY
# LIKE WATER

### Mark Henderson

If the classic "tip" of the stockholder to his or her client is "buy low and sell high," then what would be the perfect suggestion of the successful businessperson to someone starting out? Find a product that's cheap and sell it for a lot? In the case of Mark Henderson of Montreal, he couldn't make, much less find, a product at a lower price: His product was water, which he bottled and made millions from. It didn't hurt to have the support of a faithful father, either, and inspired salesmanship also helped. But what could be more basic than good old $H_2O$?

Mark Henderson, model-handsome in his dark blue suit, hasn't got a grey strand showing in his thick head of hair, and he's in his late 40s. But why should he? In 1984 he sold his Labrador Spring Water Ltd. to one of the largest food conglomerates on the planet, Nestlés, for a very large sum of money. "I've never worked for anyone else in my life," he states almost apologetically in his corner office at Goodhost Foods, a division of Nestlés, in Don Mills, Ontario, where he moved in 1985. And when one hears his tale of hard work and brilliant success, one quickly understands why he's never wanted to work for anyone else.

Henderson, an only child, was born in Vancouver in the

summer of 1938. Not long after, the family moved to Montreal. His father had been an entrepreneur in a small oil business, Bardahl Lubricating Ltd., which he had cofounded in Vancouver in 1942. But the major market in Canada was still in the east, and his wife was from Montreal, and so they moved. "It must have been a tremendous influence on me to see my dad found a business," Henderson says today.

He learned two basic things from his father: If he wanted success, he would have to work hard. And he must treat other people as he would wish to be treated. (His father, who died a few years ago, was an "extremely religious" Christian Scientist, who filled his son with a profound sense of business ethics and honesty. "I've often been asked why I don't put more money into my pocket," Henderson says. "Why I don't milk the till.")

Henderson's father never gave his son an allowance; it was understood that he would have to go out and work for it. Like many children, young Mark delivered newspapers and sold magazines, and he swears that, during the 1950s, from the age of 13 on, he was never with less than $600 in his pocket each year. And the moment he turned 17, he bought a car. Although his father ended up with a franchise operation which he sold back to the company, and made a good living, he "never lived high off the hog." The family lived in a duplex in Montreal, in fact.

At the age of 18 Mark Henderson gave up his father's religion, "but I didn't give up the ethics." He joined the United Church. (A generation later, his two daughters are rebelling in their turn.) He went to Bishop's University in Lennoxville, Quebec, and flunked out the first year. "I took arts and played," he recalls. "All I wanted to do was work and *sell*."

As a teenager, the lad had read an article in *Canadian Business* about a vending company in Toronto. He picked up a phone and called the owner. "I told him that the business fascinated me, that vending seemed like the coming thing in the 'sixties. I told him that I'd like to see him for an interview."

The boss must have been impressed by a kid who would call him from Montreal. Henderson took a train to Toronto and got "hired on the spot." "He saw a young man full of piss and vinegar who had a dream: I wanted to sell."

He began by taking a training course and serviced the

machines, but soon was given the opportunity to sell them—lease them, actually, to companies of 150 employees and more. But it wasn't very long before the words of his father, who had retired at the age of 58, came to him: "If you are ever interested in going into business for yourself, talk with me."

In addition, a concept was growing in the minds of each of the Hendersons: It was evident that supplying machines to offices should speed up the coffee break. But everyone was still taking a kettle to the washroom, which is time-consuming. Father and son wanted to provide a machine that supplied not only continuous hot water but also the packets of coffee. "My hook to selling it was, you save time! Press a button, take a cup, pour in the ingredients, and go back to your desk!" And this product, unlike the vending machines he'd been selling in Toronto, would be sold to companies with as few as 5 employees, up to 20.

Henderson's dad put $92,000 into the fledgling firm, and J. A. Henderson & Son Ltd. was born. Mark Henderson sold for seven years, but by the time he had 400 clients it became evident that they were paying too much for coffee from General Foods, among others. Since his father owned an industrial motor oil called Labrador and had a trademark for it that included "Picture of Dog," he already had a name for his latest idea.

In 1963 Mark Henderson began purchasing coffee in 50-pound bags and putting it into little packets. He did the same with hot chocolate, iced tea, and lemonade, and packaged them for their firm. Understandably, they were able to sell the packets to their clients at a greater profit for a much smaller price, which is what capitalism is all about, isn't it?

In 1964 he married, but was still taking only $45 a week home. "I was earning a third less than my friends—I always took a low salary—and they must have thought, 'Boy, Henderson is conservative!' "

But not so conservative as to be unaware of further potential and possibilities for growth. By 1968 he had 1,000 accounts and could readily see that the business could grow no further without another line added to it. "It was obvious that we should go into bottled water," he declares, as if it were as plain as water in the tap.

So Mark Henderson did what many people do when they

want to buy something—although it's usually bicycles or couches: He put an ad in the paper. (He had tried to buy a competitor but couldn't raise the money; his father refused to put any more cash into the business. "I spoke French, but Dad did not. And the Quiet Revolution was getting noisier.")

The advertisement read, "SPRING OR ARTESIAN WELL WANTED, WITHIN FIFTY MILES RADIUS OF MONTREAL." He received 82 responses. Henderson started going through them, but it was clear by the time he reached number 18 that this was an exercise in frustration more than geography or business. He was dealing primarily with farmers, and their wells often had iron in them, or smelled of sulphur. "In many cases," he says, "the water was just plain shitty."

So Henderson, Sr., managed to dig up old books on the City of Montreal before the aqueduct system was put in. "The city is a good area for springs and wells," notes his son. They began exploring old bread and milk companies, as well as soft drink manufacturers, who had used water from wells. Nothing came of it. And the cost and complications of going into Molson's parking lot and obtaining a capped spring well were overwhelming.

Meanwhile, an offer came from what would soon become his chief competitor: Laurentian Spring Water, which had sales of nearly half a million dollars annually at the time, selling five-gallon bottles to offices and homes, and had been around Montreal for nearly a century. They offered to make Henderson a partner, and he would have doubled his salary, but he refused the marriage offer.

Finally, in desperation, Mark Henderson went to well-drillers and asked them bluntly, "Where are there good springs and wells?" He eventually paid $3,500 to have a well drilled for him, and worked out a deal with the farmer who owned the land: He would pay the man $10 a month for a fraction of an acre and access to it. It must have seemed like found money to the farmer, but it was a dream come true for the city slicker.

It wasn't all that easy; they drilled several other wells, which came up either cloudy or filled with too much iron. But with this farmer, they had clicked, and the well was only 40 miles from Henderson's plant—coincidentally, just where the

Laurentian mountains start. It was to be where the Labrador fortune would begin.

"Literally, we struck gold!" says Henderson today with a grin. "Because it was a *gusher* of water. Water poured from it at a rate of 1,500 gallons an hour, without pumping!" Water, of course, is free; all the costs are in the transportation and packaging; tank trucks would haul it in. And, *bien sûr*, Henderson had it tested and just knew that this was great water.

The president of the moist firm is well aware that he had "great timing and luck," and not merely in finding the Hemlo of Water. Although there was only one other spring water company in Montreal at the time, today there are 33 companies selling either spring or mineral water in the province of Quebec!

Within 18 months at least 90% of his 1,000 accounts were taking bottled water from Henderson's firm, happy to have the cleaner taste for their coffee machines. But there were other reasons for Labrador's success. "We were aggressive," Henderson emphasizes. "We showed interest in our clients where many others took it for granted that they had a customer."

For instance, he insisted on "polite, clean-looking, well-dressed delivery men." There was regular contact with all customers. And if anyone should ever cancel their order, "we'd write thank-you notes for their business." Henderson worked long hours—often until 9:00 at night, 5½ days a week, and it paid off in, suitably, a Niagara Falls pattern—except that the profit line flowed *up*. From 1969 to 1984 they had a growth rate of less than 30% only once, and that year it was 20%. When they went into the water business, their sales were $300,000, with three or four employees. When Henderson walked out the door, in February 1985, the sales were over $8 million, with 40 employees and a fortune in highly automated equipment. "We were bottling seventy four-litre bottles every minute," he states proudly.

There is a happy sideline to a flowing well: It can be pumped 24 hours a day, day in and day out, at up to 6,000 gallons an hour. And that's 48 million gallons a year. By 1974 Henderson purchased the land, three acres in total, from the happy farmer, for $7,500. When Nestlés finally purchased it from Henderson, they put down the value of the spring *alone* at $300,000.

In the meantime, Henderson was hardly striking it rich; his salary did not creep above $30,000 until 1979, and he lived in a $36,000 house in Montreal. Yet with all his self-denial, "it was a tremendous job to finance the growth of the business. I had to mortgage my car, my house, to retain ownership." He was right to do so; he owned 100% of Labrador Spring Water Ltd.—his father had $90,000 in preferred shares—when he sold out. By that time, the food industry, always looking for a new trend, saw bottled water as having a high profile. "A. C. Nielsen had bottled water on the top of their list," Henderson says, happily.

Mark Henderson always showed remarkable marketing ability; witness how he created his coup of being the first into supermarkets with a one-gallon and a litre-and-a-half container. ("That's what *really* took off," he declares. "Small groceries, health food stores, and finally large supermarkets.")

"I used a small businessman's way of using his clout." After getting into Steinberg's supermarkets, he went to an ad agency in 1971 with a mere $5,000—"just peanuts." For this amount, he had 180 billboards made up and placed on the sides of buses. "We wanted to let the world know that we had bottled water available at leading supermarkets."

Careful readers will note that Henderson did not have his water in all supermarkets; only at Steinberg's. But note his plan: "Eventually, I got secretaries, employees, everyone I knew, to go and see store managers with their shopping carts half full, and say, 'I've bought Labrador at other markets; where is it here?'" Within a year and a half, every supermarket in Quebec was carrying Henderson's brand. Laurentian ended up sticking with water cooler rentals and larger spring water container sales.

By 1978 his firm broken $1 million a year in sales and had a 16,000-square-foot factory. And by 1981 he was approached by, and refused to sell to, five major firms, including Nestlés and Quaker Oats. "Why sell out?" he remembers thinking. "There is no reason to sell. I'm young, active, healthy, enjoy the work; I've got a great team."

But after Nestlés approached him three times in a single week, and when he was about to go into a business of creating the molding of his own plastic containers—and triple his plant size—things began to get tense. For one thing, the interest rates climbed rapidly up to 21½% in August 1981, and Nestlés put it rather crudely: "Everyone has his price, Henderson. What's yours?" When interest rates went up another ¾%, he wondered to himself, "Will they go to 30%? Will I be ruined?"

So Henderson named a price and vowed that he wouldn't vary a cent from it. After three months more of discussion, Nestlés told him, "Switzerland has accepted the total dollar figure but will give only 60% on Day One, and you'll have to be on an earn-out over the next three years." Since the president of Labrador had projected growth at 30% a year, he said yes—and ended up receiving 104% of his asking price, because sales were so good. He went home, probably a millionaire—he won't say how much he got from Nestlés—and redid the kitchen for his wife. For himself, he bought a Porsche (a used one costing $47,000).

Henderson may have sold out, but he is still proud as a papa over what he created. "Labrador was always first!" he enthuses. "First into supermarkets. First into smaller packages to compete with European products such as Evian. And first into computerization in 1974."

Henderson's other genius, beyond selling water to a country which overflows with the stuff, was his ability to motivate other people. Instead of a week's salary bonus at Christmas time, he and his vice-president would go out to department stores and buy $3,000 in gifts—toasters, hair dryers, electric frying pans—all between $30 and $60, and at the company party, they'd pick numbers out of a hat. "There was a table covered with forty feet of glitter!" he says. "They couldn't get over it."

In thanks and appreciation to his three dozen employees, he would give trips out, to Mexico, Nassau, Florida, as many as two or three a year, TO THE BEST TRUCK DRIVER, and so on. Once, he gave Casio watches to every man in the bottling room, shook their hands, and sent them all home early. On another occasion, at the end of a nondescript week, when no one would expect it, he bought a pile of vouchers at restaurants and bought cases of wine for them.

"I had the golden business," declares Mark Henderson, now on staff, along with 155,000 others around the world, at Nestlés. "I'm sorry I sold out. There are a lot of what if's but I did cash in." And there are other changes as well: "I *can* work for someone else," he says. "I'm the only VP of my division. Anyway, I'm not working for money anymore. I always dreamed of having it, but once you have it, there's a new range of values. I happen to like work."

But the greatest satisfaction one can get, according to Mark Henderson, "is not the money you take home; it's the business, the equity you're building." Besides, he says, if he does well at Nestlés, he'll get a 15% bonus. "Of course, if you're on your own," he says, darkly, 'it's *limitless*.'"*

# HAVE YOU SEEN THE MMMUFFIN MAN?

### *Michael Bregman*

The 1980s, as is only too well known, have been the burial ground for thousands of small businesses across Canada. Restaurants have opened and closed like so many dull Broadway plays, and various franchises have gone belly-up faster than you can shout, "Over 50 Billion Served!"

Then there is mmmuffins, Inc., which opened its first store in the last month of the last year of the 1970s. As of the end of 1987, exactly eight years later, there were over 90 of them across Canada. (There is also a second concept, Michel's Baguettes, a bakery-restaurant, which opened its first door in April of 1980. Today there are 12 of them across Canada. The 23 in the U.S. recently sold to a competitor, Vie de France. Let's put it another way: Sales were $4 million at the end of their fiscal year in September 1981; sales were $36 million at the end of 1987.

But that is merely the entrepreneurial glory of Michael Bregman, 33 years old and a graduate of the renowned Wharton School of Finance in Pennsylvania, and Harvard Business School. To fully grasp the majesty of the Bregman legacy— and there are now over 2,200 men and women who receive paycheques, due to his creativity in business—one must reach

---

*By the end of 1985—are you surprised?—Henderson had split from Nestlés, and was looking for a new business to buy into. Thus are the ways of entrepreneurs. By early 1987, he owned a minority interest in The Water Man, Inc., of Hawaii, doubling sales from $1 million to $2.2 million, and purchased 50% of a water-softening company in Quebec, Aqua D'or Inc., the biggest in the province. Eat your heart out, Gunga Din.

back into the nineteenth century, and the country from where so many who have changed the face of North American culture, entertainment, and finance have come: Russia.

The grandfather of Michael Bregman worked in a bagel factory in the Old Country, where the product was extremely popular. As it happens, the Revolution was not, and the young baker came to Canada in 1919. Toronto was still an outpost of the British Empire at the time, and the Jewish community was extremely small—only a few thousand, compared with 125,000 in 1981. And like most of our parents or grandparents, Max Bregman made a living, but little more. He worked endless days, going from bakery to bakery, baking bagels for each. As his son and grandson would discover years later, there was a need that cried out to be filled: In Max's case, a wholesale shop of his own would make his life a lot easier.

Starting downstairs from where his wife and five children lived, Max Bregman began his new business in Toronto's Kensington Market. By the middle of World War II he was supplying 15 stores around the city, and did well enough to open his own bagels-and-everything-else bakery.

Now, to the second generation of Canadian Bregmans: that of Lou. Even before his bar mitzvah, he was slugging it out in his father's business. ("I think I was *born* baking bagels!" Lou says today, handsome, chunky, smiling.) Dropping out of school before completing grade 9, Lou Bregman worked with his father until 1947, then went off to California to work as a bagel baker in Los Angeles. After a few more years baking in Miami, he returned to Toronto in 1952, borrowed $500, and leased a small shop on Baldwin Street. He wisely joined up with his chief competitor, and by 1954, the year his father, Max, died, they were selling up to 900 dozen bagels every day and 2,000 dozen on Saturdays.

And then, the biggest move yet, and the riskiest: In 1957 he and his wife of five years—with future muffin king Michael in tow—sold their home in suburban Toronto for $3,500, moved in with her parents, and opened the Bagel King, "the first retail bagel shop in North America."

Remember King Midas? The Bregmans seemed to have the same effect on bagels. It was an instant success, with wife Yetta working cash and Lou doing the baking and one waitress waiting on the ten stools. In the first four years of operation, the place was enlarged four times; by 1961 the Bagel King seated 120, employed 45, and sold more than 3,000 dozen bagels in 15 varieties every week.

Some anecdotes from this period: Some fights occurred when one man asked for a few dozen bagels, and the person behind him in line would scream that he was being piggish and didn't need so many for himself. And what of the woman from Florida who dumped her clothes out of her suitcase and ordered Lou Bregman to fill her now-empty luggage with bagels (requesting paper bags to put her clothes in)? Or the requests from Ottawa, Vancouver, even *Alaska*, for 10, 12, 15 *dozen* bagels at a time?

(Before one comes to the false conclusion that bagels have some kind of grotesque effect on people of the Jewish faith, let it be pointed out that the vast majority of Bregman's clientele were not Jewish. As Lou Bregman told a *Toronto Daily Star* reporter back in 1967, "There aren't enough Jews in Toronto to eat all the bagels I make." He estimated that three out of four customers were not Jewish, suggesting just how much the taste buds of Canada have been ethnicized by men like Lou Bregman.)

From the meteoric success of the Bagel King restaurant, there was no looking back. More Bagel Kings sprang up in two other suburban Toronto locations, a wholesale business was purchased, and two pie specialty shops were also opened. And then, in his beautiful wife's charming words, "the sardine swallowed the whale."

The sardine was, of course, Lou Bregman, who was doing about $2½ million worth of business in 1971, slightly up from the few rubles a week of his father, Max, back in the USSR. The whale was Canadian Food Products, a subsidiary of the giant Kellogg Company of Battle Creek, Michigan, which had an annual revenue of approximately $20 million from its Hunt's and Woman's Bakery stores but was none the less losing money on them. In an attempt to cut costs, CFP asked Lou Bregman, from whom it purchased kaiser rolls, to lower his price. Bregman said no, but was kind enough to offer a possible solution to their problems—he would buy them out.

Not alone, mind you. Bregman, another baker named Moe Arbus, and the Toronto real estate firm of Del Zotto Enterprises Ltd. combined to come up with the purchase price of about $4 million. Bregman became president, with 25% of the business (soon become 35% when Arbus sold out), and the man who had started Bagel King with two employees in 1957—one of them his bed-partner—now found himself with 2,000 employees, selling products to 130 retail stores and 370 supermarkets.

Once again, Lou Bregman's touch was golden. A new plant was built in Weston, Ontario, and Hunt's and Woman's Bakery stores prospered as never before. But for all the joy of adding challahs and bagels to the shopping lists of hundreds of thousands of Ontarians, there was something missing: He had lost touch with small stores, with the feel of dough rising beneath his fingers. In 1978 Lou Bregman got out, selling his 35% to the Del Zottos, and planned to retire. (Fat chance. His son Michael, then 24 and fresh out of Harvard with his M.B.A., urged Lou to start up a new business with him. They opened a bakery-restaurant called, of all things, Bregman's, which did magnificently from the moment it opened, and continues to thrive today, even after Lou sold out in 1983.)

Which brings us to the third and latest generation of the Brilliantly Businesslike Baking Bregmans: Michael Bregman. If a grandfather could make a go of it, baking in the Old Country, and continue in the New, and if his son could become middle class at 35, be rich at 40, retire at 50, and unretire at 51, with a grade 8 certificate from a Toronto school, then would two top-notch business degrees necessarily ruin the business and baking sense of Michael Bregman? Not at all. (There is irony galore in all of this; please read the words of Lou Bregman, interviewed by a newspaper reporter in 1961, when he was in his early 30s: "It's just too hard. You can make a wonderful living from it, but it's just too hard. I'm here from ten each morning to four the following morning, seven days a week. It's a big headache. It's not a business I want my son to be in. No sir!" But with franchising, who says his kid's got to be in the kitchen all the time?)

The hero of the third generation of inspired merchandising certainly looks the part: tall, curly-haired, athletic (he plays hockey twice a week, tennis regularly, squash in the winter, skiing holidays in Switzerland), father of three. Indeed, Michael Bregman is so handsome, one might expect him to rush forward and save the princess—except the ones saved are, in fact, those lucky or wise enough to afford the $100,000 + to set up a mmmuffins franchise, of which $20,000, plus 6% royalties, goes to his still-in-infancy corporation, mmmuffins Inc.

The origin of this North American conglomerate is not very original, but that in no way lessens the magnitude of its success. Michael Bregman, fresh out of Harvard, started in corporate development at Loblaw's, helping coordinate the no-name products launch, and was partly responsible for what he calls the "huge success" of the supermarket's photo-finishing operations. Bregman had seen how supermarket photo-finishing had taken off in the United States and wrote a brief proposal to Dave Nichol, then the president of Loblaw's. The logic was easy: By taking advantage of a service counter already at the store, people could drop off their film and pick it up the next time they were shopping. Within four months Bregman had found a finisher and received promo support in the Loblaw's weekly ads, and the supermarket chain became one of the largest photo finishers in the province of Ontario. "Working for Loblaw's," he says, "I could try out things in a big-company environment without putting out any money of my own."

Which leads us to the muffin miracle. And the baguette boom. And the croissant craze. (This could go on forever.) There Michael Bregman was, writing up a report on how to improve the Loblaw's bakery department, when in came a fellow with some giant muffins, which he wanted to sell for 45¢ each. But at the time, Loblaw's was selling "wee little things," hermetically sealed in plastic, at 89¢ a half dozen. Everyone thought it was lunatic to try and sell muffins at such a high cost, but Bregman gave it a shot, out in a couple of affluent supermarkets. They sold—dare we say it?—like hotcakes. "They couldn't get them in fast enough," he recalls today, and the response was not lost on the future millionaire.

"People didn't mind spending an extra buck on high quality," Bregman says. But what really gave him a glimpse of the future was his trial of the premium-cost muffins in Oshawa, Ontario, a factory town of General Motors and Ed Broadbent fame. They took off there, too. "*Then* I realized that muffins had mass appeal," he avers.

But Michael Bregman was not about to enter the field half

baked. He and father Lou approached the Scurfield family of Calgary, the principal shareholders of NuWest Group, Canada's biggest home builders, and with them as very silent partners—he finally bought them out in 1985—he decided to go First Class, all the way.

While his young wife went through a stack of recipe books for six months, testing oodles of muffin flavours, Bregman hired Don Watt & Associates, arguably Canada's best commercial designers, to help develop the first store, which opened shortly before Christmas, 1979. Over $75,000 in expenses, on design, construction, and equipment, went into the Eaton Centre location. The opening results were "unspectacular," but then, after about six slow weeks, it all exploded. "At the half-year mark," says Bregman, "we were up to what we had expected at the end of the first year; after ten months it was double of what we had hoped."

From the very start, Michael Bregman hoped his muffins would prove to be a good franchise concept, and soon after the first store opened, he went to work on his franchisees' operating manual. In quick succession came the mmmuffins stores: in the Yonge-Eglinton Centre in Toronto; Oshawa (God bless those trendy factory workers); Winnipeg; Thunder Bay; Longueuil, Quebec; Red Deer, Alberta; Ottawa; Calgary; Hamilton; Edmonton; Kamloops, B.C.; Regina. Let's put it in a more impressive manner: In the week of August 2–8, 1981, six stores opened across North America. Or in this way: mmmuffins went from zero to 26 stores in its first 24 months of operations, which is a lot faster than a car I used to drive.

In the meantime, Michael Bregman got the idea for his second major store concept, Michel's Baguettes, when he and his wife were honeymooning in France in 1978. (The name Michel is not so much a Frenchified Michael as a necessity; Bregman discovered that "La Baguette" could not be trademarked, since it's a generic term for a kind of bread.) The couple fell in love with the croissants and baguettes they ate there and vowed to try a bakery-restaurant if the muffins concept succeeded. Michael even imported a Marseilles baker from Washington, D.C., to teach his staff how to make the baguettes. But, in spite of Lou Bregman's faith in the bigger idea, he was fearful of "two concepts at once." It was only after the first muffin store was a runaway success that they dared to turn their hand to croissants.

The bakery-restaurants cost over $500,000 to open, so it is understandable that their growth was slower than the mmmuffins franchises, but they have recently taken off, due to a wonderful joint-venture ownership which Michael Bregman worked out with the Sara Lee Corporation of the United States—Sara has $8 billion in sales and 93,000 employees, by the way—in May of 1985. Bregman and Ms. Lee had planned to develop Michel's Baguettes across North America until they sold the U.S. stores last year.

Now, $36 million is a lot of Carrot Nut, Chocolate Chip, Banana, Blueberry, Oatmeal Raisin, Apple Cinnamon, and Cheddar Cheese muffins, not to mention croissants and baguettes. But one must remember that the vast majority of the stores are franchised, bringing in only 6% of their sales in royalties; there are but the company-owned mmmuffins and company-owned Michel's Baguettes but these bring in profits of well over 10%. (And profits are certainly why franchisees love the business as much as customers love the product: A 75¢ muffin is about 30% ingredients, 20% labour, 5% packaging, and 25% overhead and rent. The rest—nearly 20%—is profit. So thanks to Michael Bregman's smart/stolen idea, many franchisees are making very good money, often paying off massive loans within months of opening their store.)

There have been *some* disappointments, although they've been minor. For instance, although Bregman constantly tests new products to keep up consumer interest, they don't always pan out, pun intended. One flop was a flat bran muffin, called a "muffinwich." "We thought they were terrific, but they sure didn't sell," says the president of mmmuffins, Inc. There were bigger mistakes, as well. A number of mmmuffins didn't do well in the United States, whether due to weak mall traffic or a lack of love for the product. But nearly 1,500 Canadian employees isn't bad.

What could ultimately threaten the huge business created by Michael Bregman in barely over half a decade would be the dreadful ebb and flow of consumer fads and fancies. "Nothing is faddier than food fads," moans Michael Bregman. "I'm continually reminded that the life cycle of *anything* in retail is limited." And so he hops around to various cities regularly, looking at new concepts in food. He reads all the industry journals and walks endlessly around shopping malls in quest of new sales techniques. But he does not fear muffin saturation, since while many stores have gone bankrupt, the sales and profits of *his* firm have soared. Indeed, he insists that "competition is helpful, since every time a major chain promotes muffins which are inferior to ours, that helps promote us. We get a lot of free advertisements."

With controlled growth, diversification—"I can see additional concepts in the future, other restaurants and retail ventures"—and continual addition of new products to his two chains, it is clear that the fresh-baked-right-before-your-eyes gimmick is really no gimmick at all. Nor is quality a gimmick, either: "OUR BREAD AND ROLLS ARE MADE WITH FLOUR, WATER, YEAST AND SALT ONLY!" blares the sign in every Michel's Baguette. "NO SHORTENING, SUGAR OR ADDITIVES!" And each brightly coloured bag labelled "mmmuffins" proclaims haughtily, "Made only from the finest ingredients—whole eggs, buttermilk, honey, whole-grain flour, bran, fresh fruits and nuts. mmmuffins . . . a natural choice." White bread and muffins may not be exactly health foods, but they certainly lack the guilt-inducing effect of such products as doughnuts, cookies, and ice cream (which haven't done too badly either; see the next two profiles).

Lou Bregman leans back in his chair—he is still very involved in the running of mmmuffins, Inc., as an executive without portfolio—and beams at his oldest child. "I ran it with my back. Michael here runs it with his brains." "The old-style business mixes with the new," adds Michael's mother, Yetta.

It certainly does. Max Bregman looked at a bagel and saw a living. Lou Bregman looked at a bagel and saw a dream. Michael Bregman looked at a muffin and a baguette and saw an industry, rising faster than the wet dough in the calloused hands of his Russian-born grandfather.

# CHOCOLATE CHIPS OFF THE OLD BLOCK

## *Tara and Gayle Hallgren*

Greeting cards are mailed back and forth across Vancouver and the country along with huge boxes of cookies with such declarations as "IT'S BETTER TO HAVE EATEN AND GAINED, THAN NEVER TO HAVE EATEN AT ALL." "MAY THIS ROMANCE LAST LONGER THAN THESE COOKIES." "A BOX OF COOKIES, A JUG OF MILK, AND THOU," with credit given to one George Khayyam.

Huge ads in Vancouver papers cry out, "BECAUSE YOU CAN'T EAT FLOWERS," followed by "George doesn't believe that 'Romance is dead' . . . it's just resting . . . To wake up the romance in your life, send someone a 'Flower Box by George' this Valentine's Day. It's a dozen and a half of your choice of Cookies by George, all wrapped up in a genuine florist box—complete with green florists' paper, ribbon & a Because You Can't Eat Flowers card. All for an incredibly romantic Twelve Dollars. Barbara Cartland—eat your heart out! And don't forget—we DELIVER!"

As probably everyone on the west coast of Canada knows by now, there has been a small but growing firm called Cookies by George which has been in Vancouver only since January 1983 but has taken that city by storm, with its witty ads, zany promotions, and fine quality cookies. As their first advertisement, in the *West Ender*, on March 31, 1983, read: "Just when you thought it was safe to let your sweet tooth wander the streets again . . . Cookies by George has opened its doors at the corner of Denman at Davie. Indulge in our Classic Chocolate Chunk, Pecan Papaya Chunk, Coffee Walnut Chunk, Peanutty Peanut Butter Chunk, 'Reverse' Almond Chunk, and Oatmeal Coconut Raisin Cookies."

Is this any way to run a business? For instance, Tara Hallgren, 32, is the president of Great Cookies by George Inc., not because she is the eldest partner—she is not—but "because the other two were in New York. The lawyer asked if I was the president, so I said 'yes.' " (The third partner is

Noreen Kenney-Campbell; more on her later.) But to go from one store to eight stores in the first 2½ years, including one all the way out east in Edmonton, Alberta, and break sales of $1 million less than two years after they began, suggests far more smarts than such anecdotes imply. And with 15 stores and $2.2 million in sales by February, 1987, and 30 stores by year-end. . . . "We were always the girls with the bright ideas," declares Gayle Hallgren, as blond as her younger sister (and two years older), with hair to her shoulders and a face wonderfully like Meryl Streep's. "Everyone warned us not to go into business. Our family supported us, but people who didn't know that we had this desire to succeed thought that we'd fail." Adds sister Tara, abruptly, "Gayle, your problem is, you're kind of flakey!" And these women are running a successful business?

You bet. Both were born in Vancouver and grew up there. Tara went to the University of British Columbia, graduating with a B.A. in economics. Gayle also went to U.B.C., after starting at Simon Fraser in fine arts. She recalls getting her degree mailed to her, stamped "No Commercial Value." "How right they were!" she laughingly agrees.

The future cookie queens worked at the Keg & Cleaver as waitresses, and Gayle would do store windows for various Vancouver firms. (At the age of 15 Tara had pumped gas for a while, suggesting an open attitude to the work market.)

Then the two Hallgren sisters went off to Iran, where their father was a consultant to various industries. Gayle got a job working for Iranian radio and TV and tried to start a business selling decals to place on cars, trucks, and machinery. "If the Shah hadn't been overthrown," pops in Tara, her face oozing irony, "we'd be *big* in decals, now." A thought which probably haunts the Ayatollah.

Tara, during this time, was a stewardess for Air India, from 1976 to 1978, at which point she returned to finish her degree at Simon Fraser but spent her summers with her sister and family. It was a rough life: "I used to go to Dubai, play tennis all day, and drive about in a Mercedes." But all good things must come to an end, as the Shah's family learned only too well.

Gayle had seen some cookie stores in New York shortly before—no one ever said that entrepreneurs must possess originality—and was prompted to visit her sister in Dubai.

"Leave this lap of luxury," she ordered Tara. "Come home and make cookies!" They returned to their native city in 1981. (Not that it had been all play; Gayle had actually written a political thriller with a girfriend during that period, about being caught in the Iranian Revolution. It was published under a pseudonym, and she insists it did well.)

Gayle had fallen in love with New York, but, as she puts it, "I wanted to get a good idea from the sharks and then go and swim in a smaller pond." They claim that they had no money back in Vancouver, so Gayle did window displays with friends who owned a clothing store, and Tara swept the floor at the Pacific Centre, which is a long way down from the tennis-and-Mercedes scene in Dubai. "I'm not creative, I can't do anything," Tara used to tell Gayle.

Then Tara met Noreen Kenney-Campbell, who was to be the third of the unholy trinity. Born in New York, she had gone to Ohio State University, where she earned her B.S. in industrial design. She worked at an ad agency in Ohio, got married, and followed her husband up to Vancouver, where he was hired to design the roof for Canada Place. She had moved to the Canadian city in 1982, a year after her husband, and within three weeks met Tara at the art department of the YWCA. Of such moments are great partnerships made.

The cookie concept moved toward fruition. Noreen was saddened to discover that the two sisters couldn't bake, so she began to do the dirty work on the boat she lived on. "I made bunches of cookies," she says, while her two tentative partners kept talking about opening this cookie store.

In the meantime, Tara and Gayle opened a design store called Intac (short for Intentionally Tacky) Design. "We did retail stores, credit unions, and lots of promos," they say. "We did make money and had clients," insists Tara. But a moment of truth had arisen. As Gayle says, "We had this company and great clients, but we couldn't find a space for our cookie store and no one would finance us. And we didn't know how to finance things. So we sat down in a coffee shop one day and said, 'Are we gonna do this or *not*?'"

The answer was quickly in the affirmative. Tara and Noreen found a location, a place in English Bay which is now their flagship store. "We put our money where our mouths were," says Gayle. "We put in $15,000 each." Noreen did all the graphics and art work, and they tested cookies endlessly.

They painted the store themselves, grouting the tiles, and while they were making all this mess, Vancouverites kept coming into the signless store and asking for half a dozen cookies.

Then there was the name problem. "Gayle and I wanted a name for the cookies, but not our own names," says Tara. They considered Dante's Cookie Inferno. No. Theodore's Cookie Kitchen. Feh. States Noreen, "I didn't want it named after *any* guy if it wasn't going to be named after *us*." "That was the toughest part—the name!" declares Gayle. Then, Noreen's husband suddenly piped up, "Just call it 'Cookies by George'!"

But it wasn't all names, painting, and fixing; there was research that had to be done. They flew in Mrs. Field's Cookies and David's Cookies and tested them, turning them over in their hands, looking at them. "We wanted a cookie *better* than theirs!" They worked at their cookie recipes at a restaurant each night, staggering in with bags of flour, sugar, chocolate. ("You only have to *ask* people to find out where to get ingredients in this city!" exclaims Tara.) There were long, lonely hours at the ovens. Tara recalls, "After one week, as we were cleaning up our messes at one A.M., and we could barely move our hands, I cried out, 'I left Dubai, and a houseboy, for *this*'?"

They opened the first Cookies by George on March 29, 1983, a day that will live in infamy at Weight Watchers of Vancouver. The store was 827 square feet in size, but it was large enough for smells to waft out of it. From the very first day they had planned to have more than one store, and they quickly fulfilled their promise: The second store opened in November of 1983 in the Hudson's Bay store in downtown Vancouver; the third opened in April 1984 on Burrard Street, the fourth in Gastown in May. Their only franchised store, in North Vancouver, opened that June; then stores at Oakridge Shopping Centre in October, Richmond and Edmonton in summer 1985, and Burnaby in spring 1986. Of their first 15 stores, 7 were franchised.

"We've never borrowed any money from any bank to this day," says Noreen, proudly. And Hallgren *père* computerized his daughters in 1984. When the first store brought in $325,000 in the very first year, they knew they had a winner.

In 1985 they developed Ice Cream by George, with the

hope of opening separate outlets for the cold stuff only. And they now even have their own line of gourmet coffee. And they see, as so many others have before them, that franchising is the best route for them to take. "We have commitment, enthusiasm, great ideas, and a business system that works!" says Gayle. "We want the network to support our stores. We'd rather grow slowly and do a good job. We haven't changed the quality of our product since the beginning, and it's paid off."

There's oodles of competition, of course, and not only in the States from which they lifted their idea. "But if we do it first, we're always ahead of the others," says Gayle. "My brochure design was stolen, right down to the colour and shape," by a store in a city in eastern Canada "that shall be nameless," exclaims Noreen, who almost, but not quite, subscribes to the belief that imitation is the sincerest form of flattery. But they replied to all this by copyrighting their name and logo in the United States, England, and Italy, as well as Canada. Not in Dubai, however; potential pirates there still have a free rein.

What makes Cookies by George so exciting, ultimately, is the way they have made the concept fun. For instance, the three women hold Bright Idea Contests, in which they give $50 to the employee with the best new idea, such as how to sell their T-shirts better. And, of course, they are always trying to improve what's out there. "We don't have a patent on cookies," says Gayle. "We hope that you can do better than we can. But we try to raise the most common bakery product—the cookie—to a higher level, and we've succeeded."

The success is also thanks to the fact that the women behind Cookies by George "are not merely cookie sellers; we sell a gift idea." They've done this by, in Gayle's words, "putting a lot more whimsy into the cards. And by a delivery service." They even send a box of crumbs to "the crumb of your choice" at that special time when you do *not* wish to send the very best. (One woman sent the crumb box to her ex-whatever, with a card reading, "So long, cookie!!")

"We can think of a concept, work out the promotion, do the graphic design, and promote it," says Gayle. "It's a new wave of merchandising specialty foods. You have to make it more fun." Adds Tara, "Cookies are a 'good feeling' product."

The good feeling is spreading, since there are now up to

four dozen people at any one time on the Cookies by George payroll. And they have not encountered difficulties because they are women. Notes Gayle, "If we have any problems, we think *nothing* of picking up the phone and asking for help. We *rarely* encounter sexism."

Yes, they were a bit giddy, even silly, in the early weeks, but "we've become very sensible entrepreneurs since we started the business," states Gayle firmly. "We look at decisions *not* on emotions but on—forgive the hackneyed phrase—the bottom line. At the beginning we had all this enthusiasm. But we recognized quickly that it's not enough to have a great idea; we had to run the business as a business." (Although one might question whether it is a businesslike statement to declare, "Every customer is king and should leave our stores with a smile.")

Whether Cookies by George and its vivacious, attractive, and bright creators and owners will have hundreds of stores around the world in the years to come is still open to question, but there is *no* question that Gayle and Tara Hallgren and Noreen Kenney-Campbell are having the time of their lives.

"We have the best job in the world!" enthuses Gayle. "We sell a fifty-cent product to people! And it doesn't take much to make people happy!"

Nor to make the people who started the business well-to-do. After all, it wasn't so long ago, in a Vancouver bank, that Tara Hallgren received the following reply: "Cookies? *We* won't loan you money for *that*!!"

"Now," says Tara, with a knowing grin, "the banks are saying, 'Ahhh, *cookies*!'"

## KING OF THE VENDORS

### Earl Barish

When one encounters those kids in over a hundred towns and cities across Canada and the United States, pedalling their ice cream bikes, from Nanaimo, British Columbia, to Bismarck, North Dakota, and Selkirk, Manitoba, to Rochester, Minnesota, one does not think of high finance. Nor, for that matter, do images of 40 Billion Served come to mind when we see a Space Jumbo Bar ("SMOOTH CHOCO-LATE SURFACE GIVES WAY TO A PLANETARY CORE OF SOLID ICE CREAM") or a Space Split ("THICK BANANA ICE CREAM WEDGED BETWEEN COMMAND MODULES OF FUDGE. UNIVERSALLY LOVED FROM ONE END OF THE GALAXY TO THE OTHER").

But they should. For all this seeming kid stuff has made Dickie Dee Ice Cream of Winnipeg the largest seller of ice cream novelties in Canada, outside of supermarkets, who sell in six-packs and never give the money to thousands of cash-hungry teens every summer. What's most surprising of all is that the 12 million to 15 million ice creams sold in the summer of 1986 (at around 55¢ each), for a total of $8 million in sales, flows from a country with a four-month-long selling season. Indeed, Dickie Dee knocked 'em cold in Whitehorse but dried up in Arizona, where the weather contrast is too slight, and everyone stays inside, windows closed, air-conditioner on.

Earl Barish, his curly hair greying, his mustache glistening, his paunch suggesting that he loves to taste his product, was born in Fort William, Ontario, in the summer (naturally) of 1943. His father was a butcher, until they moved to Winnipeg when Earl was two. Earl's early years did not suggest a business which would spread across North America; he delivered for a drugstore at 12, working behind their soda fountain years later, and used to take the garbage out for Winnipeg's famed Kelekis Restaurant, for which he was paid in hot dogs and chips. But he was clearly bright, skipping grades as he went through school, going into university at the age of 15, straight out of grade 11, and graduating from the University of Manitoba before he was 20.

In 1957, at the age of 14, he pedalled an ice cream bike for a man who had eight bikes, getting paid 20% of sales. He would sell an average of $60 worth a day, when the bars sold for only 10¢, which suggests his skills at peddling calories as well as pedalling the bike. After two summers of this, the boy was told by the man—who had recently purchased the tiny business from its original owner, Sam Dvorchak (known as Mr. D), who had started Dickie Dee in the 1940s—that he wanted to sell.

Earl Barish brought home the idea of the business to his father, who had recently been wiped out in the stock market and had moved from butcher to cattle buyer. The man wanted $2,000, which seemed steep even then for eight little bikes. Barish and dad put up half of it and talked Toronto-Dominion into loaning the other half. So in 1959, at an age when most teenage boys are trading baseball cards and checking for acne, Earl Barish had himself a little ice cream business.

It wasn't long before problems arose: One of his sales-people appeared on the streets of Winnipeg on a bike with a different name on it! Earl Barish would not stand for this dastardly act, as he relates it passionately today, over a quar-ter century later: "Every business needs an owner who has *guts*—who makes important decisions!" The teenage entre-preneur marched off to Chicago and met with the man who made the only ice cream bicycles in North America, and told him that he wanted the rights for Canada, "so we'd be the only ones in the country with them." The man replied, "If you buy twenty-five bikes a year for the next three years, I'll give you the exclusive."

The bicycles cost $200 each, and the kid was faced with a Big Dilemma: It was true that they had expanded to 12 bikes, but this would mean an expansion of six times their present size. "That's where the guts came in!" booms Earl Barish. "We decided, if we can sell ice cream in Winnipeg, we can sell *anywhere*!"

So Dickie Dee expanded into Regina, where they put 15 teenagers on the streets, where they belonged, moved into Moose Jaw with 2, and added 8 more to their Winnipeg dozen. "I spent the summers involved with the growth and development of the business with my father," says Barish. He was paid $50 a week out of the profitability of the com-pany, the only revenue of which came during the four selling months of summer.

It was rather primitive, as well, in those first few years, because the Barish family made their own ice cream. Well, their own ice cream bars. "We'd buy a brick of ice cream, cut it into six slices, buy Christie wafers, and put the slices inside." Mrs. Barish was the Chief Slicer, and the business was run out of the garage of their Winnipeg home. They eventually incorporated Dickie Dee Ice Cream Ltd. in Mani-toba and registered it province by province as they spread out across the country.

Earl Barish opened Edmonton himself in 1962, putting

ten units into that northerly city. But, more relevant, he graduated from U. of M. in 1963. He was newly married (to his first wife) and decided that it made no sense to work four months a year; he needed a more substantial career. So he went into management for the Hudson's Bay Company at the age of 19. He worked there for four years, in linens, sporting goods, toys, Christmas decorations—all things which had little to do with his eventual return to ice cream peddling but everything to do with marketing and sales. In 1967 he moved to Eaton's as a store manager, working his way up to $18,000 a year when he left in 1970, "which was big bread then!"

Dickie Dee had not lain down and died while the boy wonder was away making a real living; when he left the little firm in 1963, his older brother moved into the company and had spread it into Western Canada and to Hamilton, Ontario, in the east. ("If we'd done a study of Vancouver, with all those hills, we wouldn't have gone there," Earl Barish notes today.)

The older Barish child decided to open the Ontario market fully, where there might be trucks and not bikes, and he started Dickie Dee Ice Cream (Canada) Ltd. in that province. And Earl Barish reached a deal with his father. "If he met the eighteen Gs I was making at Eaton's, I'd move back into the company." The 27-year-old began to acquire shares in Dickie Dee, eventually purchasing all of his parents' interest, to the point where he is 100% owner of his company and his older brother is 100% owner of his.

"It just kept growing and growing," declares Earl Barish, whipping some ice cream bars out of his freezer, sitting by his Winnipeg swimming pool (in summer, of course). That fellow in Chicago eventually went out of the bike business, so Barish started making his own in the early 1970s, building between 500 and 800 over the years. "We own all our equipment," he adds.

The best years for Dickie Dee have been years of recession, since you need a treat all the more when daddy's unemployed. And the firm has been most profitable in years of inflation, since "we are committed to raising prices a nickel at a time, making the inflationary cycle open a good margin for us." Not that it's always been easy; Barish wanted to quit soon after he put his three depots and ten bikes into Edmonton, with all that crummy weather. But "it's now our largest market!" The key, he claims, was his father's "driving force." "Dad instilled in us the drive to overcome all problems." And selling ice cream in Canada has many.

Dickie Dee is actually a 12-month-a-year business, with its busiest season being the off season, even though 95% of all sales are made between April and August. The other months are spent lining up distributors, who, in turn, get the next summer's kids, etc.

Barish finally moved into the States in 1980, since "I was busy developing Canada until then." He is in no less than a dozen states now, as is his brother, in different ones, and in every Canadian province, although weakest in Quebec. He owns and operates fully 1,500 bicycles in North America.

The kids on the bikes do a lot better than Barish did when he was 15. They make 25% of sales; distributors make 30% on top of that. The "top kid" made about $8,000 in the summer of 1986—in the Maritimes, it was—while the best in the west earned $7,137 in Surrey, B.C. The average is between $15 and $25 a day, with eight students to each bike, due to holidays, school, summer camp, etc. "They're all independent agents!" exclaims Barish. "It's up to their own initiative to go out and sell." (They should listen to and watch the boss in Winnipeg; at a Jehovah's Witnesses convention in Vancouver in the summer of 1984, Earl Barish managed to sell $975 worth of ice cream in a single day, topped by $2,686 in one day during Edmonton's Heritage Days, in 1985, and $1,785 in the next.)

Today, Earl Barish is pushing deeper and deeper into the United States, which has a longer summer than we Canadians do; he has also looked at, but rejected, Australia. "It would be ideal, with the different season, but it's too far away." He's still checking into openings in Colombia, though.

As his firm has grown, Barish decided that it would be necessary to get involved in other aspects of the ice cream industry. For instance, he has created his own molds for his Space Fleet Line (lick your lips over the first paragraphs of this profile, above), which now has six items. "I developed the concept! We have the most exciting new concept in the development of single stick novelties in Canada!!" He still makes no ice cream of his own, since distribution is too costly, and has dairies across North America do the chilly work for him.

Barish does not franchise, although it may look that way. He offers, instead, "a reasonable package," renting bikes and freezers and trailers at a good price. A ten-bike operation can be obtained for as little as $3,000. "We provide the opportunity for young people to make money!" he declares. "I've had operators make between $75,000 and $100,000 over a single summer!" (And, touchingly, it often includes kids who would rarely find jobs elsewhere: many native people, a lot of physically and mentally handicapped youth, even deaf young adults. "They point to the picture of the ice cream," says Barish. "And as long as they can make change, they all do fine. To earn money is a whole new business experience for hundreds." Up to 10% of his workers are disabled.)

Since dry ice is not available in many cities—have you ever been able to track any down in Terrebonne, Quebec, or Fort St. John, B.C.?—Barish developed a brine cartridge a decade ago. It's a round or square stainless steel container, two inches deep, with especially prepared brine inside. It is frozen, and as it thaws, it absorbs heat from those poor, suffering Space Shuttles and Space Jumbo Fudges. "It allowed us to expand to all kinds of climates, even [alas!] Arizona!" He's gotten the price down to only $25 a cartridge, and a set of 12 of them is rented with every bike.

The kind of mind that could put tens of thousands of kids to work, possibly hundreds of thousands since the early 1960s, could hardly stop at ice cream bicycles. "I always wanted an ice cream store," he cries; "I love hot fudge! And the only way I could get what I wanted was to open a store of my own!"

Which he did—Dee-Liktables—in Winnipeg, in which there was Fantasy Island, "a whole new concept of eating ice cream!" There was a freezer in the middle, with eight types of ice cream in it, along with a row of fresh fruit and toppings. "You took a bowl and filled it with as much as you wanted!" He charged 15¢ an ounce.

As the past tense implies, the store opened in April and closed in December 1984, since Earl Barish was "an absentee manager." "We had the lowest prices in the city," he moans, "double scoops for a buck! And it was rated by the CBC as the store with the best assortment and quality ice cream in Winnipeg!" But he just couldn't be at the store enough. Still, it was a marketable idea, and he won't let it grow cold. "I plan to franchise the concept; I've patented it and the name in Canada." There will be *ten* Fantasy Islands in Edmonton along, in 1987, and he expects to be in Winnipeg and Toronto in 1988—and then, across the U.S.

And then there is D'Best Hot Dog Company, founded in 1982, with its all-beef product. "I was in Miami Beach and saw hot dog carts on the highways." Most cities in Canada used to have health restrictions against that sort of thing, but this has recently been changed. "I wanted to overcome the staid quality of downtown!" says the saviour of Winnipeg. "Outdoor vending is now more accepted."

So he purchased hot dog carts in New York, three of them to begin with, at $5,500 each, Canadian funds, and set up the company with the following goals: to sell the best hot dog on the street, and to overcome the attitude that vending is inferior. (All-egg baked buns and top quality sauerkraut should put an end to that heresy.) All three were placed in Winnipeg. He had two competitors that first summer, but neither is in business now; one sold his two carts to Barish, in fact. He now has a total of five.

The way Earl Barish began his business, in late August 1983, shows that the showman still lives and breathes in him. He sold the hot dogs for 25¢ each, and the price was quickly picked up by the newspapers. "I sold 3,000 hot dogs, and lost maybe $2,500," he recalls, "but I got great publicity." He is buying five more units for 1986. "I've decided to be the hot dog king of Winnipeg!" he proclaims, still not satisfied with being the ice cream bicycle king of North America, and the Master of Fantasy Island.

Dickie Dee now has over a million dollars in equipment, and Barish feels that it could be doing a lot better in the States, but with his three children and new woman friend, his plan "is to enjoy life. I have no great desire to do much more—the store, the hot dogs. . . ." He still works 16-hour days in two 8-hour shifts in January, February, and March, going home after one, eating, sleeping, and returning for his second shift. It's not easy, dealing with ten different dairies in the United States and Canada, but he is helped by his five "very, very good" sales managers in Winnipeg, Vancouver, Saskatchewan, and Colorado.

Like a number of entrepreneurs, Earl Barish is thrilled with what he has created: "Think about it! We are affecting a large part of the Canadian population for four months every summer! An ice cream bike on every street of every town or city, all summer long! We provide a fair opportunity for an aggressive, hard-working person! It's the *best* training ground for parents to teach their children what business is all about."

This summer, as every summer since 1959, but in smaller numbers, upwards of 12,000 "kids," from 14 into their 50s, will mount their Dickie Dee Ice Cream bicycles and start or continue their training, thanks to Earl Barish of Winnipeg, Manitoba.

## POOR BOY MAKES GOOD

### *Bernard Cyr*

When people can trace themselves back to 1800 in Canada, one assumes that they are part of the Old Boys' Network, with lots of connections and lots of money. But when that background is Acadian and the individual concerned is the second child of ten, with a truck-driving father and a homemaker mother, in a town of 13,000 on the Gaspé Coast, to become a multimillionaire has the stuff of magic.

Such is the life of Bernard Cyr, born on Magdalen Island, Quebec, in 1948. There are many clues to what made this young man an entrepreneur, not the least of which is the astounding fact that all ten Cyr children went to university. "I personally got it from my mother," says Cyr today. "She was shy and never said too much, but she had a drive. She was the one who pushed us all through college." But since most of his siblings are teachers, one in nursing, another in lab technology, another a C.A., this doesn't quite explain what gave Bernard Cyr such a mind for business.

Even as a child, he "always used to make things happen," organizing baseball and hockey teams. For instance, when he was only seven or eight, Cyr was determined to have a bicycle. So he'd get up at 5:00 A.M., would catch cod, cut out their tongues, and sell them, $2 per gallon. "I got my first bike from the Eaton Catalogue," he laughs. "I had the best bike on the island!"

Cyr went to Moncton University, where he studied business administration (and where he still lives today with his two young children and beautiful wife). After university, he went to work for General Electric in Montreal and Toronto, doing financial work and employee relations. During these years, Cyr was in contact with his "old buddies from university," and some of them had approached a local man who owned two small pizza outlets. They bought them, named them Pizza Delight, and planned to franchise them, since, at the time, "franchising was starting to become quite popular." It was the late 1960s.

As early as 1970 the men invited Bernard Cyr to join them, but he turned them down. He was 20 years old and felt that he had a bright future at GE. Furthermore, he still wanted to learn English, a language he had yet to conquer. Then, in 1972, they invited him to climb on board again. This time he accepted, becoming operations manager. (There were already 25 stores by then.)

At first, Cyr did not buy in, but within six months the original partners in Pizza Delight split, and he was invited to join Bernard Imbault, the father of the chain. When Cyr went to the banks for a $5,000 loan to buy shares into PD, he was turned down, and for good reason: The company was "technically bankrupt" that year. In fact, his first paycheque bounced. "But I felt that the company had great potential, with the proper growth," says Cyr today, in his office in Moncton. So he paid $30,000 for 15% of the shares.

Throughout the early 1970s Bernard Cyr started to put the system in place, and planned expansion across the Maritimes with the pizza chain. They soon went from 25 stores to close to 200, right across Canada, by 1979, biggest in Ontario (75) and strong in Western Canada as well. But in that same year he resigned as the president of Pizza Delight. He had spent seven years hopping from coast to coast, as well as marrying and starting a family. "I wanted to be local and start on my own," he says.

So, like any good writer, he began with what he knew best. He bought the four operations in Moncton, N.B., selling his shares back for the opportunity to obtain them. The 16-hour days and 7-day weeks paid off; today he owns nine Pizza Delight franchises—four in Moncton, one in Dieppe, one in Oromoncto, one in Saint John, one in Shippagan, and one on his native Magdalen Island. Since 1979 he has built and sold many others, and claims that he could easily have close to 20 now had he chosen to do so. "It was a good business move to build a store for $175,000, make $60,000 a year from it, and sell it shortly after for $250,000," he says. "I always have two or three on the grill at any one time."

All this cash flow allowed Bernard Cyr to move into real estate. He owns a shopping centre on the island and land in Moncton, and he runs a firm that distributes products to Pizza Delights across the Maritimes. So, although he owns absolutely nothing of the massive pizza chain, he owns 100% of his own operation, which distributes $7 million worth of ingredients "for family dining" throughout the Atlantic provinces.

And there's more: Cyr has recently become involved in waterslides with three others, including one in Shediac, which was a $1 million project. One can see his attraction to such projects; Pizza Delight had had a "midlife crisis" back in 1979, when Cyr had chosen to move on, and it sold the Ontario market to Robin Hood Multifoods. "It saved the company," Cyr claims, but it also was a sign to go elsewhere. The 225 stores have over $100 million in sales, but one can see that Cyr is happy with his own slice (anchovies, green pepper, hold the onions, please). His nine stores bring in close to $5 million in sales each year, with 250 employees—a far cry from cod tongues.

And then there is the training school founded in New Brunswick in 1984. It's called Galryc Ltd., and it does research, development, and training in the food service industry. "I started it due to the huge need to prepare people to get into this industry. It's the fastest-growing industry in the country."

He developed the school with a partner. A private school, it doesn't advertise in the marketplace, since it is used on a contract basis. "But we're busy," says Cyr. "People come to us and want to develop a product and a recipe. We develop it and sell it to them." (It shares the building with the main office of Cyr Enterprises.)

And Cyr Enterprises is always on the lookout for new properties, new concepts. For example, Bernard Cyr opened a new bowling centre on his native island in 1986. "I own it myself; there's a need for one." And, as he puts it, "Over the past decade, I've always had three, four, or five things on the go."

But there's on the go and there's ON THE GO!! Bernard Cyr is very much the former. "I don't dream to be a Paul Desmarais or a Conrad Black," he confesses. "You have to learn to enjoy life, too. You can work your life out, turn fifty-five or sixty, and *then what*? I have no desire to make Cyr Enterprises twenty times bigger." No. it's not the hours, either: "It's when you go home and try to relax, and find yourself thinking business. . . ."

So what made Bernard Cyr so successful? "If you have the basic qualities of leadership," he explains, "and you have a desire to—not get rich—but achieve something on your own. I was the son of a truck driver who had a good heart but no money. And I finished university without a penny in my pocket."

To future entrepreneurs, Cyr urges that they "don't expect miracles. One doesn't get rich overnight; you've got to build equity." Like nearly all successful business people, he paid himself a small salary for years, "ploughing everything else back into Pizza Delight, as well as into my own enterprises."

There's a country home, 25 miles outside of Moncton, and the Jaguar Sovereign, and that beautiful wife and kids. And a continual awareness that you can be second of ten children in a tiny Gaspé town and make something of yourself—while providing jobs for hundreds of others along the way.

## EAT YOUR FAST FOOD, IT'S GOOD FOR YOU

*Hal Gould*

As every poor person will tell you, it pays to have money. And as every wealthy person will tell you, it's much easier to turn $1 million into $2 million than to turn $100 into $200. With those thoughts in our minds, let us now turn to the uneven, yet ultimately explosive, success of Cultures Fresh Food Restaurants, and its rich but still battered creators and owners, the Gould family of London, Ontario (no relation to the author).

Although many people in this country think of the brilliant pianist Glenn Gould when they see that name (alas, notes the author, also no relation), they probably think in their subconscious minds of another Gould whose name has been on a million billboards over the past half-century: John M. Gould. Gould-Leslie was founded back in 1913, and it grew steadily into one of the largest outdoor sign advertising firms until its sale, in 1981, for $4 million, to Vancouver's colourful Jimmy Pattison. Born into this wealthy London family were three children; the oldest, Hal, born in 1950, is now the president of Cultures. (One brother and a sister followed; the former is a partner in the restaurant venture.)

"We were all inspired in business by my father," says Hal Gould, with his round glasses, brown hair and mustache, continually lighting up Rothman's Specials. "He took that firm from relatively nothing and it became preeminent around the world. To this day, Canada is regarded as in the forefront of outdoor advertising."

But the father of the family died at the age of 49, when Hal was 25. He had gone to Bishop's University in Lennoxville, studying business, "feeling that I was best suited for it. I wanted to follow in the footsteps of my father in that I wanted to be successful in business." After he graduated in 1973 with a B.A., he went to work for Pitfield Mackay Ross as a money market trader. "I loved it; it was very exciting!" Yet like so many of us, he was aware of a certain negative aspect of it all: "It was incongruous," he recalls. "We'd deal in millions of dollars and get a pittance!" From such thoughts are independent businesses born.

With the death of his father, however, "someone had to run the company, which had a rough time after he died." So the eldest child did so, going in as president of Gould in early 1976 and remaining there for seven years.

But this story is not about Gould and his outdoor signs; it is about an inspired idea that he and his family carried to fruition. How it happened is almost comical: The mother of the Gould family, while on a trip to New York City, saw some frozen yoghurt being dispensed. She thought it was "fun," so Hal Gould flew down to investigate. At first he tried teaming up with a fellow who had four units of frozen yoghurt, but it didn't work. "In those days, no one liked yoghurt," Gould says sadly.

But he realized that frozen yoghurt would "develop a middle ground between European and North American tastes.

It was a confectionery product. We thought it had a good application as a healthy thing." (Healthy. If God had really wanted us to love carrots and green beans, She would have made them taste like Chocolate, right? More on this problem later.)

What the Goulds did—brother Jay, four years younger than Hal, joined in the concept—was to develop a menu to complement the selling of frozen yoghurt—soups and salads. Their first location was in a downtown shopping centre in Hal's native London, Ontario, about two hours west of Toronto. "It was all we could get; most considered it a fad, that it wouldn't work." It began with Hal Gould's $7,000, as a subsidiary of John M. Gould Ltd. Advertising Signs.

"It wasn't a runaway success, but there was enough sales performance that we decided to open a second one in Kitchener, with help from the bank." (Number 2 cost $75,000.) But they were losing money. "We had no restaurant experience and didn't know how to control costs!" he moans today. Yet they were helped in one important area: "We were more involved with customer reactions."

What also helped Hal Gould *et famille* is the simple fact that they thought big—really big. Mordecai Richler might say that they thought American. "We wanted one hundred of them!" declares Hal Gould, lighting up another cigarette. "The fun of putting together something that had mass application! We never wanted two, three, or four Cultures. We felt that if we put it together properly it would have *fabulous* application! We wanted to build something *big*!!"

Big in hamburgers, perhaps. Big in deep-fried chicken, possibly. But in yoghurt and cottage cheese plates? As my 13-year-old son likes to say, "If I want to eat healthy, I can get that yuck at home!" And, indeed, it was not all roses. "When we went into spinach salads, *no* one would buy them!" declares Gould, exasperated. We could have told him that. "It was in the *early* days of Participation."

One could smile that away, but the thought is profound: In the late 1970s, who could have known that health and good food and exercise would become the sex of the 1980s? Hal Gould may not have known, but he had hitched his wagon to a nutritional star anyway. "We weren't big health food freaks," he insists, and as he lights up again, we are forced to believe him. "But Cultures was generated to grow with healthy attitudes."

The first store was only 550 square feet in size, although the average now is around 2,000. And the sales, though not the profits, quickly grew to match the store sizes: In 1977, with 1½ stores, they had sales of $250,000. By 1980 they were up to 7 stores, and "a few million." By 1983 their 14 stores were bringing in around $5 million, and as of the end of 1987 60 stores sold $27 million worth of chef's/spinach/Caesar/garden/chicken savoy/cottage-cheese-plate salads, tuna/chicken/ham and cheese/ham and swiss/roast beef sandwiches, soups, frozen yoghurt cones, sundaes, shakes (Smoothies), and fresh-baked muffins, carrot bread, banana bread, and pastries. God bless sugar; it makes health palatable.

Cultures are currently opening at a rate of one a month. And by 1990 Hal Gould has no doubt at all that he will reach the 100 stores he had originally planned for, across the States as well as in Canada, with sales of $50 million. (Average yearly sale per store: $550,000–600,000, although the bigger ones bring in "well over one million each.")

There is competition in the United States, but Hal Gould has every intention of surpassing them: The Fresher Cooker (cute name) has 20 stores down there, and 40 Carrots (even cuter) has quite a few as well. Indeed, the name for the Gould restaurants has been a continual sore point. "Cultures connotated bacteria, and we didn't want to be thought of as health food restaurants!" So they added, in big letters below every CULTURES sign, FRESH FOOD RESTAURANTS. (Whew.) "Our big thing is the fresh," says Gould. "We play on people's consciousness. But if it wasn't good, they wouldn't buy it."

As so often happens in the world of business, if the Gould family knew what the hell they were doing, they wouldn't have been as successful. "If we had been meticulous restauranteurs, we would have stopped growing," he admits. "We made *all* the mistakes!" Such as? "We believed that the public would come to us. And the banks gave up on us in 1980 and made us come up wtih $350,000 in forty-eight hours."

Gould managed to scrape together the money—thanks to his talented and successful family—but "I was angry, and haven't worked with [a bank] since then, to borrow anything." He had to sell some property to pay up, and this moved him into franchising.

At that time he was up to 11 stores, all company-owned, in London, Kitchener, Oshawa, Hull, and Toronto, mainly in the latter. So he started franchising some of the existing stores, and Hal and his brother Jay moved to Toronto (75% of the stores today are franchised). Perhaps surprisingly, there were advantages to starting out in a relatively small community: Silverwood Dairies was there, so Gould was able to create his yoghurt concoctions by taking the Canadian dairy people down to the States, showing them the stuff he was impressed with, and stating, "We want this formulation." And yoghurt was *the* major portion of their sales when they opened; now, interestingly, it is less than one-fourth, maybe 20%. Even the word *Smoothie*, for their yoghurt shakes, was stolen. "We picked it up from a little place in Seattle," Gould confesses, although the potentially ruinous name "Cultures" was thought up by a designer back home in London.

Although there has been no major change in concept since Cultures opened its first store in 1977, the menu "has expanded incredibly," according to Gould. It had a mere two salads plus yoghurt at the start. Today, one can buy nine different salads, nine different kinds of sandwiches, quiches, two daily choices of home-made soups, and all those baked goods.

The number of employees reflects the huge expansion: At the beginning, there were half a dozen workers on the Cultures payroll; in late 1987 the total is over 1,200. And with a profit of between 15 and 20% before taxes, there should soon be a lot more. It isn't cheap to buy a Cultures franchise; there is a $20,000 franchise fee ("We used to lose money on it"), along with a 5% royalty and 2% for advertising. It costs up to $200,000 to put up a store.

At the present time, Hal Gould is talking with major food service companies in the States to help his original dream of 100 stores to reach fulfillment soon. In 1984 there were stores only in Ontario, Quebec, and Alberta; by the end of 1985, Cultures had spread into Saskatchewan, Manitoba, British Columbia, and Nova Scotia. In 1987 they were in every Canadian province except New Brunswick, Prince Edward Island, and Newfoundland.

Yet those who feel that the Gould good fortune is totally

due to the earlier Gould fortune are mistaken. "We were losing our shirts with finance costs at the beginning," the president recalls. "We lost money for the first four years. We needed the credibility, not the money, that our father's business gave us. That track record was necessary, or Cultures would not be here today. And we were able to use that credibility."

By the time they started to franchise like rabbits having rabbits, they had built up their own credibility as a successful restaurant chain. But there were still those tough times: "There was a distinct possibility that we could blow it all. We had to get the banks off our backs and realign ourselves. I thought I'd lost it all in 1980." And, like the Great Depression's effect on tens of millions of North Americans to this day, the memories of that year are still with Hal Gould, even as his stores rake in the millions: "In my eyes, it's *not* where I envision it to be, and I still have sleepless nights and worry. It's almost a self-perpetuating disease."

But it *will* last; Hal Gould has no doubts about that. "Absolutely. It's a concept, not a fad: Fresh, healthy food. It won't go away in the public mind."

The big dreams of Gould for Cultures won't stop, either. He sees it as capable of "lining up with all the other fast food alternatives on the same block: Swiss Chalet, Pizza Hut, McDonald's. We're a clear alternative to most of them, too."

In the tradition of most small-businesses-grown-large, Hal Gould and his brother were "never the highest paid employees" of Cultures. "The people we hired were!" No, the success of the business had to come first; then the equity would be there. Hard as it may be to believe, Hal Gould's salary was $30,000 annually for most of the eight years of Cultures; even today it is only $40,000, although that equity *has* been growing.

There is some profit sharing among the managers and assistant managers, and the nine stores that are still company-owned also share in the profits. But what's most important in the mind of Hal Gould, who has never really wanted for money in his 37 years, is the fact that he has *created* something:

"We've developed this business in Canada of healthier foods. We are in the forefront of it. And we've created the products and even the containers for them ourselves." You see, the industry was not developed for salads as full-course meals, so Gould actually designed the top for plastic see-through salad bowls. "With the top, people can toss their own salad by flipping it over."

A little thing, perhaps. But so is the silicon chip. And beyond researching and financing, Hal Gould reaches for the magic word to explain the success of Cultures: "Quality is the most important thing. If you can afford to put a product on the market that is well made and consistent, your chances of success are enhanced."

Yes, Hal Gould and his family were the inheritors of a major outdoor sign business, but the gutters are filled with men and women who received money and either threw it, or blew it, away. Not the Goulds, once of London, now of Toronto. "People who have survived in every business are those who give good value and good quality," says Hal Gould, president of Cultures, the Fresh Food Restaurants.

# AGGRESSIVE
# CORNED BEEF

### Bruce Druxerman

It's like a Hollywood scriptwriter's fantasy: three brothers and a neighbourhood deli Writ Large; could they make a go of it? You bet your roast beef on rye, they could. In October 1976 the first Druxy's opened in a closet-sized 500-square-foot space in the Royal Bank Plaza in downtown Toronto. As of the fall of 1986, just one decade later, there were over 50 Druxy's, with over 700 employees, bringing in over $40 million in sales a year. And that was only in the cities of Toronto, London, and Ottawa; the rest of Canada and the United States lay open to the Attack of the Nitrites, at a rate of one store a month—and all company-owned. But it didn't come from Hollywood; it came from Winnipeg. And it looks like NOTHING CAN STOP IT FROM GROWING MORE AND MORE AND MORE!

Bruce Druxerman, president of Druxy's, was born in the fall of 1943, in Belleville, where his father was in the Canadian Air Force. Then it was off to Montreal and finally Winnipeg, where dad went into real estate ("He made some money and was comfortable"), and Bruce and younger brothers Harold, now 37, and Peter, 35, grew up happy, upper middle class, and healthy. The oldest went to the University of Wisconsin in Madison for degrees in science, commerce, and business administration, considering either medicine or dentistry before deciding that he "didn't want school for another six years!"

After graduation, Bruce D. worked for the New York office of the Mercantile Bank of Canada for three years and "enjoyed it," and then went back to Winnipeg. His father, by that time, owned The Fireplace Restaurant, a swimming club, a motel, and a par-3 golf course. The firstborn ran the complex, spending a lot of time in the restaurant, "developing it," using it as the eatery of the swim club. He ran it six years, tripling its size, and turning it into, in his words, "the hottest night club in Winnipeg." Considering the weather there, it must have been a blessing. There was folksinging, dancing, and bands galore.

It was now 1973; Bruce Druxerman was turning 30, and he went off to Montreal for six months to work for Hosthouse Foods, which ran a chain of restaurants. "That's when I started to realize the concept, as they went from single units to multiunit operations." And he always thought as a businessman, not as a restauranteur: He looked at food costs, how to develop menus, doing it all scientifically with the help of computers and operation manuals. "I didn't want to operate like ma-and-pa places," he says. After a year, his "eyes opened up," he had picked up enough knowledge to go into business for himself. He was transferred to Toronto soon after and spent a full year researching the concept.

Now we get to the good stuff. After visiting different cities, Druxerman decided that there was a crying need for "fast-food sandwich operations, and delis connotated quality image. Think of the deli department in a grocery store," he says. So he approached J. J. Barnicke Realty in Toronto to lease one unit in the Royal Bank Plaza in 1976. "All the good locations are gone," he was told. "Your guy can't cook there, anyway, since there's no exhaust." "Hey, I don't *want* to cook," replied Druxerman. "Cooking implies grease, and I'm after *healthy* food." (Deli is healthy? Wait till my wife hears this!) The real estate company refused to lease to Druxerman; he had no track record. "Where are your *other* locations?" they asked him snidely.

"I thought to myself," recalls Druxerman, "my dad used to deal with the Royal Bank!" So he called up the bank's chairman of the board, who had just retired, and who had known papa back in Winnipeg. The son outlined his problem, and the next day the deal was cemented. (We never said that true entrepreneurs *couldn't* have money or connections in order to get started; it's what they do after they start that interests us.)

After the tiny kiosk opened in the fall of 1976—dad, who had been called Druxy by a neighbour, loaned his son $60,000—there were quickly two more locations, one in the Eaton Centre, one in the suburban Sheppard Centre. "It was horrendous running three locations!" he recalls, hiring 20 staffers almost overnight. He called an old friend from Winnipeg to come in as general manager, and the outlets began to multiply. By the end of 1978 he was up to 8 locations, all in Toronto; by the end of 1979 there were 13. "That's when the crunch came; it became a whole different business."

At the start there was no office; Druxerman was in the stores constantly. When he hit eight stores, he had a little office with another two people. "I'd always wanted to build a business as large as I could—but we actually opened five delis in one summer!" He realized that he had to have a strong financial person on board, so why not brother Harold, a C.A. from Winnipeg? Baby Peter came on board in 1981; he's now VP, management services. He has a commerce degree from Queen's and an M.B.A. from Harvard, followed by a stint at Procter and Gamble. "I would have stayed longer," Peter recalls, "but I wondered if I should join Bruce at Druxy's." He now recruits management trainees.

"With family, I've got people I can trust looking over my accounts," says president Bruce, who added four more units by the end of 1981, bringing his total up to 17. The original concept was small kiosks, the first of which earned $250,000 a year. But then the one in Eaton Centre brought in $600,000 a year, leading him to exclaim "*Hey!* This is *phenomenal*!! We're bringing in more than one thousand dollars per square foot! It's *unheard* of!" And then he was bombarded with requests for franchises.

"But my attitude was, you *start* a business, you *run* a business," declares Bruce Druxerman. So rather than franchise, he runs it strongly in operations: management meetings every Monday night with the three brothers and other top staff, with "Ninety percent of the talk on how best to serve the customers. We don't spend a lot of time discussing locations."

That's because they've never had a bad one, which is part of the genius behind Druxy's. For one thing, they changed every one to a restaurant, with 2,000 to 3,500 square feet, with seats (except one, back in the TD Centre in Toronto). Three of the five in the head office work in the stores, which means they know every problem that arises and can react instantly. "We recently added second slicers and cash registers to improve the flow, and added four or five more coffee machines in each," says the president. "Store managers don't have time to come up with ideas like that; guys from the head office *can*. I avoided franchising because of my concern for quality; I'm a stickler for details and work in the stores one-half of the time myself." When they discovered two design flaws in the bottoms of cups, making them wobble, and another in the lids, they corrected all three, along with a different size on the foil wrapping the sandwiches.

The first year, sales were half a million dollars. By the summer of 1985, they were $20 million, and with the 35 stores in mid-1986, nearly $30 million. "Some stores are bringing in close to $1½ million a year," says Bruce Druxerman, "with many up to $750,000."

They see themselves opening one Druxy's a month over the years ahead, with perhaps half a dozen more in Toronto. In the downtown core of that city there are 20 Druxy's between Front, Dundas, Church, and University, which is a remarkably small area. Which brings us back to LOCATION. "I feel that I pioneered the development of a chain-operated, family-owned, family-run, nonfranchised series of restaurants *in office buildings*," he says, beaming. He is pleasant-looking, with black hair greying around the ears. True, his delis are in most major malls around Toronto, but the menu "was *designed* for office people. You give them good value, but you can't price it crazy." The average ticket is $3.50.

Yet Bruce Druxerman insists on the whole white tuna, mixed daily, all bread and pastry thrown away at the end of the day, all salads made right there in the store, and no premade sandwiches. "Everything is prepared made-to-order." Take that, Ronald McDonald.

The future of Druxy's? Probably to Vancouver and Calgary in the near future, and then into the States, always looking at office buildings first. "That's our appeal. Shopping centre landlords are too greedy, anyway." Bruce Druxerman feels that to own and operate in a city, he needs to open five or six there. "I want to go to Boston; it's close, and it reminds me of Toronto." He wants to be there by the end of 1986 and have a half dozen there within three years. "If it goes well, there are other cities in the U.S.!" he says with a smile. And, he adds, he's seen the delis in New York City, and "*no* one is doing what I'm doing!"

It costs over a quarter of a million dollars to open each unit, but it takes under three years to pay back the investment. By 1990 he estimates that there will be at least 85 Druxy's across North America, and possibly as many as 100. Since they try to show a profit margin of close to 10%—"It's an industry standard"—profits should be well over $3 million in 1986. But then, the Druxerman brothers have been spending $4½ million a year on expansion, so it doesn't last long. And expansion doesn't come cheap when he insists on solid oak counters, tile everywhere, sparkling new equipment. "I wanted a classy-looking place," he says.

There were some mistakes; in 1977 Druxerman also opened what would be five Burger Expresses, but he found that he was spending too much time on the fresh-made hamburger joints. They made money, but not like Druxy's, so they got out of it by 1983, when they were up to 20 locations on the delis. "With Druxy's, we *are* the market," he says.

It's still a busy life, with Bruce Druxerman working from 6:00 A.M. to 9:00 P.M., five days a week. On Saturdays "I look for new locations." He didn't start paying himself "a good salary" until 1981, but since ownership of the business is evenly divided among the three brothers, he shouldn't have to worry.

"An entrepreneur is someone who makes something out of nothing," says Druxerman. "I don't care if he had any money before. With his mind, he creates something. By the end of 1985 I had four hundred and fifty employees, twenty million dollars in business, and was paying a hundred thousand dollars a month to the provincial government and another hundred thousand to the feds. We pay our fair share to them.

"I certainly opened the marketplace," he confesses happily. "I've always been very aggressive. When I was told back in 1976 that I couldn't have a location, my first thought was 'Who do I know?' I showed other entrepreneurs that there's money to be made here. Michel's Baguettes, Cultures, and McDonald's are all moving into office buildings now, too! You know, I feel *great* when I walk into a Druxy's and see a huge lineup. 'Hey,' I say to myself, 'they like my concept!' "

## MORE THAN A COLONEL OF SUCCESS

### Oscar Grubert

On the wall of the outside lobby of the office of Oscar Grubert, the chairman of Champs Food Services Ltd. of Winnipeg, is a framed restaurant bill labelled "Our First Customer." The big spender at Champs Kentucky Room had a Spanish omelette (90¢), one open-faced chopped sirloin sandwich ($1.25), one shrimp cocktail (85¢), and two coffees (20¢— we knew that one would grab you, if the price of the shrimp did not). The total was $3.20, and beneath the modest, no-name tab, three Canadian one-dollar bills and two dimes are glued on the sheet.

Not far from that modest beginning is a massive painting, entitled "The Pursuit of Success," with portraits of Oscar Grubert, partner Bill Goldberg, and none other than Colonel Harland Sanders of finger-lickin'-good fame, plus a list of the various restaurants created by the two Canadians of the three: in 1958 Champs Auto-Dine, in 1959 Champs Kentucky Fried Chicken (the first in Winnipeg), right on through over a dozen other restaurants, including the 20th Kentucky Fried Chicken outlet, which opened in 1976, the first Mother Tucker's Food Experience, opened in 1975, and the 20th Mother Tucker's, opened in Bloomington, Minnesota, in 1983. Grubert's original investment was $50,000 (as it was for the two other partners at the time); sales from all of his restaurants in mid-1987 were in the neighbourhood of $80 million. All this, from a native of Winnipeg, Manitoba, a short, double-chinned, soft-spoken lawyer with receding hair. Of such men are mighty restaurant chains and restaurant concepts born.

Oscar Grubert was the first and only male of three children born to an immigrant from Poland who came to Canada in 1926. "He had just enough to buy a loaf of bread and two cans of sardines when he landed in Halifax," his son relates. While his wife was having children (Oscar was born a few months before the stock market crash of '29), the father dug basements in Saskatoon, peddled from Winnipeg to the east and west in an open wagon, and opened a general store outside the Manitoba capital. "He was pretty industrious," says Grubert. "He cut pulpwood and shipped it to a paper company in Manitoba as well." But, unlike his very successful son, "he accumulated a good name more than anything else" before his death in 1975.

Seeing the Canadian dream in action, even without riches, had its influence on the young boy: "I picked up the work ethic, and the feeling that a good name was important." (One feels, in spending time with Grubert, that the 1984 International Man of the Year award from an American publication, *Nation's Restaurant News*, and his 1985 Man of the Year Award from the Jewish National Fund mean far more to him than any financial reward his career has had to offer). Like many an immigrant's child, he graduated in law (from the University of Manitoba in 1954), and like many lawyers, he didn't go into it to practice. "I always had the feeling that I wanted to go into a business and build something." He did practice law for a half dozen years, but it was during that period that he was struck by "the enormous traffic" in his north end of Winnipeg neighbourhood. "My God, there's no drive-in restaurant around here!" he exclaimed to himself, and a future restauranteur was born. "I can't say that I *chose* restaurants," he claims, but the fact remains that it was the lack of a drive-in, and not, say, a movie house or a milk store, that struck the young, newly married lawyer.

So Grubert decided, along with two partners—one was later bought out—to put up the missing drive-in. The name, Champs, was "a stroke of luck," suggested by an architect. The three put in a mere $15,000 between them, as noted above, along with "overspending" another $5,000. (The entrepreneur notes here that he recently did a *renovation* of a Kentucky Fried Chicken store that cost $350,000, implying that times have indeed changed. "That shows how difficult it would be today to start out," he warns all you potential millionaires out there. "We were lucky," he adds modestly.

"We got in on the ground floor of the fast-food trend." Indeed he did.)

The original Champs Auto-Dine, which broke even in its first year of existence, survived only briefly and was later torn down. But as he was slowly moving into the treacherous business, he attended a seminar on franchises in Winnipeg that same year. Two or three names were mentioned, and only one stuck in Grubert's mind: Colonel Sanders, of blessed memory. "Having lots of time, I went back to my law offices and wrote him a letter." Yet today, nearly three decades after that fateful relationship began, the former lawyer explodes, "We didn't know what we were *doing*! How does a boy from a kosher home run a restaurant?"

Not well, at first. They thought that they would offer a full menu at the drive-in, and "it only confused the kitchen. So instead of one, two, or three good items, we did twenty bad ones." But in the meantime, there was that special meeting with the gentle colonel. There are today, a quarter century later, 25 Champs Kentucky Fried Chickens in Manitoba and North Dakota.

Grubert kept trying different things during this period. There was a brief stint in the hotel business—Champs Motor Inn, 1967—but he soon realized that "unless I had a chain of hotels, the capital costs were too great to make a decent profit." He sold out three years later. "We decided to stick to restaurants, even though we made little money."

All the Champs K.F.C.'s are company-owned franchises, with the first one costing $10,000 to put up and the latest costing half a million. Grubert and his partner pay a franchise fee to run the stores. "By 1965 we were in full flight," he says, referring to himself and partner Bill Goldberg.

And like a true creative entrepreneur, Grubert was never satisfied with the wildly successful fried chicken restaurants. By 1970 he began to work on developing a specialty group of restaurants—Mother Tucker's Food Experience. "I wanted to create a concept that would expand," he says, opening the first one in Winnipeg in 1975. His excellent idea can be summed up in a simple phrase: If a restaurant will do well in Winnipeg, it will probably do well anywhere. "Winnipeg is a difficult market," he explains. "It's very conservative, with a large middle- to blue-collar class. There's not an overabundance of money, and people were not sophisticated in their choices of eating out until recently."

And, until recently, many of the Grubert inspirations failed mightily: He tried gourmet hamburgers way back in the 1970s, and "now it's the rage!" he exclaims. He also tried "lighter foods" back in the mid-1970s, which are "now very successful," but they didn't "take" in Winnipeg that early. But Mother Tucker's Food Experience was "the most substantial, with the broadest appeal and value-oriented," he says. There are now 21 of them in "every major Canadian city and across the United States," and his plan is for up to 30 of them by 1990. They are "complex" restaurants, costing $2 million each to put up, but Grubert feels that they will continue to go from strength to strength. "I have a small but very effective group of people with me," he declares, "and I pay them well to keep them from going other places."

Grubert is also looking for acquisitions that would "fit in with Mother Tucker and add fifteen to twenty in one shot. Picking up a small chain of restaurants would be ideal for us."

Although Grubert briefly considered going public back in 1970, he pulled away when the market dropped. Today he is in "no great rush; I want to control my destiny." And, indeed, it has all worked out to his advantage. He is able to finance the remarkable growth of his restaurant empire out of cash flow and lease-backs, so that, "as our net worth increases, it costs only about three to four hundred thousand dollars to build a Mother Tucker's, not two million."

Oscar Grubert is not a daring man. For instance, he renews his lawyer's licence every year "out of a sense of insecurity; it's my Jewish background!" And during those dreadful recession years of the early 1980s, when the interest rates shot up so high, "we immediately stopped expansion. It was good for us; a chance to take stock. A lot of failures at that time were from people overexpanding."

He shows his conservatism in his negative reaction to that greatest of all restaurant profit-makers: booze. "We've never become too liquor-oriented. There's as much profit in food as in liquor, if you handle it right. We like the ratio eighty–twenty or seventy-five–twenty-five, maximum. Besides, the liquor-drinking public is very fickle. Canadian Club tastes the same at our place as the next place."

Yet for all his seeming lack of risk taking, he was never

one to stop at a single restaurant. "You make up your mind: are you running one or a chain? If I ran one, it would be no challenge, and it would be monotonous! I needed to build a chain that would be recognized in the industry. I felt that we could do as well as most."

Grubert's Champs Food Service Ltd. is now ranked in the top 20 in the food industry in Canada. "A lot of those out there are big," he says, "but not as successful as we are in the bottom line. We limited that by staying private but keeping our eyes on the ball."

While claiming that his style is "pragmatic and realistic," Grubert also claims that "you need to take chances," pointing to the number of ventures that were not successful. "It took me to the age of fifty to stop making emotional decisions." It was fortunate that his youth paralleled preinflationary times. "In the early days, it was cheaper to be right," he says. "You could afford to be wrong in the old days. The trick is to change from free-wheeling, fly-by-the-seat-of-your-pants style of business to the more sophisticated input by boardroom." He feels that he has been most effective over the past five years.

The entrepreneurial spirit continues in the Grubert family. His son, Nolan, 31, a graduate of Western, is vice-president of Mother Tucker operations. And while his daughter, in her early twenties, is not part of the Champs staff, she runs a small restaurant, Baked Expectations, in Winnipeg.

Champs and Grubert have come a long way in less than three decades; his restaurants can be found in such un-Canadian locations as Phoenix, Dallas, Minneapolis, Chicago, and Atlanta, and they average sales of over $2½ million a year each. The entire operation has close to 3,000 employees, which does not go unappreciated by the diminutive chairman of the board: "It's scarey at times to think of how many people depend on me making the right moves."

And a business of his kind can't run "unless gut feelings are involved," says Grubert. "That's where the entrepreneur comes in, since the true one works mostly from his gut. That's why most companies should sell out after they reach a certain size. It takes a certain type to start a business and another to run it."

Then how has Oscar Grubert managed to be both? "I've surrounded myself with capable people, and forced myself to listen to them when they speak." He didn't have that luxury at the beginning, but he does now. "I needed help with Mother Tucker's Food Experience," he says. "I needed some creative assistance," especially after a half dozen specialty restaurants that preceded had failed to click. "At this stage of the game, I need people who can advise me and insulate me against pratfalls."

The 18-hour day and 6-day weeks are over now and have been for a decade. The goals today are somewhat different: "I've set certain goals for myself regarding being able to work for charities, and I haven't achieved them yet. But I've made commitments to them and hope to free up money and time to fulfill them."

But money, as noted above, has never been the real motivation. At the age of 25 Grubert considered becoming a millionaire by the time he was 35. But when he was 30, and told that he was, he asked, "Then why can't I buy a pair of pants?" He was a millionaire only on paper.

Today, the paper is printed by the federal government in Ottawa, and Oscar Grubert is truly rich. No, more than that: "The difference between rich and wealthy is that rich is money; wealth is achievement and happiness. We've made our mark. We haven't changed the industry, but we've made a mark and had an effect."

And there's always room for more. Grubert walks over to the large painting in the lobby and points to some of the names of restaurants in the history of Champs Food Service Ltd. There was Big Smokin' Joe's Bar-B-Q (1982); the Newport Pub in Florida (1981); Gabby's Texas Steak House in the same year; T. Bones Food & Beverage Co. (1980); G. Willaker's, an O'Toole's-type roadhouse restaurant that didn't take—it was also ahead of its time (1977). His finger stops at The Garden Creperie, which opened in 1977.

"That's still in existence," says the still-registered-as-a-lawyer Oscar Grubert of Winnipeg. "It's a good little restaurant. And it could become a chain someday. It has real potential."

As does Tommy Lasorda's Ribs and Pasta in Marina del Rey, California. Grubert expects that this latest creation, done with the manager of the L.A. Dodgers, which opened in February 1987, could well be the first of many. And so it grows.

# TAKING THE
# NEIGHBOURHOOD BAR
# ACROSS THE CONTINENT

*Gord Metcalfe*

Walking into an O'Toole's Roadhouse Restaurant is rather like being carried back in time. Loaded with old gas pumps, road signs, and movie posters, O'Toole's has a very visible fascination with '50s and '60s kitsch. It may not be everyone's idea of a fine-dining atmosphere, but as a suburban eaterie, O'Toole's is one hot spot. "We're developing the market," declares Gord Metcalfe, 41, president of O'Toole's Food Corp. of Rexdale, Ontario, who is also watching over a spanking new chain of (fresh!) fish restaurants and combination donut-and-deli stores, exploding like neutron bombs and leaving profits intact. "We are the neighbourhood bar," he says. Some big neighbourhood. There were 63 O'Toole's across North America as of the fall of 1987, and the entire system has some 3,000 employees. And the corporation is growing faster than you can say. "*You* drive; I've had a little too much."

Gordon Metcalfe, who has no doubts that he will become the Colonel Sanders of the bar, fish, donut, and corned-beef-on-rye world, was born in the fall of 1945 in Ottawa, the first of two children. His father was with the Department of National Defence; his mother did periodic office work. From 13 on, he had "lots of jobs," such as paper routes, working as a soda jerk, and, presciently, delivering beer. He studied town planning at Concordia, in Montreal, and taught geography from 1967 to 1971 in Cornwall, Ontario, and then two more years in Etobicoke, in suburban Toronto.

By 1971 he moved out of teaching, which he enjoyed but "couldn't stand the politics of the boards. And chances of promotion were next to nil." A principal of his had run a travel agency which sent students around the world, and Metcalfe started to get fellow teachers interested in the program. After 18 months of working for the travel firm on the side, he "decided it was fun" and went into it full time. For a brief period, it was the largest charter company in Canada, sending up to 50 DC-10s across the ocean over March break.

Metcalfe kept moving farther away from those noisy kids, becoming the chief operating officer for Supplies Camden, a division of Ideal in Chicago, and one of the largest manufacturers of electrical components in the world. (While in the travel business, he did direct-mail marketing, and Supplies was into that.) After his 18-month contract was over, he hopped over to Shillcraft, a U.S.-based company, doing mail orders for craft kits—macramé, needlecraft, and so on—where he was C.E.O. from 1976 to 1981.

As we have noted occasionally in this book. Necessity is often the Mother of Great Ideas, if they are nursed very carefully. Well, the necessity which drove Gord Metcalfe to go into the food service business is almost silly in its origins: "My staff at Shillcraft had no place to go for lunch, so we opened an eaterie. We wanted a concept to get them in and out in forty-five minutes," and with a plant of over 100 workers in northwest Toronto, it had to be not-too-slow fast food.

The original place was called Stash O'Neill's—"I stole a name that I saw in the States"—and it opened, with the help of a partner, in September 1981. You can guess what happened. They hit their "optimum sales peak within sixty days" after they opened the doors. In the first year alone, the restaurant had gross sales of $1.3 million, with profits in excess of $200,000.

It was't all chicken fingers and beer, since Metcalfe had some disagreements with his partner, and they split some six franchised restaurants later. It was an "acrimonious break-up," complete with lawsuits, and it saw Metcalfe buying the flagship, changing the name to O'Toole's, and starting over in February 1983.

Yes, ladies and gentlemen, you read right. One restaurant in early 1983 has proliferated/expanded/exploded/rocketed (you choose the proper verb; it's a multiple-choice quiz, and we warn you, they could *all* be correct) to number 34 in the Top 100 of the 1984 listing of *Foodservice & Hospitality* magazine as of September 1985, up from number 72 in 1983, with $53.8 million in revenue, already shooting past such other chains in Canada as Taco Bell, Pizza Hut, Pizza Delight, Country Style Donuts, Baskin-Robbins, and many more. The three dozen-plus O'Toole's are now spread across Ontario, Manitoba, and Alberta, with eight stores opening in Atlantic Canada over the next three years, a test store in Drummondville, Quebec, and an extraordinary response down in the States, where the first roadhouse opened in Baltimore in late 1984. There are now over 15 across the United States, including 8 in Ohio, 3 in Denver, 2 more in the Washington, D.C., area, a few way out in California, and even one in Bruce Springsteen's beloved Asbury Park, New Jersey. "We won the award as the fastest-growing food service company in Canada in the fall of 1983," Metcalfe says, his big, round, and youthful face beaming like a proud daddy's. But whatever happened to single births?

Clearly this hasn't all been luck, nor have 25 million Canadians and ten times that many Americans been sitting with their tongues hanging out, waiting for a neighbourhood bar to open nearby where they could take the wife and kids without shame. (And we mean it about the family; part of the genius behind O'Toole's, besides the generous portions and reasonable prices, is the fact that every store goes after full utilization of its floor space: the business crowd at lunch, salesmen in the afternoon, a family and singles dining trade, and then, later in the evening, when the disk jockeys arrive to spin the Top 40, they all turn magically into bars, in an adult—but not filthy— version of Cinderella's pumpkin.)

No, you don't get gross sales of $72½ million (from the restaurants) and another $11 million (from the construction of all the stores) for a total of over $83 million at the end of 1987, up a bit from zero in early 1983, without hard work and careful planning. What happened was that Gord Metcalfe, formerly of the classroom, sat down and decided to "explode the concept" back in late 1982, and for the first six months of 1983 he developed all the operation manuals—they total over 1,000 pages—all user agreements, all paperwork, all systems, and franchised like mad. By August of that first year O'Toole's went public, selling 11 million shares at 25¢ a throw on the over-the-counter market. Exactly one year later the shares were worth $1.75 each and split three for one. Metcalfe owns about 70% of them, which sure beats teaching geography—or even higher math, which could come in handy to read his tax return.

Let's turn to his fish and donut-deli concepts next, since

their history gives some insight into the workings of Metcalfe's mind. He was approached in 1985 by the Old Fish Market of Toronto to buy them out, and after studying the operation, he "got so intrigued by the fresh fish concept, I aborted the deal but gained tremendous insight into the seafood business." For instance, the researching Metcalfe discovered a 300 to 400% increase in seafood-eating-out in the United States. (There were no statistics available in Canada, alas, but we are rarely far behind our southern neighbours in eating fads and fancies.) He also noted that there was no franchise concept in seafood, with the exception of the Red Lobster chain. "And fresh fish is a scarce commodity in Canada, despite the fact that our country is a leader in the fishing market." He promptly came to an agreement with suppliers in North America and moved ahead.

"Fish is *perceived* as a difficult product," says Metcalfe, but he disagrees. He went off and hired two Cordon Bleu chefs and built a $300,000 kitchen to teach his franchisees, chose the name Dockside Seamarket "out of the air," and built and opened the first one in London, Ontario, in September of 1985. "It's been a phenomenal success!" Metcalfe claims, anticipating $2½ million annually from that one, and every one in the future. (There is also a fresh-fish counter in each, and he had three fish restaurants, all in Ontario, by the fall of 1987.)

OK, that takes care of O'Toole's, where the food is "simplistic"—hamburgers, chicken fingers, steaks, sandwiches—and the fresh fish idea of the Docksides. "Our systems are virtually foolproof!" Metcalfe declares. But what's this about donut-delis?

Don't *ask*. Donuts Plus, as they are called, "is an orphan." You see, Metcalfe, always on the lookout for more food ideas to franchise, "decided that donuts are so strong, we should take a kick at the can." He did an analysis of the donut business and found that donut stores make 85% of their income between the hours of 6:00 and 9:00 A.M. and over suppertime. "Yet they pay $600,000 an acre to support a five-hour business!" he proclaims. Oh yes: Fully 55% of all labor costs goes to the midnight-to-6:00 shift making the greasy little things. "So the bulk of the overhead goes to making the donuts, and one-half of the square footage is used for the making!"

Metcalfe and his men and women at the head office in suburban Toronto decided that "this is *crazy*! If we can give people a fresh donut and one of the finest sandwiches in Toronto at a lower price, all in seven hundred to a thousand square feet, and *not* let ourselves be held ransom to a baker, it would be profitable!"

So in June 1985, O'Toole's Food Corp. of Rexdale, Ontario, opened Donuts Plus and began importing smoked meat from Montreal. They soon discovered that they were moving 200 sandwiches a day, and fewer donuts than they had expected. "So we reoriented to the sandwich, which had been the orphan."

There were four Donuts Plus in Toronto as of the spring of 1986, and—surprise!—Metcalfe plans to open 30 more by the fall of 1987. That's right, *thirty*. T-h-i-r-t-y, all within 25 miles of the Toronto International Airport. "We take the stores to industrial parks, where there are no places for lunch, and they are open from 7:00 A.M. to 5:00 P.M. We're the stationary coffee truck!" (And if an owner of a coffee truck is reading this, change jobs *quick*.) The Donuts Plus truck brings in fresh donuts twice a day, just as fresh as the neighbourhood donut place, but without those costly bakers and all that expensive kitchen space. "There is a central commissary for the fish and deli restaurants," Metcalfe explains.

"The way things are going now, our success is in direct proportion to staying awake!" (Metcalfe logs 15 to 20 hours every day but is always home for dinner with his wife and two children, even if he has to leave again, which he does.) "There are holes in the food market that you can drive a truck through!" he proclaims, "and a *lot* of people are stale!" (Unlike his donuts.)

Now to the longer-range plans. Sit down again. "I see eighty O'Toole's in Canada, and five hundred in the U.S. by 1990, each bringing in $1.15 million per year." (Before you whip out the calculator, please note that all these multiplying restaurants are franchised, returning only 5% in royalties to the mother corporation.) "And if the fish restaurants take off, there should be over a thousand in North America by the end of the century." Yep. One thousand.

And Donuts Plus? "That's a sleeper. If we can get the right amount of energy, we should have seven hundred to eight hundred Donuts Plus in Canada. It will permit hundreds of people with $15,000 for a franchise fee to open their own successful business. And we could put one every few blocks in every industrial park across the country." One of the original Donuts Plus is turning close to $200,000 a year in an industrial park in Toronto, yet it is open only nine hours a day, five days a week.

Development is expensive, of course. Metcalfe shelled out half a million dollars on the original Dockside Seamarket before he put in the first nail, hiring staff, developing trading manuals, building the test kitchen, etc. But there are always backups in the fertile, hungry mind of Gord Metcalfe: "With the fish concept, we can move it in if any O'Toole's doesn't sustain its strength in any area. We needn't change cash or the kitchen, so it would be only $100,000 to redress the place into a Dockside." Meanwhile, he didn't advertise any O'Toole's roadhouses for two full years, since business was so strong. And Donuts Plus? He ran a test ad in September in the *Globe and Mail* and had 183 responses. "We could put up another thirty stores overnight!" he asserts. And he means *that* literally, too.

And what of Gord Metcalfe, himself, who could be earning nearly $50,000 a year if he'd *only* stayed teaching? And we sense that he isn't kicking himself for getting out of the classroom, either. How has he managed to produce such wonders almost overnight?

"I think entrepreneurship is genetic. There's a certain type of person who enjoys a challenge—creating something, and *making it work*. The entrepreneur is blessed with special skills to grab on to a concept. I've always enjoyed looking at businesses, ever since I was a teenager. If you're blessed with energy, you *go* for it. Anyway, it's *not* the money, it's the *achievement*."

# FROM SHARING AN EGG TO FEEDING EDMONTON

**Saul Reichert**

The stories that have come from the world of night that was the destruction of European Jewry are many, and since tens of thousands of survivors came to this country after 1948, it is hardly surprising that many of them are worthy of inclusion in any book on Canadian entrepreneurs. This is one of them, and it overflows with irony and tenacity.

Saul Reichert was born shortly before Christmas, in 1930, in Zgierz, one of the thousands of Polish *shtetls*, or villages, which covered that tragic land between the wars. Reichert's family had a paint supply store, and of the family of eight—his parents, himself, and five sisters—he was the only one who would survive Hitler's Final Solution. He was eventually shipped to the nearby Lodz ghetto, and in August 1944 Reichert was sent off to Birkenau, the death factory, to be murdered with the millions of others there.

But he was liberated by the American army and eventually found a place to stay in Germany. Reichert recalls going, with a cousin, to a farmer, and being offered a single egg to eat. "It was hard to share one egg," he says.

After Saul had worked for the American army for a while as a KP boy—he was only fourteen at the end of the war—a soldier suggested that the lad should try to go to America. But the quota was full, and he had to wait, along with tens of thousands of others. Finally, in 1948, as one of over 1,000 orphaned children redeemed by the Canadian Jewish Congress, he arrived in Halifax. There was a quota for each Canadian city; some went to Montreal, others to Toronto; Saul Reichert went to Edmonton. "I looked at the map and got frightened! 'Where are you taking me, to Siberia?' But they told me that everyplace else was all booked, and I had to go." He negotiated for Winnipeg, failed, and decided to give Edmonton a try.

A member of the Canadian Jewish Congress met the orphan in Winnipeg, brought him out to the Siberian portion of Alberta, and took him into the family. The young man had "taken some schooling in the ghetto," followed it up with some more formal scholarship at Alberta College, and "muddled through."

Fortunately for Reichert, his sponsor was a bit of an entrepreneur, as well as being a good soul, and the man purchased a restaurant called Teddy's. The appreciative ward worked there for $35 a week, 11:00 A.M. to 1:00 A.M., seven days a week, for ten full years. "It was *everything*!" he says, and how could one disagree? (He had gotten married in 1956, at which time he slowed down a teeny bit, but the restaurant was, undoubtedly, "the focal point of my life.")

As in any rags-to-riches story (except his rags had been provided by the Nazi regime), Saul Reichert began to buy bits and pieces of the booming restaurant. In 1956 he became a 50% owner of Teddy's; by 1960 he was the full owner of his own establishment in Edmonton, Alberta. "I was the waiter, manager, everything. I swept the floor, took the cash. . . ."

In 1955 his future partner had decided to open Patricia Lunch, followed by Malta Lunch, and then the Carousel Restaurant, all three purchased within two years. By 1960 Reichert had purchased a portion of the other three, along with the full ownership of Teddy's. He eventually sold out Patricia and Malta, trading the equity of the latter for that of the Carousel.

Years later, the proud owner of two restaurants, the immigrant joined with prominent lawyer and businessman Joe Shoctor to become a partner of the Saxony Motor Hotel. He has worked with Shoctor on various projects since 1966.

Most recently, Saul Reichert opened a seafood restaurant in his chosen city—or rather, the city that was chosen for him. It's called the Pacific Fish Company, and "it was *my* idea!" he exclaims. The idea being fresh fish, cooked on mesquite, in the middle of the dining room before the hungry and fascinated customers. (He is 50–50 in the project with a friend from the Carousel.) By 1986 there were three in Edmonton, one of them the famous Carousel.

In 1979 Reichert tore down the old Teddy's, and he recalls with great pride that the *Edmonton Journal* had a big spread on this "landmark" restaurant of the city. "It was old, had lots of character, and it was a unique place! City artists used to paint murals on the walls, and the people loved it!" But it only seated 50, and the new Teddy's seats 290, so progress had to take place. And upstairs, as of 1987, is a new dinner-mystery theatre.

The story of the Carousel underlines the entrepreneurial flair of the survivor from the Old Country. Initially, it was a coffee shop, and "they didn't want to give me a liquor licence; I was a little guy." Eventually there were "headlines from coast to coast," according to Reichert. And he went before the liquor commission to argue his case: "Why do one hundred-seat places get licences and not fifty-seat places?" He got the licence.

Saul Reichert has always been a risk-taker; not surprising,

considering the risks he had encountered hourly during the Holocaust. "That Saxony was a risk," he says. "Pacific Fish is a risk. And people say I'm crazy, with Edmonton in the shape it's in." (The restaurant cost $600,000; the risk-taker put up nearly a third; the Ghermezians of West Edmonton Mall fame helped with the line of credit at the bank.) With 90 seats in the lounge and another 140 in the dining room, the old-warehouse-type restaurant appears to be on the road to success.

Reichert has four daughters—and two new grandchildren, as of the end of 1987—along with over 200 employees counting on him at the Saxony, Teddy's, and the "fish places." "I've had so many brainstorms that if I did them all, I'd be either a multi-multi-millionaire or poverty-stricken!" he jokes, implying strongly that the former is closer to the case. "I have inspirations! I'd sit in front of the ocean, watching the waves come in, or see a great movie, or sit in *shul* [synagogue], and I'd want to *do things*."

Which he has. "When you have an idea, you've got to believe in yourself and push yourself to new heights," Reichert claims. "It takes a combination of things: to want to succeed, and to want to do something different." The fish restaurants are "exciting" to Reichert: "To bring fresh fish in from the east and west coasts! To have a new concept of cooking and design!" And, of course, "the challenge of making an extra few bucks." So he runs from store to store, still, but he has managers now. "I *love* to plan and build them, but I'm *tired* of running them! What I love to do is design concepts!"

Not that Saul Reichert has achieved his goals yet, as he moves into the second half of his 50s. "I'd like to go out and build more restaurants. I'd like to put up two or three in Phoenix; I've got a place there. And I'd love to build a Teddy-style one in Vancouver, with a great bar and great food. I don't know *anybody* in Edmonton who's been in the same place as long as my Teddy's!"

The basic desire, then, has not changed since the teenage Reichert came to Edmonton in 1948: "To do something new, and to explore." When the hook with his nightmarish past is pointed out, Saul Reichert hesitates for a moment. "I never consciously think about it, but there *is* some truth about the impact of the Holocaust and the murder of my family on my life. I mean, I had one English pound and two American dollars when I came to Canada. And I feel *good* when people say to me, 'Saul, you're a self-made man!' "

# SANTA CLAWS ARE COMING TO TOWN

## *John Risley*

Are you familar with Clearwater Lobster Ltd.? If not, you shouldn't be too surprised; this Halifax-based company sells only a small percentage of its shellfish to Canada. But in much of Europe and the Far East, they are the General Motors of lobster, with between 55 and 80% of the market. (They're big in Japan, too.) And when you talk with young and sassy John Risley, its hard-driving, driven president, you feel as if you are talking with Lee Iacocca—except that Risley doesn't turn companies around; he creates madly profitable ones. Opinionated, bright, controversial, Risley sounds almost like a con man. Except that there is no conning in catching, raising, and exporting lobsters—or in canning either, for that matter. There's big money in live lobsters, and John Risley is making it, hand over claw.

John Risley was born in the spring of 1948 in Halifax and was shipped off to a small private school where the headmaster was a Scot. "You'll be a successful businessman" he told the "particularly lazy" student. "He must have seen something that no one else saw," Risley declares today.

He took three years at Dalhousie University but "was too anxious to go out and make money. I studied nothing and didn't learn a thing," he mocks. "I knew more before I went." Indeed, he had always had "base, material ambitions," which he insists have changed substantially since those youthful days. A friend in university whose father was a stockbroker was making money in the market and in real estate, and Risley quickly began to watch carefully. He "wheeled and dealed," doing $100,000 deals by the age of 21, and had "a few six-figure years." He pooh-poohs it today: "Back in 'sixty-six or 'sixty-seven, any fool could make a buck," he claims.

"I had no perspective," he says, looking back on those good old/bad old days. "My vision of the future was the balance of today and tomorrow." When the stock market settled back, and winnings turned to losses, the appeal of real estate grew. He would buy houses in Halifax, Dartmouth, and environs, fix them up, and sell them quickly, doing deals with his brother. But, as he soon learned, when you go into the land development business, you need "a tremendous wad of cash." When a downturn came in 1973–74, he had a number of developments he was unable to sell. "I went bust," he says. "All the creditors were paid, but I lost all my money."

But brass times can quickly turn to gold in the mind and actions of an intelligent, aggressive entrepreneur. "I always had an affinity for the sea, like a true Nova Scotian," Risley says. A friend had a property in Bedford that was ideal for seafood, and he had a chance to get into it for little or no money. He eventually lined up three loans of $5,000 each and began Clearwater with his brother-in-law, who was a plumber's apprentice. It was initially a retail fish shop, buying lobsters in Cape Breton and selling them in Halifax.

After they made a good profit over the initial six weeks, Risley tried to borrow money from a bank to pay back the loans to each of his three friends. It turned him down. So for a long time he went through a "real financial fight," looking at his watch each day, hoping a cheque would come in the mail to cover his loans.

They felt that there was no room for them in the traditional lobster business, and saw an opportunity in Europe. "There was not a lot of interest in Canadian seafood and creating new markets, though," he says. Risley and his brother-in-law were "naïve, ambitious, and would do anything to get orders," and they went knocking on the doors of the three or four major importers in Europe, France, Holland, and Belgium. "We told them, 'See us! Low overhead! We'll extend the lobster season! We'll pack them ourselves!' "

By the second year, sales hit $3½ million. "They built quite a business on our backs, and we on theirs," Risley laughs. But, alas, Clearwater began to get dependent on them, and "they began abusing our relationship on price. Because they were 80% of our business, they forced us to get a customer base which put more value on service and less on price."

Risley was not about to take this like a lobster facing a boiling pot of water. So he turned around and went to the importers' customers themselves. "They were middlemen," explains Risley. "So we went directly to the wholesalers, all thirty of them, and shipped straight to them! That worked fine, and we built a great business."

Which is all well and good, but there is a further problem, endemic to lobster sales: It's a very, very seasonal business. The industry has attempted to get around the lack of fresh lobsters by tidal pounding, which entails putting the lobsters into enclosures in the ocean when no fishing takes place.

But Risley had convinced his customers that Clearwater was commited to quality and growing volumes, and had hoped that they could just work harder and pay more attention. It wasn't enough, especially for a single-item distributor. "The roadblock was, tidal lobster pounds are not totally effective in providing good lobster on a year-round basis," declares Risley.

So the two partners quickly began to develop new technology: dry-land pounding. Since 1978 they have had a facility with a capacity of over a million pounds of lobster in a totally controlled environment, with exact water temperature and everything necessary. "So we could go to our customer base and state, 'Here is good quality product that we'll sell three hundred sixty-five days a year!'" It's a technology still in its infancy, and Risley notes that research and development is "a significant element of our cost base."

There were rough times, understandably. "We almost lost the company back in 1980," he says, but he refuses to blame the interest rates. "It was naïveté, immaturity, bad business sense," he admits. "There is no excuse for bad management. But we stayed with it and saw it through."

The numbers are staggering: Sales were up to $21 million in 1984, and by the following year they had increased to over $30 million, with 350 employees. Their 1986 expectations were $60 million, with 500 employees. Shockingly, they ended up at $115 million—with a projected $240 million by the end of 1987, due to numerous acquisitions. In early 1987, they had over 2,100 employees!

Clearwater doesn't catch the fish; there are independent fishermen who do that for them. But they pick up the distribution chain and carry it through to the consumer. They currently have a distribution centre in Brussels, and another in the United Kingdom.

In 1984 Risley and his partner had to make a decision: Would they keep it family-owned, or take advantage of various opportunities of business? "We think there are a lot of opportunities, and room for aggressiveness," he proclaims eagerly. "We're on a critical path to grow the business substantially. We won't even rule out going public."

They plan to grow in their distribution operations across Europe and the United States, and to grow technologically. "Every month we learn more," he declares. "We want to establish ourselves as the leader in this lobster technology." They even hope that, one day, they will become a culture operation, growing their own lobster from, let us say, scratch.

Risley has also recognized the importance of some kind of diversification into other shellfish products. "We've just built a crab plant in Liverpool, and we are producing a unique line of crab products," he says. "Crab business is a real whore business, and we were scared to death when the margins went way down. But we decided to carve out a niche. We have become unique suppliers to a unique customer base. We've also hooked up with a Scottish company, also young, and close to us in size."

They've gotten themselves carried in such stores as Marks and Spencer, and "are now selling crab products to people in Europe who've never bought Canadian products before. But we convince them that they can make money selling our shellfish."

Risley and brother-in-law Colin MacDonald, who is vice-president of Clearwater Lobster, have a three-year plan, but he's reluctant to "blow our horn." Yet he's willing to brag about how "we've done *nothing* but take risks! Someone told me recently, 'It looks like you come to the office for five years and roll the dice double or nothing every day.' "

All this expansion and worldwide success has not come from leisurely work habits. For the first two years in the business neither partner took even one day off, even Christmas or other holidays. They would not go home for days at a time. Risley still gets up at 4:00 A.M., goes running, gets to the office at 6:00, runs home, and goes to bed by 9:00 P.M.

He is aware that they are too big now to not involve

others; they've got a number of people managing and involved in planning, especially in 1987. "We're more professional now, rather than just a two-man show," he admits.

Anyone who could go from a $15,000 investment to $115 million-plus has rather strong views about his country and his fellow countrymen. "It's very disturbing," he says solemnly. "As a country, we're in a lot of trouble. We've been slow to realize just how aggressive the world market has turned."

Risley is also concerned about the Canadian work ethic, and the confrontational attitude that exists between business and labour. "It's unhealthy," he says; "just south of the border, there are tremendous examples of the two working together."

He is pleased with the good personal relationship he has with his hundreds of employees. "They see *us* work hard, and not just nine to four-thirty," he declares. His own personal philosophy on work is soon offered: "People *like* to work hard," he insists. "People who don't, feel they've cheated their company, or themselves, and they are unhappy. It erodes them. So it is incumbent on good employers to make their people work hard, so they will be happy." Wait till Bob White of the U.A.W. hears about John Risley.

Like most self-made men, lobster-growers or otherwise, Risley is a wonderful mixture of bravado and modesty. "We've established a direction in the industry," he says. "But anyone with time, money, and effort could have done it. We're not particularly unique. We're just concerned about continuing to grow and staying ahead of the competition."

Yet how could any competition compete with Clearwater Lobster? "To tell you the truth, I'm not sure whether others have tried to grow their own market niches and respond to them like we have," he states. "They've got to beat their heads against the wall; that's the role of small business."

Is it a success, then? Are all dangers past when you zoom into nine figures? "Success is the result of one's own perspective," says John Risley. "We'll measure it against how we achieve our potential." Yet he pulls back once more, not unlike a lobster fisherman dragging in his traps. "Our success is yet to be established, and I'm not sure if I belong in your book. We'll call ourselves successful in five years' time if we've honoured our commitments."

# THE VERY BUSY GOURMET

### Susan Mendelson

Turning childhood hobbies or interests into a business is usually considered the worst possible move for any entrepreneur to make. If you love something, you should keep it to yourself, preferably in the evenings and over weekends, and not go to banks to finance your game-playing from 9:00 to 5:00.

But what, then, would we tell Susan Mendelson, one of the mainstays of catering for the city of Vancouver, and the author of a number of successful cookbooks which have had her taste, if not her name, on the lips of hundreds of thousands of Canadians from coast to coast?

Born in 1952, she soon moved from her native Toronto to small-town Saskatchewan (Nipiwan, to be exact), then to Syracuse (where her father taught anesthesiology), and then back to Toronto in 1963. There were four children in the Mendelson family; she has an older sister and a younger brother, and a twin who made it into the world some six minutes before her.

And, as suggested above, young Susan Mendelson cooked "all the time." She would stand on a chair as a child, making cinnamon honey butter and French toast. She was also fascinated by her grandmother's cooking, about which she was once told by a friend, "When the deep freeze was invented, your grandmother took it on as a challenge!" She still chuckles at that line, and took it to heart, as well as to tummy. (Although she has a lovely figure today, she was "very overweight" from the age of 15 into her adulthood. "I had a severe weight problem," she admits, which isn't as bad as Madame Curie getting radiated, but it *is* an occupational hazard for cooks.)

While Susan Mendelson's grandmother kept fantasizing about having a small bakery, her cooking-crazed grandchild didn't think about any career in particular. She slaved in a coffee house at the age of 15 for 50¢ an hour ("I worked like a dog"), and she used to have bake sales in her backyard to raise money for charities, but she never considered the latter as anything other than her favourite thing to do.

Then, at 19, she moved to Vancouver—"Mecca!"—because she had heard that "that was where it was happening." Although it would take a long time before Ms. Mendelson knew what was happening as a future entrepreneur. She studied liberal arts at U.B.C. and "explored everything that Vancouver had to offer," still coming first in her class. She lived in a communal house and, yes, she did all the cooking for the five fortunate souls. "I did gourmet dinners every night," she states. In her third year—"I had gone into honours English and it was *very* dull and boring"—she worked with disturbed kids and went off to Europe.

When Mendelson returned to Mecca, she finally realized that she needed to have a career, and at the age of 24 she finally graduated with a bachelor's in social work. In the evenings she worked at the Vancouver East Cultural Centre, and to make some money, she (you guessed) made and sold cheesecake and carrot cake, and, eventually, Nanaimo bars, those awesomely delicious and caloric concoctions out of the west coast. "People began calling and reserving pieces of cheesecake for intermission, and critics began to review my baking that night!" she laughs. Canadian theatre never received so much respect.

Then came a kind of breakthrough, and, as in the case of many business people, it had to do with the media. CBC radio asked Susan Mendelson to come on and talk about her cheesecake. (She was hardly getting rich from her creations, by the way; she was selling them for $7.50, and they probably cost nearly half that to make. "But in those days, every little bit helped," she says.) After she spoke once, people started phoning in, pressuring the station to have her back on. So she began to talk on such subjects as "seductive dinners for Christmas and Valentine's Day," and was soon raking in $25 an appearance.

Then it was every other week, and she was nicknamed "CBC's Ace in the Kitchen." Hundreds phoned in for recipes, and—so she swears—"phones went haywire all over downtown Vancouver." (Author's note: Susan Mendelson has utterly magnificent blue eyes, so that it is quite impossible *not* to believe what she has to say.) Then she sat down and wrote a cookbook, *The Lazy Gourmet,* and it is a measure of her entrepreneurial flair at that time that it remains *un*published. She even left the Cultural Centre, where her baking had received bigger raves than the shows, and took a full-time job as a social worker in the field for two years, at $400 a month. Some business geniuses are simply very late bloomers.

Then came 1976, and Habitat. Susan Mendelson ended up catering all the opening nights, and got great PR from that. Then she was asked to cater the food for 200 performers—breakfast and lunch every day—at the Vancouver International Festival for Young People. This forced her to "learn the whole food business—I tracked down food suppliers, bakers, and got to know the health department." And she got a lot of publicity for that, too.

Small catering jobs followed, and she finally—*finally*—created her own firm called The Lazy Gourmet in 1979, with friend Deborah Roitberg. "We conceived it as a new kind of catering that Vancouver didn't have then." Roitberg had worked with Mendelson in the same house with delinquent (albeit well-fed) teenagers, and they used to hang out in the kitchen and cook together. "She's a great cook!" says Mendelson about her partner. Their new store was to be a kind of take-out gourmet, a type of catering where people would bring in their own serving dishes and thus could pretend that they had made the food themselves. No one has been able to trust another person in Vancouver since her place opened.

Sales the first year were "over $100,000," with just the two young women. Sales in 1985 were up to $700,000, with 25 employees, including a sales department, a cooking department, a retail storefront, catering, and wholesale desserts to about 15 restaurants. At the end of 1986, there were *three* retail storefronts, over 50 employees, and well over $1 million in sales. And in mid-1987, they were looking to build a large bakery. Imitators began flattering them like crazy. "*We* created lox mousse, and everyone else has it, as if it were *generic!*" she howls, but to no avail. All is fair in love, war, and catering.

Then came more publicity. Mendelson began to appear on CTV's afternoon talk show, first with Alan Hamel, then with Alan Thicke, and finally with Don Harron. Then she and Roitberg did "The Vancouver Show," every other Friday night.

Mendelson's first cookbook was *Momma Never Cooked Like*

*This*, a combination of recipes gathered from her first five years on radio. "It was really easy to write," she admits, and it came out in the fall of 1980. The history of publication shows the growing success of the growing empire of Susan Mendelson. "The publisher took a huge risk and printed seven thousand copies," she recalls. They sold out in a week, with people lining up and begging her personally for copies. The second printing of 15,000 sold out in six weeks; it's up over 50,000 copies sold now, and continues to sell upwards of 5,000 copies a year (up to $9.95 from the original $6.95). *Let Me in the Kitchen! (A Cookbook for Kids & Other First-Timers)* was out in early 1982 and has sold over 30,000 copies.

But cookbooks and catering are prosaic compared with the remarkable creativity of Mendelson. For instance, she began Song and Dance Cooking Shows for children at her old hangout, the Vancouver East Cultural Centre. There would be singers, a magician, and 90 minutes of cooking with Susan Mendelson, for eight sell-out performances. We bet that *you* didn't think of that. "I did it to promote the cookbook," she admits, grinning.

More recently, she created a chocolate book with her partner, *Nuts About Chocolate*, which has sold over 40,000 copies, and a new one, with all fresh-fruit recipes, in 1986 hit the stands. (It's called *Fresh Tarts* and is *not* about the hooker problem on Vancouver streets.) Her latest writing project was nothing less than *The Official Expo 86 Souvenir Cookbook*, which had the awesome good fortune of being the only cookbook on the site. "They called *me* to do it," she remarks gleefully. It contained lots of salmon, seafood, and other west-coastish recipes. Both Roitberg and Mendelson were working on *The Lazy Gourmet Cookbook* in 1987—"a big, colourful hardcover."

Future plans are equally exciting. Mendelson and Roitberg may open a second location of The Lazy Gourmet soon, which would be a prototype of future ones: "It would *start* sleek, slick, and designed to make money," which is how her original one did *not*. She still thinks only in terms of British Columbia, which she feels she knows from the stomach out. "Our food is home-made style, and everyone can relate to letting someone else do their cooking for them." She can imagine four stores in Vancouver, in all. Mendelson is determined to expand catering and have a central commissary to produce the food for all the outlets.

And when these women cater, they *cater*. Romeo and Juliet should have had such an affair. The opening of Cineplex, 700 people. Board meetings, office parties, weddings, bar mitzvahs, with good-sized parties running $3,000 and up. They even catered "one of our *great* parties," one for food writers from all over Canada, which must have been pretty terrifying—the catering equivalent of trying out before Johnny Carson. "But that's what keeps it *fun!*" she exclaims.

Still, it's a long way from backyard bake sales to one of the most successful catering and cookbook-writing industries in Canada. To what does Susan Mendelson owe her fabulous reviews? "Believe it or not, it's simply paying attention to the customers. They must feel that they are the most important person in the world and responsible for my success. They must be looked after all the time. In a service-oriented business, you lose touch with *that* and you're *lost*. And keeping the staff happy, so they'll be loyal and want to be here."

Yet "billions of dollars is not something I aspire to," says former-fatty and present-beauty-and-entrepreneur Susan Mendelson. "Quality of life is what is important to me. I don't want to work harder than I do, and I need to take off ninety minutes a day and go swimming or practise yoga. Those are as important as everything else."

One more thought is added: "Be aware of your roots, and remember who believed in you." Grandma is never forgotten, she who found it a challenge to fill that freezer with cooked food as quickly as she could. And it's all paid off, even if a bit late, and on the other side of the country. "The *luxury* of this business," Susan Mendelson gasps. "They come to *us!* We just keep bringing in more and more phone lines!" And sending out more and more fine food.

# FILLED WITH ENTREPRENEURIAL SPIRITS

### Anthony von Mandl

Sometimes, there are glimmers of a person's future calling early in his or her life. In the case of Anthony von Mandl, president and chief executive officer of the Mark Anthony Group, Inc., of British Columbia, a firm in the fine wine, spirits, cider, and refreshment beverage business, the glimmer is almost comic. When her secondborn and only son, Anthony, was still a child, Mrs. von Mandl went to a reception in Vancouver, where she met neighbours from many blocks away. Every woman there said that she knew her son, Tony; "He's the one who picks up all our pop bottles!" Recalls son Tony today, from the office of his multi-million-dollar wine importing, producing, and distributing company: "I would go door to door, taking bottles down to the local grocery store. But I only recalled having done it after my mother mentioned it to me."

Anthony von Mandl has total recall when it comes to retelling the almost unbelievable tale of hard work, risk taking, creativity, daring, and entrepreneurial flair that is all his. Born in Vancouver in 1950, von Mandl saw both the attractions and the dangers of being a businessman by looking at the career of his father. An Austrian, he had owned a large textile business in Czechoslovakia until it was nationalized. So he came to Canada, earned a doctor of laws, and worked in the forest product industry of B.C. (He joined his son's then-tiny business back in the mid-1970s.)

Always interested in economics, the younger von Mandl earned his B.A. in the "dismal science" at the University of British Columbia and had a strange, and hardly profitable, dream at the time: "I wanted to work for the World Bank and be assigned to some distant Third World country and make decisions over the hydroelectric plant to be built!"

It was not to be, mainly because the lad was "always fascinated by wine and food." Both his parents were European, and he had gone to school as a youth in Switzerland, picking up much of that continent's respect for the good things in life. He also picked up a sense of good business practice: Between his third and fourth years in university, he worked in a German town in marketing. "The company was involved with newsprint, and I gleaned some fundamental things about production. I discovered why the German government uses one-fifth the pulp to make newsprint that *we* use in British Columbia: It had to do with the tolerance of the equipment, and the fact that the people who operated it had a commitment. It was *their* company, and they felt that *they* owned the business."

It was a crucial lesson, but what was even more salient

was that he met some "wine people" there who invited the young Canadian with the Austrian name to introduce their wines into British Columbia. So Anthony von Mandl went back to university, while working in sales and marketing of wine. The company he began in his native province was 51% owned by him, 49% by the German wine-makers. He was 22.

But don't be impressed. "I had nothing, not even two cents!" he exclaims, serious-looking with his glasses and thick brown hair, in his Vancouver office. The deal was that he would provide the talent—"unproven at that point"—and they would provide $1,000 a month, of which half was salary and half was office and travel expenses. The name of the firm was Josef Milz International Ltd., a registered British Columbia company.

The problem was that it didn't register with the powers who could help the young man make it work. Von Mandl was initially enthusiastic because he saw how few imported wines were listed at the time in the liquor control board stores. People weren't drinking much wine in those days—"it was still pre-white-wine boom"—and the wines he was handling were 30% less expensive and of better quality than the ones available. But then he visited the liquor board.

"I was thrown out on my ear," he says bitterly. "Actually, it was on my ass. I didn't realize how the system worked at the time." Apparently, there was no real purchasing policy, but "the last thing they wanted to do was to buy from some kid."

So von Mandl—who really *was* "some kid"—was only allowed to sell to private clubs as special orders. He went to many people, threw wine tastings, and quickly sold more wine via special order than any of the listed German wineries. (And people had to wait four months to get von Mandl's product, too.) "It only infuriated them," he recollects, adding that their response was essentially a Canadian one: "We'll show *him*!" The men at the board kept getting hundreds upon hundreds of these special orders, and "they hated the extra paperwork!"

Anthony von Mandl was getting totally frustrated when he was befriended by one of Vancouver's best-known columnists of that era, Jack Wasserman, who died tragically some years later. The newspaperman at the *Sun* decided to give the lad a plug in his column, and he ended up doing much more. On

March 3, 1973, he wrote an entire piece dedicated to the wine importer's plight, and it had a great effect on business. (It was much later that von Mandl learned that he had been blacklisted by the B.C. liquor board.)

His first "real" client was CP Air, which he landed when he managed to prove that "my wines were better quality and cheaper than the ones they used on their flights." He sold them "a lot," giving him enough money to move briefly to Toronto, get on the Liquor Control Board of Ontario list, and land Air Canada and eventually Wardair. Then he picked up a customer in California and began to sell into the States.

His business acumen continually growing, von Mandl "realized intuitively that I needed to diversify," so he began to search for companies with similar profiles, offering real value and good quality. He "started from scratch," flying again and again to Italy and France, and trusting that there would be a big market in the United States.

He managed to obtain a federal and a California wine and beer importing licence, rented a bankrupt oriental rug store in Los Angeles, stuck newspapers over the windows, and slept on a cot in the back. He shipped in German wines and sold door to door, as well as visiting countless retail stores.

The year was 1975, and it was not a good one for wines. He had no success in Los Angeles and "tried hard to keep from starvation." He thanks the heavens for the cheap fares prevalent at the time, which allowed him to fly back and forth between Toronto, Los Angeles, San Franciso, and Vancouver at bargain rates. "I kept flying around and around, trying to sell enough wine to make a living."

The first dozen years were "pretty gloomy," recalls von Mandl, who kept taking every penny and pouring it back into the business. He had expanded his product line, which allowed him to start covering his expenses, but suddenly one French company and a California winery pulled their agency and gave it to a larger firm than von Mandl's. "So I was shafted," he says. "It was a humiliating experience, but a valuable lesson." He recounts it as teaching him two things, in fact: "It told me that I could develop my own brands, and that I would have to develop a contract on my own terms."

What really launched the future wine magnate was the former. He chose "a name I thought would work"—St. Jovian, a Bordeaux Appellation white wine. He designed the label and the packaging, and it must have worked. This, from his latest list: "ST. JOVIAN BLANC DE BLANCS. A best seller and still a great buy. Crisp, smooth, light-bodied and well-balanced, this is a distinguished wine with remarkable finesse—B.C.'s best-selling white Appellation Bordeaux. Unlike any French table wine, St. Jovian is *vintage dated*! Look for the *new* 1.5 litre bottle."

Von Mandl is justifiably proud and immodest. "I anticipated the white wine boom!" he declares. "I read the market and the future correctly. St. Jovian was dead-on in taste, price, and value!" (The foundation principle was, and still is, quality and value. "I knew I had to provide both," he says.)

It was 1977, and the young man, still in his 20s, did not even find it necessary to advertise. "Overnight, everyone was drinking it. People were looking for it." He craftily had blind tastings, and the liquor board found itself with a rather embarrassing problem: "Too many of my wines were winning the tastings!" He was quickly listed, and added French and Italian listings as well: eight in one fell swoop. By the end of that year, he had shot up to $150,000 in sales.

"Something fundamental happened in those years," says von Mandl, underestimating the case. He bought out the German company's 49% interest—"they were desperate financially"—and he took over their other wine products. So he founded, in 1978, Mark Anthony Wine Merchants Ltd., a name which is less romantic in its origin than it might suggest; von Mandl's first two names are Anthony Mark. "Now I had my own company!" he exclaims; "they were all Mark Anthony products!"

From the very start he was "totally innovative in approach," acting as if he were an American or European merchant. "I was aggressive, always on the ball, always with new promotional ideas, always getting into the press," he states emphatically. "The word of mouth and the restaurant community supported me."

He was soon going after listings in other provinces, and by 1979 some of the leaders in the wine trade approached von Mandl, inviting him to take over their distribution in Western Canada. ("I never imagined that they would let me in their front door!" he claims.) The companies will be familiar even to teetotallers: Mommessin of France and Deinhard of Germany. "That catapulted sales!"

It's typical of the true entrepreneur that von Mandl was never driven by money. "I wanted to make a success!" he proclaims, underlining the word *wanted* three times with his voice. He learned to do everything, even preparing the ads for the latest additions to his line.

The first office in Vancouver cost $19.95 a month. It was a 10 by 10-foot room in the back of the Queen Elizabeth Theatre, "around the corner from the men's washroom." His next office was two rooms, costing $79.95 a month, and for many months before all heaven broke loose, he had trouble making the payments.

By 1980, however, von Mandl's firm had become very profitable, and he became determined to fulfill a long-time dream: to produce world-class wines in British Columbia, the way Ziraldo and Inniskillin had done it in Ontario. Not only that, but he was concerned that "being in a strictly import business was risky. I remembered how my father had lost everything when his firm was nationalized in Eastern Europe."

So on June 1, 1981, the son risked everything by buying the only privately owned winery in British Columbia for $4 million. "It was in a terrible state, with no wine-making staff." He changed the name of the old firm to Mission Hill Vineyards, since it sits atop that beautiful hill in Westbank, in the Okanagan Valley, about 300 kilometres east of Vancouver. He brought in an expert to help run the winery, giving him 7% of the business, leaving von Mandl with a still-substantial 93%. The banks put up most of it: It was "a leveraged buy-out before the word was coined; before it became a science."

Anthony von Mandl worked day and night at this new subsidiary, always and still a bachelor. "I worked endlessly, breaking only for sleeping." It took 18 long months before they released the first wine under the Mission Valley label.

Then, in December of 1981, another "window of opportunity." Von Mandl noted that "no one was producing premium quality cider" in the west, so he launched the Okanagan Cider Company, producing both apple and a unique pear cider. They were B.C.'s first premium ciders, premium priced. As the president puts it, "sales grew exponentially." The earlier facility sold 18,000 cases a year before he bought it; in the first year, he sold 100,000 cases; in the second year, 200,000; in the third, 300,000. "It took the market by storm!"

In the first four years with his own products, von Mandl and the Mark Anthony Group increased its sales many times—up to $20 million in 1985, $23 million in 1986, with expectations of over $30 million by late 1987.

Part of the reason for such enormous sales was that, in 1982, von Mandl "went against the trend, fought hard, and obtained the first distiller's licence granted in B.C. in fifteen years." He found himself stuck with large amounts of grapes which were not up to his Mission Hill standards. So he flew in a cognac-type pot still to start distilling the higher acidic wines produced from inferior grapes, and imported *limousin* oak barrels from the Cognac district in France to age the brandy. Great West Distillerrs was incorporated.

Today, Anthony Mark von Mandl and his Mark Anthony Group produce wines, spirits, and ciders galore: 100 products under 50 different labels, listed in every Canadian province and sold to a half dozen countries, including the United States, Denmark, even Japan. There are ten branch offices in Canada and an in-house ad agency. The Okanagan Cider Company keeps turning out that cider, the Mission Hill vineyards keep producing those award-winning wines, the Mark Anthony wine merchants keep importing those fine wines, and Great West Distillers also has a complete line of Scotch, Jamaican rum, tequila from Mexico, Napoleon brandy from France, and vodka. Prices range from "the very competitive" to the most expensive wine bottled in Canada—at $18.

As recently as 1985 a further coup worthy of Lebanon: von Mandl launched California Cooler in British Columbia. "Everyone in Canada" had sought out the two young entrepreneurs who had created the monster success, but the Americans chose to award it to the Mark Anthony Group, Inc., since, in von Mandl's words, "they saw in us a mirror-image of themselves." After he gained the licensing rights for the world's best-selling cooler, von Mandl's sales continued to skyrocket. Made in British Columbia to their specifications, California Cooler was launched by the Okanagan Cider Co. Division in late April 1985; by that July it was the largest-selling bottled cooler in the province. In 1986, they took it across Canada, even getting it listed in the grocery stores of Quebec.

"We're becoming even better at what we know best," says Anthony von Mandl. He claims that they are not driven by profit or a return on invested capital but by "a strong commitment to certain principles and a corporate philosophy." Like the Japanese, he claims that the Mark Anthony Group is "a company made of the people in it," to whom success comes automatically when you are committed to values in how you conduct your business.

The key to von Mandl's success is simple, according to the man who has put more bottles on Western Canadian tables than anyone except soft drink companies: "Using my intuition; having a strong belief in my success; overcoming any obstacle. It was my determination to turn every problem into an opportunity, and never giving up, despite how bad things looked at any time." (He was investing those millions and building his company when the interest rates were hitting 22%.)

It won't be President von Mandl forever, of course; he became chairman of the board in the fall of 1986. They refinanced the company that same year, bringing in "considerable equity," and the ability to expand to the east, even the Maritimes. They could be public by early 1989. But the goal has changed somewhat since he was grovelling for a listing on the liquor boards of British Columbia a decade ago, and since he was working near the men's room of the Queen Elizabeth Theatre, just half a dozen years ago: "I live comfortably. I have few needs. I reinvest everything back into the company. The goal is to build a corporation that will flourish into the next century. And it will, since I've always been committed to whatever I do."

## 2.
# THE BUILDING INDUSTRY

### Gimme Shelter

If food is the most important need for human survival, then shelter—especially our own, often frozen, country—is surely the second. And thus, our second chapter. Here we look at the lives, careers, and successes of five men who have put the actual ceiling over our heads (Stanley Diamond of Montreal), built the houses and offices we live and work in (Iggy Kaneff of suburban Ontario and Ralph Medjuck of the Maritimes), and built and run the hotels and executive apartments where we put up our feet when on the road (Maurice Rollins of small-town eastern Ontario and Tom Vincent of big-time Toronto—but both with hotels and apartments across Canada and even around the world).

As with most of our entrepreneurs, these men have as little in common as their places of employment: They range in age from 40 to early 60s; they come from both poor and wealthy backgrounds; they are both native and foreign-born (Medjuck's father was an immigrant from Eastern Europe, and Kaneff himself came over from Bulgaria in his mid-20s); their educations range from Diamond's Harvard M.B.A. down (or up?) to pharmacy dropout (Rollins), grade-school dropout (Kaneff), B.A. in psychology (Vincent: "It equipped me for nothing"), and law degree and successful practice (Medjuck).

There were hints of entrepreneurial skills in the childhoods of most of them: Stanley Diamond ran a mail-order business with his brother as early as age 13; Maurice Rollins had numerous jobs in his youth; Tom Vincent admits to "two dozen jobs since the age of twelve." And one could mention Kaneff's coming to Canada in 1951 from war-torn Europe as a daring, almost entrepreneurial, move.

Still, what they all have most in common is the choice of businesses where the product is a necessity, and where the customer is king/queen and has been treated as such. Diamond's Intalite became number 2 in the world in custom ceilings (with $36 million globally in 1985, and 330 employees) by "getting it right the first time," specializing in his area of expertise, and "identifying the marketplace." Kaneff went from a single home, built, bought, and sold, to 1,500 houses and 7,000 apartment units (and $60 million in sales in 1986 alone) by paying workers more, and, in his words, "treating the customers like a god." As with Diamond, there was an obsession with quality all the way. (Both Diamond and Kaneff, interestingly, used the word *dreamer* to describe themselves.)

Ralph Medjuck took risks, as did all these men; he built a seven-storey building on a Halifax waterfront that was considered a slum at the time, "thought nationally" and kept gleaning ideas and workmen from Toronto, and "recognized the market and needs and tried to satisfy both." To this date he has built over a quarter billion dollars' worth of buildings across the Maritime provinces, so he must have satisfied *some*. And both Kaneff and Medjuck—and Rollins, in fact—grew and expanded their construction businesses at a time when Canada was doing the same, with the boys returning from the war and massive immigration of men and women who would demand their own houses, cheap land, and wildly expanding cities. (Kaneff's suburb of Toronto, Mississauga, was a town of some 7,000 souls in the 1950s; today it is one of this country's largest cities, at over 350,000 inhabitants. Halifax grew along with Medjuck's projects, as did small-town Ontario with M. H. Rollins Construction.)

In the cases of Rollins and Tom Vincent, there was a "bright idea" as well—although there was also a certain cleverness in building quality ceilings and developing Mississauga and Halifax. Rollins thought of "building budget hotels next to Holiday Inns" way back in the 1960s but wasn't able to act upon his inspiration until 1978. And, not dissimilarly, Vincent, after relatively successful forays into travel and villa marketing, thought up the idea of setting up apartments for vacationers, eventually developing an international network. Why not stay for a month in a three-bedroom townhouse in Vancouver (or Newfoundland, believe it or not) for a grand or less, instead of a (possibly claustrophobic) hotel room for upwards of $100 a night?

Both Rollins and Vincent latched onto wonderful ideas, according to Sam Adelstein, a supervisor at Pannell Kerr

Forster Management. "The big hotel chains had only one type of service into the eighties," he says. "So good budget hotels created their own market, especially at the height of the recession in 1981–82; they helped people to not spend a lot of money at hotels." And the fact that chains such as Ramada Hotels have begun to create a range of places (with Ramada Inns on the budget end and Ramada Renaissances on the high end) shows how Rollins's Journey's End and Vincent's Executive Travel Apartments must have been attractive ideas.

Each of our sheltering entrepreneurs has his own explanation for his success, from Stanley Diamond's "tell the customer that you appreciate his business" to Vincent's "drive to do something—anything." But it is summed up best by Maurice Rollins, who has gone from 3 hotels to 60 in less than a decade (after building and selling some 10,000 homes in Ontario towns): "I wanted to show I could *do* something and be successful."

These five businessmen *did*, and *are*.

# THE SKY(LIGHT)'S THE LIMIT

### Stanley Diamond

When Stanley Diamond began Integrated Lighting— it became Intalite "as a handle" in the early 1970s—he soon identified an area of activity in the ceiling field. He got an order for a major job in Toronto and was asked by the engineer, "You're gonna make a *business* out of *ceilings?*"

You can bet the roof over your head on it. From total sales in 1960 of $180,000, Diamond has made a profit *every single year* since then, hitting over $6 million in Canada in 1985 and (get this) in excess of *$30 million* "globally." Yes, globally, since this Montreal-based firm, which now has about 250 employees across the globe and another 80 in its home province, exports ceilings with the ease of Brazil exporting coffee.

Stanley Diamond was born in the fall of 1933 in Montreal, studied commerce at his native city's McGill University, and graduated from Harvard with his M.B.A. in 1958. (His father manufactured clothing and inspired the man when he was young; as early as 13, Stanley was in a mail-order business with his brother, selling pants, shirts, and accessories.)

Intalite had started in 1960 as a distributor for a U.S. manufacturer, but not for long. "I concentrated on building a business with small jobs, and planting roots broadly, rather than make a name for myself from special jobs, like the ceilings of Terminal One" (at the Toronto International Airport). When that was being bid, he made "a carefully considered decision not to chase it." There were fewer than half a dozen employees back then.

"You *have* to reinvest in order to be able to build a business," insists Diamond. The Dorval Airport Terminal was his first job in his city, and it's still there. "If you manufacture quality goods that will last the life of a building, then you never have to apologize, do you?" he asks rhetorically.

So, from the start, he refused to sell plastic ceilings ("they crack, and go yellow, and can catch fire"). He subcontracted manufacturing in 1963 and finally opened his own factory in 1966. He borrowed money from his accountant's brother-in-law and his father-in-law, as well as hitting the banks for a loan, but it was less than $100,000 all together.

The creative thinking was always there: "We concentrated on manufacturing those products that we had to produce in a way that others lacked expertise in, and we wanted to control the technology." Louvre ceilings were the main product area in 1960, and the expertise involved in manufacturing them was purchased. But "by buying expertise and technology, we realized there was no company that we wanted to turn it over to, or could manufacture it with the quality we demanded." (A belief that gains credence when you consider the "cost of replacing a one-cent part in the field can be many thousands of dollars." And the field, for Diamond and his booming business, could be in the heart of Africa.) "You *must* try to do it right the first time, in ceilings," he proclaims. "You've got to solve a mistake *quickly* because it's so *apparent*!"

Although sales progressed on a regular basis over the years, starting in 1970—"a critical year!"—they found themselves cannibalizing their own sales in Canada by opening manufacturing facilities around the world. When they obtained the order for the ceiling of the fairgrounds in Düsseldorf (for $350,000), the potential cost of ocean freight and duties moved them to invest in a small factory in Holland, and shift the order there. (They had started exporting to Europe as early as 1964.) And they determined that the competition in Europe would squeeze them out unless they were locally based. Intalite has factories today in Australia and Japan, as well as Holland and Montreal. As we've noted elsewhere in this book, it ain't only the Yanks who are into imperialism.

And speaking of Yanks, Diamond acquired a U.S. distributing company in the States in 1980. "Doing business in the States is so simple, there's *no need* for a factory there!" exclaims Diamond. Tell that to Mulroney. Their literature reads: Intalite, Illinois. "We foster the image that we are an American company," he says with a smile. "Why create a problem that doesn't exist? The Americans like to do business with U.S. firms."

Over the years, Intalite has benefited from marketing other people's ideas to some extent. One of their key products was created by an architect in Denver, and another came from London, England. In-house, an invention by the manager of the Dutch company was the most important turning point in the company's history. "But you have to learn from your own mistakes!" exclaims Diamond. When he lacked a local management team in the factory in Holland, it didn't work. They had tried to expand into another area where they lacked the technology, and it was too labour-intensive and needed hands on. They had to write off $700,000 in investment over a two-year period. They now subcontract that particular ceiling.

Intalite today does business in Hong Kong, Singapore, Indonesia, and the Middle East, as well as Europe, Australia, and North America. There is even an office in Panama, where they also just love ceilings. "We are number two in the world in custom or decorative ceilings!" declares Stanley Diamond proudly. (Number 1 is the firm they acted as international licensee for, from 1965 to 1976.)

All this because Diamond worked briefly for a next-door neighbour who had a plastic ceiling business, before he went off for his Harvard business degree. After he earned his M.B.A., he noted that his friend was having problems; plastic wasn't working. So Diamond began his own company, with a partner in Montreal and himself in Toronto. By 1963 he bought the partner out, meaning that the fellow will never get to have his name in this book.

Even the exporting came by chance: He had received a letter from Australia, Diamond wrote back, and he soon had the man selling his products. "We found ourselves exporters in 1964!" says the cofounder and director of international marketing of Intalite. "Australia was our very first external market, and it's so far away!"

"More than anything," says Diamond immodestly, "we differed in our single-minded dedication to a specialized area of expertise, and an area of opportunity that we saw. It's a positive thing: We've created an identity as the leader and founder of the concept of the open-cell ceiling field as a separate business."

You know the Queen's Quay Terminal, by the Toronto waterfront—that basket ceiling? An Intalite product.

Market Place, and the mirrored overhang of the O'Keefe Centre in that city? Intalite. Those gorgeous ceilings in Abu Dhabi? Kuwait? Damascus? Hanover, Germany? The domed, leafed ceiling of the Communist Party headquarters in Paris? Yep, Intalite.

The Baghdad Conference Palace? It's got $2 million worth of Intalite ceiling in it. "But we'll even do twenty-five square feet," claims Diamond. "Our philosophy is, 'If you don't do the small ones, you'll never get the large ones.' " And the Baghdad Conference Palace is very, very large.

Stanley Diamond became a half-owner again, back in 1968, when he merged with another company. They had gotten into a patent suit in the Centennial Year, and there "wasn't enough room in the Canadian market for two of us." His partner is now down in New York, his forte being administration and finance, whereas—good fortune here—Diamond's has always been marketing and sales. "We grew through the use of the talent of each of us."

From the first day on the job, Diamond has "made it a practice to identify with the agent and distributors in the field. This was *long* before *In Search of Excellence*! There are no secrets to it; it's basic, basic stuff. You've *got* to identify with the marketplace, letting the customers know that you appreciate their business. I reply to telexes every day, to tell them this.

"It's not that we're so brilliant. You have to understand what makes people support you!" says Diamond. "In the Middle East, for instance, your word is your bond. We gave up *many* opportunities to make quick bucks, in order to protect our distributors in the Middle East."

Since the moment that Stanley Diamond opened his doors, a quarter century ago, his firm was the largest in Canada, with the broadest line. About 40% of his Canadian-manufactured products are exported to the United States today, which is perhaps one-fourth of his total business, which is moving toward $40 million in sales. His number 1 competitor in the States, noted above, was acquired by a gigantic American firm in late 1984, and Diamond is far from threatened.

"The history of that is, those companies go downhill. The absence of the entrepreneur who led the company has had *disastrous* effects on those firms that are taken over. That change in ownership from one man with a strong will—it'll change the nature of the company! All they'll have is hands-on managers, instead of a dedicated dreamer."

Stanley Diamond is, as you probably guessed, our home-grown Canadian dedicated dreamer. "To be number one! To achieve an even larger portion of the U.S. market!" (With some time out, occasionally, for the wife and three daughters, skiing, and organizing the fastball and softball teams he's run for the past 38 summers.) So when you see him leaning back, staring up at ceilings around the world, it's not just day-dreaming, you can be very sure of that.

In 1986, Diamond and his partner became "philosophically divided," and he decided that it was time for a career change. He sold his 50% interest in Intalite that June, and has been doing international marketing consulting ever since, even serving on several Department of External Affairs Trade Committees. He has most recently been investing in five different hi-tech start-ups in Montreal, "providing my expertise." Also serving on the advisory board of a group for young entrepreneurs, he is looking—as of late 1987—for a new business to join in, "to spend 75% of my time with."

# THE SHEPHERD TURNS
# TO CONSTRUCTION

*Iggy Kaneff*

There are certain things in the grandiose offices of Iggy Kaneff on the seventh floor of the handsome Kaneff Centre in Mississauga, Ontario, which are a dead giveaway about his Eastern European origins. The book labelled *Bulgarian Engineering* gives a strong hint, but even more so are the framed pictures of the president of Kaneff Properties with (then) Prime Minister Trudeau and with (now) Prime Minister Mulroney, as well as a letter of praise from the former. Who else but an immigrant has such respect and admiration (and lack of cynicism) toward our political leaders? Kaneff, more than native-born Canadians, knows only too well how lousy it was back in the Old Country, and how good it can be over here. And Iggy Kaneff has made it *very* good over here, for himself and thousands of others.

Short and square-faced with closely cropped hair, Kaneff was born in 1926 in Gorno, Ablanvo, Bulgaria, a town of about 5,000 people. His father was a farmer in the small town, and involved in a farmers' co-op and store. His father also had "three hundreds sheep and a half dozen horses," and they had cows and mules as well. "He wasn't poor, but we never had money, because you couldn't sell nothing. The whole country was in a depression! We had no money to buy gas; oh, it was a very poor country, Bulgaria!"

Iggy Kaneff "sometimes watched the sheep too," which hardly prepared him for his future calling in the New World. He finished grade 8, and then this fourth of seven children went off to Austria, where he had some relatives, and worked in market-gardening, selling fruits and vegetables for 2½ years, taking school part time. He stayed in that country until 1951, when Bulgaria tracked him down to draft him into their army. "I didn't want to go," says Kaneff, with good reason: "When I saw the way the Russians were acting when they came to Austria, I thought, 'That's not the way the system should be!'" So Kaneff and his first wife sold what they had and came to Canada.

When he arrived, on April 18, 1951, Iggy Kaneff spoke German, Russian, Bulgarian, and Croatian, but neither English nor French. "The biggest Bulgarian group outside Bulgaria is in Toronto, but I couldn't find any who spoke Bulgarian! It was a very, very difficult time, since I didn't possess the language." That fact was appreciated by a Toronto native, however: the cab driver who picked up the Kaneffs and drove them from Union Station to Queen Street, a distance of perhaps three blocks, for all the money Kaneff had in his pocket—$5. "I didn't know what was going on!" he says today, laughing. "In Austria then, I could travel across the whole country for the same amount of money!"

But once out of cabs, Kaneff found nothing but kind people in his adopted city. He had never gotten paid for the land he sold, but the first job he landed was with G. S. Shippe, one of the major builders of homes in Toronto at that time. During the war, when Austria was bombed, the city government had made Kaneff and others repair the houses that were damaged, and Kaneff had *"liked"* that idea!" So he had come to Canada with the specific plan and hope to work in some kind of construction. Indeed, his father had built houses for himself and his relatives in Bulgaria.

Kaneff began as a floor sweeper, "using a broom," at $38 a week. His lack of English continued to hurt, as when he said "yes!" to whether he was willing to work on Sundays. After three months he was a carpenter, earning $1.75 an hour, and the following spring, 1952, he was up to $2 an hour. He also picked up English quickly.

The awesome success story begins right about then: In November 1951, the first year he was in Canada, Iggy Kaneff bought a small lot in Port Credit, a western suburb of Toronto, for $300. "I didn't even have the eight dollars for legal fees!" he admits today, but he managed to borrow it and pay the man back the following week. He built a little frame house—"it's still there!"—for himself and his wife. Then he took a loan against the house, and he purchased another lot in 1953. "As soon as I saw how houses were built, I learned how to do everything but electricity," he claims; "plumbing, roofing, *everything!* I'm a self-learner!"

A quick learner, too. He built the second house for less than $10,000 and sold it quickly for $16,900, which enabled him to borrow much more. Then he bought a third lot, built a house on that one, and sold it right away, too.

Then, in 1954, Iggy Kaneff quit his job at Shippe and built three more houses, hiring two men to help him. He then lined up subcontractors and acted as a contractor for that year and the next one. His sales were between $10,000 and $15,000 the first year, as he edged into the role of "custom builder of homes."

By 1955 he was buying several lots at a time in a new subdivision in suburban Toronto, building a total of seven houses that year. The year after, he built another dozen, all in Mississauga, but "I was still a little guy then."

And little guys don't become big unless they deny themselves weekends, Sundays, holidays. He would work from dawn to dark every day, and it soon paid off; in 1957 things really started to happen. Kaneff built a commercial building—an auto dealership—and late that year, his first apartment building, with a grand total of nine suites. "Everyone thought I was crazy," he says with a grin. "Such a huge building! Who will rent it?" As you may have guessed, it was entirely rented out even before it was completed.

A few highlights of the rigorously capitalistic career of one Iggy Kaneff of Bulgaria, Austria, and Mississauga, Ontario:

1958—30-suite and 45-suite apartment buildings.
1960—over 50 more houses and 2 more apartment buildings.
1963—another commercial building and a GM franchise, which he ran in his spare time and sold four years later. (He was building an average of 50 to 60 homes a year throughout this period.)
1967—almost exclusively into development and building high-rises, including 2 large apartment buildings of 105 units each (and no doubt about whether anyone would rent them).

To jump ahead: By 1985 Iggy Kaneff had built over 1,500 houses and apartment buildings with a total of over 7,000 units, along with numerous commercial buildings. Sales in

1986 were $60 million and in 1987, should be $75 million, with another 150 houses and up to 500 apartments.

Kaneff eagerly lists the things that made him such a remarkably successful construction entrepreneur. For one, when he started out, "I didn't jump to build ten houses; I built one! You put the seed in the ground and prune the plant. You don't plant a tree!" Furthermore, institutions (and banks) saw that Iggy Kaneff was "dedicated to the community." As early as 1956 he borrowed $2,000 in order to donate to a new hospital. "They saw I was honest and kept my word. Anyone who buys a house from me—to me he is a god! Today, people say that their house is Kaneff-built, and they get thousands more for it!"

He always borrowed heavily from banks, and still does. "Without banks, it's impossible!" And he kept in mind a proverb of his: "Bread goes bad. Property gets better all the time!" So he has managed to "keep a lot of our products for future investment."

Another key to Kaneff success has been the way he has treated his staff. His secretary has been with him for 26 years; his senior VP, 18; his second VP, 17; his comptroller, 13; his property manager, 15. "I pay them more than anyone else; always, from the beginning," he says. "Shippe paid *me* fifty cents an hour more than anyone else, too! He demanded better workmanship and expediency; he was my teacher!"

It was not until 1985 that Kaneff moved back heavily into single-family homes, building some 400 in Mississauga. "For mass-produced homes, they are built with material, quality, workmanship, and design as good as custom-built homes. Yet they don't sell for more! Maybe $100,000 to $140,000. And they're big, four-bedroom homes! We presold a hundred and twenty-five houses in a ninety-day period!" And with most of the customers being ".relatives of previous customers," he can count on nonstop demand. "Houses will always sell," he insists. "Canadians like to live in single-family homes, especially when they're newcomers. They like the opportunity to have their own house, that they couldn't have in the Old Country. The immigration of this country created my business!" And his employees as well: As of 1987, he had over 200 full-time employees, and "maybe a thousand more" employed indirectly through subcontracting.

And it created Iggy Kaneff, builder *extraordinaire*, as well.

He has sprinkled family throughout his organization—his first wife's nephew, his adopted son and daughter, an adopted niece. (Back in the late 1970s, Kaneff brought a new wife back from Bulgaria, with whom he has two young daughters. "It's important to have biological children," he says, nodding eagerly.)

Kaneff Properties has grown along with the town/city that he has helped to grow. When he first started building in Mississauga in the early 1950s, it was a sleepy bedroom suburb of Toronto of maybe 7,000 souls. Today, there are over 350,000, making it one of Canada's top ten cities. Tens of thousands of those people have lived and worked in Kaneff-built apartments, homes, and offices.

"It's instinct," he says. "I'm a dreamer. I want to do better things, better buildings." (Among the better things: Since 1970 he has worked on behalf of the mentally retarded, running a golf tournament that has raised many, many thousands over the years, with Kaneff himself donating about $10,000 annually to the cause. Nor are his good deeds limited to his chosen city; he built a kindergarten in the Bulgarian village where he was born—and where his siblings still live—and fixed up the church where he was christened. "The whole country knows me!")

There have been some risks, although Kaneff insists that "I was *very* careful *all* the time!" In 1981–82, when interest rates "were unbearable," he "carefully manoeuvred and planned," even selling valuable property, including the office building, Kaneff Centre, in which he has his office. But the city he has helped hasn't ignored him; there is a Kaneff Crescent in an area of Mississauga where he built 1,850 apartment units.

Lives and successes like that of Iggy Kaneff are stunning in their magnitude, but what can we expect from a man in his 62nd year of life who continues to go every morning to the sites of his new projects, looking at them and wondering how to improve them, and asking himself, "What can I do for the community today?" (One thing is to continually find immigrants and help them find jobs and "get them set up.")

Like all immigrants, he is suffused with love for this country and its endless—at least to people like Ignat Kaneff—possibilities. "Once you start and see that your effort is rewarded, and the opportunities are there," he begins, then stops suddenly. "This system allows you to exercise your abilities and political freedom, and the economic conditions are suitable for success."

Not that it has gone to his head. Not Iggy Kaneff. "I don't live extravagance," he says. "I chum with the same people that I chummed with when I was poor. Of course, thirty years ago, I didn't sit at parties with Conrad Black. Today I do."

## THE BUILDER OF
## THE MARITIMES

### *Ralph Medjuck*

It is rare that any one person can be said to have built a Canadian city, especially in the second half of the twentieth century. But most Maritimers are aware that an entrepreneur named Ralph Medjuck, of Halifax, has done more than most to put that city, and many others, on the map of Canada. Tens of thousands stay in his hotels, live in his apartments, work in his office buildings. And if things go as planned, they will soon use gas and oil from his offshore discoveries. What can you expect, anyway, from a man who, as a young lawyer, hired a new grad student named John Buchanan? The firm was called Medjuck, Buchanan for ten years, and the junior partner went on to become the premier of the province. And the senior partner? Read on.

Ralph Medjuck was born in Halifax in 1932, to a man who came to Halifax in 1929 from Glace Bay, Nova Scotia, "a modest businessman" with a corner grocery store. Ralph's apparent inspiration was when his father went into second-hand furniture. "I loved the idea of buying something for twenty dollars and selling it for fifty dollars! It sounded like *found* money!"

Medjuck went to Dalhousie and graduated in law, being admitted to the bar at the age of 21. But he had already had his first taste of real estate: An uncle bought him "my first property" for $2,000 when he was still studying law, and he began collecting rent in the early 1950s. He practised law full time for many years, but he promptly began adding to his tiny inheritance. "I bought slums in Halifax, fixed them up, and rented them out. The idea of home ownership in the slums was not there at that time." So he would occasionally visit Toronto, where he was struck by what he saw: Young men were building whole streets of houses, up to 100 and even 200 a year! The idea intrigued him, and in 1960, still in his 20s, Medjuck found his first apartment to build in Halifax.

"I approached *every* financial institution I knew in Canada that year, and not one would loan to a Maritimer. I wrote and solicited every one. It was like sending a manuscript to publishers!" At one point, he began to make a package offer to London Life, but he was so discouraged he decided not to. His secretary urged him to do it, and a few weeks later the insurance company agreed to a $2½ million loan. "They gave me my start!" he says. And years later, London Life eventually opened a branch office in Halifax.

Ralph Medjuck began his career in the 1960s by using Toronto architects, tradesmen, and concepts, and "transferring them to Halifax." He felt that the local equivalents were "quality people," but back in 1960 none had experience in developing. "There were *no* high-rise offices or apartments in Halifax at the time," says the man who built most of them. "Before I got organized, there were few elevator buildings! Three-storey walk-ups like Quebec were common."

And he insists that he began "with no money" of his own. "It was the beginning of putting down an option and taking a mortgage. I recognized the difference between the actual cost of a building—the assessment of land, bricks, and mortar that would have economic value—and the economic value of the building when it would be completed as a revenue-producing property." Mortgage companies would lend Medjuck 100 to 110% of the cost of a building, and he would "cash out." "Those days are gone forever," he sighs. But he would "roll from one building to the next," building a whole series of high-rise apartments and office buildings. Elevator companies should have flattering pictures of Ralph Medjuck on their every wall.

The "revolutionary" move came in 1963. Ralph Medjuck came to the corner of Sackville and Water Street in downtown Halifax, where his father had had a store since 1929. He persuaded his father to move out—no, not into the cold—and put up a seven-storey office building on the waterfront. "It was a slum area," he says today, "filled with old fishing boats." Today, little over two decades later, the Halifax waterfront is prime land. "It was exceptionally risky," Medjuck admits, adding that "I didn't know any better." It sure seems that way; he had no tenants for his building before it went up, but "we somehow just filled it up overnight."

There were many difficult times. In 1966 he had expanded to the point where he was "locked into a chasm of doom," and he needed help from heavies in Montreal and Toronto. "I was overextended," he confesses. "I had beautiful properties, but I had overruns!"

Another boo-boo was when Medjuck got involved with "social housing," such as that for students and senior citizens. He was approached by people at St. Mary's University in Halifax: "We desperately need student housing!" So he built $15 million worth of housing for students, taking the university's land and borrowing money from the CHMC to help him pay for it. "But that system was always heavily administrative and highly suspicious of developers," he growls. "The CHMC never understood our social housing, and eventually put us out of the business."

Medjuck admits that he built for profit but was willing to operate the housing without any profit for the next 50 years; "They didn't understand." What almost sent him "to the brink" in the early 1970s was when Medjuck built a 1,000-unit subdivision in the Cowie Hill section of Halifax, consisting of 400 townhouses—"innovative housing," he calls it. "It was *so* innovative, it just about *ruined* us!" He can laugh about it today.

He had taken 50 acres and put the deal together. But there was a construction strike in 1973 which lasted five months, and he had committed to sell the units at a certain price. Meanwhile, there was a high inflation rate as well. By the time the strike was over, there was "a *major* leap in costs! The CHMC recognized *some* of the increase in costs, but not all." Units that Medjuck had agreed to sell for $16,900, he wanted to raise to $19,900, but to no avail. "We lost over two million dollars on that project," he sadly recalls. "It just about ruined us again!" But there is now tons of housing for students at St. Mary's, and in the Cowie Hill section of Halifax. (Oh, yes; he also built two senior citizens buildings and lost money on them, too, when CHMC refused, once again, to recognize his increased costs.) "I said that I'd never deal with CHMC again," he swears, and he hasn't.

Back in 1963 Ralph Medjuck also became involved in the hotel business, as a partner with the Orensteins of Toronto, who had built the Seaway hotels. He acquired their interest in the Citadel Inn, one of Halifax's finest hotels, in 1980. "It's always been successful," he says. So much so, it recently became the Citadel Halifax, still managed by Medjuck's company but in a new relationship with CN Hotels. And since 1986, the 218-room Prince George, a new hotel attached to the Halifax Trade Centre. "Hotels are interesting," he murmurs. In July 1987 Centennial Hotel Management Limited will have the largest number of rooms under administration in Halifax, thanks to the Cambridge Suites, a new, luxury, all-suite hotel.

But what has been clearly most exciting has been real estate itself. "It's *creative!*" he declares. "It's *exciting* to find a piece of land and have an interest in it. I always went into a project when I became enamored with it." And he clearly fell in love a lot.

A wheeler-dealer like Ralph Medjuck is bound to have more than his share of disappointments, for all the love affairs. He admits to having been in projects priced as high as $50 million that were never built. But he estimates that, as of the mid-1980s, he has managed to get built over $250 million worth of buildings throughout the Maritimes: in Fredericton; the Saint John City Hall; office buildings in Moncton; senior citizens buildings in Saint John; nursing homes in Baddeck, in Dartmouth, in Halifax. "Basically, most of my buildings have been in Nova Scotia and New Brunswick," he says.

All this has led to much respect in the community. He has been a visiting lecturer on urban planning at Dalhousie since 1961, and brings classes of up to 30 students to his office to talk about the field. "Students are much more expert these days; they get stimulated by the stories of development." He also speaks at the Technical University on development, "which has been rewarding, too." Paying the community back, he has "always found time for everything": chairman for United Way, chairman of Israel Bonds, the United Israel Appeal, and Camp Kadimah, where he served as a counsellor, years before.

But why such awesome success in Maritime real estate?

"It was a recognition of markets; recognizing a need and trying to satisfy it. I took risks that others wouldn't take. I often miscalculated the process, and that often took longer. But most of all, it was the ability to think nationally and adopt what was happening in Toronto and Montreal to Halifax. That was the fundamental key. Oh, and to learn how to deal with financial institutions!" Eventually, he grows semi-modest; "It's been a fluke of perseverance, continuity, flair, recognizing opportunity."

In the tradition of the "location location location" gag (about the three things important in buying a house), Medjuck praises his own understanding of "the location aspect. My sites are always the *prime* sites. I paid top price, but I got the best locations for my buildings." (To be fair, he seems to be the only one who looked at that run-down Halifax waterfront and saw gold. Not that he was always so prescient; he recalls the 400-unit building he built many years ago for $5.3 million, which he sold for "a few hundred thousand more than I had paid for it." It recently sold for $18 million.)

No mistake, though, in his latest venture, in association with another major Halifax law firm. It's Cornwallis Place, the first phase of a major downtown development on the waterfront—immediately across from One Sackville. A quarter-century after his big risk, in that location, there will be a $25-million, medium-sized office building which will be "the newest and most prestigious of its kind in Halifax."

If Medjuck has any major regret about his real estate career, it is that "I didn't think north/south! I never looked at Boston or New York, and I should have! I thought east/west, since it was more familiar." He is disappointed that he "*never* built a project in Toronto, and yet I go there all the time! That was a mistake; you couldn't go wrong in that city in the late 'sixties and early 'seventies." Now he tells us.

Ralph Medjuck appears to be unable to go wrong in the "newest phase" in his life, either: "the energy factor." The story behind what "could be a mega-opportunity" flows with the same kind of luck and brightness shown in his land development. In 1980 his son Brian came to him, fresh out of law school. The young man had friends who had acted for a group in Toronto who had made applications for oil leases offshore. No oil leases were being granted at that time, since various ownership questions were still being considered in

Ottawa. "If we could help them get licences, we could get an interest in it," son told father.

"It's naïve," said Ralph Medjuck. "That's oil, and we're in real estate and we'd get lost."

Weeks later, the son asked again, and daddy refused. "No, I will *not* inquire from the government; find something we *know* about!"

Brian Medjuck came back a third time, and hit psychologically below the belt: "Dad, you've always told me to do something in life. Well, you're not being supportive in this."

"Now it had become a father/son issue!" declares Ralph Medjuck. "It was not just financial any more!" Still, he had no faith in the concept but reluctantly made an inquiry about the status of offshore drilling.

Ralph Medjuck was surprised to discover that the moratorium had been lifted in 1978, and he quickly made arrangements to pick up provincial licences for "a lot of acreage off the shore of Nova Scotia." He had been told not to spend any money, but he formed Scotia Energy Resources Ltd. and gave his son Brian interest in the company, "since it was his idea."

Then, "a unique thing happened": During the constitutional debates, there was a "tremendous rapport between Ottawa and the provinces," and the feds asked the provinces to give provincial licences to large companies. The door opened and closed, and Medjuck's company was the only private one that had federal *and* provincial licences to 2.3 million acres offshore, on the Scotia shelf and Sable Island.

They eventually made a "farm-out" with Husky/Bow Valley and drilled two wells, at the cost of $55 million each. The first was dry and has since been abandoned (Glooscap). The second, 22 miles from Sable Island, was a significant gas discovery, made in 1984, which "basically put us into business." They bid in March of 1985, were awarded adjacent lands, and made the commitment to drill three additional wells. Medjuck *et al.* have "put in very little money" to this date; they are carried by other companies. And they will eventually have to "put in our share and do some financing." Then there's the coal R & D, with Scotia Liquid Coal, where Medjuck claims they've "had brilliant technological success, but not economical." That company owns a piece (10%) of another "very interesting company," Bantrel, which has 700 employees and was awarded a $50 million job in B.C., doing petroleum work, back in 1985.

Ralph Medjuck is positive that offshore oil and gas discoveries *"will* take place in Nova Scotia"; only the timing is uncertain. "It's a multi-billion-dollar industry," he rejoices, as a man who has only been involved with multi-*million*-dollar deals before now. "It's almost like a new career, and a new involvement with new people who look to Nova Scotia to do business!"

The man who helped build the Maritimes is still building, only it's on less firm ground, and underwater, but with even greater potential. "It's so far removed from real estate development it's funny!" He laughs. "You know, Jews were always merchants, and sometimes into real estate, but there are very, *very* few Jewish people in the oil industry!"

True. And there were once no blacks or Latins in major league baseball.

## LET 'EM EAT CAKE ELSEWHERE

*Maurice Rollins*

Maurice Rollins, 59 in the spring of 1986, is one of Canada's more impressive entrepreneurial one-man stories. From working in construction in eastern Ontario, he created his own firm, becoming one of the largest in that area of the province. Soon he was putting up all sorts of complexes, opening his own building supply company, and had sales of $20+ million annually, with over 500 employees. Then came his concept for Journey's End Motels—"budget-luxury," if you please—going from 3 small motels in the early 1980s to 36 hotels at the end of 1985, including 5 in the United States, with sales of $24 million, and $38 million more in construction. And in 1986? So glad you asked: $45 million in room rentals and $40 million in construction, with profits in the range of $5 million. The end of 1987 should find them with 68 hotels; 1988, *98* hotels. And they talk about *American* Running Dog Capitalists?

Rollins was born in Tweed, Ontario, in May 1927, eventually moving to Belleville, not far from Ottawa. His father ran a lumber yard. (The business later went bankrupt, and the man became a sheriff after he turned 60.) Maurice has a brother, one year younger, who has been working for him, building houses, for the last quarter century. "I was very much the entrepreneurial kid," says the stern-looking, white-haired, bespectacled gentleman from small-town Ontario. "If it snowed, I shovelled it down the street; in the fall, I raked leaves." By the age of 12 he was a parcel boy for Loblaw's after school.

He went to grade 13, studying pharmacy, leaving about halfway through when he decided that he didn't like it. "Anyone can pour twelve ounces of liquid!" he proclaims, recalling writer William Faulkner's line about why he quit the post office in Mississippi: "I'll be damned if I have to serve anyone who has a lousy two cents for a stamp."

Faulkner never became a millionaire builder, however. After working briefly in a hospital pharmacy in Belleville, Rollins wheeled cement as a carpenter-helper for a contractor, followed by two years for an engineering firm as a sewer/water layout man. For five years more he was a sewer and water superintendent and estimator in Picton, Ontario, but, after the long hours, became a partner in a hamburger stand at night. "My family was poor," he explains; "I supported myself since the age of twelve or thirteen." In a nutshell, "I wanted to get ahead."

Rollins was saving money during all this time, and after building three houses after hours and on Sundays, he realized just how lucrative this business could be. So in 1955, still in his 20s, he founded Maurice H. Rollins Construction Ltd., building single-family houses. Then it was land development, from Oshawa to Ottawa. "I did quite well," he says, too modestly. "I had various development companies, getting into townhouses and high-rises, strictly subdivisional work. We serviced them all," putting in streets, pipes, and so on, proving that working as a sewer layout man after dropping out of pharmacy school can pay off.

His firm built in over a dozen locations, including Port Hope, Brockville, Cornwall, "a fair number of houses" in all, since "the local suppliers couldn't keep up with us!"

By 1962 Rollins started his own lumber yard, recalling his own father's failure in the same, calling it Rollins Lumber Ltd. (He was married by this time and now has five children, with three active in one aspect or another of the motel business.)

Then there were more development companies in larger areas, building up to 1,000 units of houses in a single year across eastern Ontario. "That was quite a feat!" he says, smiling. "In Toronto, it's easier. But to do seventy-five in Belleville, ten in Tweed, twenty-five in Cornwall, the majority in Kingston, Peterborough, Brockville. . . ." In total, Rollins was directly responsible for putting up 10,000 units since the start of his firm.

Then came the Bright Idea: "It really happened in the 1960s," he recalls. "It came to me: Somebody should build a budget hotel next to every Holiday Inn in the country! Let them eat and drink over at the Inn!" The problem was that Rollins had gotten so busy—80- to 100-hour weeks—that he had "no time to concentrate on that sort of thing."

So he didn't consider it again until 1978, when he was thinking of selling Rollins Construction. Interest rates were sky high, and he was aware that the housing development demand was lessening. "I could see that the baby boom was over," he says. "With all the land I was accumulating, I should get into something else."

The something else was the building and running of motels. He built the first three in 1978, 1979, and 1980, with Joseph Basch of Kingston joining forces with him in 1978 and Tom Landers of Belleville in 1981, as partners. And in 1980 he finally sold everything he had built up over the years—his development company, the lumber yard, all the unsold land—to Steve Roman's Standard Trust, for "close to $10 million." Not bad for the poor boy from Tweed.

Journey's End started off slowly, with one motel a year. Then he and Basch, who had been involved with the building and management of several high-rise apartment complexes, decided to increase the numbers rapidly. So in 1984 they put up 10 motels, bringing the total at that time to 23, with most in Ontario, 1 in Nova Scotia, and 1 in New Brunswick. By the end of 1985 there were about 50% more, including 5 in Quebec, 3 more in Ontario, and 1 each in Buffalo, Rochester, Syracuse, Utica, and New Haven. The negotiated lots for 1986 include 15 more, bringing them up to over 50 motels and nearly $50 million in sales. And we've *told* you about the near-100 by the end of 1988.

"We build according to our ability to finance," says the president of Journey's End Motels. "We could build many more in a year, but we want it to develop on a sound financial footing." (Only four of the dozens of motels are franchises—in Sarnia, Cornwall, Kitchener, and Brockville—and they manage many others.) "We hire only experienced people," he states, with a manager in each motel reporting directly to the head office in, of all places, Belleville. "I work out of an old office of Rollins Construction," he says. There are over 300 employees, a number which should ·double by the end of 1987.

Somehow, in the highly competitive world of hotel/motel building and running, Journey's End has found its ecological niche. Relax Inn, for instance, built a few in Calgary and has since come east, but "we have larger rooms; much larger!" And Venture Inn, whose investors recently encountered major financing problems, did well, but changed its philosophy away from Rollins's: "They are going into high-rises with more amenities, and are therefore getting more expensive."

Yet Journey's End's creator feels that "it's quite conceivable to have over one hundred units by 1990, and well over one hundred million dollars in sales." But how? Is it all a gimmick of low price for low frills? For under $50 a night, a traveller gets a good-sized room, queen-sized bed, phone, TV, radio, loveseat, work table, free coffee, and nothing else. You wanna eat or swim, go over to the nearby Holiday Inn, Colonel Sanders, or YMCA. Two-thirds of the rooms are directed toward the businessman or woman on a cheapo expense account, and those people travel 12 months a year and not just over Christmas, Easter, and Spring Break, as do most families.

It's been a remarkable career for Maurice Rollins of Belleville, and in many ways it's just beginning (again). All he had started with was his own savings and one house. He took the profit from the latter and built another. And so on. And so on. And so on. "The fifth and sixth houses came so quickly, I hired my brother as superintendent and never got back into the sewer again," he declares. All this with no loans—although you could purchase a lot for a mere $200, thirty years ago. "When I was forty, I was probably a millionaire, but I was too busy putting it back into land and wasn't aware of it," says Rollins.

"There's one thing about motels," Maurice Rollins says. "They're actually an extension of the building business! If you build and rent a house, you get so much return. You rent an apartment, and it's smaller. But you build smaller units [e.g., motel rooms], and rent them by the night, and there's *more* revenue per square foot of building! It's a natural progression from the rental market! I don't know *why* other builders didn't think this way!"

But they didn't, apparently. Rollins denies taking any risks in Journey's End, but he certainly did with Rollins Construction. Back in 1975 he once bought a chunk of land for $4 million "at one crack"; it's still being developed into high-rise condos. And another time, he put up 250 houses totally on speculation. "If they hadn't sold, I could have gone under."

One time he lost. In 1966–67 he started a factory about 12 miles from Dover and built houses in England, Switzerland, and France. He eventually closed up, due to lack of business, at a loss of nearly $150,000. "I had seen a market for timberframe houses, which would take three months to build instead of one year for concrete. They were the first in England with storm windows and asphalt roofs." Today, nearly two full decades later, he is putting the same roofs on his dozens of motels as he had used in England. Nothing is lost in this field; nothing.

Why such a success, Maurice Rollins? "I had drive, and I was willing to put in the time and effort to get ahead. I had *ambition*. You know, I had *no* idea that I'd been accumulating any money at all! I just wanted to show people that I could do something and be successful!" You did, Rollins, and you still are.

# AN APARTMENT HOTEL IS A HOME

### Tom Vincent

When we stay in a city other than our own, we tend to like hotels, and for good reason. We get a phone, daily cleaning, room service, and all those other amenities which make life on the road such a pleasure, although costly.

But Tom Vincent of Executive Travel Apartments, with its over 6,000 suites in 22 cities around the world, has created a brilliant concept which should expand continually in the future, and which asks a simple question of employees, employers, and accounting departments everywhere: Why pay up to $150 a night to put up Charlie in Toronto, where he's taking that management course, when he can get all the same service, and more, for $490 a week, and in Rosedale, yet? And why should Debbie spend $120 a night in a hotel in Vancouver, during that monthlong deal, when she can have a two-bedroom apartment, with all the space she needs for conferences, for $1,950—a mere $65 a night—for the full 30 days?

The way the president of Execupart Ltd. reached his present level of business acumen is as roundabout as his apartment hotel idea is inspired. Tom Vincent was born in Toronto in 1947, the first of three children of an engraver and an Avon salesperson. (Both are now involved in his apartment business.) He had "over two dozen jobs since the age of twelve," including working in a beer store, doing duty as a delivery man and a paper boy, trying the lawn business, etc. A more memorable one was a car wash business ("LET TOM CLEAN YOUR BOMB"), where he placed flyers on cars in the neighbourhood and washed them from 7:00 A.M. to 5:00 P.M. each day, charging $1.50 per car. "My parents taught me to be self-sufficient," he says simply, a man with glasses, half-grey beard, and thinning hair, sitting in one of his many Toronto furnished-apartments-for-rent.

Vincent went to the University of Toronto, graduating in 1971 with a B.A. in psychology, which "equipped me for absolutely nothing." Then, after a moment's pause, he adds, "Actually, university does help train you to think." Then it was off to England for a year—"My dad says that I went to find myself"—and he clearly did, soon starting the first of a number of often successful businesses.

"I wanted to retire at forty-five," he admits immodestly. "I want to be able to do what I want to do, *when* I want to do it. I had a drive to do something, anything. You know, naïveté is a great thing in life. If you haven't been trained in business. . . ." The implication is, it seems, that there are great advantages in not knowing what on earth you are doing, and a look at Vincent's career only proves his point.

While he was "tooting around Europe," Vincent ran into a fellow who had a "guest room concept at five dollars a room." The Canadian offered to be the man's exclusive representative in North America. He returned to Canada and founded a firm in 1975 called EuroLondon, which would provide guest homes, bed-and-breakfasts, in London. He started with an office in his parents' home, got written up in travel columns, and soon had an accredited inspection system covering 150 homes. "We got two hundred letters a day!" he exclaims, still excited about the idea after all these years.

Then it began growing on Vincent: "I kept being asked for help with flights and cars as well. What am I doing, *referring* all these people?" It was one of those proverbial epiphanies of business. "Old naïve me!" he says. "I decided to get into the travel business and hang a shingle!"

There were no travel courses in those days, according to Tom Vincent, so he put an ad in the travel section of the newspapers: "AMBITIOUS YOUNG MAN WITH WHOLE-SALE BUSINESS WANTS TO LEARN TRAVEL BUSINESS." He received 15 serious replies and set up Vincent Travel & Tours, opening it in 1973.

The Bahamian government approached him soon after: "We have a lot of guest houses," they told Vincent; "handle us." He flew down and found them of inferior quality, so he said no. Later that same year, the Jamaican government showed him their villas, and "they were gorgeous." So he negotiated a deal to be the representative for the Jamaican Association of Villas and Apartments. They had 200 villas in that country, but there was, sadly, potential political turmoil in the offing. So he went to Barbados, which had villas but no way to market them.

Another blow for Canadian capitalism. "I put together 15,000 villas and apartments throughout the Caribbean, Mexico, Hawaii, and Europe," says Vincent, calling it Worldwide Villa Vacations. "I was a pioneer!" he proclaims. "I was the first person to put together a villa marketing company in this country." Considering our weather, it's rather surprising that no one thought of it earlier.

"It's the greatest concept in the world! You get a cook, a maid, a gardener, a laundress, a butler, and a private swimming pool, and it is all cheaper than staying in a hotel!"

But the best-laid plans of mice and Canadians, to coin a

phrase: The problem was, Sun Tours began mass merchandising, and travel agents were wary, and Vincent lacked the money to produce a brochure of 15,000 properties. By the time he contracted a charter series with Air Canada to Jamaica, "it was my downfall." There were riots and killings, and suddenly, no one wanted to go to Jamaica. "We were going down fifty percent empty, and I lost $150,000 personally." He eventually collapsed the company, which had a dozen employees, in 1980. "It was the worst day of my life, having to call in the staff and tell them, 'I'm sorry, this is it.' I paid off my creditors, including Air Canada, and never stranded a single passenger, but it hurt."

Still, ever hopeful, Tom Vincent "knew I'd be back in the travel business." And while he still was, he began his present company in 1977, which, he admits, "evolved from the travel concept." What happened was that the Canadian government and Air Canada invited him to set up a special-interest product across Canada. He replied, still up to his neck in villas, "Why not set up apartments for vacations?"

It was called Ventures Canada, and he researched it thoroughly and put a program together: People could stay in Calgary, Vancouver, Ottawa, Toronto. The new problem was that he needed a lot of money to change people's attitudes: Why would people *want* to stay in an apartment on a vacation? Most of us want the glamour of a hotel!

How true. And in his research, Vincent discovered what most of us still think: that most apartment hotels were of poor quality and had no services. So he went to Greenwin, one of the major builders in Toronto, and leased five apartments, of which two were already furnished. It cost him $9,000 to start Ventures.

The first thing he did was to let people know that they were available. Next, he went to other apartment hotels and asked them who their clients were. They actually told him (!). In 1979 he went to a bank for $25,000 to furnish 20 units in another location in Toronto, and the bank turned him down. Why? "We don't understand your business, and we don't think it'll go."

"You bastards!" grumbled the rejected Tom Vincent. "That put a fire under me!" he roars now. He went off to the Federal Business Development Bank, which charges a higher rate of interest and which told him, "This is one of the best small business presentations we've ever seen." Two days later he had his $25,000 to work with.

In the meantime, one more glorious concept which quickly turned sour. Vincent raised $1.2 million to open the first retail time-share sales centre, Timeshare Investment Vacations. He lined up properties in St. Lucia and in Florida, which he planned to market to frozen Canadians for $5,000 a week. He did everything: videos, brochures, top salespeople. But, as the fates would have it, he had "an irreconcilable dispute with a partner; we couldn't agree on ads, and the board of directors backed him." Vincent went to court, but in six months the firm was bankrupt. "As I predicted," he gloats. "He was taking $14,000 ads across two pages of the *Globe and Mail*!" rages Vincent, still angry about the dream gone bad.

But all was not lost. True, the travel business had gone belly-up, he was still in the courts over the time-sharing partnership, and he'd lost all his dough. But his father had been overseeing the apartment hotel concept since 1977, and in 1980 they had opened a total of 25 units in Toronto. So he decided to go back into that business in 1981 and run it full time. The sales that year were a mere $250,000, but they still managed to make a $10,000 profit, so the possibility was there. His father had a stroke, which also forced the issue: In executive apartments lay the future.

To jump to the present and that future, the idea certainly clicked: By 1985 sales were over $2 million, with a "very, very good net profit" of "well over ten percent." By the end of 1987, they were considerably over $4 million and will be "well over ten million dollars by 1990." Clearly, he has been doing something right.

The first right thing Tom Vincent did was to visit cities around the world, seeking a good-quality product. "We wanted the best places available, offering the finest services for the corporate traveller. We deal with relocations, short-term assignments, training programs, and so on." For instance, Nesbit Thomson books 20 apartments for a full month on four different occasions every year in Toronto, since they have various sessions with employees from across the country coming in.

Vincent's Executive Travel Apartments has daily, weekly, and monthly price lists. Some examples: Manoir Le Moyne in Montreal—one bedroom from $86 per day, from $532 per week, from $1,550 per month. Plaza 1881 in Halifax—two bedrooms $70 per day, $455 per week, $1,650 per month. Nova Park in Zurich, Switzerland—three bedrooms from Sfr 275 per day, from Sfr 1,925 per week; and if you want to stay a month, you'd better ask.

Most rent on a monthly basis, of course; that's where the real savings are. And Vincent wisely puts in telephones, charges no monthly deposit and no security deposit, offers housekeeping and nearly everything (and often more than) a hotel offers, and accepts payment by credit card. (He still had the name Ventures Canada, but "it didn't mean anything," so he changed it in 1979 to Execupart Limited. Unfortunately, "no one could sell it, say it, or pronounce it," and it didn't say what they were offering: furnished, short-term travel apartments, not unfurnished apartments on an annual basis. So they went with Executive Travel Apartments.)

The biggest inspiration was most certainly Vincent's desire to seek out other places in such locations as New York, London, and Paris. He decided to "put an international network together like I had done with the holiday villas!" It was a brilliant transference of learning: By signing a marketing agreement with other properties around the globe to market them, offering each a chance to become part of "this international concept," he finally had a winner. "Our brochure is the first directory of furnished apartment properties for corporate travels in the world!" he exclaims, beaming. He printed 50,000 at first, and quickly put out another 100,000.

In summer 1985, Tom Vincent received a telex from Air Canada, asking him to mail 1,000 brochures to corporate travellers in Zurich, from which they would mail another 20,000 to various corporations across Europe. "We pay Air Canada a commission if they get bookings for us," he notes.

Now 40, Vincent has become a landlord, marketing other people's properties, managing still others, and merchandizing them all. Naturally, all this took a lot of money, so it was fortunate that he met a man in 1983 with a concept for small business development. They made an offering that year to business people who wished to invest in his company, for which the government would give back 30% on each dollar. They have now raised $14.2 million, to buy properties, furnish them, and rent them out to corporate travellers, as well as manage them. Over 2,000 investors purchased the $10 shares, and he hopes that Executive Travel Apartments will go public by the end of the decade.

In Toronto alone, Vincent's business has 150 apartments or condos, all fully furnished, of which he has an interest in about 30; the rest he leases. They rent for an average of $70 per night on a weekly basis, and he nets 20% across the board in profit. In New York City, his firm is the exclusive marketer of 1,500 apartments in eight buildings. In England, where he once flogged $5-a-night bed-and-breakfast places, Vincent is now the exclusive marketing rep for 47 Park Street, which has a three-star Michelin-rated restaurant. "I'm talking about *class*!" Vincent brags. "Rich Little stays there! So does Charlton Heston! One bedroom goes for one hundred and fifty pounds a night!" Indeed, Vincent can even get you up to 1,800 square feet in Toronto's Rosedale or Forest Hill for a mere $150 a night; you can't get much more than a closet for the same price in the best Toronto hotels.

In all luxury units there is a fully equipped kitchen, china, cutlery, two phones, a working desk, maid service, parking, catering, and—get this—complimentary limousine service each morning. Tom Vincent's face beams as he tells one of his favourite anecdotes: An executive stayed in his Rosedale "home" and was taken by stretch limo to his meeting at the bank offices in downtown Toronto. The president of the bank saw him arrive and checked into the man's travel and accommodation expenses, assuming that he must have been padding his bill. He was shocked to discover that the man was spending less for his executive apartment than the president was at his hotel. "And ours is in the heart of Rosedale, surrounded by million-dollar houses!" boasts Vincent.

Much of his success is because Vincent is "good at research." For instance, he was aware that major firms such as Ford Motor Company, out in the suburbs of Toronto, were paying $85 a night to put up staff many miles away. So he recently built 15 townhouses in Burlington, near Hamilton, and by the second month after they were completed he had 97½% occupancy. "We give them a three-bedroom townhouse for seventy-five to ninety-five dollars a night," Vincent says, "and the price drops to fifty dollars over a month."

Vincent has built three properties in Toronto since 1985. A 30-unit in Mississauga, a 50-unit in the northeast section of the city, and up to 150 units in the heart of downtown

Toronto, at Bay and Bloor. It was a $12 million project. (Not that he starves when his clients hop down to New York or over to Europe; he gets around 20% commission when they stay in the places which he has not built or doesn't own.)

What he has now is remarkable flexibility: He can develop a property as a condominium, can run it as a furnished apartment for the best cash flow anyone can get on an accommodation, and can sell it if and when the market peaks. "If you run a hotel, you can only run it as a hotel. But I have the option of selling in pieces, or a dozen, or a whole building. It gives me the greatest flexibility in real estate today, and I'm still in travel!" (And a lot of travel, too. Vincent has the only condominium property in St. John's, Newfoundland, with 11 units, and he somehow manages to keep it at 90% occupancy.) In May of 1986, he opened in Ottawa, as well.

There are now nearly two dozen employees at Executive Travel Apartments, and Vincent claims that "it is solid. I've built up a good capital base through conservative investments. I'll go from a small- to a medium-sized business over the next few years." And he feels he can't lose, with most of his clients being "The *Financial Post 500* types."

It hasn't been easy, according to Tom Vincent. "It was tough at first. People don't want to pay you to market their properties. But I could promise to fill their last fifteen percent occupancy, so how could they refuse?" And how could he not found one more (last?) business, when he saw all the people he was missing? In November 1984 he started Executive RentalSearch, which broke even in its first year. "People were staying with us, and they kept asking for assistance to find houses, apartments, and condos. So we've now got six hundred houses in a directory." He charges $450 a day for the service, and it should have three full-time employees soon. "No one else does it!" he declares, which is as good a reason as any to start another firm. And since 1986, he owns 100% of everything.

Next, he expects to form his own real estate firm: "We'll buy a house and lease it and furnish it for you! People will come to us for furnished and unfurnished apartments; I can see that happening. It's a natural transition; everything fits like a glove."

It's taken a while to get a glove that fits, but Tom Vincent seems to have it at last. "We've created the industry in

Toronto," he claims. "We're creating an awareness of the product: the concept of travel apartments. Within the next three to five years, whenever travellers go to a city in Canada, they will think of hotels *and* apartments!"

Vincent doesn't spend a penny on advertising, aside from his brochures, and why should he? The word has been getting around the business world about what he has to offer with those 6,000 suites in those 22 cities. "There's no magic," he insists. "If you do your research, it leads to good planning. There are other apartment hotels, but I offer the best service at the best cost. I never forget the customer, I'm just doing it right."

And, he adds quickly, "I'm forty; I've still got five years to go" to meet his retire-at-45 deadline.

# 3.
# BEAUTY AND FASHION

## *Move Over, Ralph Lauren and Helena Rubinstein*

This is the field dominated by women; in the dozen beauty and fashion businesses profiled, 8 of the 15 entrepreneurs discussed are female. This might seem self-evident at first, in terms of makeup and handbags and *haute couture*, but let us recall how much fashion has tended to be dominated by men, from Max Factor to Calvin Klein to Canada's own Alfred Sung.

The strongest female hook is not the number of entrepreneurs, but the massive move of women into the job market, and the tremendous effect this has had on retailing, as women have demanded more fashionable clothes and accessories. A single statistic from StatsCan tells much: Between 1979 and 1983 there was an increase of 15% in the number of women in the Canadian labour force, to a total of 52.7% of the female population; the increase of the number of men in the labour force during the same period was a mere 4.2%. (In 1971 only 39.9% of women worked outside the home; this was up to 44.8% by 1976 and over 53% by 1985.)

Other factors in the growth and success of beauty and fashion industries have to do with an increasing interest in personal appearance, sparked by a higher proportion of single adults. To quote from Alistair McKichan, the president of the Retail Council of Canada, "Single people tend to be more concerned with their personal appearance than married people."

This chapter, like the others, has a certain inner, if quirky, logic. We look at successful entrepreneurs in skin care (Jack Marley of Upper Canada Soap and Candle), Caryl Baker (of Visage), Jacques Carriere (and daughter, Celine, of Société Jacquar), and Brigette Manning (of Colours). Basic covering for that perfect body of yours are touched upon by William Cline (men's shirts) and Frank Katana (women's shoes). Accessories include Paul Cormier (La Mine D'Or—jewellery), Peter Leunes (Tannereye—designer glasses), and sisters Barbara Twaits and Peggy Hilmer of Maggi-B (garment bags, slippers, travel doodads).

Women's clothes? Liisa Nichol (of Pirjo-Liisa). The *avant garde*? Nicola Perry and Harry Parnass (of Parachute). *Haute couture*? Zonda Nellis (designer *extraordinaire*).

There is no geographical centre for these fashion-conscious people; they range from Charlottetown to Moncton to Montreal to Toronto to Kitchener to Winnipeg to Vancouver. Nor a common age— Carriere and Cline are 61; Cormier is 30; the rest are sprinkled fashionably in between.

Nor do they have educational backgrounds which are similar. Manning was a cocktail waitress, Cormier a first-year university dropout; Nichol has a degree in speech pathology, and Parnass has a doctorate in architecture and urban design from Harvard.

What these women and men do have in common is an ability to take a skill of their youth (Baker modelled; Katana was apprenticed to a shoemaker in Yugoslavia; Nellis used to "make things" at her mother's sewing machine) or take an *un*original idea and run with it in a creative, highly entrepreneurial way (Marley "put romance into packaging" little nostalgic-smelling soaps; Baker set up beauty salons in malls "with no other stores near"; Manning saw someone doing colour consultations out in California, slashed the price, and franchised it like wildfire; Cormier brought discounting to jewellery sales in the Maritimes; Leunes got the idea of leather eyeglass frames from the Chinese, who had used it 1,500 years earlier; Twaits and Hillmer noted—in discussion with their mothers-in-law—that "no one made decent cosmetic bags"; Nichol went the classic "home party" route made famous by Tupperware and Mary Kay, but with women's clothes). And these people take special care, because nearly half of them have their own names on the label, and thus literally on the line.

Every one of these Canadian entrepreneurs had something else, of course: a quickness to see trends and capitalize on them—free demonstrations, medium-priced products (with some exceptions; Parnass, Perry, and Nellis are *très cher*); product pride ("better buttons and holes and better seams" in Cline's shirts, for instance), quality more important than price; thinking nationally or even globally; long, often torturous hours at the office, with little money taken home; and, perhaps most of all, in the words of Zonda Nellis, "not [leaving] your fate in the hands of other people."

Some of their businesses have one or two dozen employees; others have many hundreds. Some have only recently broken $1 million in annual sales; others do that every week or two. But every one of them echoes the paraphrase of a famous French expression by Celine Carriere: "If you don't risk, you don't gain anything." Or, as this author would put it, "Beauty—and fashion—are in the eyes of your bank manager."

# FROM LITTLE ACORN SOAPS, MIGHTY BUSINESSES GROW

### Jack Marley

The image of going from your basement to a multi-million-dollar business is a financial fantasy which captivates North Americans as much as being discovered by Hollywood while serving sodas in a neighbourhood restaurant. The image of Wozniak and Jobs creating an Apple which fell very far from their original tree is a haunting one, as, for that matter, is what happened to each of the computer genii. The story of Jack Marley, vice-president, general manager of Upper Canada Soap & Candle Makers is hardly in the Apple league; far from it. But the way he started, developed, sold out (that's why he's not president any more), and continued to lead his growing firm is a tale of great persistence, wit, and wisdom.

Marley was born in New York in 1941 and came to this country when he was about 17, in 1959. His father was in financial advertising for *The New York Times*, and was transferred to Toronto. "I really grew up here," Marley says from his Mississauga home. He went to a private school in Toronto and to the University of Ottawa, where he was "not a particularly stellar student. I was educated in the school of hard knocks." (His daughter and son are currently attending the business school at Queen's; let's see if they get it right.)

As a youth, he was always in little businesses, usually of his own making: gardening, window-washing. And he once had three newspaper routes at one time, which may suggest something. No matter; from 1963 to 1969 Marley was an account executive with Foster and NCK, advertising agencies. And it was during those years that he first got interested in "the soap business." The initial impetus was a position paper he wrote for Colgate on bar soaps; they were looking for a new niche in the market. He wrote two sentences on the specialty soap business in 1967, and he noted—who didn't? —how all of Canada was caught up in the Centennial year celebrations.

"I liked the idea of soap related to nostalgia," he says today. "I talked about it for a year with the other guys in the office, but did nothing." (He may as well have been born in Canada, the way he first acted.) While with NCK, he made propositions to his fellow workers to try out his incubating idea. He then became the marketing manager for Whitehall Laboratories for three years; they're the people who cure our running noses and walking headaches with Dristan and Anacin.

He decided on the somewhat coy, drawn-out name Upper Canada Soap & Candle Makers since "I wanted a name that harkened back to the old days. And it seemed to fit." (He added "candle" in the hopes of future expansion.) It should be noted that, during this same period, Marley had "about fifteen" ideas on paper for restaurants, ad companies, and oodles of other business concepts, but never acted on any of them.

But, he says with a decidedly flavourful metaphor, "The soap thing was something I thought I could sink my teeth into." He asked his potential partners for $10,000 each to start the new business, and, to paraphrase a great Canadian humourist, they leapt upon their wallets and rode off in all directions. "Instead, I put in about five hundred," remembers Marley. (He had been married in 1964 and had three children by this time.)

So, in September 1969, somewhat late to take advantage of Canada's Centennial year, Jack Marley contracted a private-label soap company to make 500 bars of soap for him. It was he who provided a fragrance, working with several houses who create such things. "I wanted it very scented, reminiscent of the pioneers." (Thank heavens Marley had never walked behind a horse and plough.)

It is interesting that Marley was "really into nostalgia," a soon-to-take-off fad *cum* obsession which had not yet occurred in Canada. It cost him only 15¢ for each bar and wrapper

("The cost would drop to a dime if I had made more," he adds). His total investment, as he remembers, was "exactly eighty-six dollars," although production, material, and logo ran another $500. Hardly big business, but wait. Wait.

There was a gift shop near where Marley lived in Mississauga, just west of Toronto, and a gift show was coming up. He made a deal that he could have a card table in their booth. He piled about a gross of the soaps on the table and sold them for around 25¢ apiece.

At the worst, Marley thought, he would be stuck with a lifetime supply of nostalgic-smelling soap. But he sold $900 in orders of the little things, which were ingeniously placed in tiny wooden boxes. "I was in Seventh Heaven!" he exclaims. "It was like picking pennies off the street, it was so easy." Later, it was not so easy; the first two customers didn't pay him.

By February 1970 he had two kinds of soaps, two candles, and a men's cologne (bayberry-scented)—five products in all, all made for Jack Marley. But although he did not make them himself, he "put a lot of work into their packaging. I put romance into all this stuff."

By this time he had his own booth at a gift show, and he attracted the attention of one of the largest giftware distributors in Canada, who wanted to handle his merchandise. He negotiated with them for a while, giving them a discount off his wholesale price. (He was still working at Whitehall with the healthy noses and heads.) After two and a half years of relationship with this distributor (N. C. Cameron, which had a Canadiana division), he found that he didn't make much money, but he was being provided with a coast-to-coast network of salesmen, plus space in all those gift shows. And he gradually kept adding items to his line.

In May 1972 there was a bit of breakthrough in the halfhearted, but romantic and nostalgic, career of Jack Marley: He left Whitehall and spent that summer creating over four dozen new items for his Upper Canada Soap & Candle Makers company: shampoos, hand lotion, bath salts, bath oil, bubble bath, and much, much more. A mile away from his house he rented a barn, and he had a warehouse in his garage and his basement. "Teenagers in the neighbourhood all had keys to my house," he reminisces today. "Kids wrapped soaps and filled orders." (He recently ran into a woman who had started her career in his basement; she is now a lawyer. There is a moral here, somewhere.)

He continued to develop more and more products, and went to a private contractor who manufactured soaps, perfumes, etc., for others, including large cosmetic companies with private labels. "Some big companies wouldn't even talk to me," he says. His hook for his products was always crafty: "natural, fresh, fragrant merchandise, usually with a fruit or floral aspect—strawberry, green apple, etc." All had packaging themes, and "*were* made with extracts!" Marley adds determinedly.

And all this was before the herbal essences so heavily advertised with millions of dollars in the early 1980s. "They took the price right down," he says, "but I had about two years on them!"

In September 1972 Jack Marley launched his new, yet old-fashioned, product line. He did business with gift shops, health food stores, and, thank the Lord, Eaton's. In fact, he sold that department store chain $28,000 worth of products in the month of December alone. In 1972 he managed to reach $100,000 in sales.

By 1973 Marley was up to $350,000 in sales, and at the end of that year, he began to take "a minor salary." After three more years, selling over $500,000 worth of products in each, he moved into an industrial unit of 4,500 square feet in suburban Toronto, with half a dozen workers, all basically involved in packaging.

Here we come to one of the funniest aspects of any business: the tobacco heir who is allergic to smoke; the health food scion who lives on chocolate bars. In Jack Marley's case, it was his latest concept: "tiny soaps in the shapes of rosebuds, seashells, daisies." What's so funny is that Jack Marley despises the product. "I hate them! You can't wash with them! People enjoy putting this awful stuff in their bathrooms, and I've never allowed one into my house!"

But who cares if Colonel Sanders was a closet vegetarian! And the same with the attitude of Jack Marley; he was on to something big with those small, bitty soaps. "Now, we've got soap teddy bears, hearts, scallops, shells, butterflies, Santa Clauses, frogs, ducks—I can't stand it!"

But he can, since the baby soaps are now in 20 different colours, and, more importantly, are a full 50% of his business.

"The Bed, Bath and Linen Show in New York City in June 1978 launched us," he remembers with pleasure. His expenses were $10,000, and he sold only $2,250 in soap, but it was the Big Break. "We stuck with it and learned the U.S. market." He had some bad reps, but he hooked up with one fellow in Minnesota who knew good reps in Dallas and Michigan, and helped Marley to line up solid workers across the States.

It didn't start rolling until 1979. "Business doubled overnight," he says, adding ruefully, "mainly due to these awful soaps." His inventory doubled, and his need for cash trebled, leading him to rely on outside financing. A bank wanted a mortgage on his farm, and "it was disconcerting. I had to sign that we'd lost the keys to the ranch!"

But, as can happen when small businesses are growing into larger businesses, and thus out of control, he met some people who knew of Finlayson Enterprises, then a public company on the unlisted Winnipeg Stock Exchange. With the sales of Upper Canada Soap & Candle up to $1 million a year, he was an attractive takeover target.

He was sold in November 1980, signing a five-year contract to manage the business as vice-president, general manager. It wasn't sold for very much money, but it allowed him to get out of debts of many hundreds of thousands of dollars. "And," he adds happily, "I got the keys to the ranch back."

In the past six years Marley has increased the business more than sixfold; sales in 1985 of Upper Canada were over $6 million. "I was spending thirty percent of my time dealing with bankers, assholes, and accountants," he cries; "I wasn't trained for it! Since the takeover, they have all the computers, accounting department, and collection and credit departments, which is the key to all this!" Marley gets a salary, an incentive, and "a reasonable part of the profits." There are now 30 employees, up to 60 in the fall, using 25,000 square feet of warehouse.

It's ultimately a happy story, since Jack Marley doubts that he would have survived in the early 1980s, nor would his ranch have, either. "In 1981 I was paying two percent over prime, so I would have been paying twenty-five percent interest for a time. And then there was that seven-week-long postage strike! We would have gone under, that's for sure!"

The two thousand products of Upper Canada Soap &

Candle are now distributed across the United States (over 50% of sales, in fact), and 12 to 15% more to such territories as Australia, Scandinavia, England, France, Germany and Switzerland. Those "bath pearls" sell for only 7¢ wholesale, so "to make a million-dollar business out of them, you can *imagine* what we sell!"

In all, there are over 2,000 items, and 10,000 accounts across the United States and Canada. And, not to ignore the name of the firm, Marley has a man in Bracebridge, Ontario, making candles for them, which are now about 25% of the business. "We have the volume to make soap and candles ourselves, but I don't want the hassle," Marley says. "My expertise is in the field of marketing, of coming up with product ideas and getting them on the shelves of gift shops and bath boutiques."

There have been failures, of course, and some are quite amusing. For instance, miniature dollhouse furniture. In the early 1970s Marley went to a California gift show twice a year and "saw this stuff. It looked fascinating! I wanted to be the first and biggest in Canada!" It ended up being "the biggest, *dumbest* thing I've ever done!"

It took 65% of his time and ended up being less than 25% of his revenue. "People would fuss over a dollar-and-twenty-cent item and end up wanting only three of them!" He did end up selling out all his inventory—he had brought it in from Mexico, Korea, and Taiwan—but it was a pain.

A positive example of Jack Marley as his most creative best is moustache wax. You read right. He somehow came across moustache wax in a jar—a nostalgic men's line, of course—and he placed it in a shop in Banff. He lined up six skiers and had three of them place the stuff on their moustaches; the three returned with icicle-free whiskers. Marley had a poster made and labelled the stuff, "Moustache Anti-Freeze." Sales in 1984 increased ten times over 1983, and he sold over 30,000 pieces.

Marley imports some toiletries from England that can run up to $15 and $20, but it's basically a nickel-and-dime business. But nickels and dimes can add up to plenty when the product sells in the tens of millions. For instance, the teddy bear mould: He purchased three moulds to make teddy bear soaps, which would retail at 50¢ each. They cost a towering $15,000, which he amortized over six months by adding a penny to each teddy bear cost. He recently sold 1,500,000 teddy bears, and the costly moulds have clearly paid off.

Other times, it's just recognizing a possibility. For instance, a glove moppit, which he came across in England. He pays a royalty for the product, which doesn't really "fit in" with the rest of his line. "I sell $100,000 worth of the stupid gloves every year!"

Jack Marley has managed, as president—and later as vice-president, general manager—to make his crazy, nostalgic ideas work as a small business. A small business which threatens to become a fair-sized one; he expects to do over $10 million in sales by 1988. "I like finding funny things, like those mops," says Marley. "I look at it as a challenge: finding items that will sell, bringing them to customers, and finding more. I can pick up trends and can communicate them to people who will package them."

Is there any end in sight? "I'll go on as long as I'm able to keep generating new ideas," says Jack Marley, of Upper Canada Soap & Candle Makers of Canada. Just don't insist that he wash up for dinner with any of those impossibly minuscule soaps.

## PUTTING ON AN ENTREPRENEURIAL VISAGE

### *Caryl Baker*

Why some men are delighted to work for the company store and others have a longing to own their own; why some women have been happy to stay home with the kids and others climb the wall and look for infant businesses to nurture—these are questions for psychologists as much as for the author of this book. In the case of Caryl Baker, mother of three children *and* of 35 Visage salons, she was very much the latter kind of woman. Hers is a story of tenacity and risk, high goals and high demands. And one senses that this is only the beginning, or perhaps the middle, of what could become a worldwide empire of cosmetics stores, sales, and schooling.

Caryl Baker, née Fruchtman, with thick blond hair, a very square face, severe but pretty features, and a voice that makes Barbara Frum sound like a soprano, was born in Toronto in 1942. Her father was in the textile business with her grandfather, and she was the firstborn of three (one brother is in interior design; the other is at Oxford, completing his doctorate).

Even as a young girl, she "never wanted my parents to do anything for me. At the age of five, I begged them to let me have piano lessons. At the age of fourteen, I went out and enrolled in modelling." She studied psychology at the University of Toronto but "felt that it was not for me," and got married (the first time) at 18. Even then, although she had her family "quickly, I always felt that I had to do something else."

The young mother had done "a lot of modelling," although she was not tall enough—5'4"—to succeed the way she wanted. So when she had had two of her three children—and with the third on the way—she declared to herself, "I *can't* sit around and do nothing, even though I'm pregnant!" So when she saw an ad for people to run a modelling school, she ran off and did it, for six months. It was one of the Jeanne Rene Charm Centres, which she still believes was "run by someone in the underworld. I worked for one of the franchises, and after selling a few, they vanished!"

But young Caryl "loved it, and got a taste" of two of her favourite things: modelling and teaching. But the only thing that came out of it was that she had learned of a makeup company, Fashion 220, which had sent its products to the school from Chicago. She called them and offered to sell the cosmetics, and they agreed. "I was on commission," she recalls, so she arranged parties, starting them in her neighbourhood and eventually working her way across Toronto. "No one taught me how to do it," she admits proudly. She was soon making up to $300 a week from just a few nights at it.

Yet, following the same pattern of dissatisfaction with school and staying at home, she "loved what I was doing, but I hated the quality of the makeup." It was the perfect coming together of "a bit of a shit-disturber" and a potential future career as a seller, and eventually a manufacturer, of cosmetics. "I'd pick up an order and tell them how they could improve it," she remembers. "And my success made me realize that I was good at selling and presenting makeup." Furthermore, she "really liked the attention of fifteen to twenty people at a party!"

One day, still in her mid-20s, the very active mother of three happened to speak with a friend in New York, who told her, "With so many jobbers here, why not pick up a line and sell it yourself." So she went down to New York, tore a leaf from the Yellow Pages, and went from place to place of those who manufactured makeup. One gentleman eventually took her under his wing, recommending cleanser, moisturizer, freshener. "I put a thousand dollars of our money in, and my father signed for a loan of another three thousand," she relates. "The whole thing cost less than five thousand dollars by the time I was done."

She opened her first little store in the fall of 1969, calling it Visage Cosmetics. ("I picked up a French dictionary and went through it," she admits. "I felt that only French cosmetics sold well!") It was a storefront—125 square feet—and when she opened her doors, "no one came in," except a few relatives and friends. So she went to see a friend in the cosmetic business, telling him that she had "a line of cosmetics and no money. What do I do?"

"Why not keep the selling party plan?" was the reply, and she quickly realized how right it was. So she ran an advertisement and soon had 300—yes, 300—young women working for her. From 1969 to 1974 they were selling her kits of cosmetics "long before Mary Kay!"

Although the young entrepreneur was filling little bottles of lotion from bigger bottles, her sales were more than satisfactory. She sold $50,000 worth in 1970, and by 1974 she was up to a "few hundred thousand." She was also now up to 800 square feet in the same place as before.

But, ever dissatisfied, she "got sick of it! With two hundred girls, maybe twenty worked; with three hundred, thirty worked! Only ten percent actively worked!" So she began going out and doing wedding parties and fashion shows herself, with only one person helping her—the wife of one of her brothers. Then, a striking turning point: A fashion magazine invited her to run an ad in their pages, and she wrote an inspired one: "You'll know why Caryl Baker can charge $200 a face, when you have *yours* done free at this month's clinic!" She got over 300 phone calls and ran free clinics for the following three months.

She created a makeshift school, sitting down a dozen women in a room and proclaiming, "OK, everyone, take out your cleanser!" "I didn't *need* three hundred girls to work for me [or the 10% of them who would *really* work]; people were now coming *to me*!" And she found that she was selling between $200 and $400 to the dozen women in each "class." "Our sales really picked up!"

This triggered Caryl Baker's first retail store. Once again, the spark came from outside, as it had from her New York friend and her cosmetics cousin: The new Hudson's Bay in downtown Toronto phoned her and said, "We really like your ads; they've got class." That's when her second husband, Alan, got involved. "Let's go for it!" he urged her. It cost $20,000, and they had to borrow from a bank, but both bank and Bakers were pleased that they had. Still, "It was really scarey," remembers Baker; "I don't like to go to banks." Stephen Leacock was not alone.

In December 1974 the first store opened: CARYL BAKER VISAGE. "You couldn't trademark 'face,'" she comments. And no sooner had she opened, when she saw a Revlon booth just down the aisle. "I had a fit!" Baker recalls. The Bay had promised to send out ads to all her clients, but the tough cookie told them "no"; she demanded $20,000 to cover her loan. And they *gave* it to her (!). "It was the talk of the mall," she says today with a giggle. "Oh," they'd say to her, "*you're* the girl who got the twenty grand!"

But what's 20 thou to a booming business? "Sales were incredible," Baker declares. "People were lined up inside the store, trying to get close." She didn't want a counter, and it was a brilliant move. "I wanted to feel close to the customers," she says. "I was used to parties, where there is nothing between you." It's like what Naisbett says about Hi-Tech-Hi-Touch; in a society overflowing with machinery and technology, never underestimate the growing importance of feeling, touching, patting, rubbing. They become all the more needed, and even demanded, by customers.

Baker continued her golden feel/touch/pat/rub. She put up a sign, FREE DEMONSTRATION, and "we couldn't *cope* with the business." The first week, sales were at least $1,200, and "the profits were astronomical, since this was *retail*! I didn't have to sell to my girls at fifty percent off!" Her husband, bushy-haired, moustachioed, bespectacled, now co-owner and operator of the Visage cosmetic salons, asked her if she should have another store. Within six months— June 1975—it was open; then the third, then the fourth. Caryl Baker ran the four stores herself, and she found that she was "going crazy; I lost the personal touch." Not only that; she was still bringing in that guck from New York, labelling and assembling it. Then, more inspiration from without: Baker got a call from Prince Albert, Saskatchewan, from a woman who wished to open a Visage store there. The boss said no, feeling that it was too small a city, so the woman happily moved to London, Ontario, and ran a new store there, as a franchisee.

To jump to the end of 1987: 35 salons, in Ontario, Quebec, Manitoba, Alberta, only 2 of them now company-owned: Eaton's Centre and Hudson's Bay, in Toronto. The number of employees is up to 175, and *all of them work*. "We could have grown quicker, but we've never stopped serving stores," says Baker. "We want to grow only five stores a year." (And that includes "a *lot* of inquiries" from the United States and Australia. Besides, Caryl Baker thinks that her system would be ideal in France as well.)

The thriving businesswoman feels that she has no competition because her stores offer "special service. I'm in malls with *no one* nearby, while Clinique, for example, is in department stores with competitors right next to them. We *care* more," she insists, and has shown this by opening five schools which train women to be cosmeticians with Visage, as well as to work for other companies. The schools are all registered with the government, and she gives a recognized diploma. "I cater to the masses, not to the classes," claims Caryl Baker. And the schools are "*very* profit-making!" Over 250 students in Toronto alone pay up to $1,800 for the course, which includes a kit worth $800.

The stores average $200,000–600,000 each, making total sales over $9 million by late 1987. And Caryl Baker sees herself with 200 stores in the foreseeable future. And those healthy sales come from stores which range from only 225 to 325 square feet in size. Franchisees make up to $75,000 and even $100,000 a year, and Baker brags that "we have never closed a store." (One daughter is a supervisor with Visage; another also works inside the company; her son is a promising young actor.)

Caryl Baker and Visage now have manufactured their own skin care and cosmetic products, up to 70 different kinds, including 40 various colours of eye shadow, and probably a grand total of 300 to 400 items altogether, most of them exclusively made for her. But the secret is, as always, "the one-on-one relationship with the clients. It's the right way to market a good product to a woman. We've shown cosmetic companies that women *want* this personal attention, and you're seeing more and more demos in department stores now. Every cosmetics store has a chair today!" (Baker also hopes to get into men's cosmetics, and to start making a small line of men's skin care, offering the same service to husbands, boyfriends, and so on. And what *man* resents feeling, touching, patting, rubbing? Would any cry sexual harassment?)

Looking back on her phenomenal past decade, the woman with her name above the title pats her own back: "If you get too much help, it's not easy to make it. You've got to find your own successful road. I did the parties myself, and no one was there telling me what to do. It was a matter of hit and miss, but I *never* gave up. And if I *want* something, I find a way to *do* it!"

# THE SWEET
# SMELL OF SUCCESS

*Jacques Carriere*

Jacques Carriere of Montreal, 61 years of age, does not feel at home speaking English, so his daughter, Celine, 30, does most of the talking. But Carriere *père* certainly always felt at home in the world of business, as this profile will show.

After completing high school, Montreal-born Jacques Carriere started to work in distributing various products in drugstores in La Belle Province. They were pharmaceutical, like Band-Aids, and not related to his future work in cosmetics. He started young, and soon moved up to sales rep for the large firm, when, in 1952, at the age of 26, he "saw no other opportunity there to being my own boss!" And he knew the drugstore market very well.

So he founded Société Jacquar—a combination of his two

names—beginning by importing and distributing baby gifts, toys, *Tintin* books, and sundries to drugstores across Quebec. By 1962 he was successful enough to buy Desbergeers, a pharmaceutical company, which he eventually sold in 1977. Its prescription products were sold to all clinical pharmacies, and to the growing drugstore chains such as Shoppers Drug Mart. With his two laboratories, he started to distribute two lines of French cosmetics, when "we saw the opportunity of putting a line on the market to correspond to *Canadian* needs of consumers and customers [the consumer being the ultimate buyer; the customer, the retailer]. It's always more interesting to manufacture than to distribute!" Celine exclaims.

By the mid-1960s, Carriere founded his Anne Marie company, a complete line of skin treatments and cosmetics, ranging from $2.00 to $9.95: nail polish, lipsticks, eye shadow, mascara, blush. "They were and are medium-priced, targeted to the middle market," Carriere says.

By 1972 another company, Marie France, was created, producing cosmetics for teenagers, ranging from $1.69 for nail polish to $5.99 for eye shadow. Then he bought Canada Drug, which under the gentle persuasion of Bill 101, became Droguerie Canada, which began to manufacture and distribute Michel Robichaud perfume across the country (ranging in price from $11 for a small bottle up to $36 for a good-sized one).

Almost from the beginning, the three companies under the umbrella of Société Jacquar have grown by 10 to 12% a year, covering the province of Quebec with their multitude of cosmetic products. By the early 1980s they had broken $5 million; 1987 saw them at $7.3 million in sales. The 1987 projection is over $8 million. And what is so impressive is that Carriere was taking on such names as Max Factor, Maybelline, and Revlon in the province of Quebec, fighting for space on those very limited drugstore shelves.

Yet somehow, over the past two decades, Société Jacquar has become the biggest cosmetic in Quebec drug stores. "And there's a lot more competition today than when we got in!" says the founder's daughter. So how did he manage to do it? "My dad is not a dreamer," says Celine Carriere. "He is a very soft person. He's just a businessman. You could say that he must be very lucky to start a cosmetic company and be successful at it. But thirty years ago, he had a certain market sense which didn't really exist back then. For one thing, he was an experienced distributor, and wisely chose to put his products into pretty bags."

Pretty bags? Is that all? "He has a keen sense of marketing and selling," the daughter says. The initial investment of $60,000 (for low-priced trial packages of various lotions and bath oils), along with $35,000 for samples and $40,000 for inventory capital, was earned back in less than a year.

Not that there weren't failures; there were a number of them. The Carrieres put a few cosmetics on the market and within a year they were forced to discontinue them due to lack of demand. And sometimes there could be an *embarras de richesse*. For instance, the inspired move to invite Michel Robichaud to be the first Canadian designer to put his own product on the market. "That was a real success!" Celine Carriere declares. "But we sold it too fast! We ended up one week before Christmas almost entirely out of the perfume!"

Yet Jacques Carriere had no money when he began his business, and no one to help him. Today, there are nearly 50 employees in his various firms. There were over 200 when they still owned their labs. Finally, the man himself reluctantly agrees to speak: "First of all, you have to work! Show aggressiveness! Not be afraid to make decisions, and take some risks! But they must be *calculated* risks! And always renew your ideas; you can't sit back at age forty-eight or fifty-one! And choose good people around you, to be your key managers. And see potential in them!"

Like his young daughter perhaps? For if anyone can help spread the cosmetic products of Société Jacquar from sea to sea, it will probably be Celine. "Up to now, we've sold mostly in Quebec," she says. "But not for the rest of our lives! There is a limit here; a certain saturation, with six million people!" So she has begun to track down more and more accounts outside the province, selling the Robichaud perfume in a number of small chains in Ontario.

"I want to make this country grow and grow and grow!" enthuses the second-generation Carriere, who is the vice-president, marketing, having joined the firm full-time after she graduated with her Bachelor of Commerce degree from Concordia. She is determined to get Anne Marie, Marie France, and Michel Robichaud cosmetics into drugstores right across Canada, just as they have swept hundreds of stores across her native Quebec.

"We have a saying in French," says Celine Carriere, kindly translating. "If you don't risk, you don't gain anything."

# MAKING MONEY
# BY THE SEASON

### Brigette Manning

The numbers are as straightforward as the concept, and even more impressive: In 1978 Brigette Turner Manning began to do colour consultations out of her spare bedroom in Toronto; by late 1987 there were over 135 franchises in such suburban Toronto locations as Australia, New Zealand, Scandinavia, Greece, England, West Germany, the United States, all of Canada, and South Africa, where, as we all know so well, colour is all.

The concept is so simple that it seems embarrassingly obvious: Men and women look better in some colours than in others. The origin of the idea can be traced back to Bauhaus artist Johannus Itten, a half century ago, who noted that artists gravitated toward colours in tone with their own skin pigmentation. A theory gradually evolved that each of us has a unique skin colouring, based on the percentages of melanin, carotene, and hemoglobin in our skin. But to leap from the colour wheel to dozens upon dozens of successful businesses around the world, employing hundreds of people of all different nationalities, backgrounds, and—yes—colours, is the kind of entrepreneurship which one does not normally expect from ex-cocktail waitresses from Newfoundland.

Which is where Brigette Turner was born, in November 1949, in the town of St. Brendan's, to parents of English and Irish background. The second of six children ("squished in, with a girl before and four boys after"), she had a happy childhood, continued in Toronto before she was a year old. Her mother was a wireless operator, later a housewife; her father an iron worker. "Raised in a family of six, if you wanted extras, you had to work for them," she exclaims. The family was "very religious," and all went to parochial schools. Brigette Turner baby-sat, washed hair in a hairdresser's, worked for a cleaner's, and became a secretary after graduating high school.

A turning point was when she became a cocktail waitress at 20, since she learned that she "could make a whole lot more money through service." After three different waitress jobs, she married Jack Maniscola, who often used the name Manning in his work of managing rock concerts and, later, distributing videos. As he began to do well in his various businesses, she started travelling with him, once spending five months in Los Angeles.

"I wanted pocket money, and something to do outside the house," she recalls, "and I didn't want to ask Jack for money." (Ironically, it was in her house that her future business began.) While in Los Angeles, she met a friend who knew of a woman in San Francisco who did colour consulting for movie stars. This was in 1977, yet even back then the woman had the nerve/gall/chutzpah/genius to charge $300 a session.

"Hey, there's something I could do in my own house," thought Brigette Manning, in the tradition of the light bulb appearing above the character's head in the comic strips. Manning had designed her own clothes since she was 16, and "had a flair for makeup," but this, in itself, would not create a million-dollar business.

"We researched the Itten theory, studying the colour wheel," and began charging $50 a session in her home. "I did it as cheaply as I could." As with many cottage industries, Manning began with her friends, "as many as I could!" The delightful result: "It works! When people saw it, they wanted it! They were looking younger and fabulous!"

During the 90-minute consultation, Manning would take off the woman's makeup, and work with her natural skin tone. She would use daylight, or simulated daylight, and study her skin, working with a range of 140 basic colours from an 800-colour source, holding swatches of different-coloured cloth up to the client's face. Eventually, it would be narrowed down to 30 or 35 colours "that really work." True, most people have a general inclination toward their own pigmentation, but Manning and her growing number of clients quickly realized that knowing their "season"—cool colours with blue undertones were categorized as winter and summer; warm colours with golden undertones as autumn and spring—fine-tuned the whole procedure of choosing wardrobes, makeup, accessories.

The *Toronto Star* did a story on Manning's home business, and she soon became so busy she had to move to another location, in the first floor of a building where her husband had a business in downtown Toronto. By 1980 she upped her price to $60 per consultation and had two other people working with her. "It was still fun, but there was no big money in it yet," she says, pretty and attractive in her Toronto world headquarters of Colours, Inc., and so right in her proper colours. "But I was doing better than any job I ever had."

Like many small business proprietors, Manning was totally unprepared for what started to happen: "People began to ask to open their own stores. I would tell them, 'Please, I don't want to move so quickly!' " She adds, nodding, "It's very artistic, and I understood why they wanted it."

Artistic, but also potentially far more lucrative than what had occurred in the first three years. (By 1979 products began to appear in the Colours repertoire, such as scarves and makeup, which Manning had made for her. A painter would paint on silk for her, and she would sell the scarves at $35. And, of course, a complete line of makeup, colour-coordinated for each season, was soon available. The price today for a "complete travel kit" is $130, which includes foundation, brushes, eye shadow, lipstick, mascara, etc.)

The first place was in Beverly Hills, of all places, followed by Halifax and Vancouver—each run by close friends of Brigette Manning. And each of those women kept getting inquiries: "How can we do this in *our* area?" "And I thought to myself," says Manning, light bulb flashing, " 'Hey, I could franchise!' " Not that she did it like a graduate of Harvard Business School; not by a long shot: "I began to do it as I went along. I asked what each woman wanted to pay, and I got the price that way." The price was $10,000 then (now it's $17,500), plus 10% of royalties (now 8%).

Within one year after Colours spread beyond downtown Toronto, the number of franchises was ten. "We've doubled each year," Manning says. By 1984, during which year around two dozen stores were opened around the world, sales were about $3.2 million, including the consultation, now $80, the scarves, the hosiery, the necklaces, the belts, the sweaters, and, of course, all that makeup—each, as Ecclesiastes told us, in its proper season.

"In 1985, it was up again," Manning says, somewhat reluctant to discuss exact figures. But much of those rapidly growing figures also came by chance: "People *wanted* scarves and makeup," she says, while manufacturers kept offering the young businesswoman their products as exclusives.

Not that it is only Brigette Manning who is growing wealthy in changing the 1970s line of "what's your sign" to a 1980s version, "what's your season?" For instance, "the girl" who opened one of the early Colours in Canada took home $90,000 for herself in 1983, after taxes, and $120,000 in the following year. "And *her* top consultant made $40,000!" declares Manning, who could have saved many a Nora from bad marriages a century ago (and there *are* Colours in Scandinavia today, thank heavens).

By 1981 another brilliant concept was added to Colours: Style, dealing with lines, proportion, illusion. With this service, women could get professional help on hem lengths that would be most flattering, jacket lengths that are best for their bodies, hat shapes and hair styles that "work," etc. About half of the Colours locations have Style available as well.

There are many $1,000 sales, but the average one is about $250, which is a lot more than McDonald's gets for its hamburgers and fries. "Women won't walk out without makeup or a few scarves," says Manning. And the customers flow in without advertising, since the word of mouth is so strong.

Today, Brigette Manning Consultants and Design Inc. owns 100% of Colours, and it seems that there is no limit to future numbers: "Whenever someone opens a Colours in Denmark, Switzerland, Germany, or Great Britain, it boomerangs like crazy!" she declares. (Imagine what it does in Australia.)

The number of employees who make a living from one service or another, thanks to the development of Colours by Brigette Manning, now numbers over 400, and "that would be conservative," she admits. But why be conservative, when over one-half of the human race is not? "Women shop like crazy," says Manning, "and they want to look good."

And they *will* look good, if Brigette Manning has anything to say about it. "We're moving state by state" across the United States, and by the end of 1987 she expects to have "many, many dozens" more stores. "I won't let it die," she exclaims. "I'll keep creating things."

There are other colour-consulting stores, *bien sûr*, but Manning doesn't consider that she has any competition. Only a few of them are franchising, although it seems that "people are always coming in, stealing ideas." Not without spending at least $80 for a consultation, I'll bet.

Anyway, Colours is "way ahead of anyone else." There's a two-week intensive training program, with an internship. "They must know it well before we give them a certificate," much less a franchise.

But the real genius has been Brigette Manning, who admits that she did it in "very unorthodox" fashion. "I didn't think about it; it just happened." Still, she soon discovered "that I was a lot better businesswoman than I knew." She belatedly went to franchising seminars and discovered that she'd "done everything right, without knowing."

And why? "I'm extremely perceptive about people's characteristics. It's a talent I have. I have a good visual memory." But most of all, Brigette Manning has got "a great sense of timing" that tells her "it's time to do this, and we can't do that yet.

"I held off franchising until I was ready; I'd had requests for a long time before. I took products on when it was the right time to do so." Yes, she's made mistakes, but "none that have hurt me."

To go from 1 to over 130 stores in less than a decade is almost scarey, but not to Brigette Manning, who's never taken any business courses which might have held her back from spreading an inspired concept right around the globe from her Toronto home. "It's happening too fast to live in the future," she states; "I live in the present." And fortunately for Manning, her hundreds of employees, and her hundreds of thousands of satisfied customers, both the present and the future have four distinct seasons. And everyone, but everyone, has a body covered with skin.

# A SHIRT-SLEEVES OPERATION

## *William Cline*

The story of William Cline of Cline & Co. Shirt-makers, of Kitchener, Ontario, is not one of dozens of stores and millions of pieces sold. But it is an entrepreneurial tale of intelligence and the desire to make a better-quality product that is worth telling. "Here I am," Cline says today, immaculately dressed, with brown horn-rimmed glasses, square face, and central European good looks, "a small Canadian company surrounded by multinationals." Yet he is thriving, and the reasons for that go right back to one of the central themes of this book: People are willing to spend more money on products if they are well made.

William Cline was born in 1926 in Hamilton, Ontario, the oldest of three children of a sales manager for Burlington Steel and his wife. (His grandfather was a Methodist preacher who crossed the Niagara frontier in the early nineteenth century.) "I was a *very* average child," he claims, although he "tended to be a leader" in organizations such as the Boy Scouts, where he quickly rose to be a patrol leader.

He went to McMaster, graduating in 1950 in history and economics, as part of a prelaw course. But he "wanted to go out in industry," ever aware of his father's frequent complaining "about the irritation of having a boss." He had reached a watershed: He could go ahead academically and become a lawyer, which his father had always wished for him. "He saw it as an economic insurance policy." Or he could move toward industrial relations, which had begun to fascinate him. But there were few industries that had formal industrial relations, so he was not sure what to do. During a few summers he was a sewer and water maintenance worker for the city of Hamilton, and, after staying in the job after college, he chose to make contact with Studebaker, of blessed memory.

The car company wanted Cline to be the editor for their house journal, and since he had been the sports editor for the McMaster paper, he joined up. Eventually, he became the assistant to the sales manager there, and then an interesting chance arose: Cluett-Peabody, the parent company of Arrow Shirts of Kitchener, had gone through a renewal and wanted an industrial relations department. Cline applied but had no experience. After three months, and still with Studebaker, he got the call: "You still interested?"

So in 1950, all of 24 years of age, William Cline was the personnel manager of C-P, where he stayed for 17 full years, working his way up to VP, manufacturing. Unlike many entrepreneurs, and unlike his father, he was "quite content in the corporate structure." Then he jumped to Forsythe Shirts in the same city, as its CEO. "I was happy there, too," he admits. He was waiting to become the president of Cluett-Peabody and had become bored. And here was another company in some difficulty! "It was moving three blocks and climbing a mountain," he recalls today.

Ever the corporate man, Cline spent a full decade at Forsythe, coming home each night to wife and two children— the son's a lawyer, by the way, so the plan succeeded in the next generation. (Actually, Cline had come in as executive VP, but he was the CEO at Forsythe; he wasn't called the president, so it wouldn't look like a Cluett-Peabody takeover.)

Forsythe was hardly a tiny organization; they had $10 million in sales when Cline came on board. But they "ran out of cash" while turning the company around, and the outside directors felt that the firm should be sold. "I agreed fully," says Cline today. Among the candidates who were interested in the business was Dylex, the giant clothing conglomerate, and an agreement was reached in the mid-1970s, with Cline staying on to run Forsythe.

With the restraints of money off his back, Cline brought Pierre Cardin to Canada, and generally thrived, but began to feel the irritation that had bothered his father decades before: "I was generously treated," he says, "but I was part of a large corporation that believed in managing by committee. I spent a great deal of my time at meetings and decided that I wanted to be *more* than a hired gun. I wanted to see if I could *initiate* things."

But there was the certain matter of a contract, which "chained me to the company for life." A lawyer informed Cline that it would take three years to get out of the deal, but he somehow negotiated his way out in the summer of 1977. The major restriction was that he stay out of the industry for a year, which was just fine for Cline; he would spend the full 12 months thinking about the shirt business and renewing his knowledge of manufacturing.

In 1977 Cline & Co. Shirtmakers, of William Cline Co. Limited, was incorporated, with between $75,000 and $100,000 in seed money which the successful company man had managed to save up from his bonuses over the years.

He looked about for rental space, leased 15,000 square feet, negotiated a bank credit line, and took additional equity through the Small Business Development Corporation to supplement his own capital. It took a year to establish the plant, and he hired his first people in March 1978. The first Cline shirt came off the line in the fall of the same year. "We began in Kitchener and went out in concentric circles, with the concept of high-quality shirts made in my city, out of a background of Canadian consumer wishes."

The success is made clear by the numbers: In the first year, ending in June 1979, sales were already $600,000; in the fiscal year ending in June 1987, sales were over $3½ million. The handful of original employees moved quickly to nearly two dozen; today there are 70. "We've grown fifteen to twenty percent every year, and as fast as we could," says Cline, noting proudly that he has made good profits for the last four consecutive years.

All this in an industry "which is slowly collapsing from the onslaught of government indifference to secondary industries, and low-cost imports" from overseas. The reason is clear: "I chose a very narrow, specialized base. I asked myself the all-important question: 'What *is* it I wanted Cline & Co. to be?' " The answer is clear: "If I could conceive of a product that is of higher quality than most shirts, and in the old-fashioned tradition. . . ." Cline knew that if it sold for a few more dollars than other shirts, retail, people would still buy it. "I'm fussy about the quality of fabrics," he says. "The kinds of lining in collars, even if they don't show." (Those are imported from Switzerland.)

Next came the marketing: "I'd go to specialty stores and not the chains or department stores. 'Here's a no-name shirt by Cline,' I'd say. I kept selling out my rising capacity. And even as the Depression descended in the early 1980s, the concept of a better-quality product, distributed on a specialty basis, continued to grow."

There were moments of concern: "Cline? Never *heard* of it!" And moments of humour: "Italian storeowners would say, 'Cline? Never heard of it, but I'd like one of those Ce-lee-ne shirts!'" "The product sold," Cline says, "because independent retailers cared about their customers and would recommend it."

William Cline denies that there's any sophistication to his concept: "It's just common sense. You've got to reach the people who are the last two feet from the cash register, and give them some reason to buy! I expect my product to be explained and to be sold. I don't print claimers, like Tilley." (See story in this book.) What Cline also has in his corner is an interesting fact of which most of us are unaware: "The selling people on the floor of clothing stores are *so* tired of the indifference of most manufacturers! The salespeople are *anxious* for product knowledge!" And along comes William Cline of Kitchener, who keeps visiting them, explaining how good his shirts are, and what are their selling points. "I go personally to explain what the shirts are about," he says, although he has some agents who do it as well.

Cline Shirts are now carried in specialty stores and independents across Canada, and he has evolved three names, three labels, and three merchandising concepts: Daks, an English-styled shirt which he makes; Gant, an American, "Yuppie, traditional Ivy League style"; and Cline, "no-name indigenous. The three labels give us broader scope: I see us evolving into thirty percent Gant and twenty percent Daks. But I'm not out to build a monument to my name; during these rough times, you develop a survivor complex. If it ends up forty percent Gant, that's fine too."

So William Cline has plugged himself into the generous resources of Daks (Europe) and Gant (U.S.), "which are very useful in helping me tie into a scale of purchases that a smaller company cannot achieve." He even buys his material through Gant. The average price shirt today in your friendly neighbourhood department store is between $25 and $35. Bargain Harold might hit you for $15 or $25. Cline's spread is $35 to $60, for an English, two-ply, 100% cotton shirt. "I end at the top end of the middle for volume, and reach for the top end."

There are between 150 and 200 specialty stores in Canada which are Cline's target market. Back in 1978 he had declared, "If I could reach seventy-five percent of those stores, I could sell three million dollars in shirts," which is precisely what he has done. But such a successful businessman is not about to stop with shirts. For instance, he recently discovered "the best raincoat in the world," which will sell for $495. And he's begun to represent Jaeger sweaters from England. "I'm going to use my marketing base to push these top-line raincoats and sweaters," he says, importing them from the United Kingdom. "If I could find the world's greatest chili con carne, I'd sell it to the stores as well," he says with a smile. "We're always looking for things to balance what we make in Kitchener."

He's also got to worry about "product pride." "You can't make a better-quality product and hire cheap people," Cline says. He has established piece-rate and incentive conditions for about half the work, and hopes to move that up to 80% incentive soon. Yet he "never expected to make a lot of money. There are no quick killings in the needle trade. I wasn't ready to retire, and I wanted to make something better and be independent." Not that being independent comes easy in his industry. "Margins are tight, due to competition pressure." On a $30 shirt, a profit of $3 would be "a miracle"; $1.50, or 5% is "almost respectable."

The next five years will tell which way Cline & Co. shirts will go. Will he continue as an independent company? Merge? Sell to a large conglomerate? One thing William Cline is sure about. "The business will be more than the shadow of one person."

The shadow should grow larger; he sees $5 million in sales with the plan he now has, and another factory holds no interest. "Largeness doesn't attract me; I've been through a large-scale company!" No, what *does* attract William Cline is quality—better buttons and better buttonholes, better seams, a better product. "With all of that, I have an edge on what the others are making," he says. "As long as I can make a product in Kitchener to the quality level that I can sell, I'll do it." And no one in Canada, in law or in industrial relations, can make a similar claim. Or make a better shirt.

# NO BUSINESS LIKE
# SHOE BUSINESS

*Frank Katana*

One of the best advertisements for capitalism can be given in a single sentence: In 1957 Frank Katana came from Yugoslavia to Canada without a penny in his pocket and but a few words of English in his vocabulary. In 1987 he co-owned a major shoe-manufacturing company with sales of close to $7 million and over 125 employees. Both the painful memories of escape and resurrection in the New World, and the drive that made it possible, are still there.

Born early in 1932 in the Croatian part of Yugoslavia, to parents who were farmers, Frank Katana apprenticed with shoemakers after the war. (Both his older and younger brother are still on the family farm in the old country.) "I was the only one who could never really adapt to that life," he says today, in his huge Celebrity Shoe factory in an industrial park in Scarborough, east of Toronto. "I was always looking for something easier than farming. I always wanted to achieve something on my own."

The hometown had only about 1,000 people, so Katana went off to Zagreb to earn his licence as a shoemaker, obtaining his master diploma in 1949 at the age of 17. By the age of 19 he had two people working for him, and soon joined a company making specialized shoes by hand. After two and a half years there, he decided to leave the country. "Life was real tough in Yugoslavia. I wanted something better, whether in Austria or somewhere else."

The someplace else would be Canada, but not without the kind of horrifying close calls so familiar to people who attempt to leave Eastern Europe, and so unknown to most Canadians: the police taking away his two friends; the one-way trip to close to the Austrian border; the police who refused to believe his story about meeting a girlfriend there ("I got suckered! She was a good-looking girl!"); the leap from the train ride back to Zagreb and the ten-minute search for the defector in the bushes; the camp in Austria, overflowing with refugees from the Hungarian Revolution.

Katana had wanted to go to Australia, but friends who had gotten out had written to him in Yugoslavia, "We're being eaten by snakes and mosquitoes!" He had read a bit about Canada, and he was accepted into our country with the understanding that he would go to Winnipeg and work on the railway there. But when he arrived (sick) in Halifax and was told that Winnipeg was cold for six months of the year, he was attracted to Toronto. "Well, it's a big city," he said to himself. "I'll have a better chance here."

When Katana stepped off the train at Union Station, he decided to sit and wait until he heard someone speak Croatian. Eventually, he overheard two men conversing in his language, and he begged them to take him in for one night. (All he had was underwear, two shirts, and a toothbrush, so when the men offered to carry his light-as-a-feather suitcase, he cried out, "No, no!" When they picked it up, they asked him, "What have you *got* in there?" and laughed. "You are *another* rich one!" They were off by only two decades.)

The next morning, hoping to get the $15 a week that Immigration was giving to new arrivals, he was told that he would have to go to Winnipeg or get nothing. So it was off to a Croatian church—really a gymnasium—to find someone who would let Katana live with him for a few weeks. (Precious memories abound, such as the first day, when he took a streetcar to his new job, putting springs onto mattresses for 60¢ an hour. The streetcar cost 10¢, but since he knew no English, he stuffed his only dollar into the container.)

Katana recalls seeing the others at that job drinking Coca-Cola and orange juice, while he feasted on water and dry bread. "If only I could get that!" he murmured. After a few weeks, he looked for a shoe factory where he could put his education to use. A Ukrainian-owned place offered him $1.30 an hour, but the boss was an alcoholic and had a mere $10 to give him at the end of the week. So it was off to another shoe factory, this one paying 90¢ an hour—but at least it paid it—and after 18 months he was a foreman, and after three and a half years he was raking in $2.25 an hour.

There would be false starts, such as when, with a partner, Katana opened a small business in 1959, making shoes by hand and repairing others. They printed ads, taking them door to door, and the immigrant lived in the back of the shop. But it didn't go well, and he had to keep his job at the factory. "After a year, I could see it wasn't for me, so I sold it to my partner for five hundred." After a further six months at the factory, he opened another small shop with another partner, to make summer sandals, borrowing a few hundred dollars from friends to do it. But after six months this concept did not work, either.

Then, as luck and talent would have it, two men at the factory decided to join with Frank Katana in 1961 to open their own shoe factory. A lawyer recommended a name—"Why not call it Celebrity Shoes?"—no expensive name-search here—and a new Canadian business venture was born. The cost: $17,000 in capital and 2,500 square feet of space. "With such little money, it was a tough time to start!" exclaims Katana today, handsome and tall, with a full nose, curly hair, and a huge, toothy grin. The banks weren't too anxious to help out, so Katana bought old machines and repaired them. One partner designed the ladies' shoes, but the three joined together to agree on what they would manufacture. The other men were older, and they "wanted cheap, to sell. But I stressed *quality*!"

After a year, one partner got out, and Katana brought in a friend from Yugoslavia who is still his partner. The experiences with the banks are illustrative. One of them: A partner told the bank manager that his share was worth $7,000. Frank Katana told the man that his share was worth $125,000. "Why so much?" asked the bank manager, taken aback. "Because I wouldn't sell my share for $125,000. I'm *sure* I will succeed; I believe in myself!" The men had been asking for $10,000, but the manager gave them $25,000. "My confidence won him over," says Frank Katana. (The banker also gave the immigrant some nice Canadian advice: "Never write a cheque if you don't have coverage.")

In 1961 there were the 4 partners and 3 employees, and sales of their ladies' shoes were $40,000. By 1965 sales were up to $200,000, and the 15 employees had moved to a place double the size. By 1970 sales were $700,000, with 45 employees. By 1980 Celebrity Shoes was down to 2 partners but up to $5 million in sales and 90 employees. There has been some increase every single year since its birth in 1961. Indeed, even in the "tough time" of 1981 they expanded, doubling the size of the building—although unable to double sales of shoes. The $7 million today suggests that the expansion was right, even if risky.

Today Celebrity Shoes sells close to 250,000 pairs from coast to coast, most of them "in better shoe stores," primarily independents, although Eaton's carries them as well. "They are upper-quality, all-leather shoes," says Katana, with an average price of approximately $70.

The reason for the success is clear to Katana: "We built our place in the market, and we're holding it. We give quality, service, and value. Retailers know that they will make money when we give them our shoes to sell." Good marketing skills are also involved; Katana says that if they sell 1,000 pairs to a store, and five styles sell well and five styles sell poorly, "we gear to repeat the more popular style." Obviously, perhaps, but apparently not all companies do that.

If shoes retail for $70, the stores get them for half that, which leaves less than 20% profit for the manufacturer, but it hasn't troubled Frank Katana. "We didn't take much money home before 1980," he states. "When we had four partners, most wanted to take everything out." But the partner he has had for the last dozen years "wanted to put everything back," just like Katana. They would work 16-hour days, no holidays or Sundays off, and his wife from the Old Country, whom he married the year he began Celebrity, "complained from the start." But the kids didn't turn out badly; the son, 21, is studying economics at Western; the daughter, 23, has finished her degree in French at York, and was recently sent to Zagreb, "so she could learn her roots!"

Not that the partners have kept their eyes only on ladies' feet; the partner is involved in a new company which makes aircraft parts, and Katana has been buying land around Toronto since 1980, with a half dozen properties being developed at this time.

A number of shoe companies have closed their doors over the past few years, but not Celebrity. "My success was believing always in what I'm doing. I was always confident! I never feared that I wouldn't succeed. I believed in myself, and had a good partner (Joe Avsenik), which is 50% of my success. We've never had an argument in twenty-five years!"

As with most successful business people, Katana's goal was not the money. "It was to be successful, to be comfortable. You want to build a business; money comes by itself. I love to work with people, and if you treat people nice, they give it back.

"You've got to be specialists in something, and known for something," he adds. "We've become known for our fitting, and for quality women's shoes. And we're always improving the product."

It's a long way from the Eastern European family farm to suburban Toronto, millions in sales, and ten dozen employees. But Frank Katana puts it succinctly: "Canada has been a good country for me."

# THAR'S GOLD IN THEM THERE MARITIMES

## Paul Cormier

Paul Cormier's late father was a doctor, and he must have been upset with "the wildest" of his five children, who was always teasing his two older and two younger siblings so unmercifully. And when he saw Paul give up on university after two months, he must have given up on Paul. But he should have noted such little things as the way the lad, at the age of 8, used to send his younger cousin to collect bottles for him in his wagon. When the child would come to Paul with $7 or $8 worth, the crafty older boy would pay him $1. "He needed me to tell him to do it," says the 30-year-old owner of one of the most successful independent jewellery stores in Canada, with over $1.8 million in sales in 1986, in Moncton, New Brunswick. "It took him a few months to learn to do it himself!" That slow-to-learn cousin is now an engineer, and we already know what happened to Paul Cormier.

But the way it happened is what's *really* interesting. The Cormiers are of Acadian background, having been in the Maritimes since the seventeenth century. It was a middle-class family that witnessed young Paul go off to Montreal for grade 11, live in a monastery in Oka for a year, pass grade 12 back in Moncton, drop out of university, and then move on to be a waiter in a "high-class French restaurant" for three years. A waiter! But as any doctor can tell you, a lot of fascinating people came to eat at Chez Jean Pierre, in Moncton, N.B.

Such as the customer who distributed jewellery, a friend of the restaurant owner. For some reason, Paul Cormier, then edging out of his teens, was charmed by the man and his profession, and asked if he could have some gold chains to sell. His mother had a bridge party, and "I sold them all—a half dozen—in *minutes*! I made a profit of $100 in less than a half hour!" Cormier quickly noted that it took him two nights of long hours to make similar money at the restaurant, and, furthermore, "the women really *did* appreciate the jewellery! And I saw it was easy to sell!" A future millionaire capitalist was born.

No fool, however, Paul Cormier continued to work at the restaurant as he began his extremely fledgling career in jewellery sales. He borrowed $5,000 from a bank and began to buy a product from Montreal, basically lower-priced jewellery, which would sell from $10 up to $200. He spent nearly all of the bank loan—less the plane ticket—on the products which he just *knew* would continue to sell as they had done at his mother's bridge party. He went to a printer to have business cards made, and, noting a place called The Golden Nugget, he decided on *La Mine D'Or* (The Gold Mine), a prescient choice, as well as a sensible one; Moncton is nearly exactly one-half French-speaking, and the other half would have no trouble with a name like that.

Nor with the image of a kid selling jewellery out of a suitcase. He created Tupperware-type parties—"It's been done before, but it was one way to start out"—and he carted his suitcase to beauty salons, hospitals, nursing schools; "some earrings, some rings, mostly chains." It took him less than four weeks to sell the initial $5,000 order.

And how could he not? He'd line up two dozen women in a church hall in daytime—as the head waiter, he was still busy at night—and he lined up house parties, where women would invite their friends over to look at Paul's stuff. He would give 10% of the sales—in jewellery—to the woman who opened her doors; an extra 5% if another woman booked. In 1978 he sold $20,000 worth of jewellery out of his suitcase for the initial six months.

But there was always that drive, that pushing, as exhibited with his innocent cousin over a decade earlier. His mother would take appointment after appointment during the day, and "for one call—even if only one woman wanting a chain—I'd go there." Cormier, with his thick, brown hair, moustache to match, and piercing eyes, smiles as he speaks, making the writer want to pick up a few deals for his wife. "Business grew like a chain reaction," he says, ignoring the double entendre. But little else was ignored.

It was, to quote the entrepreneur, "quite hectic!" He was still at the restaurant every evening. So he decided to open "a little store," ignoring his father's warning. ("No! It'll cost you too much!") It was a good street, with a McDonald's, gas stations, and banks sprinkled along it. He opened his store in May 1978 at the cost of a few thousand dollars. His sisters helped make the signs, his mother made the curtains out of a bedspread, and in all its glory, it was 300 square feet. "A closet!" Paul Cormier huffs.

Then he began advertising. Like mad. And in French and English. And it worked. "At Christmas time there were line-ups that made us look like a McDonald's at suppertime!" His sales were around $200,000 that first year, with profits of over $50,000, proving once again that we can't listen to our parents about *everything*. Sales then jumped to $300,000 the following year, then to $500,000 (at which point he finally gave up his waiter's job), to $900,000, to the present $1.8 million. "I defy all Statistics Canada averages!" he brags. "I've always grown between thirty percent and one hundred percent every year." And it was mainly because he advertised a lot—and, in his words, "I'm a discounter!"

But you can't discount very successfully if you are paying too much for your product. As his business grew, his suppliers had always helped Cormier, but in 1979, when he wanted to buy direct from the manufacturers, "to get a better deal for my customers," he was told, "Sorry, we only sell to wholesalers."

No problem. Cormier sat down and formed Eastern Jewellery Ltd., which would be his wholesale company, so he could get extra discounts from the suppliers. And they were good to him once again; he was given a hot tip that gold was about to take off like a rocket. So he risked all, buying over $100,000 in gold chains at $367.50 U.S. per ounce. (He had made a new bank loan "with difficulty.") It shot up to $800 almost overnight, and the young jewellery entrepreneur "overdoubled my investment!" So when his building came up for sale, he bought it and moved upstairs from his tiny basement store. It was now over 1,000 square feet in retail space, with Paul Cormier living next door in a place he also owns. And there is parking for 20 cars as well.

In 1985 he more than doubled the size of the store once again, to 2,500 square feet, at the cost of a quarter million dollars, providing more room to sell his crystal, dinnerware, and Rolex watches, which he had been selling since 1982. "I'm known for having the biggest selection at the best prices in the Maritimes," he declares.

La Mine D'Or now has over three dozen employees, over half full time, up a bit from the original two. And he wants to see that grow as his profits have done: "I've done some preliminary work on franchising," he says, as well as having been burnt once on a store in Halifax which went under, at the Mic Mac Mall. "I get a better discount than most jewellers," he says, and he continues to advertise far more than most: Around 8% of his sales go into ads on radio (25%), TV (ditto), in newspapers (40%), and "miscellaneous." He opened a second store in a mall in Moncton in August 1986, "getting solid in this city, and only then franchising across the Maritimes." His new store is 20% over projections and he hopes for $2½ million in total sales in 1987.

It's come a long way from chains dragged out of a bottomless suitcase to a possible chain. For instance, in early 1985 Cormier developed a Corporate and Scholastic Division of La Mine D'Or, which sells school rings, company pins, and more. What "more"? Well, how about that company which might buy 100 rings for all its employees? Or the accomplished fact of General Motors, which came in and purchased 48 clocks for some of their workers. "That was a five-thousand-dollar sale right there!" Cormier says with satisfaction. "I gave them a better price." He also gives better prices to insurance companies, offering discounts on replacing stolen jewellery. One smart guy, this Cormier kid.

And he must be doing something right, since two jewellers opened and closed in the past few years in Moncton. "I am the new breed," says Paul Cormier. "The older, traditional jewellers, who were craftsmen, not businessmen, are closing up right across the country. I'm the only real independent with a large volume left in Moncton." The philosophy clearly works: "Sell quality at a lower mark-up." And with a goldsmith on staff, he can make sure that the quality doesn't suffer. And the traditional 100% mark-up is easy to cut down.

It's a family affair now. The mother who once helped him

line up those parties now works 20 hours a week in La Mine D'Or, in the giftware section. And brother André is vice-president of both companies and helps in the administration (he's got the bachelor's in business from the University of Moncton, but Paul's the one who started the business, let us remember). It was 15 to 18 hours a day, 7 days a week for the young bachelor until recently, when he slowed down to merely 60 hours a week. And he claims that he is "liked by the suppliers, but I'm known as a tough bargainer. I play them against each other."

It helps to be able to speak English in Toronto and French in Montreal (and both in Moncton), but most of all it helps that he pays his suppliers quickly, getting better prices so that he can discount 25% across the board, and up to 30% on some expensive watches. The 1985 Award of Merit for Overall Store Appearance in Eastern Canada (from the Canadian Gift and Tableware Association) shows that he cares how things look, as well as how much they cost. But in many ways, it's helped most of all to be in his hometown—recognized, honoured. He was on the board of directors of the YMCA, and he was the assistant campaign chairman of the United Way, and, as Paul Cormier says, "I was born and am known here. I was known from the restaurant as well. Many of my suppliers were really impressed that a twenty-year-old knew his wines and sauces."

And his economics, too. He stresses how he took a mere $25,000 in salary over the past few years—the company owns his apartment—and was supercareful "not to spend the profits before they are earned. I used to have only one stapler in the store during the first few years!" he exclaims, as if such a tiny saving could "help keep building up inventory." And maybe it could. Watch for La Mine D'Or very possibly opening in a mall near *you*. Paul Cormier is out to prove that Moncton is a lot closer to Montreal, Toronto, Winnipeg, Edmonton and Vancouver than it appears on any map of Canada. It is just a wagon-ride full of pop bottles (and jewellery and giftware) away.

# NO KINKS IN LEATHER

## Peter Leunes

Sometimes a simple statistic can say more about good entrepreneurship than 10,000 University of Western Ontario business studies: In the early 1980s Tannereye Ltd. of Charlottetown, Prince Edward Island, had more employees than anyone on the island, with the exception of the civil service. And the fact that a firm dedicated to the making of high-cost leather eyeglass frames could succeed on that postage-stamp province primarily known for potatoes and tourism shows how aggressive business practices can lead to international respect.

The main character is Peter Leunes, a bushy-haired, moustachioed grandson of Greek immigrants, whose parents first settled in New York City, where they had their first child in 1939. A few weeks later the family moved to Honesdale, Pennsylvania, a town of 5,000 not far from Scranton. The Leunes parents were in the restaurant business, and young Peter finished high school and spent only a year in college, "barely taking the basics. I was an athlete."

The Canadian connection first began in 1967—he's been a citizen of his new Home and Native Land since 1980—when Leunes saw an ad for "book salesmen" up at Expo in Montreal. Over a seven-week period he sold Grolier Encyclopedias, during which time he was "fired two or three times, but they always hired me back," suggesting either an uneven performance or an unknown Canadian version of George Steinbrenner.

Leunes met his future wife in Montreal, "travelled around for a year," and then started a leather business in Mexico, with a partner doing the manufacturing and Leunes doing the marketing. They made and sold belts, wallets, hats, and purses—"I spent some time with a leather-maker friend" —and they soon moved into jewellery. "It was my own company; I designed it and others made it." The business was called Little Fingers Design, and it did "reasonably well," in the words of the boss: In its last year, the three people involved sold $250,000 worth of their products across North America.

The Leuneses were in Mexico only from 1969 to 1971, when they moved up to the Laurentians, north of Montreal, flying down to the centre of operations every six weeks. A chance trip to P.E.I. led to the American's buying land in that beautiful province in early 1974, at which time he started a retail store, finally terminating his work in Montreal and Mexico and moving there in 1976.

He had converted a boat into a store, which he suitably named The Albatross, and he ran the business for three difficult years—"It was a nightmare, actually." They had to keep moving the 65-foot scallop dragger around the mall, and the damned thing weighed a ton a foot. "Everytime we moved it, we needed three cranes," he moans today.

All those years in leather making hinted that a future still lay in that ancient craft, and when a friend suggested the name Tannereye, Leunes decided that he liked the hook with leather and eyeglasses, and dug up $7,500 to incorporate. The idea was a good one, if hardly original: "The only reference I'd ever heard was that the Chinese wore leather glasses fifteen hundred years ago. I thought that they would look as good as the leather earrings I'd been making and selling." And if the ancient Chinese had a letter of credit for over $80,000, and an initial order for $81,000 worth of product from Optique Dumonde of New York, they might still be making them.

With some small grants from the provincial government and Ottawa's Industry, Trade and Commerce, and Employment and Immigration, Leunes "got a factory together." By the end of 1978 sales were over $200,000, and "we more or less doubled every year after." Sales were up to half a million by 1979, $1.2 million in 1981, and a peak of $4.3 million in 1984, before dropping to $3.2 million in 1985. (One customer in the Middle East, where the leather frames were selling like shashlik and tabuleh, suddenly discovered that he had a huge overinventory, and all projections were abruptly cut in half. "Within sixty days, we lost forty percent of our sales," says the president of Tannereye.) By the end of 1987, sales should be over $3½ million.

Which leads to the obvious question: How on earth does a tiny business in Canada's tiniest province come to sell glasses to the royal family of Kuwait, as well as hundreds of thousands of other customers in 100 countries around the world?

The answers lie, of course, in a clever product—and one which the company is constantly changing—and in very daring, impressive marketing. (During one month Leunes and New Brunswick-born vice-president Michael Jardine visited 23 cities in 28 days, lining up customers in all four corners of the globe.) Another answer is that "we make the best-quality frames in North America." The price range for the leather ones runs between $85 and $125 U.S., with the most expensive being the Porsche models, which run over $400 Canadian. "It's a difficult situation to nail down, but since ours are hand-made, we can be flexible." The frames cost more to make, so Leunes sells them "to people who care more about quality than price." (Interestingly, this is a statement which is frequently made by the successful business people profiled in this book.)

Also wise has been the frequent diversification of Tannereye: As its name implies, it was all leather at first, but since 1983 Leunes and his 150 employees have been making plastic frames as well, which now make up nearly 40% of the business. "A significant percentage of manufacturers in plastic are drying up in North America, since it's not easy to compete with the technology of the Orient." And since the competition is so rough, "we have to make a better product."

The key is innovation, such as that move into plastic, and Tannereye's doing inlays with semiprecious stores. And the latest diversification is in some ways the most promising: For more than half of 1985 Leunes and his partners were busy making leather watchbands, and have been creating samples for Timex, Bulova, Longines, and Citizen. "It seems like we could do business with some or all of them," he says hopefully. By going to just two major shows, one of them in Switzerland, Leunes has managed to show his samples to "over sixty percent of the people who sell watches."

The whirlwind/worldwide trips are fewer, now, although Leunes goes to Europe two or three times a year, having set up distribution in the United States, where most of the product is sold, followed by Europe and Japan. "We have a reputation for being aggressive marketeers," declares Leunes proudly. "With just one product, leather glasses, we have sold over $100 million in retail—over one million frames—in the past seven years!" (Tannereye is already up to 9,000 frames a month in plastic.)

One of the charming aspects of the island firm is the fact that over one-half of the employees are related to each other, leading to a closeness and loyalty to Tannereye (and each other, one would hope): "There is a lot of unemployment here, and the word got out we were hiring. Everyone has a brother or sister working here."

The fact of being nowhere near anywhere has also been a boon more than a handicap. "Part of our success is good delivery, and we're in the top echelon of delivery schedules. Everything goes by air, and the factory is tantamount to duty-free," since the $1 million in Bausch & Lomb frames can be shipped in, coated with leather, and exported out, without being hit with taxes. "It takes *less* time to do business here," Leunes insists.

The new Canadian admits that it's easier to get money in the States for a good idea, and that "it took a long time to get help from the banks here," but one does not achieve success in this northern clime—or anywhere, for that matter—without hard work. "Before I came to Canada, I sold out of the trunk of my car for over a half dozen years," Leunes recalls in his home on the island. "You made a sale or you didn't sleep in a motel the next night."

But that was then and this is now: over a dozen dozen employees, two major factories, and "reasonable expectations" of $5 million in sales a year. And that's mainly in leather, since he recently sold off the plastics, now called Phoenix Eyeware, to his partner and is beginning to work with leather-covered sculpture, as well as eyeglasses. Which, as anyone who lives in Prince Edward Island can tell you, is no small potatoes.

# WOMB MATES
# STRIKE IT WICH

### Barbara Twaits and Peggy Hillmer

"Sisterhood is powerful" runs the feminist line. "Sisterhood is profitable" runs the thought behind the line of products from a remarkably successful Toronto firm, Maggi-B Ltd. Barbara Twaits, 40 (nickname, "Auntie B"), and Peggy Hillmer, 35 (a/k/a "Maggi"), have created a company which is successfully producing and selling garment bags, slippers, and travel accessories by the hundreds of thousands, right across Canada, and, you can be sure, across the United States as well. Undercapitalized, out of daddy's basement, hit-and-miss concepts—they seemed to do everything wrong. But almost since the day they moved out of the house and into the real world of factories, labour, and cost control, they have been growing as rapidly as any two brothers in partnership have done. And they haven't touched a needle in years.

The wonderfully pretty and bright sisters were born in Calgary, raised in Montreal, two of five children of a man who "heads a large American manufacturing firm." Like many a son, the two daughters were "encouraged to get into business for ourselves. Everyone in the family was expected to go to university and make our own livings—*especially* if he or she got married!"

Peggy, the younger sister (but president of Maggi-B, although they are equal partners), studied business at Ryerson Polytechnic in Toronto; Barbara, now secretary-treasurer, "never finished home ec at McGill." They were both soon married, with children, and in creative fields of which they both soon tired. Peggy was in advertising and "didn't want to stay in a client-is-always-right environment." Barbara did TV commercials and some performing, and also wanted "to be independent in my own business. Not to answer to someone—well, to the bank, you answer!"

In brief, they both "wanted something more permanent." So in 1976, with the assistance of their father, who obtained them a line of credit of $10,000 at the Canadian Imperial Bank of Commerce ("they've been great!"), they incorporated and took no money for the next three years for themselves. Not that there was that much money to sneak from the till, since they were working out of daddy's basement and began with a number of weak marketing concepts. They started making Christmas ornaments out of imitation bread dough, but that was limited in financial reward. Then they did "funky pins that were way ahead of their time," such as molded and hand-painted hamburgers, etc., which didn't become a fad until the early 1980s. Their first-year sales weren't much more than that line of credit from dad, so they knew they had some more searching to do for the right product. (And real, cooked hamburgers had already been done.)

Finally, in 1979, they tripped over the idea they had been looking for, and which would win them a Province of Ontario Industrial Achievement Award in 1984 ("for accomplishments in selling in Canada"): No one seemed to be "making decent cosmetic bags." So they developed a line of sewn bags out of quilted cottons, and "they caught on like wildfire with small retailers! It started to build and build and build!" As did the women's business acumen and product line: Along came eyeglass cases, little travel robes with matching slippers, shower caps, and, as of the end of 1985, three dozen different items in over half a dozen different fabrics.

"When we started the sewing of the bags in 1979, we had a goal of perhaps one million sales a year," says sister Barbara. "We achieved it far sooner than we thought." The first reason for that—and there are many—was the fact that their father retired in 1981 and wanted to sell their rather large home. "It was time to go legit, ladies, and get a real plan!" they say, laughing. So they opened their first factory in northwest Toronto, "right in the middle of the Italian labour pool." Although sales were still "slim" right into 1981, they began experiencing 50 to 70% increases almost every year thereafter, approaching the $5 million mark in 1986. Projections for 1987 are for 20% more.

"It was going legit—having a factory—being one of the guys," says Twaits. "That's what did it." And having a product which was clearly satisfying a need. (Not that there was any formal market research; they had only interviewed their mothers-in-law, who claimed that PEOPLE NEEDED THESE TRAVEL ACCESSORIES. So much for jokes maligning that genre of women.) Not only were all the products made from durable, machine-washable cotton (the fabric version of healthy, fibre-filled food), they were all colour-coordinated in bright, charming designs. (The latter is relevant; the fact that this eyeglass case matches that travel bag pushes many a consumer, consciously or not, to make more than one purchase.)

Within a few short months, Maggi-B products were in hundreds of small retail stores across Canada; today more than 1,000 boutiques carry many of the products of the two sisters, including such other retail stores as Eaton's, Hudson's Bay, Bowring, Cara's, Birks, and hundreds of drugstores carrying private labels which were developed by Twaits and Hillmer.

The 10,000-square-foot space at the northwest tip of Toronto has already been outgrown; a new 20,000-square-foot factory just opened in Woodbridge, Ontario. And how could it lose? "You don't give a shower curtain for a gift," says Twaits, recalling one of their early failures, "but you *do* give a cosmetics bag!" (Their large version, selling for $21 retail, is their number 1 best-seller.)

Today, about 70 people have jobs working for the Maggi-B sisters—up to two-thirds of them sewers, the rest in packaging and supplies. "We *are* the market in Canada!" they proclaim. "We are *it!* The number one supplier of cosmetics bags to Eaton's and Hudson's Bay. We sell the best and the biggest amount!" Which leads us to the tiny, underpopulated country just south of the 49th. They already have California "covered," with showrooms in San Francisco and Los Angeles, and their products are selling like crazy in Dallas, New Orleans, Boston, Detroit, and Denver. (Every province in Canada has a salesperson on the road, of course.) And sales are "taking off" in France, Switzerland, and Belgium.

The work is divided between the two women. Barbara does the outside sales and marketing; Peggy does the production and finance. They are continually visiting trade shows—in Milan, London, Frankfurt, Paris—always together, looking for colour trends, styling changes, the kind of things that could help them, or hurt them, over the following months and years.

One could say that the women often act impulsively. "We're rather creative and spontaneous workers" is the way they put it. For instance, they called their accountant in 1985 and declared, "We just signed a lease for twenty thousand square feet." And that was that. But "we have a gut feel for business. We are controlled in planning, but spontaneous at the same time. We say that it's time to move and then *we do it.*"

Twaits and Hillmer feel that there is too much envy in Canada, too much of what they describe as "the old WASP work ethic: If you succeed, *why?*" ("We're Catholics, but not very good ones!" jokes Twaits.) Not that they could ever let their success go to their heads. As children in a family of five, if any one of them got "too bloated, the four others would scream, 'Oh, look how great *she* thinks she is!' " (Canadian banks, of course, can be counted on keeping us small-egoed, as well. When some bank managers asked if the two sisters would bring in their husbands for their signatures, Twaits and Hillmer protested, "How relevant *is* that? Let's *move on*! If *our* signatures aren't enough. . . ." Take *that*, male chauvinist bankers!)

But being women in a male-dominated industry hasn't hurt, because the women always felt, "If we didn't know about it, we hired it! And our lawyer and accountant have been *marvelous*." And their attitude to bouncing back is as healthy as that of anyone in the business world: "If this product area ever faltered, we'd just move into something else. That's why we are always travelling, looking for new trends in colourization and fashion." They are importing more lines, including soft luggage and even lingerie.

Twaits and Hillmer don't profit-share, since the bulk of their sewers are piece-workers, but they pride themselves on how many jobs they have created. The key to the runaway success of Maggi-B is, ultimately, "an instinct, the practicality of our styling, and the ability to know what the customer wants in look, feel, and practicality. And we know that a budget's a budget. You can't spend more than you make." (If that were true for all of us, Dagwood and Blondie would have been cancelled years ago, and Master Card, Visa, and American Express would be waiting in line at the soup kitchens.)

Finally, the sisters are "global in our thinking; we're *not* provincial at all. Today, Canada; tomorrow, the world." And how can 5 billion people get *around* that world without colour-coordinated travel and garment bags?

# LITTLE SISTER MAKES GOOD

### Liisa Nichol

Siblings of successful men have always tended to vanish into the woodwork. Need we remind the world of the brothers of presidents Johnson, Nixon, and Reagan? Which is why we shall mention, only in passing, that Liisa Nichol has a brother named Peter Nygard, the founder and chairman of Tan Jay International Ltd., one of the largest manufacturers of women's wear in the world. But that's all, for him; we're looking at how his sister did, and is doing, and how she is making it *herself* in Winnipeg, and in Canada.

Liisa Nichol was born in Finland during the war and came here with her parents and older brother in 1952. Her parents' dream was to have their own bakery, and to give their children an opportunity in Canada. They didn't start their dream until both children were in university, but it achieved rapid success. "Ladies would send taxis to get bread there!" she relates, her shoulder-length blond hair and white teeth shining.

As a young girl in Winnipeg, Liisa would always do babysitting, and she was filled with the feeling that "I had to earn my own money." (The feeling was not only instilled by her parents; she recalls being 11 or 12 when she borrowed some money from her older brother, and he collected it a few years later *with interest*. It was two finnmarks.) There were many other role models, including cousins in small business, back in Finland. "My grandfather was a direct seller, as I ended up," she declares. "He was an amputee and sold clothing out of a trunk on a horse and buggy! I only recently realized that I had seen him do this back in Europe!"

Liisa Nygard went to the University of North Dakota, graduating with a Bachelor of Science, majoring in speech pathology. Throughout her career, having become Liisa Nichol, she had four children, "two of each," ranging in age from 13 to nearly 21. Her husband, Russell, had studied business, worked at the Bay, then moved into the garment industry with his brother. He eventually joined his successful wife in her new business in the fall of 1975, until they recently separated.

Nichol's last child was not well, so the mother stayed at home but "wanted to work badly." So she began a direct-sales, home-party business. Hardly original, but in Liisa Nichol's case, it was to be highly successful. "A girlfriend asked me to sell Coppercraft, and another suggested clothes. I realized that the latter is more natural for me; I was a seamstress, and I had a brother in the business." (*She* mentioned him this time; we didn't.) So she was familiar with the manufacturing end of it, and, as she correctly notes, "As long as there are people, there will be a need for clothes." (Especially in Winnipeg.)

Her first decision was to sell "good-quality clothes, but at reasonable prices. I targeted my market for the average Mrs.

Canada—not impoverished, but not wealthy, either." She went on the premise of less mark-up but more volume. "If you want to sell volume, you must *buy* volume." She chose "keystone" marking—you buy for $10, sell for $20. "Most retailers in clothing charge more than that," she claims.

She began with $2,000 in clearance goods from Tan Jay, but within the month she was calling on other factories as well. Today she uses over 100 suppliers, with Tan Jay making up one-fourth to one-half of the sales to her.

Liisa Nichol did everything by herself, initially, and then had two friends join her. (They had one kit, and it rotated.) Within five months she had 5, and then 7 workers. In June 1975 she incorporated Pirjo-Liisa Fashions Ltd., the title of the firm being her complete name. There were 12 workers by then, plus a little warehouse. "My basement had grown too small," she says.

Everything else has grown large. She is now responsible for the paycheques of up to 300 people, with over half of them, all independent salespeople with goods on consignment, working at any one time. She refuses to give her commission rates, but she notes that "our girls [*sic*] often make more than their husbands. It depends on how entrepreneurial they are. There are no restraints on them." (Except maybe from husbands who resent their "girls" making more money than they.) There are no territories in the plan of Pirjo-Liisa Fashions; the women go from province to province, if they wish. And Nichol insists that it is "*not* a pyramid company; we give bonus points only for bringing in a recruit. It's strictly *running your own business*, which is what I like about it."

The party concept appears to work as well for clothes as it has always done for Tupperware and Mary Kay. The saleswoman finds out the sizes of her friends beforehand, inviting anywhere from 15 to 20 to the home. The women try on, discuss, and eventually buy there. "We bring a little store to them," says Liisa Nichol. "Usually it's two garment racks, with about eight to ten thousand dollars retail in clothes." Prices range from $5 to $100, with the most popular items under $35. Most of the stock consists of bottoms and tops, with blouses and sweaters often selling in the $30 to $40 range.

What keeps the prices so low, of course, and what is at the core of Nichol's success is that in her concept, *everyone* comes out a winner (except, naturally, Eaton's, Simpson's, the Bay, and Dylex): Nichol does well as the owner; her husband as VP, finance; the saleswomen, in commissions; the customers, in getting discounts they've rarely seen before; and—let's not ignore them, folks, since they make it all possible—the manufacturers, who are getting rid of stock which they feared they'd be stuck with.

"We buy overcuts from manufacturers," explains Nichol, "and I take them all. I may get no size fourteens sometimes, but I get good discounts." She is now committed to several factories that way and is offered clearances "all the time." The factories are now spread from Vancouver to Montreal, each one probably ecstatic that this woman in Winnipeg is always there to buy their mistakes, overruns, boo-boos, even at extremely low prices.

And even though Nichol buys "all these clearances," she keeps building "a fashion story," matching blouses from one overrun to a skirt from another. "You can buy a whole wardrobe at a party as cheap as fifty dollars," she says. "We sell a lot of wardrobe packages." And the customers love them. Business doubled for the first few years, going from $500,000 to $1 million, and onward. She peaked at $8 million, before the recession hit like a ton of overruns. "Alberta was our mainstay for a while, and it got tougher to sell there in the early 1980s." But even the rough times were good for her. "We were comfortable, and we were forced to examine ourselves and streamline our management."

As often happens in stories like this one, friends tell friends who tell friends. For instance, Ottawa began when "the fourth girl" in the company moved there. The cities being flooded with Pirjo-Liisa Fashion parties now include Calgary, Edmonton, Regina, Saskatoon, Winnipeg, the Vancouver area, Thunder Bay, and yes, Ottawa. There should be a half-dozen stores in southwest B.C. by the end of 1987.

What came later, but now makes up 50% of her business, is her own chain of actual stores. She opened the first one in the late 1970s in order to clear out the clearances from her parties. But it took off, and now there is one in each of her "party" cities, with two in Calgary. Called Pirjo-Liisa Warehouse Discount, the stores are thriving. "We locate in unorthodox places, usually near airports," she says. "Some retailers pay twenty-five dollars a square foot for space; we pay between two-fifty and seven dollars!" The parking is good, but the stores are not fancy, with open ceilings, pipes showing, etc. "But we pride ourselves on Holt Renfrew quality and service, joined with discount-store prices!"

There is smart business sense going on both at the head office and among all those party-throwers. Nichol has developed a relationship of net 60 days with her manufacturers, making sure they never have to call for the bucks. "We've become well known in the industry as good payers."

So too with the "girls." They throw two to three parties a week, for up to eight months a year, and can earn $16,000, $18,000, even $20,000. "One girl earned $40,000 in a single year," Nichol is delighted to report. They must put down a modest refundable deposit "in the $500 range" when they pick up the clothes, but we don't hear any of them complaining.

There is a real sense of women-helping-women in what Liisa Nichol has created. "Some couldn't *imagine* themselves in the field and are now my biggest sellers!" she exclaims. "One of my biggest thrills is seeing the women who were terrified and have now become self-confident." (One "girl" began in the warehouse and is now assistant to the VP of merchandising. The company has so many girls in it, it's surprising that it hasn't been closed down under child labour laws.)

There are actual children working there, too. Nichol's two sons have worked in the warehouse, and the oldest child, Angela, has sold in the stores, was employed by Tip Top Tailors, and now runs the booming Vancouver operation. The boss recalls her father running after a bakery truck in order to land a job. "All that builds the fibre in a person," she says, and every mother knows how important fibre is to us. "There *are* opportunities in this country; I wish Canadians would realize that! We tend to be followers instead of leaders, and are too conservative by nature. We've never gone through a war here."

And Pirjo-Liisa Nichol almost didn't make it here, either. Her father had put down his name on lists of immigrants wanting to go to New Zealand, Australia, the United States, and Canada, when Winnipeg had come up. "We had an aunt in Minnesota, and on the map it looked close!"

Success is more than close now for Nichol. "To the best of my knowledge, my business is the largest and longest-standing of its kind in Canada." June 1985 completed her tenth full year in business; she knows of nearly a dozen other similar concepts which started and quickly sank from sight. Not Pirjo-Liisa. She sees herself still doing this in ten years, and beyond. She's even looked southward, but there are all those border problems and red tape. "We were seriously considering Minneapolis but found that we'd have to purchase there, and not export. With all the tariffs, Canadian manufacturers can't be competitive."

Nichol feels that she "made it look a lot easier than it is!" She worked 17-hour days at the start, 7 days a week. "I had warehouse babies!" she jokes. And how many businessmen can say *that*? And she is resentful that many believe that her brother is in any way responsible for her success. "He treats me tougher than all my other manufacturers! I took a credit line with Tan Jay for net thirty, and in thirty days, I had to pay it!!"

The goal is now $8 million, a solid growth up from 1986's $7 million in sales. But "we could have $100 million now if we wanted to. If we did, however, there would be no family life." Unlike most male entrepreneurs, Liisa Nichol declares passionately that "to be happy in business, we must be happy at home. So we've tempered our growth." She finds time to be "heavily involved" as a volunteer in women's gymnastics, since a daughter is a gifted athlete, and Nichol is a judge as well. She hopes that she and her daughter will be spectators at the 1988 Olympics.

During the interview, Pirjo-Liisa ("it's like Anna-Marie"), glasses hanging around her neck, her blue eyes gleaming, numerous rings on her fingers and bracelets on her wrists, keeps looking around the restaurant as she speaks. "As I sit here, I'm watching how the women dress, looking for new ideas. I'm always thinking one step ahead and always have an alternate plan ready—or can come up with one quickly. And I can turn things around rapidly, to my advantage."

That's for sure. Nichol, who has never taken a course in merchandising ("It's all intuitive"), once made a dreadful mistake. When her firm was still tiny, she ordered 144 units of slips. When it was too late, she discovered that she had ordered 144 *dozen* slips by mistake. (She was unaware that slips sell by the dozen.)

"They were all soon sold," she declares.

# PARACHUTING INTO THE STATES

## Nicola Perry and Harry Parnass

There is an ancient, honourable tradition of Canadians playing Americans in theatre and film, whether it was Alexander Knox as President Woodrow Wilson or Raymond Massey as Abraham Lincoln. But the tradition of having the Yanks wrap themselves up in the latest—and wildest—Canadian fashions is more recent.

Which brings us to two Montrealers who have taken New York and Los Angeles by storm, with fashions as brazen in the '80s as Quebec politics were in the '40s: Nicola Perry and Harry Parnass. Perry was born in England in 1948 and studied in a British fashion design college. She came to the States on a travel bursary and was offered "a good job" in Montreal in 1971, eventually ending up at the Chateau chain of youthful fashions. "We realized fairly immediately that there was more than we could do at Le Chateau."

We? That brings us to Harry Parnass, and the father of the couple's daughter, Talia, born in the spring of 1984. He was born in Germany in 1935, coming to Canada in 1964 after being educated at Columbia and Harvard in architecture and urban design. He taught at the University of Montreal, eventually becoming a full professor in his chosen field, and is still there. With his own architectural and urban design practice, he became the consultant to all municipal, provincial, and federal programs in his expertise, and, he says, he "redesigned many Canadian cities, by having an influence on most downtown plans." He has been a consultant to projects in France, the Middle East, and the United Nations as well. Somehow, he came to Le Chateau, where he was VP of that organization "for several years," meeting and joining up with the very beautiful and talented Ms. Perry.

OK, we've got them together at Le Chateau. Then what? "I left Le Chateau with Nicola because we were interested in more *avant garde* clothes than that chain could handle." So with an investment of $10,000, the two began to design their very, *very* bold and different clothes. There were a number of "false starts"—licensing designs to manufacturers and letting *them* hire salesmen ("It didn't work")—and they found themselves "screwed by all the whores of the industry," in the words of Parnass.

So Perry and Parnass opened a little store, a furnace room, really, doing it all by themselves in a small store on Crescent, in Montreal. They found a Lebanese lady with a sewing machine, purchased bolts of fabric, and began designing. "It took off!" exclaims Parnass. "Suddenly people all over America had heard of our store!"

Oh, yes, that name: "We needed something bilingual, and the military look was big at the time [it was late 1977], and we wanted an action-sports word. And our clothes designs were risky in terms of fashion, and you're not supposed to jump out of a plane without a parachute, are you?" So Parachute was born.

For all the wit of the name, there was still "a *big* risk" involved, according to Parnass. "We soon learned that the nature of our designs outstripped the ability of the Canadian market to absorb them."

Which is why the two partners/lovers went straight to the heart of it all—New York, New York—and opened the largest single designer store in that great city's history—10,000 square feet. (The largest one before was Ralph Lauren, with under 7,000.) Who says that Canucks don't think BIG?

"My own feeling as an architect is that the greatest urban luxury is *space*," states Parnass. "We made a statement that way. We gave people in crowded New York lots of space to watch videos and read magazines. It was a totally advanced environment for 1979." And it attracted everyone who was anyone. Peter Gabriel, one of the major rock performers of the last decade, has been writing original music for Parachute stores, and, to quote from Ms. Perry, "we sell to well-known people all the time!" Cher is visiting Parachutes frequently, as is Mick Jagger, once of Sonny and, and the Rolling Stones, respectively. Michael Jackson—remember him?—wears a Parachute leather jacket often, and Bob Dylan—still blowin' in the wind—bought a few thousand-dollar items. "We do interesting clothes that attract interesting people," comments Perry.

"We design very special clothing," says Parnass, so the music must be designed carefully as well. (They do their own videos of their fashions being modelled.) "People like to come in and there's no hassle. We've become the meeting places that the Italian piazzas were back in the sixteenth century."

When they *also* dressed pretty classy in certain circles. A second Parachute store opened on Columbus Avenue in New York in early 1982, followed by a third one on Melrose Avenue in Los Angeles later that same year, later closed, with a new one four times the size on La Brea Avenue in the same city, followed by one in Chicago at the end of 1983, and one in Beverly Hills in early 1985. In spring, 1987, there was a new store in Dallas. The single store in Montreal in 1978–79 brought in maybe $250,000 in sales; in 1984 Parachute clothes sold over $27 million retail around the world, with the money still pouring in at the end of 1987.

Why such overwhelming success? Many people are happy to buy T-shirts and sweatshirts for up to $20, but pants and shirts for $80 to $200? Leather coats for $1,200? "The key thing was," explains Nicola Perry, "that we enjoy being designers and holding the whole thing together. Every day we do something new. The investment is in big spaces and creating dramatic clothing, and not taking it safe. And opening beyond the pale—outside Montreal!"

The head office is still in Montreal, and it has over three dozen people there. They do a little wholesaling, mainly shipping to their stores. The partners are "continually updating and improving" their fashions, creating five seasons a year, mostly in natural fibres, but "occasionally switching over."

"We run our business like all companies mentioned in *In Search of Excellence*," declares Harry Parnass. "You do what you can do best, and all the rest, you farm out." And what Perry and Parnass do best is designing the clothes, the stores, conducting the market research in fabrics.

There are now literally hundreds of people sewing Parachute goods, and up to 35 employees in the giant New York store, making a lot of people depend on the trendy but obviously gifted talents of these two Montrealers. Oh yes—the St. Catharines store in Montreal burned down, and they've had one in St. Lawrence since May 1986. "The Canadian market is not right for our goods," says Parnass. (Sorry, big spenders in Toronto; they won't carry their full line there. *You* don't make it, either.)

"It's *very* time-consuming," says Perry. "We don't take

holidays, and it's a seven-day week, since we tend to bring it all home." The first stage was easy, they claim, and the rip-offs were coped with from the beginning. But there were risks galore: "Every opening of a new store is a risk," declares Perry. "We have *such* a specialized product!"

But not too specialized for the glitterati and hoi polloi who keep beating paths to their doors across North America. There are a number of franchisees who want to get in on their successful act, and a store in Milan (Italy, if you please) looks "pretty definite." "We did it with conviction," says the female partner. "We offer a lot of choice and styles of clothing, and convince customers that we know what we're doing. Few clothing stores have videos that have such creativity to them—it's a whole new development." (Last spring they shot one in Hawaii.)

The danger, as always in this sort of thing, would be to compromise their taste and styling by growing too big and expanding too fast, and the two struggle against it. In the meantime, that major Parnass/Perry production, Talia, "has generated a very successful line—baby and children's clothes!" There you have it: Motherhood is the necessity of invention.

## TAKING CRAFTS TO THE BANK

### Zonda Nellis

One of the most exciting examples of turning one's hobby— childhood interest, really—into a financial success has been the meteoric career of Zonda Nellis of Vancouver, whose red-haut couture is being worn proudly right across North America by thousands of women whose taste buds and wallets combine to afford them. (Two-piece outfits begin at around $800 U.S., and one client at a major boutique in Arizona has *six* four-piece outfits, since, in the words of their creator, "they are so comfortable and elegant, they are hard to resist."

Born in Woodstock, Ontario, in 1950, Nellis was an only child of parents who had "a little greasy spoon" in Ingersoll when she was a child. "Being around a restaurant means you're involved," she recalls today, from her home 3,000 miles to the west. "I did my homework at the tables, and carried dishes." But it was not the kitchen that inspired the future designer, but the fact that as an only child she had a lot of time to herself. So she sat at her mother's sewing machine, figuring out how to sew, and "made things" throughout her childhood.

After finishing high school in Oshawa, Nellis moved to the west coast to community college, and headed off to Europe at the age of 17 ("Everyone was doing that in the 'sixties"). She stayed there for a year, living and working in Sicily for six months, coming back to Vancouver and studying anthropology and English, and making tie-dyed clothes with a woman friend. "We designed dresses and earned one thousand dollars in only three weeks!" she exclaims, with a voice that still betrays her excitement at the time at having made *so much money*, selling the clothes to students and staff at the art school in Banff. Then it was back to the Vancouver School of Art for a year. "I wanted to weave and do fabric design," she says.

Still no entrepreneur, Zonda Nellis found a woman to teach her to spin, taught craft programs at the Vancouver Art Gallery, and spent five years improving her craft. "For most people in the arts, making money is not the most important thing, but just doing what one wants to do." But money still came, in spite of its not being the most important thing: She began selling her designs at craft shows, and soon discovered that dozens of customers were coming specifically to buy her clothes. "Mine were good," she states immodestly. "I thought to myself, 'Why sit around here?'" Indeed, even in those lean days of the early 1970s, when Nellis was still in the first half of her 20s, she was doing "unusual things," which would soon become usual for her: "I sold coats for three or four hundred dollars, even as early as 1975." Yet she was earning only enough to live, since it took a very long time to make each one.

So it was off to the states—San Francisco, California, to be exact—where she exhibited at the Renaissance Fair, and quickly discovered that "no one was doing what I was doing." She displayed her wares there for three years, zapping back and forth to her home in Vancouver, selling her hand-spun woven coats for up to $500, and her original scarves for as much as $70.

But even in the rarified atmosphere of an American crafts

fair, Zonda Nellis asked, like Peggy Lee, "Is that all there is?" She looked around, saw crowds of up to 30,000 paying $10 each to visit craftspeople like herself, and knew that there was Something More. "Why sell my clothes for a few hundred dollars?" she recalls asking herself. "I could sell to stores for more." Furthermore, she had once again grown tired of the entire dubious concept of the crafts fair: Too much depended upon the location of her booth, and she "didn't like having my fate in the hands of other people."

So Nellis took her fate in her own hands, as most successful entrepreneurs must do at one point or another. She went to Saks Fifth Avenue in San Francisco with, believe it or not, a selection of her handmade clothes in a bag, and asked to see the buyer. The woman was impressed with what she saw, but, understandably, was taken back by the fact that the young Canadian had names for her styles but no specific sizes. Yet it was still the morale breakthrough which Nellis had longed for and needed: "The fact that they'd even *look* at my things!" she enthuses today. "They wanted a dozen, but I didn't think in such big amounts."

Nellis returned to her home in Vancouver and began developing a new kind of fabric—a blend of cotton, linen, rayon, and silk. "It's unique-looking, but high-fashion," she explains. She realized that what she did was limiting, and knew that she needed to hire people to weave *for her*, for a change. The creation of the new fabric took a number of years, but they were as well spent as those of any restauranteur researching the demographics of a mall.

She had, furthermore, the kind of incentive which many creative women do not have: Having never been married, she had to support herself. "Many do crafts for the sheer joy of it," Nellis says. "I wanted to make a profit from mine." The development of the new fabric was a further breakthrough, and she knew that she "didn't want to sit and make coats myself." She showed Saks her first real collection, and they asked her to be one of a new group of designers they were introducing. It will warm the hearts of our frozen countrymen to hear that because of Zonda Nellis's involvement, the Americans changed the name of the group from "California Designers" to "West Coast Designers." All this without the assistance of a Reagan-Mulroney friendship or free trade.

"I did jackets, sweaters, skirts—all very elegant, selling

for about $1,000 an outfit retail, with myself getting about half," she says. They sold well, and Nellis started getting press in Vancouver, with local stores eager to promote her, including Monique Gabin, an exclusive boutique there. She was still sewing at that time—1979—and had one weaver.

By the following year, Zonda Nellis "actually made money!" She was able to sell to a number of stores across her chosen city, and she "just *knew* it would be successful; people wanted my clothes!" With such confidence, she took off around the world for nearly half a year, with a male friend. Soon after their return, her lover suddenly died of an illness, and she "threw herself into the business a hundred and fifty percent." Since she wanted to have workers who would stay with her for a long time, she hired two Tibetan women, who, incidentally, are still with her. "I wanted people who had weaving in their culture."

The Bay in Vancouver now picked her up, forcing her to extend her collection. She would now do at least 20 different styles in her line, as opposed to less than half that previously. And it forced her to develop good sizing. By 1982 her sales were only $27,000 for the entire year, and people seemed to stop buying during the Great Depression, Part II. Stores were reluctant to buy sweaters priced at over $500. So Zonda Nellis found a storefront, and set herself up in a more accessible location, West 10th Street, in Vancouver. "It allowed me to build my image and make me more visible." In the meantime, she did a trade fair in New York, which she attended with the promise of no orders whatsoever. "But I was sure of my vision," she declares. On the first day she received $40,000 in orders, and she was on her way. Returning to Vancouver, she realized that she needed an agent, and responded to the offer of a "sensational" woman in San Diego.

As of the end of 1987 Zonda Nellis was selling close to $1 million a year of her designs, up somewhat from the $27,000 of three years before. Original Zondas are sold in over four dozen major stores across the United States, with Canada somewhat ignored, for not-unexpected reasons: "A vice-president of Holt Renfrew told my major buyer once, 'Nellis's things are lovely; the only trouble is, she's Canadian.' " Sound familiar?

Nellis states, with some bitterness, "Americans are more visionary; in Canada, the buyers ask, 'What will the public buy?' " So it's been easier in the States, whether at Sakowitz in Texas, Bergdorf Goodman in New York, Denallo in Beverly Hills, or Therapy on Madison Avenue. She employs about 20 people now, including her two Tibetans; a number of Greek women weave in their homes in Vancouver, and 6 employees work in her studio, where the sewing is still done.

Zonda Nellis sweaters, coats, dresses, jackets, and scarves are being snatched up and worn proudly across North America, but Our Lady of the Fabric has no five-year plan. "I could easily sell more than a million dollars within the next few years," she thinks. The number could come sooner rather than later, due to Nellis's latest interest: "I'm beginning to work on fabrics for interiors. I can design fabrics for interior decorators and keep my weavers working." In 1987, Canada's most prominent interior designer, Robert M. Ledingham, began using her fabrics. Indeed, with the same overhead she has now, she believes that she could "easily do thirty percent more business."

Zonda Nellis realizes that, being located on the west coast, she lacks direct access to the mills of the east, but business has never been better. "We created a market where nothing existed before, and our customers are very happy." And some of the customers get around; her clothes were on the television show "Dynasty" in the 1984–85 season and appeared on "Hotel" in 1985–86. More recent, but still rich and famous clients included sit-com giant Norman Lear, for his wife, a movie costumer purchasing for a Glenn Close film, the characters on "The Colbys." And every week, in the opening credits on "The Bill Cosby Show," guess what his TV wife is wearing?

"It used to really bug me and make me furious that I had to go to the States," she says, adding softly, "but the Canadian fashion industry is young." The real pleasure lies in the fact that she has created "something that no one else has, and that I have control over each piece!"

Craftspeople certainly can be entrepreneurial, insists Zonda Nellis. "I started something from nothing. I had no backing, no money, nothing. Three years ago, I couldn't get a Visa card; I was a single, self-employed woman. And just the other day, I got a gold American Express card mailed to me." (And two years ago, in October 1985, a beautiful child, Alexandra Elisabeth.)

## 4.
# RETAILING

*More and More Stores*

One of the major business phenomena of the last decade has been franchising: taking a store or service and spinning it off across North America. The classic image is McDonald's or Colonel Sanders, but people in the know realize that Canadian Tire Corporation and Shoppers Drug Mart built their empires in this fashion, and for countless other businesses it seems to be the most satisfactory way of expansion. (But not the *only* way; for while franchised businesses are common throughout this book, including mmmuffins and O'Toole's in an earlier chapter and Molly Maid in a later, there are still many, many successful businesses with dozens of stores which have refused to go the franchise route, like Druxy's, and a number of companies in this chapter, including Alan Perlmutter's Micro Cooking Centres and John Park's Hi-Fi Centres. "I don't believe in franchising," says the latter straightforwardly. And there are still others, such as Peter Friedenthal's House of Knives, which have a healthy mix: of his approximately 50 stores, just over one-half are company-owned, the rest franchised.)

"Franchising: A boom that just won't quit," screamed the headline on the front page of the *Financial Times* on November 19, 1984. Some numbers will suggest how correct that headline was: In 1981 Statistics Canada reported that Canadian franchise operations accounted for a massive $46.8 billion in sales, up from $20.1 billion just half a decade earlier. There are over 400 Canadian companies listed in the 1985 Franchise Annual, out of St. Catharines, Ontario, which are actively seeking franchisees—and another 2,000 in the United States. A positive quotation comes from the Asa brothers, who have turned one tiny camera store in 1959 into over 150 stores, with over $100 million in sales, by the end of 1986: "Franchising makes more people rich! It's a life-style and a happy business."

But all the businesses and their founders below are happy, whether they are franchising or not. Somehow, each has managed to build a single store into many more, often many dozens more, and frequently in the time frame of only a few years. These stores cover the kitchen (Friedenthal's House of Knives and Perlmutter's Micro Cooking Centres), furniture and decor (Bob Thorssen's Jungle Interiors and Bryce Schnare's Bass River Chair Factory outlets), and, with admitted whimsy on the part of my editor, lights (Seymour Schwartz's Lighting Unlimited), cameras (the Asa brothers' Japan Camera), and (understandably, in a book about entrepreneurs) action (John Park's Hi-Fi Express). These highly creative, driven men have few childhood parallels to draw: Perlmutter and Friedenthal both come from wealthy homes, albeit far-distant ones (the former, London, Ontario; the latter, South Africa); Thorssen's father is a professor of engineering at the University of Alberta; Bryce Schnare never went to college, whereas Seymour Schwartz has a law degree; Korean John Park studied computers at Cal Tech, and the Japanese-Canadian Asa brothers never attended university and were (briefly) impoverished orphans in Japan after the war.

What these bright and capable men *do* have in common is that same passionate drive to succeed: "When you immigrate, you *must* make it," said Friedenthal, who could just as easily be speaking for fellow-immigrants Park and the Asas. "I always had a desire to do something," says Perlmutter, for whom everything he's touched has turned to gold. "I wanted to get into my own business; I wanted to make decisions," says Schnare. "I wanted to create my own business," echoes Park.

But big deal, you may think; lots of people long to be their own bosses and create their own firms; a fraction succeed and, even then, rarely end up with dozens of stores dotting Canada. What *else* did these entrepreneurs have?

For one thing, they had good concepts. "You need a creative idea," states the highly creative Thorssen of Jungle Interiors. Friedenthal stole his House of Knives idea from Calgary, with the aid of friend Schwartz, and frenetically placed them in "Triple A" malls across Canada until no one could catch up. Perlmutter saw his mother fall in love with a microwave oven, sensed a market there, and exploited it like mad, selling "the use" of the machines, and always "quality over price" (a common theme in this book). Thorssen had a market study done on imitation plants, it came back negative, and he disregarded it entirely and pushed ahead. (So much for going with expert opinions.)

Bryce Schnare encountered the century-old Bass River chairs when he was putting together a weak fish-and-chips concept in P.E.I., and saw how attractive they were, knowing that "restaurants are ahead of society in style." John Park and the Asa brothers are in perhaps the most competitive retailing businesses on earth: stereos and cameras. And yet each has had awesome success. In Park's case, it was because of his faith in the coming of "mass merchandise discounting," which has already arrived in the States, and in which Canada is traditionally a few years behind. By eliminating warehousing and lowering overhead (a mere three employees work in each Hi-Fi Centre), and using co-op ads (where the electronics companies pay for much of them), he went from one store in 1982 to 20 stores in 1985, and expects 50 stores by 1987, with $80 million in sales. The Asas' secret was "service" as well as a marketing coup of momentous proportions: They obtained the exclusive rights to the Noritsu one-hour photo-finishing machine in Canada. And then there's Seymour Schwartz, who has helped to franchise Friedenthal's House of Knives and the Asas' Japan Camera, as well as make his in-law's Lighting Unlimited Stores take off (from 7 to over 60 stores in 17 years, also thanks to franchising and to elimination of billing and warehousing). And the way this man stole a fruit-and-nut concept—even the name!—from the States could have him arrested and shot in most countries of the world.

No, it's not originality in this chapter, any more than in the others; it's a profound desire to succeed, combined with a willingness to work long hours, take little (if any) money home for many years, and cling to their concept tenaciously. "The excitement of building something" is what drove Perlmutter and, ultimately, everyone else in this section.

# SHARP BUSINESS PRACTICES

### *Peter Friedenthal*

Often, in the world of entrepreneurship, it is not so much creating an idea as taking someone else's idea that is the key to success. Everyone knows that Henry Ford was hardly the first to build a feasible motor-driven car. But he *did* create the first mass-produced automobiles, and the rest, as they are wont to say, is history. (And when, years later, Ford refused to offer any colour but black, Chevrolet moved into a commanding position that General Motors has never given up. So much for originality in business.)

Ditto Peter Friendenthal, tall, stunningly handsome in his cowboy boots. Born in Johannesburg in 1939 to parents who had emigrated to that country in the 1930s from central Europe, he had a very upper-class upbringing: His father was busy developing the biggest lighting fixture business in South Africa, doing large residential homes, hotels, office blocks.

At the age of 18, the secondborn child left South Africa, working for an electrical wholesaler in England for 18 months, then attending the London School of Economics for 14 months. From there, it was off to Grenoble to learn French and study arts, and then on to Hamburg, where Friedenthal worked in marine insurance and banking, and attended further classes in university.

He finally returned to Johannesburg at the age of 26 and worked for his father as a salesman. "I really built the business up with him," he declares, and eventually, the family sold out to one of the largest public companies in South Africa. Even after that major deal, Friedenthal junior continued to run the company for another four years as its managing director. It was eventually called Dominec Lighting, and it tripled its sales in those years, up to $4½ million by the time the young man left.

"I always wanted my own company," says Peter Friedenthal, echoing the words and emotions of 10,000 entrepreneurs, both successful and un. "I saw the problems looming ahead in South Africa, and I wanted to make a new start."

There were few alternatives, including Australia and this country. "The States were impossible to get into," he relates. He had made a business trip to Canada and really liked it, and so, in September 1976 he chose peace, order, good government, and brutal winters over chaos, revolution, and cheap help. He was allowed only 30,000 Rand to take with him, so he left most of his money in an apartment block and various properties. He later sold them and realized little.

He did come with a wife and two children, and soon separated from them as well. (The children are both grown; the 24-year-old now works with him in his new Canadian business enterprise.) But there must have been hard times: When he left South Africa, he had been promised a position with the people he'd worked with back home, who had planned to start a lighting company in Canada. "They suddenly changed their minds, and I found myself out on a limb."

But Friedenthal came to this country with a good background in lighting, even if his money and prospects were both bleak. He was offered $120 a week by one lighting place, which he rejected. And he soon was running a small table section for Singer Lighting for a year and a half. For another year he was a general manager for Aristocrat Lamps. But by June 1978 he left that place as well, and thrashed about looking for another job.

He had been friendly with Seymour Schwartz at Lighting Unlimited, and when the latter encountered a store called The Knifery, in Calgary, he flipped. "They had only hunting knives, no kitchen utensils or anything, but he still called me, and I flew out to the city."

At first glance, Friedenthal felt that the place was "so badly put together," he wasn't impressed. But then he thought of Hoffritz in the States, which makes gorgeous knifeware, and the concept began to come together. He flew back to Toronto on Monday, and on the following day he sat down with Schwartz and a lawyer, and decided to form a company: House of Knives.

Friedenthal's initial moves were in the direction of research: He did extensive looking into all local manufacturers of knives, as well as importers, taking from June to November to do his work. In November 1978 he opened his first store in Oshawa (the Motown of Canada), a half hour east of Toronto. "It was difficult to get a site, and Oshawa was the only mall that was willing to take a shot."

The amount of space was, and is, comical: 164 square feet. "We invested thirty thousand dollars into the business, of which I put in fifteen thousand, so I had fifty percent of the ownership." He also lined up a $40,000 loan from the Federal Business Development Bank. Talk about inauspicious; the first day's sales were $7. "I think it was a paring knife and something else." He laughs. "You wouldn't *believe* what I went through!" Not only that, but he was already committed to another mall in St. Catharines, Ontario. (A bad move, in retrospect; he had so many burglaries in that store, "it was incredible." Next to drugs, it seems that knives attract punks the most. It was eventually closed, due to bad sales and all those break-ins.)

Then Friendenthal opened in Eaton Centre in December 1978, giving him three stores within eight weeks. (The store at Eaton Centre has only 135 square feet; thank heavens for folding knives.) "It's a hole in the wall, really—it was a Toronto Dominion night deposit!" Hole in the wall or not, it cost him $10,000 a year in rent; today it's almost triple that.

The first franchise of House of Knives came about when a franchisee of Lighting Unlimited offered to buy one, for $10,000 plus 6% royalties. By this time, Friedenthal had a franchise program worked out but lacked capital, so he decided to create a mix of company-owned as well as franchises.

The end of 1979 saw $400,000 in sales from the three stores. Twelve months later, there were 12 House of Knives stores, with sales of $1.5 million. In 1981 27 stores were in business, of which 7 were company-owned; sales were up to nearly $5 million. By 1983 the number of stores was up to 46, and in 1986 50 stores (60% company-owned) were bringing in $8½ million in sales for Friedenthal and his 140 employees of House of Knives. There should be 6 to 8 more stores by late 1987.

The hopes? Perhaps 65 stores, at which point the president feels that Canada will be "basically saturated." There was a test store opened in Cleveland, Ohio, which did well, "but it was impossible to run it from here." He sold it to Remington. He still hopes to move into the United States, but only when sites become available, possibly as soon as sometime in 1987.

Why such a success from such a seemingly limited concept? "We've done well because we specialize, and our staff is knowledgeable about the products," Friedenthal declares. They carry 800 items in every store, including knives, scissors, pocket knives, hunting knives, magnifying glasses, and similar products. And there are a lot of impulse items, such as flashlights and a gift line for men. "The big problem is space, so we are limited with how much we can expand," he confesses.

The average sale is around $20, and Friedenthal travels extensively to Europe, ever looking for new products. He brings in around 40% of his items himself; the rest are imported by other companies, which sell them to House of Knives.

"Other guys keep copying me, so I have to be very innovative to stay ahead," he declares. Advertising, however, is not one of the ways; a mere 2% of gross sales is spent on letting the customer know that he is there. But the franchisees appear to be happy; one fellow in Vancouver has seven stores, one in Ottawa owns three, and another in Halifax has two. There will be House of Knives stores in every province, with the exception of New Brunswick, P.E.I., and Newfoundland, by the end of 1986.

Franchisees now pay $15,000, plus 6% royalties, for the joy of running a House of Knives. They probably need close to $70,000 to run their store from the start. Friedenthal helps them with choosing product, and all the other things that good franchisers must do for their people.

As with many successful franchisers, Friedenthal insists that every store be in a "major Triple A mall." It's basically for traffic, and the fact that they carry only high-end products. True, some knives are as cheap as $1.50 to $3.00, but hunting knives can go for as much as $300.

The early years were lean, of course. Friedenthal ran everything out of his basement for the first six months, and he "nearly went belly-up when I moved into a warehouse, got the first shipment from Europe, and then had the first burglary." The sharpies cleaned out $45,000 in knives, and the shakey owner got only $30,000 back from the insurance company. (His record is eight burglaries in one mall.)

Friedenthal is an obsessive businessman, working an average of 12 to 14 hours a day, 6 to 7 days a week. "My hours?" he exclaims. "Oh my God!" And he admits that if he sold out now, barely more than a half dozen years after he opened the first store, he could obtain "a few million dollars."

"That's the beauty of knives," he says, smiling. "It's one of the oldest implements used by man, and it'll only get stronger." (Especially when women hear about them.) And now, the French, Italians, and Germans are going into coloured handles, which we've always needed but didn't know about before this year.

"We've made people aware of knives," says the president of House of Knives Limited. "We're the largest seller of the product in Canada." In fact, he expects that sales could be up to $14 million by 1990, with stores getting larger: from 600 to 1,000 square feet in size.

There are no secrets to Peter Friedenthal's success in his new country. "Tenacity, a flair for merchandizing. But it would have been a success in the States, as well. You see, it became an obsession to get into my own business and make it again. When you immigrate, you *have* to make it."

# MACROPROFITS
# FROM MICROWAVES

### Alan Perlmutter

In a little industrial park northwest of Toronto is a tiny little office with a back room filled with chairs in a circle. "MICRO COOKING CENTRES—THE MICROWAVE SPECIALISTS" says the sign, and the room is the microwave cooking school, where lucky purchasers of the product can learn how to use it efficiently. The various products around the room give no sense of the explosive and ingenious entrepreneurial skills of the creator of the chain of stores: An apron (price $11.95) hangs upon the wall. On it is printed, "I'VE GOT MORE TIME FOR LOVIN'/SINCE I GOT MY MICROWAVE OVEN." Books line the wall: *Microwave Meals in 30 minutes*. *Kids Cook Microwave*. Corning Ware Microwave sets are lined up in the corner. A sign over the door gives a clue to the concept's success: "WE WILL TEACH YOU TO LOVE YOUR MICROWAVE OR WE'LL BUY IT BACK."

There are 57 Micro Cooking Centres sprinkled across Canada (as of early 1987), and if these were the only things that 35-year-old Alan Perlmutter had created, it would be impressive enough. But they are not, which makes his youth and success all the more astonishing.

In some ways, Perlmutter was to the entrepreneurial manner born . . . and raised in London, Ontario, where he continues to reside and run his prospering business. He is the eldest of three sons (one is a lawyer, another an M.B.A.). His father was and is a C.A. who made good money in investments and property. But even the family fortune cannot explain the almost inbred business sense of the small-built, pleasant-voiced young man. "After high school, I didn't want to go to university, since I didn't know what I was going for." What Perlmutter did want was to go to Europe, so he (naturally) ended up in the charter business.

The story is Horatio Algerish in the retelling: The teenager went to CP Air's offices in London, Ontario, and asked what he would have to do to get a free flight. "The man told me that if I arranged a group of charter flights, for every 20 seats I would be given a free one." Young Alan got to London, England, free, and hung around the airport, watching people and learning the charter flight business. He somehow met the general manager of a small British airline company, who "clued me in to operations in Toronto." Perlmutter was 17 years old.

He quickly discovered that many companies were selling seats in the United States, but every flight was coming home empty. "I thought up a deal: If they would give me fifty tickets, I would go to Europe and sell them wholesale or retail. They would be thrown into the garbage, anyway."

Thousands upon thousands of seats later, Alan Perlmutter and Bill Makutra, who owned a wholesale company handling chartered flights, were partners. The kid from London, Ontario, owned 50% of Overseas Flight Services in Toronto, 25% of Albion Tours, 50% of Overseas Flights in England, and 50% of an Amsterdam company with another partner. By the age of 20 Perlmutter was, as he modestly describes it, "involved in travel." He would go to various travel agencies and sell to them wholesale. He would hire kids by commission to hand out business cards which gave coupons to flights.

"I don't consider myself a business genius by any stretch of the imagination," says Perlmutter. "Whether because of insecurity or ambition, I always had a desire to do something." When he was 10 or 11, he had three paper routes during the summer, creating contests to boost circulation: "Sign up for the *Toronto Daily Star* and have a chance to draw a free subscription." He had a bank account since he was in first grade, thanks to his first business, dirty magazines. "I found a store that would sell me adult magazines, and I would charge kids to read them." By the time he was in grade 9, he ran bus tours from London to see shows at the Royal Alexandra Theatre in Toronto. "I'd line up a bus and sell blocks of seats to high school kids."

From 1969 to 1973, Alan Perlmutter remained in the travel business, but it was "getting too easy to enter. Other people destroyed reputations of firms, since a lot of people got stranded." So he made a deal with Canada House, the Canadian Embassy in London, that if anyone was stranded in England due to a failed charter, Perlmutter would give him or her a free trip home. Over a two-year period he went back and forth to England over four dozen times.

Always the canny businessman, although barely into his 20s, Alan Perlmutter sensed that the Canadian government would have to regulate the charter business or stop it. And regular airlines began to organize charter-class fares. It was time to get out. "I won't tell how much money I made," he says, "but it was *very* profitable." (Perlmutter recalls telling his grade 3 teacher, who was troubled that the dyslexic child could not spell, "Why do I need to spell, if I can have a secretary?" He told the same teacher on another occasion that he would make a million before he was 30.)

From 1973 to 1974 Perlmutter went to the University of Western Ontario in his hometown, "taking first-year garbage" which leaned toward economics. But he soon got bored with school and "latched on to old English indentures." You see, during his countless trips to the original London, he discovered the massive amount of handwritten documents on sheepskin, some signed by Queen Victoria—old legal deeds and records. In 1975 he would go into solicitors' offices and ask if they had any old indentures they would like to clear out. "I'd pay for his time to sort through them."

Perlmutter eventually bought tens of thousands of them—three-quarters of them were rotten and unsellable—and he would peddle them "for their aesthetic value." (Don't get any ideas; recently the British government has declared that they cannot leave the country. After all, look what happened to the Elgin marbles of ancient Greece.)

The young Canadian entrepreneur travelled across the United States, hiring kids along the way, buying a new Mercedes Benz to cart both kids and indentures, and sold the old things for between $30 and $100. A lot of them would go to lawyers and judges, who just loved the thought of a deed to a castle, handwritten on sheepskin with a seal on the bottom, hanging on their walls. He did it for a year and, as always, did quite well.

Then it was back to Western for second year, followed by another six months of selling sheepskin. Then, in 1976, he went to the now-renowned business school at U.W.O., taking their undergraduate M.B.A., called an H.B.A. "I'd do it again; it was a great experience," he says excitedly. "It forced me to structure my thought. My earlier businesses were profitable, but they lacked organization." (To be fair to the once-uneducated boy, his ideas still tended to be well thought out. Staying at Hiltons helped create credibility with judges to whom he wished to sell his indentures, and even the Mercedes was a good idea; he had a serious accident at one point, and would have been killed had it been a cheaper car.)

Perlmutter finished his H.B.A. in 1978 and would soon create his most successful business yet. (He later heard from his father that, when he was in England making as much money as his father's friends when *their* children were in school, the men would tell Perlmutter's dad, "Don't worry; Alan will find himself one day.") In May 1977 Perlmutter senior was building a shopping mall, and, since business school did not take all of his time, the student began working on an idea to start a business. One of his projects at Western involved researching Litton Industries, and whether or not they should build a factory. "I saw a market totally underdeveloped in microwave ovens," he says. "I wanted to buy one for my mother, and I just knew the project was flying."

After he gave his mother the gift, Perlmutter was pleased to discover that it did far more than anyone had suspected of it. "My mom's goal in life was to make us eat vegetables and get our roughage. She fell in love with the microwave and began to use our regular oven as a breadbox. And I saw an underdeveloped market in all this."

In retrospect, it was a combination of two factors: that formal research project on Litton, and his own personal experience, watching his mom cook meals in minutes. "It was far more useful than I realized." So when Perlmutter saw a space empty in his father's mall, he put aside his original idea of a telephone store and came to a new, crucial resolution: "You don't sell a microwave; you sell its *use*. There was no way of becoming profitable in phones, where I could easily be undercut." So, two weeks before he was to open that telephone place, he opened the first Micro Cooking Centre, on May 17, 1977.

"The concept from Day One was, sell the idea that it can

cook well. Whereas seventy percent of most purchasers do not use their microwave for all their cooking, most of our customers do. We sell cooking, where others sell ovens." He first went with Litton (GSW in Canada), and after two years, he saw that Quasar was coming on the market. "I had six stores by then, and Quasar had no distribution or money for advertising. They needed me! And it was just rated the best product by *Consumer Reports*. It was a natural marriage, and we quickly took on the line."

In the meantime, everyone else was selling ovens like mad; when Eaton's sold Toshiba, other stores began to undercut them by $5. But not Alan Perlmutter of London, Ontario: His approach was to fulfill consumer needs. "I've had no competition until recently, since no one knew how to sell microwave ovens. My concept was to sell quality, not just the cheapest price. All others were pumping out low-level microwaves."

The numbers give a sense of just how right Perlmutter was in his concepts of selling use and selling quality: In 1977 there was the one store, selling a little over $100,000 in ovens and accessories. By 1979 he was up to 6 stores; by 1981, 18 stores; by 1984, 25 stores; by the end of 1985, 44 stores; by the end of 1987, 60. He has a five-year plan, based on the specific malls he wants to go into, but no set number of stores has been targeted. "They will be spread from Montreal to Vancouver; there's no market in the east."

Interestingly, every one of the Micro Cooking Centres is company-owned. "When I wanted to franchise, the stores weren't profitable, and now that they *are* profitable (they have been since 1981), I don't want to franchise!"

The profitability has come from the buying power, and it is the fact that he lacks that power in the States that keeps him from looking south. "I've been asked to go down there with the concept, but my ambition is not to die working," Perlmutter declares. "I go in at ten and am home by five, but it's the constant thinking that is tiring."

Although Micro Cooking Centres is profitable as a corporation, a store doesn't make money for the first 18 months, so the new stores are always reducing his taxes. "I've always had the philosophy, 'I'll take every good mall available.'" And there are a lot of malls out there: Perlmutter opened 5 stores during a three-week period in Montreal, and 12 stores in a five-week period in Ontario and Quebec. With sales running between $250,000 and $700,000 per store, it was a business with sales in the range of $23 million in 1986, probably $30 million in 1987.

In less than a decade, Alan Perlmutter has achieved a significant market share in line with the largest department stores, such as Eaton's and Sears. But why such a runaway success? "A triad of reasons," says the young businessman. "Good suppliers, good locations, and good, loyal staff." The latter numbers around 200, and Perlmutter is proud that he has "lost few." "They are all on profit sharing; they know my real cost and get a share of the profits." He had begun with straight wages but changed in 1981, which, interestingly, is the first year he began to show profit. "The staff wanted more money, but no profit sharing. I created a plan that said, 'You increase my profit and share in it.' That was the turning point of the business. I didn't realize it then, but with hindsight, it was."

Staff gets from 25 to 30% of the gross profit on the selling of the machines, with those who've been with Perlmutter longer selling more and so doing better. Unlike many products which allow up to 50% and even 100% mark-up, the gross margin in microwaves is only about 26%, "which is why I can't afford too many mistakes." And he has made plenty: "I've hired the wrong people, picked the wrong malls—I've made lots of errors!" And as the major creditor of the company, "no mistakes can hurt anyone but me."

Perlmutter didn't take a bank loan until he had eight stores. The first one cost about $50,000–60,000 to create, and he built and rebuilt it three times, so there was "a lot of wasted money there." And having never worked in a store before he created his own, he was "forced to organize things for others to solve them."

As with the charter flight business, Alan Perlmutter is not blind to the pitfalls that lie ahead: "In two to three years, microwaves will peak out. But then it will become a replacement market, and I think that it will be a good one." With eight million households in Canada, if one assumes that 10% of them are always buying microwaves, he figures that the market is about 800,000 a year at the present time.

Perlmutter is sensitive to other matters as well: "Penetration and saturation are not the same. Many buy ovens that are too small. It's true that the life of a microwave is fifteen years, but people get tired before that, aware of the new features which are constantly being offered." Furthermore, whether Alan Perlmutter owns the business in a decade or not, he has no doubt that his firm will be the leader in the business. "Buy from Joe, and he may be out of business in a few years; Micro Cooking Centres will be there."

After hitting 60 stores by the end of 1987, he predicts "*very* moderate growth after that," which translates into 3 or 4 a year through the decade. He spends only 3½% of sales on ads, which is rather small, but he feels that "you buy traffic that is always going through malls, and I consider part of my rent as advertising." Part of the success of the firm lies in the fact that every store has a cooking school, some of them in separate facilities such as a rented hotel room. (The only stand-alone cooking school is the suburban Toronto one, described above.)

Always, Perlmutter refers back to his original concept: "We sell the *use*. We sell them with the promise that if they have problems, they call us. If they don't like it, they can bring it back. [About one in ten does.] A free cooking school has been offered from the first day we opened, and we keep them to twenty people or less." Such service doesn't come cheap; Perlmutter describes it as a "major expense" and says that he spends hundreds of thousands of dollars a year on the classes.

He claims that everyone has schools now, but they all created them in reaction to his chain of stores. Eaton's, for instance, has around three classes a year, whereas Micro Cooking Centres has three a week, and the big department store allows 100 and sometimes even 200 in each class.

The Perlmutter personality is not surprising: "I'm methodical," he declares. "The fact that I *know* I'm profitable is more important than the money I've made. Everything is planned; nothing I do is knee-jerk. All is ponderous and thought out to the best of my ability; that's what university did for me." Not that such attributes have eliminated risk: "You never know what cities will be like. I lost hundreds of thousands of dollars in Vancouver until I turned that bastard around, yet I made money from the start in Yorkdale [in suburban Toronto]." More money will come from his own cookware, manufactured for him in Toronto. Called Micro-Mark, it will sell across North America in 1987.

One must believe Alan Perlmutter when he insists that he doesn't know how much money he's earned: "I don't keep track, because I've never cared for money. It's the excitement that drives me, not the money. The excitement of building something." There's the wife and two young daughters, of course, but the thinking never stops: "I may look at other business concepts." After dirty magazines, newspaper subscription contests, bus tours, charter flights, and century-old sheepskin indentures, there are clearly more ideas where the microwave inspiration came from. And lots more profits to share.

# THE JUNGLE COMES TO THE OIL PATCH

### Bob Thorssen

Bob Thorssen, full-bearded, ever-excited and passionate in his pith helmet and safari clothes, likes to do "little things to make people laugh." Such as the invoices for his rapidly expanding business: "HI, MY NAME IS MAGILLA. I'M THE JUNGLE COMPUTER. FROM NOW ON, I WILL KEEP TRACK OF ALL OUR INVENTORY, SEND YOU UP TO DATE PRICE LISTS, AND KEEP TRACK OF YOUR ORDERS AND INVOICES. THE KING OF THE JUNGLE THINKS I'M A GREAT APE!!" King of the Jungle is the nickname for the creator of Jungle Interiors, a concept which could well be spreading its artificial plants, wooden carvings and masks, ceramics, wall hangings, and rattan right across North America. " 'Real silk' plants for real smart people," reads his logo, implying that people who go with maintenance-free, replacement-free, bug-free, nonallergenic plastic plants are a lot brighter than those who buy the "real thing." Certainly, if anyone is "real smart," it is "Jungle Bob" Thorssen.

The background of the Edmonton-born superfranchiser with the ready laugh is hardly rags-to-riches: Thorssen was born in 1948, the third of five children (the oldest brother is currently working with the Vancouver store, a younger brother is the operations manager for Jungle Interiors, and the youngest, "an engineering and computer genius," recently wrote a program for all the company's growing inventory and billing).

Their father was a professor of engineering at the University of Alberta until he entered the world of business. He has, with partners, built shopping centres, is involved with developing Calgary, and is chairman of the board of the University of Calgary. Obviously inspired by this entrepreneurial father, young Bob went to U. of C., taking commerce for two years before dropping out. "Since he was chairman, he was upset when I quit!"

"I was always restless," Thorssen recalls today. "I hoped to make a whole lot of money. My father was still basically a professor, who didn't care about that; his ambition was to do good things." He recalls "always having ideas," but because of school, he could never put them into action. When he finally did, it made a huge splash.

The occasion was when Canada Post went on strike for the first time—"Was it 1969?" he asks—to which Thorssen responded by starting a company called Associated Delivery Service. He borrowed office space from a law firm and hired kids on bikes to deliver the mail which was not going through. He received "tons of press" across the country, once even on the CBC National News. It was his first year in university; he was about 18.

It was an exciting way to begin a business; a rock was thrown through his window, and there were threats on his life (for which he hired bodyguards to get even more press). After it was all over, he had made only around $800, "but I paid everyone," he adds quickly.

But it was only the beginning of nonstop, extraordinarily exotic adventures in the world of business. The next job for Bob Thorssen, the future King of the Jungle, was in the jungle of Bernie's Cornfeld's eventually infamous I.O.S., Investors' Overseas Services. He began by selling mutual funds in Calgary ("I did very well"), where he became the youngest salesman in the world. Indeed, he was too young to get a licence in Alberta, and when he did, at the age of 21, he promptly went on the road.

The road soon led to Geneva, where he "got driven around in Cadillac limousines," and then he sold condos and villas in Spain for the I.O.S. It may as well have been pancho villas, since "the company was collapsing around me!" He had made perhaps $20,000, but he had lots and lots of shares in I.O.S., which, as for tens of thousands of others, "led to nothing. It was real hype."

So it was back to Calgary, where Thorssen began another business while still in his early 20s: Diversified Directories, which involved putting together directories for oil companies and publishing them in ring binders, updated monthly. They sold for $150 apiece, and he did it for a year. Then he formed, with partners, a company called Roveco Resources, which hoped to get into the oil industry but ended up buying real estate.

Then, as you've probably been expecting in a strange case study like this one, Thorssen went off to Asia in 1973, where he stayed for seven years. While the following adventures and misadventures read like a cross between Joseph Conrad (*Heart of Darkness*) and Steven Spielberg (*Indiana Jones*, etc.), they were, in fact, the necessary apprenticeship for what would become Jungle Interiors, so some listing is necessary:

Thorssen's first stop was Australia, where he had a girlfriend. "I wanted to buy a diamond mine on the southwest coast of Africa that I'd heard about." But the price doubled by the time he got there, so he didn't buy it. He had a boat ticket for around the world, but he cashed it in for a plane ticket which would make "lots of stops." Next, he flew to Jakarta, where he befriended an American woman and a Filipino logger, and was invited to help with the financing of a major logging operation in Indonesia. (Who says that Canadians are dull?)

He eventually obtained the rights to a logging concession and formed the company in Indonesia, with the help of Canadian friends, investing $20,000, mostly from local banks. It was hand-logging, where men would cut trees close to streams and rivers, roll the logs into the water, pray for rain (to raise the logs above the mud and shoot them into the rivers), and float them downstream. "I made some money from it, but we all got malaria badly," Thorssen recalls.

Then Our Man From Calgary raised money to buy large tractors, big skidders, and army surplus trucks, to help produce the logs. This all took place, for those of you who are taking notes, in Balikpapan, in Borneo, right on the equator, about two hours from Jakarta.

Now, Holiday Inn has never made it to Balikpapan, which left a window of opportunity for Bob Thorssen of Calgary.

"There was no good hotel to eat and drink in," he says, "so I built a bar called the TIT." As in "have a drink at the TIT; have a bite at the TIT." Before you close the book, please note that it was an abbreviation for Teluk Indah Tavern, or "the beautiful bay tavern," since it stood on stilts over the beautiful bay of Balikpapan. Yes, Thorssen and his friends had to build it by hand, with planes and saws, since there was "no power, so no power tools."

It was a big bar which held 120 people, with "30 girls upstairs" doing godknowswhat. "It did very well," states Thorssen, but he had hard times as well. He drank part of the profits away, but the real problem was that, only two weeks after it was completed—it took a year to build it—his Indonesian partner "got control of it with knives and guns." (Who says that Canadians are smart?)

So Bob Thorssen, a long way from the oil patch, had to leave the town, spending a year fighting to win his bar back. He eventually went into partnership with "a general's daughter," came back with a letter of warning, and "booted everyone out." He stayed there for another 18 months, probably worrying his mother sick.

Then, he got into a bigger logging operation in Sumatra, near Krakatoa. Considering Thorssen's career in Asia to this point, it is surprising that the volcano didn't blow, but everything else did. Although he was producing $300,000 a month in logs, he lost that, too, and found that he "had no recourse to the courts in Indonesia."

So he left and moved back to Canada, but not before getting run over by a bus in Borneo. It was early 1979. He did not plan to stay long in his homeland, however (how ya gonna keep 'em down on the prairies, now that they've seen Balikpapan?), and he soon was sailing around the Caribbean, involved with a shark-tagging operation.

Home once more, Bob Thorssen ended up buying a tool supply and grinding business for the machine shop industry, North American Tool and Carbide, with the help from family and the bank, to the tune of $200,000. They sold tooling, high-speed drills, twist drills, etc., to such places as CN and CP Rail, expanding across Western Canada. Their first year sales were around $300,000; their second year, more than twice that.

But by 1980–81, the National Energy Policy began having

its effects on Calgary, and "the Alberta oil industry folded up. And they were my main clients." So, like many an entrepreneur, Bob Thorssen "decided that I had to quickly look for something else."

As luck would have it, he had known a friend who was involved in silk plant manufacturing back in Hong Kong. "It seemed like it could be big. I made inquiries, did a market study, and hired a firm to see if there was a market for fake plants. When I got their negative results, I disregarded them, and said, 'Fuck you.' "

Thorssen had seen with his own eyes all those thousands of plants in every restaurant, bar, mall, and office building in Calgary, and he quickly made a number of trips to the Orient. He mailed "masses of letters" to Korea, Taiwan, even Communist China, finally lining up a factory to manufacture artificial stems and silk-screened leaves. He still had some cash flow from his struggling tool business, and started developing new types of plants of better quality than those available. He photographed real leaves and made silk screens from the photographic plates, and then carefully chose a fabric that would be close to the thickness of particular leaves. "It wasn't too hard to say that *this* looks better than *this*."

During this time, he chose the name Jungle Interiors—he'd always been called Jungle Bob back in Indonesia—and started the business with $100,000 from the machine shop supply business. And his idea from the very beginning was to take it across Canada. "I never do anything small! Look at the name I gave my machine shop: *North American* Tool and Carbide!"

The first Jungle Interiors store opened in Calgary in November 1982, still a division of his tool shop. He had five people in a 1,200-square-foot location in Mont Royal Village, an exclusive shopping centre. "It cost little; it was an empty space, and shopping centres don't like empty spaces. I promised them that I'd make a garden there, and I paid no rent; just a percentage of sales."

The shopping centre owners must have been pleased; by the end of 1983 the sales were $230,000 from the one tiny store. Soon Thorssen was developing dealers out west and in Toronto. He briefly had an operation in Hawaii, where he was stopping during all those trips to the Orient, but he closed it down after a year and a half. "I have a major plan for the U.S. market, so I didn't want it to continue."

Within the first two years he got "all kinds of articles" written about his strange new business: the front page of the business section of the *Calgary Herald*; the front page of its Lifestyle section; *The Magazine That's About Small Business; Your Money*. At the end of 1984 Jungle Interiors stores existed in Vancouver, Calgary, Edmonton, Saskatoon, and Toronto.

Not that it was planned all that carefully. At first they were all dealer stores, to which he supplied finished goods, sales training, suggested prices, and the use of the name and the jungle-y logo. But each dealer owned his or her own store, kept all profits, and paid no royalties. "I had thought that dealership was the way to go," admits Thorssen, "but I quickly realized that you must supply more support."

So a number of changes took place: North American Tool and Carbide was rechristened Northrim Trading Inc., and Jungle Interiors Canada Inc., a franchise company, was set up separately. The Calgary and Edmonton operations were placed under TWK Silk Plants Ltd., with a number of minority partners brought in to help run the business. Bob Thorssen owns 100% of Jungle Interiors and the Edmonton operation, and 70% of the Calgary one.

The total retail sales of all silk plants in 1984 was $1.2 million, but the future looks far silkier: Thorssen manufactures the plants in Hong Kong, then they are assembled in Calgary and at each franchise store. "They put the leaves on, and put them into the pots, and make them into beautiful plants!" (And beautiful profits, too: A plant which sells for $125 retail would have a mere $25 worth of leaves on it, although, to be fair, there is all the shipping duty, federal and provincial sales taxes, assembly in Canada, potting, wood chips, foam, stalk, etc. The price range of the plants is from $20 to $300, with the average sale being about $75.)

Bob Thorssen had sales of close to $2 million by the end of 1986, but his five-year plan is as ambitious as trying to set up a logging operation in Indonesia (or setting up a rival postal delivery service in Canada, for that matter): By the end of 1987 he hopes to have 18 to 20 stores across Canada, with sales in the $4 million range. By the end of 1988 he expects a "start-up" of 15 stores in the U.S., "doing better than a new store a month."

The franchising is relatively standard. $15,000 fee, plus 6% royalties, as well as 2% for advertising. Most exciting, perhaps, is the major, $30,000, study of the U.S. market, which was completed during the summer of 1985: "*No* one is doing what I'm doing, in the States!" he exclaims. "The wholesale business in Canada and the U.S. is very well developed, but *not* the retail!" The reason for all the wholesalers is clear; there are a lot of florists out there who sell silk plants. But for whatever reason, no one is putting up stores which specialize in silk plants, whether franchised or in chain stores. "We're going to blow them away!" shouts Thorssen.

According to his plan, the first store in the States should be open no later than the end of 1986. And, he insists, "the concept has a lot going for it: no competition, good profit margin, and an immense market. Every restaurant, home, cubbyhole has a plant." And, perhaps most important of all, "it's fun. No three-piece suits or ties necessary!" (The standard dress for managers remains khaki, although pith helmets are recommended.) For a mere $100,000 (to cover franchise fee, opening inventory, store fixtures, working capital, etc.), dozens of men and women are clamoring to swing into the jungle with Bob.

Nor does Bob Thorssen see any reason that his crazy dream should die. "There will be no competition, since we're growing in quantum leaps; geometrically, in fact. Those who have tried to copy us see it as a hobby business, but they're not really serious about it. They're not willing to put the massive effort in that I and my staff have done." The effort, he says, consists of "dreaming it, twenty-four hours a day," as well as 12-hour workdays and weekends. "A lot of my job is the razzmatazz, the developing business contacts, finding the people who will run the new stores. And I am really pioneering here; I'm not taking from established businesses, but developing a new one."

There were a few dozen people involved with Jungle Interiors, as of the end of 1987, but Thorssen foresees over 250, when he will have 40 stores, including part-time help. So what's his secret? "You've got to be, and remain, *positive*," he proclaims. "As long as you believe you can do something and work on it, you can get there. But you need innovation—a creative idea. And you have to be able to get people excited about what you're doing. Then you've got people on your team—customers, consultants, everyone whom you do business with. They know you're really striving."

They all know, because of the monthly "Jungle Drum" newsletter, with the trips and prize programs, along with new ideas on how to sell, and the continual addition of new, jungle-related products. Lining up major accounts with dozens of companies like McDonald's, PetroCanada, Royal Bank, VW Canada, Denny's, Arby's—all of whose products taste about the same, one might note—makes business thrive as well. And for those who are not buying tens of thousands of dollars' worth of artificial plants, there are all the soapstone carvings, stuffed animals, and "jungle jewellery." "People *love* jungle themes!" says Bob Thorssen. It must be a reaction to the Canadian winter.

If successful entrepreneurship is related to faith in oneself and one's concept, then Bob Thorssen of Calgary might well fulfill his "real good possibility that Jungle Interiors will be the McDonald's of silk plants." (Over 42 Billion Unwatered?) But by then, admits the man who brought the TIT to Borneo, "I'll be out and doing something else. I like the start-up phase of things, and I'm not interested in running something for twenty years."

Where he'll probably be by the early 1990s, if all goes as planned and real plants are driven from our lives like so many killer whales, is on his yacht, sailing around the world. "I'll do it, too! I'll likely sell part of the company, and send back news bulletins from Jungle Bob in various parts of the world." After surviving Canada Post, Bernie Cornfeld, a dubious legal system in Indonesia, and Pierre Trudeau's N.E.P., there seems little reason to doubt that Bob Thorssen will do it.

# A CENTURY-OLD TRADITION MEETS MODERN MARKETING

**Bryce Schnare**

The oldest chair company in Canada was founded in Bass River, Nova Scotia, in 1860, by one George Fulton. The bearded gentleman died in 1907 and didn't live to see his factory destroyed five times by major fires, although he must have gained pleasure in watching his antique-style hardwood chairs and tables become renowned throughout the Maritimes for their value, comfort, and quality.

We now leap ahead nearly a century to the birth of a man in Halifax, in 1948, who would help to make the 400 people living in Bass River in the 1980s a lot more stable and happy than they had been for decades: Bryce Schnare. After finishing high school, he joined Dylex, for whom he worked for over a dozen years both in his native city and in Toronto, eventually becoming the regional manager for Tip Top in the Atlantic Provinces. "That's where I got my university education," he says.

But then, like many entrepreneurs, he felt that he had to leave the mother firm to "get into my own business. I wanted to make the decisions, and felt that I could have a more lucrative life as an owner-entrepreneur."

Schnare's first move was to buy an interest in a clothing store in Halifax, House of Rodney, in 1979. The plan was to buy the place when the owner retired, but after a year he realized that the old man had no such intention. So he left that and moved to Prince Edward Island, to get into the restaurant business; in particular, a fish-and-chips franchise, Captain Scott's. Although he still owns the rights to franchise in the Atlantic Provinces, it proved to be a failure. He had joined a friend, Scott Linkletter of Summerside, who had founded it, and they became partners. But within a few years, "my heart wasn't in it." In a phrase, he "didn't like the kitchen part of it."

But often, chance brings together an unhappy man and a happy product. "We were buying Bass River chairs for our restaurant," he recalls. "That's how I got to know them." It was a magic moment: "We looked at the product and thought to ourselves, with *my* retail background, we felt sure that this country look was on the move." And with restaurants, one tends to be ahead of all others in style. "If you want to know what your house will look like in 1990, look at restaurants today!" insists Bryce Schnare.

So Schnare began to go to restaurant shows, and sold the chairs to such places as the Mermaid in Toronto, the Old Spaghetti Factories across Canada, and many of the Mother's Pizza restaurants. And while he was selling the product, Schnare "realized that it had a retail home use."

And so, in 1981, the Bass River Chair Factory Outlet

Store opened in Charlottetown. Schnare and his partners, who now included Brian Eamer of that lovely city, as well as Linkletter, devised a marketing plan and went to the board of directors of the Dominion Chair Company Ltd., which had been making the Bass River chairs for over 120 years. They were understandably ecstatic, since they had "virtually no business" and were ready to close. Consumers across Canada had discovered chrome, plastic, and various synthetics back in the 1960s, and sales had dropped like P.E.I. tourism in the winter. Indeed, in 1985 Dominion chair was put into receivership, its 55 employees in far worse shape than their handsome chairs. It was eventually purchased by "someone who offered more" than Schnare, and is now on a firm footing.

Schnare and his partners put together a ten-page marketing concept, after operating the Charlottetown store for a year and breaking even in the same period, with sales of about $350,000 in 1980. "We were trying to find our way," admits the president of the firm. "And the consumers decided it for us." What they decided—and they are always right, you know—was that "chairs and tables by themselves are not exciting enough."

So they looked around, and they didn't have to look very far. "In our own backyard, Paderno Cookware was available." Brought to Charlottetown from Italy, over a half century ago, the "fantastic stainless steel cookware" was being sold to Bays and Eatons across the country, so why not at the Bass river location? "We got *that* into the store!" says Schnare. Furthermore, Grohmann, Canada's only knife maker, from Pictou, Nova Scotia, had another fine product to offer.

"We evolved into a kitchen/dining room store," says Schnare. Then came other Maritime products: sturdy wooden toys by Brocklin, quilted and homespun P.E.I. fabric crafts, lots of kitchen accessories in wood, and much more.

This wasn't all overnight: "After the first year we still were not convinced that we were on the right track," said Schnare in Bridgewater, Nova Scotia, where he was opening the 12th Bass River Chair location in the spring of 1985. "I was taking truckloads of chairs to shopping centres." But after about 16 months the Charlottetown store "finally clicked."

So the men took it on the road in 1983, opening six stores and franchising them across Nova Scotia: Dartmouth, Bedford, Truro, Moncton, Amherst, Antigonish. The sales broke

$1 million that year, but they still "put the brakes on," as they realized that, while they had half a dozen stores doing well, they had no control over the name or the locations.

They weren't happy with the design, either. So they decided to open no more stores until they were truly "ready." They obtained the name legally from Dominion Chair and hired a major Toronto designer to create the look of the stores. This took them until the summer of 1984. That fall they opened three stores: in Halifax, in New Minas, N.S., and in Woodbridge, just north of the toughest market of all, Toronto. And a "half-store" in P.E.I., where the tourist season is short.

They also developed a "McDonald's kind of franchise agreement," where people would pay $15,000, plus a percentage of royalties. In the fall of 1984 they sold one-half of the company to a Torontonian, which gave them the expansion money they needed to move more fully into Ontario.

After a lot of trial and error and insecurities, Bass River Chairs Inc. of Charlottetown appears to be on its way to glorious success. The plan is no longer hesitant: 50 stores by 1990, spread across Ontario, the Atlantic Provinces, and possibly the New England states. Of the latter, Schnare enthuses, "We should be in New England. It's very much like the Maritimes, and it's only an hour flight to Boston. In order to become a force in the marketplace, you need at least two dozen stores and five years of solid financial statements," says Schnare. "Then, it would just be people and manpower." If they were to go public, he sees Bass River growing to "four hundred stores, easily."

Schnare is well aware that his stores have evolved "during really rough retail times. And in tough times, people spend their money carefully." Part of the concept is to sell everything about 20% less than retail and have no sales. "We stole the 'COMPARE AT' line from Moore's," he admits. The Paderno cookware is, indeed, one-fifth less than it would cost at Eaton's, and "it's *all* Maritime-made, waving the Nova Scotia flag!" Schnare jokes.

The market philosophy oozes the old-fashioned quality concept: Pictures of the old plant in Bass River, Nova Scotia, are on banners in every store. "The customer perceives buying in our store as *good value*," emphasizes Schnare, but good value can differ in image from the Maritimes to the Big City.

For instance, he admitted that they "may have to drop 'Factory Outlet' from our name. The connotation means 'cheap' in Toronto, and we've got to be careful there." Indeed he does; by mid-1987, they had only "nine good solid stores" in the Maritimes alone, with sales still below $4 million. There *have* been setbacks.

As for Bryce Schnare personally, he loves the retail business, finding it "extremely exciting! Our products are fun to work with, and I can sell them with all kinds of confidence. And our stores are different; we seem to be totally alone in the marketplace. But we've slowed down, and are building a far stronger base. We are *far* more selective in our locations, and won't move into the States until 1990."

Schnare and his partners are hardly millionares yet, and the former Haligonian admits that 1985 was the "first time in five or six years that I had a buck in my pocket." But he feels little doubt that the concept of Bass River Chairs Inc. will take off across Canada, and possibly the States as well, since their average customer is a 35- to 40-year-old female, with a middle or upper income. And as is well known, whether they do the cooking or not, they *have* to sit down in that kitchen or dining room *sometime*.

# THE MAD FRANCHISER

## Seymour Schwartz

There is something in all of us that is impressed with the man or woman who starts with nothing, and is almost *unimpressed* with the inheritor, or the one who took over the family business. (And almost put off by the person who married into wealth or a successful business.)

It's understandable, as are our feelings of warmth and awe toward the highly original thinker, and near-irritation with the one who lifts others' ideas and makes a go of them, almost like a late–twentieth-century equivalent of the horse thief.

But suspend your negative thoughts, if you will, as we look at the strange, peripatetic business career of Seymour Schwartz of Toronto—bearded, youthful, vivacious—whose actions over the past two decades hardly burst with originality (and who still runs his in-laws' business, by the way) but whose creative output has created ten of hundreds of jobs across Canada, and directly created tens of millions of dollars in sales—and taxes.

The framed documents on one wall of his cramped office in the Leaside section of Toronto give only a suggestion of what will follow: A law school degree from Osgoode Hall. Membership in the Law Society of Upper Canada. And under them both, The International Council of Shopping Centres certifies that Lighting Unlimited is a regular member. More of that later.

Seymour Schwartz was born in Toronto in the summer of 1942, the second of four children. His father had come to the city from Hungary, where he was a champion wrestler, and later, the chief bodyguard of the King of Rumania. An orphan, he had come to Canada in 1935 and worked as a peddler, buying fruits and vegetables around Toronto, later ending up with a warehouse in Leamington, Ontario, the tomato capital of Canada.

The father's success is most relevant, because young Seymour worked from 5:00 A.M. to 11:00 P.M. in Leamington every summer, from the age of 13 to the age of 23. (At 16, he graduated to a truck.) He went to farms, bought cauliflower, cabbage, tomatoes, cukes, and Spanish onions, and would shlep the stuff back to the warehouse and then load the trains. "That's where I learned to work hard," he says. "By 16 I knew how to buy and sell; I was told, 'You're not going to camp; you're going to *work*!' "

Seymour never got an allowance, and it was pretty obvious that he was going to go into the business. "I really knew it well." But then he met his future (first) wife and realized that he didn't want to live in a small town. So he decided to go to law school, graduating in 1967, and was called to the bar (and away from the vegetable patch) in 1969.

But Schwartz never practised law, since he encountered a dilemma which many men and women wish they might have: He had in-laws who ran a fairly successful minichain of stores, Lighting Unlimited. His father-in-law, who had founded it in 1953, building it up to seven company-owned stores in Toronto and nearby Hamilton, had a heart attack. He had decided to franchise, so he invited his new son-in-law to join him.

You can guess the cries from Seymour Schwartz's parents: "How could you spend so many years studying law and go into the lighting business? You could have been in the fruit and vegetable field!" (Literally.)

But into lighting their boy went, and it was clearly a wise choice all round: The sales in 1970 of the seven Lighting Unlimited stores was around $300,000 per store, perhaps $2½ million in total. In 1985 there were 47 stores, 15 of them company-owned, 32 of them franchised, with sales of around $18 million. "It was a steady growth," says Schwartz. "You add a few, close a few." They are in every province except P.E.I., New Brunswick, and Quebec.

Then, a dramatic change: Seymour Schwartz's father-in-law died in the early 1970s, and he and his wife split up soon after. Since the now-no-longer-related young man owned 25% of the business, he approached his mother-in-law, Harrianne Waddlinger, and told her, "Look, I can go back into law. You want to buy me out, or should I stay? I like the business and I like you." The answer is self-evident; Seymour Schwartz and his former mother-in-law have been partners for the past decade.

Lighting Unlimited flourished. They are the top retail lighting store of their type, and the biggest strictly retail stores in North America. They did no restaurants or hotels, no discounting, although they are in the process of changing that. The average store has close to half a million dollars in sales, with franchisees paying only $10,000 for a fee, and 6% of sales in royalties.

Part of Schwartz's genius was that he "simplified everything": They run over five dozen stores with only two buyers, three supervisors, and himself. "It's the exact same number of staff as I had fifteen years ago," he proclaims proudly. Despite the small staff, however, sales have increased tenfold. They eliminated all warehousing, and the entire head office for the nearly four dozen stores is barely 6,000 square feet.

"We were told that we *had* to warehouse and have trucks," remembers Seymour Schwartz, the grey in his beard resplendent against his colorful, vertically striped sweater (no lawyerly suits and ties around *here*). "But I realized right away I wanted some cost efficiency. I told the people who sold products to us, 'You want to grow with us, *stick* with us! You've already got good volume with our seven stores; give me better discounts!' "

He eliminated billing with the stores as well. After an

opening order of $70,000 worth of merchandise with a new store, which he guarantees within 60 days, every store must handle its own orders. Stores get billed and handle all goods directly. He also worked out a rebate structure on volume, splitting it 50/50 with his franchisees. "This way, they are enticed to buy from the same people I buy from," he notes. "And we make sure that our buyers buy the best on the market. The bigger the volume, the bigger the rebate." (He supplies all advertisements for Lighting Unlimited; it runs 3% per store.)

Law school helped Seymour Schwartz a lot, in spite of his parents' worry about a possibly wasted few years at university. He does all his own franchising, leasing, and legal matters. And he always poured all profits back into the business, so when "all the trouble hit in 1981, we didn't have to borrow at all." He also paid all his bills promptly, taking advantage of the traditional 2% off in ten days, getting "the best terms possible." And he always refused to expand "unless we can generate it from income."

Schwartz never had any particular goals in terms of numbers during his years with Lighting Unlimited. "When a good location comes available, we take it," he says. "If it's out of our territory, then we franchise it." He opened over a dozen more in 1986 and 1987. "Around 60 Lighting Unlimiteds would be the maximum," he declares. "We're saturating certain markets. For instance, I've got three stores in Kitchener, Ontario, and I wouldn't put more than two in Hamilton." He has looked to the States, but "I've got enough here."

Indeed he has. Part of future growth will be on the wholesale level of lighting, which he has always avoided until 1986. "We hope to get the discount-oriented customer who won't go to a mall, where we have our stores. If someone was buying a new house, he never would have considered having Lighting Unlimited do the whole place for him. So we've never had any big action of, say, five thousand dollars. [Average sale: $70.] I'm getting into that now; it's discount, but we handle bigger fixtures, track lighting for kitchens, and so on. I'd lost that market in the past."

Now, if turning Lighting Unlimited from a small business into a good-sized one was the only thing that the vegetable-buyer-turned-lawyer-turned-lighting-businessman ever did in his career, it would be pretty impressive. But it's when we get into the "ripped-off" concepts of Seymour Schwartz that we encounter the real entrepreneur. (Picasso got lots of his ideas from African art, ya know.)

For instance, Frontier Fruit and Nut Company. It was founded by "an American guy" down in the States, and a few Canadian friends pointed it out to Schwartz, asking him what he thought of the concept. "I thought it was really fabulous!" Schwartz enthuses. "I'd never seen anything like it up in Canada: open barrels filled with figs, raisins, banana chips, dried mangos, carob—forty barrels in all!"

So what did the sneaky Canuck do? He "grabbed it," taking the name and concept above the 49th parallel. As luck would have it, the lawyer of the American founder knew Seymour Schwartz personally and suggested that the two become partners and not sue one another. "He helped us out and we gave him a small royalty," the Canadian declares.

The growth of Frontier showed typical Schwartzian magnitude: He opened the first store in suburban Toronto in 1978 and had 35 "right across the country" by the time he got out in 1984. "We did well from Day One, but I don't feel that I'm married to anything but Lighting Unlimited," Schwartz claims. "So I sold out. It was a good run. I didn't get rich, but it was fun.

"Then I founded House of Knives," states Seymour Schwartz, in much the same way as a Paul Anka would stand before a crowd in a Las Vegas nightclub and murmur, "And then I wrote. . . ." The complete story is told in the Peter Friedenthal profile in this chapter. Schwartz had walked into the Chinook Centre in Calgary and "saw a bunch of people milling round a little kiosk." He found it "very interesting," and called Friedenthal, whom he already knew and liked, in the middle of the night, back in Toronto. "Come out here! Grab a plane to Calgary! I've found a fabulous business for you! I think it's franchisable, and I can get the leases for you!" (Franchising clearly gets into the blood.)

Friedenthal saw the idea and loved it. Within a week, the two men flew to various knife places in the States, opened a promising store in Toronto's Eaton Centre within two weeks, and their first franchise, in Calgary, during the same period. Schwartz's second wife thought up the name—House of Knives—and her husband was 30% of the deal; Peter

Friedenthal has 50%. "It's a good chain," says "the origina-tor" of the theft; it was up to nearly five dozen stores by the end of 1987. Both Hoffritz and Remington tried to buy the men out during the past few years, but "they threw too many curves." But, gleefully adds Schwartz, "it's too late for any-one to compete with us! We've got the market!"

There's some incest in all this as well. One franchisee in Vancouver has six House of Knives stores, which he added to his two of Lighting Unlimited.

Schwartz's latest venture is Yü Fashions, which are little stores selling costume jewellery. As Seymour Schwartz quickly notes, with uncharacteristic modesty, "I didn't start it."

The real origins are slightly more romantic than those of Lighting Unlimited, Frontier Fruit and Nut, and House of Knives. Candace Macdonnel had a kiosk in a Sunday flea market in Pickering, just east of Metro Toronto. And "they were closing the market." A group of businessmen who knew one another got together—one was dating Ms. Macdonnel; I told you this was romantic—and declared, "This looks like a great concept! What do you think?"

When the men approached Schwartz, he thought it was "great" too, and "the race to the malls" was soon begun. "We developed the concept," states Schwartz, characteristi-cally immodest. Yü Fashions sells high-end costume jewellery, bringing in everything from offshore ("Candace feels the most beautiful stuff is from Europe").

The first store opened in June 1984 in Fairview Mall, in suburban Toronto. Then came the ever-popular Eaton Cen-tre. There were five stores by the end of that year, eight as of the summer of 1985, ten by the end of 1985, within 15 months of the race beginning. By early 1987, the number was 18. "I own 25% of Yü," says Schwartz (which frightened this reporter for a split-second). A good store will do over $300,000 a year, which is impressive when one discovers that they average 200 square feet in size. "It's almost embarrassing," says Schwartz, who would most likely be embarrassed only by a failed business concept. And such wealth from such small stores is less embarrassing when one realizes that they make them up to look like real jewellery stores. "We spend over $100,000 on a 200-foot store, which is a lot of money." Marble does tend to cost a lot.

And the idea could be risky, although Schwartz is not one

to throw good money after a bad idea. "Knives haven't got fad appeal, but jewellery is tougher. In terms of inventory, they really have got to be on the top of styles." The first ten Yü Fashions are in Ontario and Quebec right now, but they have a strong master plan: "We're heading south," declares the Canadian imperialist. "We'll be in the States in 1986. Of course, how the hell do we know for sure? It's only a year old! But we could open five or six in New York City alone, as well as one in Beverly Hills. Why go to Edmonton for just one mall? He sees Yü as "a big growth thing. There will always be a big market for costume jewellery. And we've been told that Yü is better than anything around today in North America. We're fully computerized, with gross profits daily per store. Everything is meticulous; there's nothing that they don't do. It's first class all the way." Only three of the first ten stores were franchised; the rest are company-owned.

There is no end in sight for Seymour Schwartz, as his various franchise concepts cover North America. For instance, he points out with some excitement that "no one has *really* done lighting in the States, and it could be done. I've had offers to come down. And we've considered it. With a good operating partner, I'd be interested."

But Schwartz is a Canadian, who wants to be home with his beautiful wife and their two lovely children. (And the 17-year-old from his first marriage recently moved in with them.) "I've been through one divorce; I don't want a second one." No, if you think Seymour Schwartz is aggressive, just look south of the 49th. "The Yanks are *much* bigger movers than we are," he exclaims. "In a minute, there's a hotel room and a plane ticket ready to get you to see something. That man who started Frontier Fruit and Nut once opened thirty stores in a single month! We go slower and are more conservative up here in Canada. In the States, they can't wait!"

And the Canadians can't wait to pick those marvelous brains of Schwartz. He's begun to do a lot of franchise consulting. When Japan Camera Centres came to see him, they had a mere eight stores. He did their prospectus, worked with their supervisory staff, developed their manuals, got rid of their warehousing. Every week, he meets with that firm, doing seminars with franchisees, helping the business up to over 100 stores today. Then there's Collegiate Sports, and. . .

With the gift of knowing what works in business, Sey-

mour Schwartz has no need to get to work earlier than 9:00
A.M., or to stay later than 6:00 P.M. "I'm not a workaholic," he
insists. Today, as he edges into his middle 40s, he sells in the
Lighting Unlimited stores only between November 20 and
December 24. "I love to sell!" he booms.

But this is a relaxed man today. "I'm conservative," he
says. "Before my divorce, I didn't feel that the cash registers
could work without me being there." Today, they seem to
manage just fine, in the dozens upon dozens of stores he has
created, developed, stolen, franchised, invested in—except
before Christmas, when he still indulges.

"I try to pick up ideas from other people," he says. "I see
myself growing more in these businesses. I think that every
one of them has good growth potential." Every one of *them*?
How about Seymour Schwartz himself? If you ever see his
name listed on the Toronto or New York Stock Exchanges,
remember that it was this book that gave you the tip.

And in 1986, Schwartz sold his Lighting Unlimited business to the "Home Environment sector" of Molson's, for
untold millions. He'll be with them until 1991 or so—and
then? *Don't ask.*

# FROM MUSHROOMS
# TO MILLIONS

### The Asa Family

The word *asa* is a mountain in Japan. The letters
*A.S.A.* refer to film speed in cameras. When you bring the
two together, you end up with the Asa Family of Vancouver/
Japan/Toronto, whose Japan Camera Centres number over
100 from coast to coast, with sales (including those of Asa
Corporation Limited) of over $100 million. Nearly 1,000 peo-
ple work within the system across Canada, and the story of
how three brothers ended up creating that immense company
is one of the most extraordinary—and fearful—business stories since World War II.

The war is worth mentioning, since it lies at the core of
how three young Japanese-Canadians—Roy, the president of
Japan Camera, born in 1934; Kenji, its executive vice-president,
born in 1936; and John, the general manager/secretary/treasurer,

born the following year—have worked together as if they were one. Yet if your initial response was "They must have been interned during the war," you are wrong. And in many ways, it might have been better for them if they had been.

For although the father of the boys had come to Vancouver in 1925 and had two thriving grocery stores in that city by the time his three sons were born, he actually chose to send his family back to Japan in 1939, and took the last boat out himself. The reason was logical as it was ultimately horrible, for he had been in the army, and felt that he *had* to return to his native land.

One can already guess to where the family moved: a small suburb of Hiroshima, which lost 391 of its 1,000 inhabitants when the bomb fell on August 6, 1945. Exactly three days earlier, women from the Asas' village were ordered into Hiroshima to help tear down buildings in case there was a bombing, and when The Bomb fell, Mrs. Asa, among thousands of others, was killed.

Overnight, the three teenagers found themselves orphaned. Their father was fighting in China; their mother was dead. "Either we stick together or we go to an orphanage," they said, and it became the basis of their lifelong relationship. "It's unusual for three brothers of such close ages to work together," said John Asa. Oldest brother Roy is given most of the credit for running the child-run family, as they all took turns cooking, cleaning, and going to school. They remained on their little farm until their father returned from China three years later. (Since he could speak English, thanks to his years in Canada, he interpreted for the Allied forces.) "We didn't know if he was alive!" say the sons today. "It was a blessing, since that lack of knowledge forced us to work together." The other blessing was that none of the boys ever got radiation poisoning; nor have any of their children been born with birth defects.

There was no major immigration to Canada after the war, but the word came of a mushroom farm in Port Credit, just west of Toronto, which was looking for Japanese to pick for them. "We were small, and hard workers, and so, good for the job." Their father declared, "Canada is a great country; you three go together, or no one goes." In 1954 three young Japanese-Canadians arrived in Toronto's Union Station knowing no English. Nor would they learn any at the mushroom farm, where there were 100 Japanese working, all speaking their native tongue.

The $75 a month, which included room and board, was acceptable, but not the lack of the vernacular. So the three Asa brothers studied English twice a week at night, after picking mushrooms all day. It is an insight into their mutual drive that they felt the two nights a week inadequate and soon began hitch-hiking into Toronto to take two more nights a week of English.

Eventually, the two oldest Asas declared, "We *have* to know the Canadian way of life!" So they placed ads in the Toronto papers, announcing, "SCHOOLBOYS LOOKING FOR ROOM AND BOARD; WILL DO HOUSEWORK, IN EXCHANGE FOR THE PRIVILEGE OF ATTENDING A TORONTO HIGH SCHOOL." Kenji Asa soon found a home, as did John, nearby. Oldest brother Roy stayed at the mushroom farm, since his contract ran for several more years.

As soon as they were settled in suburbia, Kenji and John Asa started a garden business in the neighbourhood, handing out mimeographed sheets which read, "Expert Japanese gardeners want to do your work!" They hired children at $1 an hour, putting them to work at different houses, and handled about 20 homes at $5 a throw. "Our secret was service," they recall today. "We would go in the middle of the night to sprinkle water on the lawns. Our houses were always green, while the professionally cared-for ones were brown!" (They also changed summer/winter windows.) This went on for two years, and they managed to save $1,500 each summer.

In the meantime, oldest brother Roy finished his indenture at the mushroom farm and began to work at the Japan Trade Centre for $36 a week, "doing everything." After a number of months, his boss there told him, "Roy, you work so hard! You should go into business!"

One day, almost mystically, the oldest Asa dreamt of a store-for-rent sign which he had seen sometime before. He went there the next day and asked how much. It was $200 a month, which was "a lot of money." He decided that it would be a camera store, although the reasons were hardly profound: "We'd taken a few pictures; that's all."

Asa Camera Store opened its doors on June 11, 1959, with a stock totalling $2,000 in value. "We made our own show-cases," they reminisce today. They didn't even know what insurance was, and were turned down when they applied. When they wanted to do photofinishing, they were told by the developers that the negatives must be brought in. So John, who had a $5 bike, would ride the film each day to the developers. It was all cash, no credit, and although the boys lived in a $16-a-week rooming house, they did surprisingly well on the tiny street off Yonge, in downtown Toronto: Sales were around $300,000 the first year.

As with Kenji's and John's Japanese gardening business, service and sincerity were all. "We couldn't advertise, so we mimeographed announcements and stuffed thousands into mailboxes of homes and apartment houses all over downtown." They looked after their customers carefully, and claim still to have many of their original ones.

They soon changed their name to Japan's A.S.A. Camera Shop, and then, after a move to Yonge Street to take advantage of the new subway which had just opened its doors, they changed it, for the last time, to Japan Camera Centre (although they sold German cameras, too).

By 1962 the Asa brothers obtained the first of their exclusives: Ricoh of Canada asked them to handle the distribution of their products. The following year they opened their first branch store in Hamilton, Ontario, about 40 minutes to the west of Toronto, which "did so much business that Roy had to commute there every day."

The expansion was hardly explosive; their third store did not open until 1965, in a mall in suburban Toronto, and "it was a bomb." With the first three stores, sales were about $1 million. In 1968 the first Montreal store opened, and by 1970 they established camera departments in seven Sayvette stores, and seven more in the Robinson chain. "But we never thought about franchising at that time," recall the brothers. "We weren't that smart."

What was smart, as well as lucky, was the chance meeting that Roy Asa had in 1974 with a man who made photofinishing equipment. Four years later the Asas once again ran into the man, and soon they were in Japan, in October 1978, working out the Canadian distributorship to the revolutionary QSS Noritsu, a machine which does quality printing in less than one hour.

Although the Asa brothers did not invent it, their faith in the machine, and the way they grabbed the Canadian rights, would be as important to the future of Japan Camera Centres as Albert Cohen's discovery of a minor Japanese firm which eventually became Sony, back in 1955. Cohen's recognition of a breakthrough in transistor radios turned his Winnipeg-centred General Distributors into a half-a-billion-dollar-a-year company, and the Asas would experience a similar explosion of success.

The Noritsu meant that 110, 126, and 135 film could be processed, printed, and paper-processed within one minilab system, and since it worked without darkroom facilities, it could be placed almost anywhere, taking up little space—less than 300 square feet. There is now one of the minilabs in every single Japan Camera Centre store, and they have sold 300, at a cost of between $100,000 and $250,000 each, even to their competition.

The machine wasn't accepted at first, and because no camera stores would buy them, the brothers started selling them to shopping centres. John Asa supplied the one-hour photo trademark, and the logo, design, merchandizing, and construction of various locations, since he kept selling the machines to people who had no retail experience.

By 1979 the Japan Camera Centres had reached a hiatus. The concessions in the Sayvette camera departments had all gone under, and they had only nine stores—"all good stores"—in Ontario and Quebec, with sales of under $10 million a year.

So they started franchising, a concept which now proved rather irresistible, thanks to the Noritsu minilab. In May 1981 the Asas opened their first franchised store in Ottawa. The fee was $30,000, as well as $200,000 in equipment, $40,000 in inventory, and $100,000 for the lease. It wasn't cheap, but by the end of that year they had 18 company-owned stores and 27 franchises, with sales of about $12 million.

In 1982 there were only 15 company-owned stores, but 46 franchises, totalling 61, with sales up to $26 million. In 1983 there were 16 company-owned and 71 franchises, with $37 million in sales, and the following year there were 26 company-owned and 87 franchises, with $50 million in sales. The end of 1987 had 155 Japan Camera Centres in all ten provinces, numbering over two dozen company-owned and over 125 franchises, with sales of over $65 million. As of the mid-1980s, the Asas were running the only national camera store chain in the country, since Black's is primarily in Ontario, Direct Film is in Ontario and the east, Astral appears in only a few provinces, and Kits Camera operates mainly in the west.

Although the stores average around $550,000 a year each, the basic breakdown in earnings is a shocker, and clearly shows how wise the Asas were to go with the minilab. Film, cameras, frames, and accessories make up only about 30% in sales, while a full 70% of sales comes from photofinishing. And what an attractive breakdown that is, since while there is, at the most, 25% profit in the former items, photofinishing offers profits of between 75 and 80%! In other words, there is up to a $16 dollar profit on a $20 roll of film, using the Noritsu.

The Asa brothers note that, by 1990, 60% of all photofinishing in the States will be of the one-hour variety, and that is a $5 billion business. "In Canada, assuming that the number will be around $600 million," says John Asa, "that means at least $300 million should be one-hour. We'll get our share!" There are technicians and quality control in every Canadian province to fix the minilabs, and the Asas have built up a substantial inventory of Noritsu parts.

What is especially promising, in a geographically absurd country with a few major population centres, is that the Asas feel there are profits to be made in smaller towns as well: "I just came back from a small place in Nova Scotia," notes John Asa. "There were only eight thousand in the town, but seventy thousand in the surrounding area. I see possibilities in small communities enjoying the same one-hour service as the big ones." Like many camera store owners, the Asas once "looked down on photofinishing," but no longer: "Now we see camera sales enhancing photofinishing." And with average new-camera buyers using 14 rolls in their first year behind the shutter, the potential is almost endless. (And it should be noted that the tens of millions of dollars in sales of the Noritsu minilab were *not* included in the sales noted above; these fall under the Asa Corporation Ltd., which, like Japan Camera Centres, is divided equally among Roy, Kenji, and John, and their families.) And there should be millions more from their entering into the selling of Ricoh 8mm video cameras, in the summer of 1987.

The three brothers from Vancouver, Hiroshima, and Toronto feel that the real reason for their success is their faith in the Golden Rule ("Jesus Christ was right," they say). "We treat staff like partners," they insist, "not as employees." There is no profit sharing, but they feel they have a close understanding of their workers, since they were never store managers and worked on the floors of their shops as late as 1976. They also have as much faith in franchising as do their franchisees: "Franchising makes more people rich! It's a life-style, and a happy business. Memories are precious to customers, and photofinishing provides them."

They certainly never bled the business: "Our philosophy is, we can only eat three meals a day and can only drive one car." When the brothers were starting their families, back in the early 1960s, they were taking home $20 a week each, while the salesmen in the stores took home between $80 and $100 weekly.

In 1959 the brothers joked with one another, "We want to be the best, not necessarily the biggest." Indeed, they never imagined having more than one store. But there are clues in that past which help explain why one store became 131, and $300,000 in sales turned into $100,000,000, in barely over a quarter century: the death of their mother, their decision to work together, their passion to learn English, their gardening service, their recognition of the Noritsu minilab, and the madly successful franchising. And one more, which suggests that work is work, no matter how much money, prestige, or future is involved:

"I enjoyed the mushroom picking too!" says John Asa, smiling. "Although Roy held the record there; he once picked two hundred sixty-one five-pound boxes of mushrooms in a single day!"

# FROM COMPANY MAN TO BUSINESSMAN

### John Park

While many of the greatest success stories in recent Canadian entrepreneurship have come from franchising stores like so many hotcakes, John Park has managed to dot the country with his own company-owned stores like so many Xeroxes. Perhaps that's because he had begun his career with

Xerox, or maybe simply because he has approached the business world like any late-bloomer: with passion, speed, and near-frenzy. "HI-FI CENTRE: THE FASTEST GROWING AUDIO/VIDEO WAREHOUSE OUTLETS IN NORTH AMERICA" read the full-page ads in newspapers across Canada. And when one hears his (rather short) story, one is reluctant to disbelieve him.

John Park, classically good-looking, immaculately well-dressed, was born in South Korea in 1938, the eldest son of four. His father was the chief of police in Seoul, his mother a housewife, and his first move away from his divided homeland was to the United States as a foreign student. He studied computers at Cal Tech and worked for Xerox, but "had to go back; I didn't like the atmosphere of Los Angeles, and all the crime." Xerox was clearly reluctant to let him go, and begged him to take a six-month holiday before he decided definitely to return home. "Look to Canada!" they told him.

He did, and decided to stick it out in Toronto, where there are about 30,000 other Koreans living today. From 1969 to 1979 he worked for Xerox in Don Mills, a north-central suburb of the city, where he countered the traditional dilemma of a man who "wanted to create my own business": Xerox treated him so well, with stock options and a good salary (up to $45,000 by the late 1970s, quite enough to support his wife and two daughters), that he just couldn't get up the nerve to leave.

Then, the downer which a man like Park would quickly turn into an upper: Xerox Canada decided to "unplug the large-scale computer systems," and John Park was laid off. It was the move he could never make himself, now forced upon him. His first business choice was only partially successful, but that provided to be good enough. He decided to open an electronic parts store for hobbyists in 1979, which he called Kyll electronics. ("That's my middle name.") He gathered all the money he had, and it went all right, but not on the component side, as he had expected. "It was very successful on the audio side—speaker parts, etc." He did about $1 million in sales during the first year, which is really quite extraordinary, but Park sold it..

"I decided to go bigger," he says, which is, as you'll see, an understatement. He next went into wholesale speakers with a partner, but that didn't work out well, so they broke off the relationship. So he opened another store, The Hi-Fi House, in 1981. It was retail. But after six months various "problems" arose, so he walked away from that partnership as well. (His wife is now vice-president of the Hi-Fi Centre chain; any future walking away from partnerships could be a lot messier.)

Then, in 1982, a mere four years ago, John Park borrowed $20,000 from his parents, who were living in Los Angeles, and started Hi-Fi Centre. The first store was in Malton, near the Toronto International Airport. There was quickly a second one, and six employees, with the two stores doing $3 million in sales in the first year. Since there have been so few years since the start, let us list the rather overwhelming numbers in sequence:

> 1983—4 stores, 12 employees, $6 million in sales.
> 1984—8 stores, 38 employees, $12 million in sales.
> 1985—20 stores, 60 employees, $24 million in sales.

True, 1986 was a disappointing year in the electronics business, and Park is down to 16 stores and about 50 employees. But it is still a strong company.

What makes the Hi-Fi Centre story so truly amazing is, to quote John Park, "I've never been a businessman before in my life! I was an engineer! I felt that I had no talent for something like this!" For instance, he had "heard that you need to use bank money, but I've never owed any bank a penny." Yes, you read right: All the growth has been "internally generated." The banks still don't know who the hell John Park is; if they did, he might have been able to save the Northland, single-handedly. As noted, Hi-Fi Centres are *all* company-owned. "I don't believe in franchising," claims Park. "The profit is so small in consumer electronics, you just can't share the profits." (Tell that to the Asa brothers, who precede this profile.) He claims that net profit is generally about 8%, which isn't very much at all.

Clearly, the "gimmick" behind the success of Park's chain of hi-fi stores is his tiny "mark-down." This means how much he is willing to make on sales. For instance, according to him, his largest competitor, Atlantic, which has nearly 150 stores, "aims for 39% mark-down"—meaning that they want to make $390,000 profit on every $1 million in sales. Another major competitor, which has 21 stores, wants 35% markdown. Park and the Hi-fi Centres will live with 24% markdown. Live? Be fruitful and multiply, to quote The Book.

"We have an entirely different philosophy from everyone else," claims John Park. "The future of the consumer electronic industry is gearing up for mass merchandising discounters. We in Canada are three to five years behind the States in market discounting and this marketing philosophy. We are a conservative market up here." (So what else is new?)

A shocker: Talk to mass merchandisers in the United States, according to Park, and the biggest did $510 million in sales. His margin was a minuscule 14 to 16%. So what's to gain from all this price slashing? "By lowering your profit margin, you get more gross turnover, more sales. Per store, I'm the highest in gross sale turnover in Canada. And because of my shorter margin, I have to come out with a system to overcome this."

The answer? He has begun to implement "the Japanese style of management." No songs or uniforms, but "the lowest possible overhead; the simplest possible paperwork—we're in the process of computerizing now—and *no warehousing.*" Japan will distribute directly to the stores, right across Canada.

With a well-chosen manager in every store, "everything is geared to performance and productivity." And with each one averaging a very high $1.5 million in sales, it is clearly working. "Because of our low-margin policy, we get lots of advertising power from cooperative ads," Park declares. In other words, if he buys $1 million worth of JVC products (Japan Victor Corporation, which makes most all of the VHS videocassette machines), they will pay $50,000 toward advertising. This can save a lot of money over the year and will allow Park to flood newspapers with his screaming cries for SHARP VHS! MITSUBISHI VCR! JVC AMPLIFIER, TUNER, TAPE DECK, TURNTABLE, SPEAKER! SANSUI TOWER SYSTEM!! JVC VIDEO MOVIE LIVE RECORDING SYSTEM! etc., etc., etc.

The 50% base salary and 50% commission seems to sit well with the rarely sitting staff, and Park gets a kick out of how "the suppliers jump like crazy when I suggest discounting," and how he has to fight the "great deal of price fixing" which is traditional in the industry. "Our philosophy is, *'Don't let people walk!'* We are open to bargaining over prices." The

Arab market has come to Canada, via Korea. Marshall McLuhan was right, as always.

The growth of the Hi-Fi Centres (and their lack of contacts with Canadian banks) is probably telling the industry something. "*Nobody* in our field has been doubling every year!" exclaims Park enthusiastically. He has managed to keep staff down to three in each store; Atlantic and Majestic have an average of five, which obviously gives them a lot more mouths to feed. "I try to sell for less by minimizing overhead as much as possible," says John Park, who looks Korean but sounds more Japanese and American by the second.

"If you are logically minded and look at the object to be achieved and eliminate all the stumbling blocks, you can do anything," says Park. "It's just like engineering." Yet, President Park of Korea insists, "I have no ego to be the biggest in the country. I want to prove to myself that I can do it. And I'd like to hit $100 million a year in sales by the mid-1990s."

As you may have gathered, as he grows bigger, his net profits keep shrinking, forcing him to "develop a way of being as effective with many more stores." In the meantime, Park flies off to Japan twice a year by invitation of the suppliers, and he watches carefully "the way *they* do it, and then I *implement* it." And "since everything is paid for, why go public?"

"I'm what they call a workaholic," says John Park, who averages 70 hours a week, with his wife in the office next door. "My accountant keeps urging me to go into real estate, and my bank manager does, too. But I tell them, 'it's my *hobby*, now, to be a businessman!' And I've found that the *best* hobby to have is to make money."

# 5.
# THE SERVICE
# INDUSTRY

## At Your Service

Readers over 40 will recall with affection that moment, early in the 1960s film *The Graduate*, when a businessman corners Dustin Hoffman and proclaims, "I have just one word of advice for you, son—plastics." Hoffman's character looks up stunned and confused, but we roared our approval and understanding, for plastics was one of the main roads to riches in the '50s, when that advice-giver probably made his fortune.

If there is any one word of advice to be given to the entrepreneur of the 1980s, it would more than likely be "service." Yes, service. And don't look like Dustin Hoffman when you read this. For the service industry is what has been expanding at the speed of light over the past decade, even more than computers. Food service, of course, which we looked at in the first chapter. But other services as well, which have taken off as women have poured into the marketplace, as the family has been shaken to the core (with fewer daddies and mommies to do many of the things they used to around the house), and as disposable income has increased, even with the inflation and unemployment of the past few years.

A StatsCan fact: While Canada's experienced labour force grew by 39.2% between 1971 and 1981, the financial, insurance, and real estate sectors "experienced the most striking growth in labour force (73.5%), and the largest numerical increase was in community, business and personal services, with 1.4 million (40.2%) of the 3.4 million gain in persons in the labour force."

In this chapter, we look at services for the home, including painting (Greig Clark of College Pro), cleaning (Jim MacKenzie of Molly Maid), and moving (Tim Moore of A.M.J. Campbell Van Lines). And service for your much-loved and rusted-out car is covered by a profile of Gary Goranson of Tidy Car. (StatsCan again: "There was a 23.4% increase between 1981 and 1982 in the automotive product and services sector.") Service for the office includes temporary personnel (Barbara Rae of Office Assistance), printing (the O'Born brothers of The Printing House), accounting (Sean Minett of MIBAR), payroll (Bill Loewen of Comcheq), and investment counselling, when you've made more money than you know what you can do with, and Brian wants to take most of it away (Philip Robinson of Eastland Capital). And, of course, when you want to get away from it all, there's Victor Pappalardo's City Express airline.

As with the other chapters, these ten men and one woman have few things they can compare notes on, beyond the fact that they have made (or are beginning to make) large sums of money, and (most) have created a multitude of jobs for our economy through offering services to the public. Their ages range from 35 to 57; they cover the country from Halifax to Vancouver; high school dropouts to M.B.A.'s and accountants—and there are a few more of the dropouts than the university graduates, interestingly enough.

What each of these bright, savvy entrepreneurs did was to enact the business equivalent of Mickey Rooney beaming at Judy Garland and squealing, "Hey—let's put on a show!" Greig Clark needed money to pay for his university education and noted that painting was an easy way to make it. (And it is; but does that explain how College Pro went from $40,000 to over $25 million in a decade?) Jim MacKenzie read up on working women and bought a fledgling Molly Maid idea from a young woman in suburban Toronto. His firm has moved into the United States and England, and has achieved sales of over $40 million annually, all since 1980. Tim Moore borrowed $2,000 to buy a pickup truck in 1971; today A.M.J. Campbell Van Lines has $25 million in sales, with close to 800 employees coast to coast. Gary Goranson had been through a dozen jobs before he became enraged that he was offered so little money for his rusted-out Meteor, and began Tidy Car; today, there are over 175 car appearance centres across North America, bringing over $20 million. Barbara Rae of Vancouver worked as a temporary for Office Assistance in 1951, became its president in 1969, when its sales were a mere $1 million; in late 1987, that number has broken $40 million, and it is the largest firm of its kind in Western Canada. The O'Born brothers went into printing in 1961 with a $500 investment; today, The Printing House has 50 stores and 350 employees, with $19 million in sales, the highest sales producer of its kind on the continent. Shaun Minett's MIBAR has gone from zero to over $2 million in sales since 1982 with his manual accounting system, up against the computers of the world. Bill Loewen of Comcheq had 1 employee in 1968; today, he prints cheques for 3,500 clients, earning $13 million, with 200 employees in 16 Canadian cities. Victor Pappalardo bought a failing airline in 1982, and in three years City Express has gone from a few million to $35 million, and from 54 to 350 employees. And Phil Robinson's story of tax shelters has to be read to be believed.

Is there a pattern in all this? You bet there is. They're all business people with their eyes on the main chance, who saw the need and market niche for painting/maid service/moving/car appearance centres/temporary office workers/rapid printing/manual accounting/computer payrolling/tax shelters/cheaper and more convenient air service—and they went for it—with long hours, often with little remuneration, but with a faith in their concepts of service that almost defies (and deifies) belief. In the words of Bill Loewen of Comcheq, "I always had full confidence in the system." And, one can say for all these servicing people, in themselves, as well.

## THE IBM OF PAINTERS

### Greig Clark

The story of Greig Clark and what he has accomplished across North America with his concept of College Pro is an impressive tale of chance, luck, struggle, faith, and ultimate reward. How ultimate? "I set a target to be a millionaire by the age of thirty and beat it by a couple of years," he says, from his handsome mansion in the Forest Hill area of Toronto, just two blocks away from the former domicile of John Turner, leader of Her Majesty's Official Opposition. Not that the story has touched everyone; after Clark wrote out the history of his young firm and sent it off to McClelland & Stewart, the namesake and, then, owner of the publishing company phoned Clark and stated, "You know a lot about business, but you write like shit."

But it is his business acumen, and not his writing style,

which has gotten Greig Clark to where he—and his 450 franchises and 4,500 painters in nine provinces and ten states in the United States—is today. Going from a $40,000 investment to over $28 million in billings in less than a decade is surely part of the Canadian Dream, and Clark is not about to wake up and discover that it didn't happen.

Athletic, winsomely handsome Greig Clark was born in Montreal in the summer of 1952—the first name is his grandmother's maiden name and is pronounced "Greg"—to an engineer father and a social worker/industrial psychologist mother. He was the oldest of six, and the youthful Clark eagerly points out that recent studies have shown that over 60% of all entrepreneurs were firstborns. There were no entrepreneurial influences anywhere in the Clark family, which moved to Brockville, Ontario, when Greig was still an infant, but the parents were bright, and the oldest child was, too. He was always the first or second in every class, skipping a grade, which made him "younger than everyone else, and so no social success." So although he was captain of his football team, he "only blossomed in university," where he went to "study economics and become the next John Maynard Keynes."

It was toward academe that Clark was heading when "a fluke of life happened" which changed his life forever. He was taking three arts and three sciences during his first year at the University of Western Ontario, in London, when he was shocked to see that his chemistry textbook cost $65. Back in the dorm, a fellow offered to sell him his coursebook for business for $5, and, providentially, that course was at precisely the same time as the too-expensive chemistry class. "The professor was fabulous!" Clark enthuses, and at the end of the first year, the man urged the youth to go into business. "For the first time in my life, I was studying things that I *loved*!" He also saw his roommate, the son of a Czech immigrant, start his own snow-ploughing business, and he thought to himself, " 'Gee, here's someone my age who's making hundreds for playing!' It was a mental breakthrough for me!"

A further breakthrough was soon to come. When he returned to Thunder Bay, where his family had moved when he was in his last year of high school, Clark faced a mathematical problem: His best prospect for a summer job produced a revenue forecast of $2,000, and his expenses at

Western would be $3,000. He had heard stories of fellows at university who started their own painting businesses, and he soon hooked up with a friend as a partner, creating Stewart & Clark Painting. The buddy's job was to do the painting; Clark's to line up the jobs. When he finally did his first estimate, he had to take a book out of the library to figure out how (multiply the length by the height). He gave a price of $390 for the entire house, and got the job.

Then his partner decided to quit, and Clark "hit the wall! Should I back down and tell people that I couldn't do it? There I was, no paint, no painter, no partner." As Clark gleefully relates it, he went to a store for the first, called on Manpower for the second, and got on quite well without the third. In that first summer of 1971 Clark had two or three painters and made his necessary $3,000. The following summer he had seven or eight painters and made $7,000. And in 1973 he had a dozen painters and made $13,000. In the fall of that year Greig Clark "realized that I was on to something. If someone could earn in their first summer what I had earned in my third, then we could split it!"

Back at Western, Clark kept "doodling" around with the concept and came up with the name College Pro. He also became aware that most union painters, in addition to charging a pretty penny, do little residential work. And as his third-year business project, his group worked on the idea of College Pro going national. He got about a 75 on it, which he would eventually hope to match in millions of sales.

In the summer of 1974 Greig Clark graduated from Western with an Honours Business Administration, H.B.A., and was on the dean's list. He had his brother Tim take over the minibusiness in Thunder Bay while he travelled around the world. Not that he was only bumming around; he kept a little orange notebook, which he divided into chapters: estimating, selling, production, accounting, etc. Whenever he had a thought, he wrote it down. It was to be the first College Pro manual.

He also developed his Chunk Theory, as opposed to the Nibble Theory. In brief, one starves all summer, but then, in early September, one gets $10,000–$3,000 for school, $2,000 toward a car, $5,000 for the bank. "It creates capitalists!" cries Greig Clark. "I love College Pro because it creates capitalists!" While still wandering around the globe, he wrote to brother Tim, telling him to line up a manager at Western so they could open their first outlet in London, Ontario.

Clark "just had to test the concept," but, alas, it was "not a roaring success." He quickly learned what drives many entrepreneurs into near despair: "It's difficult to transpose what you've learned to another individual." The fellow did enough business, all right, but Clark was losing money. "To err is human, to repeat it is stupid," cracks the young businessman.

Back in April 1975 Clark began a marketing job at General Foods, which he kept for the following two and half years. But on nights and weekends he kept rewriting that manual, trying to improve it. Yet College Pro had reached a crisis point that fall: Was it worth it to continue? He was spending one-fourth of his after-tax General Foods salary and ploughing it into stationery, flyers, and telephones. A further blow came when he shelled out over $100 for an ad in the campus newspaper: "RUN YOUR OWN BUSINESS AND MAKE $7–10,000 NEXT SUMMER." Clark expected to be stampeded; it was like offering free dope at a rock concert, he jokes. He did not get a single reply. (Even today, although the average earnings of a summer student painter is up to $12,000, he still has a problem attracting enough good-quality applicants. Clark marks it down to FOF—Fear of Failure, and FOTU—Fear of the Unknown.)

It was at this point that Greig Clark almost threw it all away, and nearly lost his chance to be a millionaire, to give thousands of students jobs across North America, and, most important, to make this book. But he "convened a crisis meeting" in his brother's room at Western, also attended by his future best man and future wife. As you may have guessed, he decided to give it one last try.

In December 1975 Clark hired two managers: one for London, and one for Mississauga, just west of Toronto. The former was a success, the latter a failure, leading him to a mighty lesson: It could succeed, so carry on. And he'd learn from the mistakes of Mississauga. The latter also provided one of his juicier anecdotes. When he phoned his Man in Mississauga that July, he was told, "We're booked about one week ahead." "Great," said the boss, "how much work did you land this week?" "Only about forty hours." "Oh, dear," said Clark, "for six guys, that's not very much." "No," said the manager, adding with glee, "but it rained three days last week, so I'm still booked one week ahead of myself!" Adds Clark drolly, "With those criteria, our happiest managers would be the ones in the Amazon monsoon rain forest. They'd never do any work, but they'd always be booked one week ahead."

On New Year's Day, in 1977, just over a decade ago, Greig Clark reached a further decision point. He had six test markets, and, like a good business school grad, he drew up a decision tree: If five or six of the test markets were successes, he would quit his job at General Foods that July and start College Pro full time. If three to four were successful, he would continue the test for another year. If fewer than three were successful, he would drop the concept once and for all, continue with General Foods, and move to Europe with his new wife. (It's worth noting that it was at this time that his "forced savings account"—now up to 50% of his $14,000-25,000 at GF—had been ploughed into College Pro and proved to be "a tremendous advantage." So many others around him kept saying, "I want to quit and start my own business but I've got this wife and kid. . . .")

All six markets succeeded; and so, in August 1977 Greig Clark launched College Pro with $40,000. He still chuckles at the face of General Food's marketing vice-president when Clark told him that he was leaving to become a house painter. That September he ran the Toronto franchise himself, to see the major problems. During that winter he rewrote the manual once more. (It's up to 600 pages now.)

Some numbers:

> 1978—19 franchises, $1.5 million gross sales.
> 1979—35 franchises, nearly $3 million.
> 1980—55 franchises in Ontario, 20 in the west, a
> few in the United States, sales $5 million.
> 1981—110 outlets, $7 million.

Jumping to 1984, 80 in Ontario, 60 in the west, 80 in the States—200 franchises in all, sales about $17 million. And in 1985, 270 franchises, in every province but Quebec plus ten northeastern states, sales of over $25 million. By the end of 1987 nearly 500 franchises should bring in $32 million.

The average franchisee earns between $7,000 and $15,000,

before taxes. Occasional "incredible managers" earn up to $30,000–40,000 over a summer, with a record of $50,000 being held in Toronto, Alberta, and the United States. The lowly painter doesn't starve, although he makes less than his father in the union: Wages are between $5 and $7 an hour, meaning that 500 hours over the summer can earn an average of $3,000. "One painter made seven thousand dollars last year," says Clark; "he's a manager this year."

Unlike most franchise operations, College Pro has no up-front fee, but there is an ongoing royalty of 12%. "I've got to stay close to the customers," says Greig Clark. "I painted a few weeks ago, and I'll paint again this summer." He stays close to the community as well; every summer for the past decade, he has insisted on a charity project in every city, painting homes for battered wives or for the mentally ill.

Like many entrepreneurs, Clark had originally seen his golden goose as a way to get him through school. Even when he quit GF, his dream was merely 30 to 40 operations, all in Ontario. "I never saw it getting as big as it is; it just took off," he declares. Indeed, he and his wife lived in a one-bedroom basement apartment for the first three years of College Pro gone pro.

Things have changed over the years. In the last two, Clark has hired "two dynamic young presidents" for Canada and the States, as he made himself chairman. And the business has been restructured along the lines of *In Search of Excellence*, with four levels of operation. "We were stagnating at a certain level, and the market is wide open in the United States! Some surveys say there is five billion dollars a year in painting down there, and even if we got ten percent of it. . . ." He hopes to double College Pro's sales every three to four years, reaching $50 million by 1990 and over $100 million a decade from now. That goal should be assisted by the creation of College Pro Window Cleaners, which has 30 franchises in Ontario, alone.

Greig Clark speaks with an almost religious fervor when he speaks of the business he has created. (His parents were Anglicans, then Quakers "after grade ten"; he now belongs to the United Church.) "Our objective is to be the IBM of painting!" he exclaims. "We have our own uniform: T-shirts and white pants. We're also the Procter and Gamble of small business. I want that people who want the best small business training in the world should come to College Pro! We have a management development program at our firm which is as intense as General Foods—ten days a year. Even McDonald's doesn't last any longer! We'll be turning out some of the best small-business personnel in North America!"

Clark realizes that College Pro was basically a one-man show for quite a while, but that he "was surrounded by good people and didn't appreciate them." No longer. "The business is now like a cat, gathering its legs underneath it! The new presidents and vice-presidents are the key. The objectives for the next half decade will come from the presidents."

Sure, it's great to live in a mansion, but Clark insists that material wealth was never the end in itself, only a means. "I've got six guest rooms here," he says excitedly. "All managers have open invitations to stay here!" No, what it comes down to is "You want to *do* something in your life that's meaningful! That makes a contribution!"

Greig Clark's greatest joy, aside from his happy marriage and three children, is the fact that he has a Little Brother whom he assists in life. When the boy was 11, a teacher asked the class, "What is an entrepreneur?"

The child leapt to his feet and shouted, "My Big Brother is an entrepreneur!"

## MAID IN CANADA—AND AROUND THE WORLD

### Jim MacKenzie

Outside the tiny, unimpressive world headquarters of Molly Maid Home Care Services Ltd. in Oakville, halfway between Toronto and Hamilton, a Buick Riviera sits, its vanity plates reading MOLLY 1. Inside, wearing his Molly Maid tie, with his open collar, his hair whiter than the Man from Glad, his black eyebrows making him look like a handsome Dick Van Dyke, Jim MacKenzie sits, quietly and assuredly spreading his empire around the world. In 1979, when he purchased the Molly Maid name from its founder, Adrienne Stringer of Mississauga, Ontario, it was less than a year old and had 10 employees. Eight years later, there are 145 franchises across most of Canada and a growing part of the United

States, with more than 1,800 Molly Maids cleaning houses and apartments right and left. Sales have broken $40 million, which is a lot of dusting. But if housecleaning was seen as merely dusting, it would be as if Ray Kroc saw hamburgers as just hamburgers, and look where McDonald's is today. And with over 50% of all women working outside their homes, one can only guess where MacKenzie's Molly Maid will be tomorrow.

Jim MacKenzie was the first of two children born to a doctor and a nurse in Toronto in 1943. As a child, he was "always interested in business," even at the age of six, when he would sell skipping stones to other children at a penny each up at the cottage. "I got a bank account from my paper routes," he says.

After high school MacKenzie studied commerce and economics at Queen's University in Kingston, since he "wanted to go to college to please my father, and gain a better understanding of business." After earning his B.A., he began working for a chemical company for a year, with the goal of "gaining an understanding of financial statements." He followed that with a two-year stint at Ralston-Purina as a plant accountant, at which time he enrolled in a C.A. correspondence course. He eventually finished four of the five years of the course.

In the meantime, MacKenzie decided that he wanted to get into sales and marketing, and was offered a sales rep job at R-P, which he held for nine months. By this time, he had bought an embossing machine, and, in his off hours, he started up a company that made placemats for airlines. "It did well," but when he was promoted to product manager, he had to divest himself.

Altogether, MacKenzie was at R-P for a decade, eventually promoted to the level of vice-president of the consumer products division. And, as might be expected, "it was always in the back of my mind to start my own business. You can make things happen yourself," he declares, sounding like a preacher. "You can get personal satisfaction in making it happen." And with his involvement in many major projects related to pet foods, and in large new plants and cross-country travelling, he had ample time to see how businesses worked.

There would be several false starts before he finally clicked with the Molly Maid concept. When he left R-P in 1979, he formed an investment company with four others, called GX Investments. They acquired the Canadian franchise of a unisex haircutting place, but "couldn't control the growth." They had planned to expand to suburban malls across Canada but could not secure leases quickly enough. So they kept looking for other investments, finally settling on a central messenger service for legal correspondence.

It was eventually the Chicago Department Exchange—there was already one like it in Toronto—but after only ten months MacKenzie was stopped from going into the States, so he was forced to arrange the sale of that business as well.

During this same time, Jim MacKenzie was an avid reader of all things related to the business world, and was becoming aware of "the large growth in working women and their participation in the labour force. I felt that this would create many opportunities in meeting the needs of working women." It was to make his fortune.

After identifying maid service as a concept for all those working women, he did a study of the maid service industry in Canada. And then, in 1979, he came across the tiny little business of a woman named Adrienne Stringer in his own backyard. "We asked if they were interested in selling, since I immediately thought that it could become the dominant maid service in Canada, if not North America."

He felt that the concept was "far superior" to anything he had seen in the States. For instance, the number of people on each housecleaning team was two. In the States, teams tended to be four strong. "The economy was better with Molly Maid," MacKenzie says. "If one doesn't show up on a team of four, it destroys efficiency. But two housecleaners can get along and be close, not leaving numbers three and four as odd men out."

MacKenzie and Stringer structured a deal within three days, giving the founder some cash up front, and around $15,000–20,000 for 80% of the business. He also agreed to pay an additional $15,000 to the former nurse, upon the success of the business. "It was very risky," MacKenzie says today. "I had to come up with another fifty thousand in working capital." In .fact, MacKenzie had to take a mortgage on his house to put the money into GX Investments and Molly Maid, and he had no other job at the time. He took no pay for six months.

When MacKenzie took over as president of Molly Maid—he insisted that Stringer stay on in charge of training, since he could see that "she would be a tremendous asset to us"—it was August 1980. Sales were $100,000, and they were losing money with their ten employees. So he sat down and developed a business plan to add 25 or more franchises per year. By 1981 sales were up to half a million dollars; by 1982, $2.5 million; double that in 1983; and double that again, to $10 million, in 1985. Molly should earn $48 million–$50 million by the end of 1987, $30 million from the United States and $1½ million from the United Kingdom.

He has a three-year plan, into 1990, but hopes go far beyond that. "I expect to reach saturation in English Canada by then, one hundred and sixty franchises, and then look at Quebec, Australia, and European markets. By 1995 I will hope to have fifteen hundred franchises in all fifty states of the United States, each with about fifteen employees, meaning twenty thousand altogether." (MacKenzie moved into the States only in 1984, with the first unit in Ann Arbor, Michigan, which went "extremely well." At the end of 1985 there were 30 franchises spread across that state, Ohio, Illinois, Colorado, Texas, North Carolina, Kentucky, Florida and California; by early 1987, there were 110 franchises in nearly twenty states.)

MacKenzie charges $9,500 to his franchisees, which includes $4,500 for equipment and manuals. They also need $2,000 in working capital, for which they get supplies, advertising, training, and more. Molly Maid, in return, receives 6% royalties on sales.

The former pet-food-pusher owns 40% of Molly Maid, since GX Investments still holds 75% of the business, and he owns 50% of that. Any discount for supplies they put back into the business, because, as MacKenzie states, "we don't feel that we should profit from the franchisees, and vice versa." Not that neither should profit at all; franchisees are usually profitable in the first year, since they earn 15 to 20% of sales. "We've got four franchisees doing over $500,000 in sales now," he says, meaning that there are a growing number of people who are getting rich on what used to be considered a lowly profession.

Or at least, growing wealthy by hiring others to do the dirty work. Not that the cleaning ladies starve, by any means:

An average houseowner will pay $38.50 for two women to clean two hours, and the women get 28% and 23% each. These cleaners earn around $225 a week each, plus the use of the Molly Maid car, which is leased and paid for by the franchisee. "Typically, it's a gal with a few young kids, who wants to be home early and doesn't want a nine-to-five job with overtime," says the guy who runs the place. By keeping his margins "lower than the competition," MacKenzie can pay his people tolerably well and give them a sense of belonging, with the pink-and-blue keychain on their fifth anniversary, the regular newsletter (*The Molly Maid Rag*), and many bonuses and awards. "These are professional cleaners, not charwomen," he underlines. (In a recent issue of the company magazine, under the heading *"Strange Requests . . ."*: Kimberlye Smith, in Uxbridge, Ontario, was asked by one of her customers, who was the award-winning makeup artist of the film *Amadeus:* "Please don't move the Oscar; it holds the bathroom door open." With Molly Maid, we get a late–twentieth-century version of the classic line about no man being a hero to his valet, thousands of times every week.)

MacKenzie denies having any competition, since "no one has the system and strategy that we have, as developed by our franchisees and managers." He is pleased that "virtually all of our franchisees are women. Women can relate to the needs of other working women." Furthermore, he looks at his business as "awarding franchises, to selling them." (And they must be getting valuable; some have been sold at a later date for as much as $70,000.)

Some of his success is due to crafty publicity moves, such as his recent tie-in with Johnson's Wax (a free Molly Maid cleaning for a full year was given away in every province in Canada). But much of it is because of his solid, no-nonsense philosophy: "We are partners with our franchisees. They are responsible for the growth and development of our business. And we will make many millionaires." Another "secret": MacKenzie sat down and talked with the dozen or so earliest franchisees on how to make Molly Maid better, and "they came back with hundreds of recommendations," many of them promptly implemented.

But there is competition, of course, especially in the Giant to the South. Maids International is the largest in the States, with about 150 franchises and 400 employees. "We'll surpass them in 1987," declares Jim MacKenzie, smiling knowingly at another blow for Canadian imperialism.

Ever aware of the importance of public service—and probably prodded into it by the more traditionally charitable sex which fuels Molly Maids and cleans its houses—the firm is involved in many charities. MacKenzie has a 36-foot sailboat which goes by the name of *Molly Maid*, and it races against *Big Mac* each year in Lake Ontario, donating $1 for each house cleaned that day. And there is the Santa's Helper Programme, in which gifts are collected from franchisees and customers for needy children across Canada (10,000 toys and games came in last Christmas). And there is a programme for underprivileged and handicapped children each summer, involving a picnic or a day out each summer. ("That was suggested by one of our franchisees," says MacKenzie happily.)

Jim MacKenzie, soon to be a millionaire, feels that Molly Maid is "firmly established" now, but admits that he "runs the danger of being complacent. So we are looking to build franchisees and assist them. The sense of achievement is being replaced by a feeling of responsibility."

Much of the achievement, if not the responsibility, came from his involvement with the subsidiary of an American firm, Ralston-Purina. MacKenzie recalls hearing "always from the Americans that they knew better. But it wasn't so." R-P was losing $100,000 a month when he joined, and when he left it was earning $5 million a year in profit. Not that it was all his doing. But he remembers sensing the feeling that "we should go into the U.S. and find out how to do it.

"The corporate mentality in the U.S. is that they are better-managed companies," he says. "But we in Canada have better opportunities. Our businesses are smaller, so our managers have a greater understanding of finance, and R & D. A senior manager in this country will be exposed to more areas than his American counterpart—manufacturing, sales, and so on. We have more generalists in Canada."

Not that everyone in Canada gets what he or she wants. Jim MacKenzie's father tried to encourage him to go into medicine, as he himself had done many years before. "But he realized that my heart was in business," says the president of Molly Maid Home Services Ltd.

## ENTREPRENEURSHIP AS A MOVING EXPERIENCE

### Tim Moore

Tall, dark, handsome, with Tom Selleck good looks and a moustache as thick as his bankroll, Tim Moore expresses some concern at being interviewed: "I'm sometimes too open." But he has much to be open about, as the old (1960) Rolls-Royce and the newer one (a hand-made 1985 Corniche, which costs $200,000) suggest. What he has done in the seemingly dull moving business in his 43 years on earth suggests that inspired business practices can be found everywhere—especially in Halifax, Moncton, Fredericton, Montreal, Gatineau-Hull, Ottawa, London, St. Catharines, Winnipeg, Calgary, Edmonton, Fort McMurray, and Vancouver, which happen to be where the branches of A.M.J. Campbell Van Lines are located.

As with many successful men and women, there were oodles of hints of his future success in the kind of aggressiveness shown in his childhood in Montreal. A firstborn whose parents were "quite strict" with him, Moore witnessed his father in the material handling equipment business, selling dollies, forklifts, etc. By the age of 11 he worked in a smoke shop, since his father "insisted that I get out and work and pay my own way."

In the summers, it was loading boxcars for the CNR, where he "always ran, never walked. I had an obsession about working hard. Everyone else knew that they'd finish early if I worked with them." By the third year he joined a chain gang "up in the sticks," laying tracks. The others were immigrants from Italy and Portugal, but Moore had no trouble keeping up with them: The only Canadian in the group, he lived in boxcars, rose at 5:00, breakfasted at 6:00, really earning that buck an hour. "I was *compelled* to work," he says today.

The family had moved to Toronto when Moore was eight, where the boy completed grade 12 at a Catholic parochial high school. Aspiring millionaires may be pleased to hear that young Tim failed grades 3, 12, and 13, since "sports were my ife." (They have racquet courts in the new Campbell building in suburban Toronto.) "My lifetime ambition was to play pro ball. I tried basketball, track, and got up to twelve and a half feet on the steel pole." At the end of grade 12, he was told by a priest to go out and work. "That hurt me," he says. "If I'm determined to do something, I can do it." But he failed the next year, and went into St. Augustine's Seminary in Scarborough, Ontario. He lasted three years, "literally locked up," with only the summers off to spend in the material world.

Not surprisingly, Moore threw himself into work during those months with an almost religious passion, putting in 16 hours a day at Expo 67, working double shifts at a dollar an hour, until he was "so run down, I had to go to the hospital." But he somehow found time to meet "a girl from Colorado" who was going to a Church of Christ college. They married in 1968 and moved up to Sudbury, where Moore taught grades 7 and 8. "I always wanted to teach, whether swimming, skiing, or any sport." After spending 18 months in the classroom without a degree, he left to study history at Waterloo Lutheran University (today Sir Wilfrid Laurier), graduating with an Honours degree in 1970. Then it was off to McGill for his M.A. in history, which isn't bad for someone who flunked grades 3, 12, and 13. "I had this compulsion to learn French!" he reminisces, although he is still two courses short of that master's degree, 15 years later. "I needed money!"

Which is where we truly enter the wildly successful moving business career of Tim Moore, who sold his car and bought a pickup truck in Montreal. (He had split up with his first wife back in Waterloo, Ontario. The couple had two sons.) The truck cost $2,000, and he had to borrow most of the money. It was January 1971. (But why moving, you ask? "I had a friend back in Waterloo who told me how much he made in a day with delivering!")

That first week in January 1971 the 26-year-old made $300. He put ads in the *McGill Daily* and *Westmount Examiner,* offering to move people for $7 an hour, and got students to help out when necessary. And it wasn't long before a second man was necessary. Not that it was all glorious: "I've seen everything. When you move people, you see them as they really *are*. One woman called and said she had 'a few boxes' to move. I told her it would cost seven dollars. When I got there, I discovered that she had three and a half rooms, and she insisted that I not charge more than my seven-dollar estimate." Yet amidst such petty treacheries, Tim Moore had decided on a goal: "I wanted to be a millionaire by the time I was forty. I've doubled that."

Within three months he bought another truck, borrowing more money and changing the name of his firm from Moore Moving to T. C. Moore Transport Ltd. two years later. In all of 1971 he made perhaps $10,000, but there were steady increases every year. "I kept no records; it was a cash business." The first big 24-foot truck came within the first two years, followed by a second big one in the next year. By 1974 there were five trucks, and there were times when their wheels must have been ready to fall off from exhaustion: "All leases terminate on either May first or July first; all Montreal moves on those two days!"

Moore operated his business out of his apartment until 1976, and had up to 30 students working for him each summer. "I never consciously undercut the other companies in price, but I knew we were well under them." His other secret was to "build a reputation for excellent service," working on the trucks during the day, with the answering service on, and doing sales at night. "We weren't in the Yellow Pages until 1977!" he says with a laugh. It was still that handful of newspapers. And, interestingly, he still has five of the movers who worked for him back in the early 1970s.

(It should be noted that all the while his little moving business was growing bigger, Tim Moore was fooling around with real estate. In 1971 he had borrowed $1,000 from a friend to buy a townhouse; he was "offered a grand more a week later, and refused." He kept buying a property a year until 1980, by which time he had gone through over a dozen and owned five. "I made money with every one but one," he says proudly.)

By 1977 the teaching bug appeared to be still gnawing at Moore, who up and sold his company to two of his workers for $80,000, after receiving a job offer to teach in Peel County, just west of Toronto. (The company eventually joined Mayflower and went bankrupt.) "I'd worked seven days a week for five years, and had $140,000 in equity [as well as a new wife, Bernardine, who has provided tremendous support—and two children]."

But fate stepped in, in the guise of his accountant, who must have been pulling his hair out after all those years of cash sales. "He offered to become my partner in a new moving business if we'd take a company, run it for three years, and sell it." The thought must have been irresistible: They bought an old business called M. J. Campbell (the "A" was added some years later, to put it earlier in the phone book), which had been established in 1934 and hadn't done much since. It had a grand total of three trucks, as well as permits to move within the cities of Toronto and Barrie (about an hour to the north of Toronto). Most important, they were one of only three movers who had permission to move soldiers to and from Camp Borden. They paid $200,000 for the business.

They bought the unpromising firm just before Christmas 1977. By the same date in 1978 they had $350,000 in sales. Moore still lived in Montreal, where he opened an office, ran a truck, and had no permit, commuting every year for the following three. "Montreal really took off," he recalls. By 1978 they swallowed up another old established moving firm for another $200,000, helping sales to move up to $400,000. And the following year they brought a tiny firm in Edmonton called Hooper's for $20,000.

By 1980 Moore opened in Calgary (after buying his partner out), and in 1981 they bought into Vancouver, doing it all from cash flows and loans. "I was working seventy-five-hour weeks, and my partner worked twenty hours a week," Moore says. "I was about to sell the company to him. I knew nothing about accounting!"

But one doesn't need to have a C.A. degree to know that A.M.J. Campbell was doing rather well. By 1981, with Vancouver on board, sales were up to $3 million; in 1983 Moore bought Tuck's in Moncton and moved into Fredericton; in 1984 he was situated in Fort McMurray, St. Catharines, and London; in 1985 Halifax and Winnipeg came aboard. He was now president of one of only two moving companies in Canada with their own offices in major centres from coast to coast. And by the end of 1985 A.M.J. Campbell Van Lines had gross sales of over $13 million, and 300 employees. By the end of 1987, they would *double* that, with nearly 800 in the firm.

You've got to be hooked into a major American company

in this business, and for a quarter of a century, A.M.J. Campbell had been part of North American Van Lines, paying them 10% for the honour. In December 1984 Moore switched lines, since "North American was competing their agents against ours! They were the only one to do that. The conflict of interest was unbelievable!" Moore was angered by their tendency to go in and say, "Why deal with our agent; *we're* the van line!" So when the contract expired in December 1984, he jumped to Atlas. "By nature, we're loyal," says Moore, "and if North American had been smart, we'd still be with them." But Atlas, of Evansville, Indiana, offered to paint all of Moore's trucks (that's $200,000 right there), give him free literature for a year, and give him a $1,000,000 signing bonus. It was irresistible.

So why such an explosive success in a low-margin, high-labour-cost business, where "it's difficult; you've got to deal with the psychological side when people move"? A major reason is that Tim Moore always stressed family, starting with friends, then their families. "We've got twelve families involved in A.M.J. Campbell, most of them owning shares," including two of Moore's brothers, Terry and Ted, his cousin Neil, and "adopted" Jackie Stewart, a $2 million producer of sales. Moore has gone from success to success, doing "all the major contracts," such as moving all the relocating employees of Xerox, The Bay, Simpson's, CIL, Kraft Foods, and many, many more. "No one does more bulk moves than Campbell Van Lines," he insists.

An example: Kraft went out to tender in early 1983, and Moore's firm offered to do all their moving for $500,000. They lost it to a lower-priced firm. Six months later the president of A.M.J. Campbell got a call: "Tim, you want all our business?" Kraft regretted going to the higher-discount place and had heard of Campbell's service level. Moore gleefully rattles off the moves for most VPs of Gulf, the contract with Mobil in Alberta, his deals with major banks, the 140 moves for Hoffman-LaRoche pharmaceuticals, Sun Life. . . .

Tim Moore is no lover of unions, and he speaks happily of how he met with the Teamsters in 1977: "I told them no way; I'd sell the company and close the doors if they moved in. I was told to take care of two union members who'd been with them for 25 years, and I agreed." He pays between $6 and $12 for helpers, but, almost unique in the industry, Moore has all his drivers on contract. "We were one of the first. They all get a percentage of everything they do. They own their vans, pay their own gas, labour, claims." The advantage? "They have a moral and financial obligation; it'll come out of *their* pockets if they don't do well. And the trend is toward this."

Moore sounds like Iacocca when he begins to spout his philosophy: "I've *got* to know my costs! I want my guys to work hard! I've got no patience for unprofessionalism! You work harder on contract, but you make more." He's right; his truckers make over $65,000 a year, and the men who own the tractors (that pull the loads) may have to pay all gas, labour, and licensing, but every single one makes over $100,000 a year.

There's profit sharing for the branches, which all get 10% of pretax profits. "*No* one in the country has family ties and stock ownership like we do!" Yet he claims that he still misses teaching, and still talks of going back. Fat chance. "I'm caught now," he admits. "I couldn't sell Campbell Van Lines; it would be selling out."

Tim Moore hasn't sold out on those seminary days, either; he still goes to church every Sunday, and his brother-in-law is a priest. "My strength is people," he says. "I treat people with respect."

But being nice to people doesn't make a company the largest moving company in Canada, nor does it explain away the fact that 8 Campbell agents are in the top 10 of Atlas Van Lines' 140 agents.

"It's my philosophy: working hard, having a good attitude. You'll never make it in life without it. I've never put an ad in the paper; we get our business through meeting people." Indeed, A.M.J. Campbell is "like a cult: We're a different breed, and we're close-knit. We're all good friends, we go skiing together in Aspen, and we work as a team. It's an unbeatable combination." Almost unbelievably, Tim Moore has never lost a single person to the competition. "They *can't* go to a better moving company," Moore asserts; "we've got the best product."

What helps it be the best product goes beyond all those family ties: People deal with Campbell at both the origin of the move and its destination. (Vancouver, Fredericton, and some of the smaller centres are franchised.) Their advertisement reads, "You deal with us here and at the other end."

Moore has no desire to go into the States and admits that he is rather tired of working 80-hour weeks. The fact that Campbell has never had less than a 22 to 25% increase in sales per year and 35% in each of the last two years seems to inspire him almost as much as that seminary. "I want ten more Campbell centres," he says. "Peterborough, Brockville, Regina, interior British Columbia—all franchised." Future sales? "We'll go to forty to fifty million," Moore says, "since we're still growing in the major centres." Another reason is their expanding commercial moving and the installation of partitions, the only moving company doing it. Sales of those divisions alone will be over $7 million in 1987.

But where does it come from? "It's inherent in you. I look for qualities in people that I see in myself. The work ethic is *so* important!" As are the little things, too, such as A.M.J. Campbell being the only moving company with a requirement meant to give "an added dimension of pride and professionalism": Uniforms and tie must be worn by all key Campbell personnel. Clearly those years in the seminary weren't totally forgotten.

## MAKING TIDY PROFITS

### Gary Goranson

When this writer first interviewed Gary Goranson, founder and president of Tidy Car ("THE WORLD'S LEADING AUTO APPEARANCE SPECIALISTS"), back in early 1983, there was a giant map on the wall of his world headquarters, just west of the Toronto airport. It was covered with dozens of Tidy Car stickers: Panama, Chile, Mexico, Norway, Malaysia, Australia, Liberia, South Africa, Manila, Indonesia, New Zealand. Close to 2,000 dealers in over 30 countries around the world were treating cars with Preserv-A-Shine, rustproofing cars with Rust-Rebel, noise-reducing cars with Sound-Rebel, stainproofing cars with Upholstery Gard 2, dry-cleaning cars with New-Matizing, cutting open cars by adding sunroofs, and even protecting cars from being stolen with Stop Thief.

Today, less than 5 years later, it's quite different. Tidy Car has moved away from low-priced franchising and begun to open Tidy Car Total Appearance Centres across North America, over 150 in the States and 25 in Canada, costing over $100,000 each, plus 9% royalties. And by the end of this decade, Goranson looks to 300 of the stores, averaging $500,000 each, for sales of over $150 million. (Sales today are over $25 million.) And the world headquarters of Tidy Car is now in Boca Raton, Florida. All this from a man whose career in selling has been, in his own rather indelicate words, "up and down like a toilet seat." (One might add, like a toilet seat at a Stanley Cup Championship.)

Nearly every article written about the plump, heavy-smoking, moustachioed, one-eyed entrepreneur—and there have been dozens over the years—begins the same way: There he was, dumped from his exciting position as a regional sales manager for Magnavox of Canada when it was taken over by North American Philips, and he lands in the hospital in November of 1975, diagnosed as a diabetic. Dashed from pushing colour TVs for high pay to pushing insulin needles for no pay, in a few short weeks!

Then, in born-again fashion, Goranson reread Napoleon Hill's *Think and Grow Rich*, and an inspiring article in W. Clement Stone's *Success Unlimited* ("The Magazine With a Positive Mental Attitude"), and he realized that *people were keeping their cars longer*, and no one seemed to be speaking to that growing market of car appearance, and, as he thought to himself, "Dammit, I'd never been master of my own fate!"

Gary Goranson was born in 1942 in our nation's capital, but after his parents' divorce when he was still in grade school, he was raised in Vancouver by his mother. When he was just entering his teens, she remarried a Saskatchewan farmer, so the future saviour of thousands of franchisees of Tidy Car from Bismarck, North Dakota, to Morvant, Trinidad, found himself growing up in Waka, about 40 miles south of Prince Albert. Like many great entrepreneurs, he "got tired of school," dropped out of grade 11, and studied to be a male secretary. Then he dropped out of the secretarial college, as well.

Then came a succession of door-to-door selling jobs that would be comical if they weren't so alternately challenging, depressing, and thrilling: He sold encyclopedias in Saskatchewan (selling one set, and feeling so bad about the "*very* high-pressure sales pitch" that he quit). He then sold heat alarms in tiny northern prairie towns (selling only one, after the little metal model he used to show how the thing worked burst into flames). And, after handing out *Watchtowers* as a missionary for the Jehovah's Witnesses in Kingston, and still in his teens, he pushed heat alarms again, this time in Ontario, for $25 a sale.

Then, after a five-month stint as a hospital orderly back in Saskatchewan (making an untidy $199.50 a month), he "realized that I wasn't getting anywhere" and headed back to Toronto, getting into vacuum cleaner sales at a generous $40 commission each. But he found that he "couldn't give them away," so he headed back to the prairies again, selling 22 cleaners in a single month in Waka—a community with a population of less than one thousand well-vacuumed souls.

Oh, yes—he was just turning 20 at this time. At 21 he met his beautiful wife (they have an infant granddaughter today), tried selling in Toronto once more ("I was told to go back to being an orderly, and I cried!"), and, in the west once more, took off like a rocket. In 1964 alone he sold 1,938 vacuums in the Saskatchewan area; in 1965 (expanded through the entire west, now) he sold 9,026; and in 1966 the number was up to 15,116. (No *wonder* the prairies are so flat, with all that cleaning going on.)

We shall spare you the failed attempt to sell nylon stockings in New York City (where Goranson was told, "You are the most *unqualified* person I've ever interviewed!"), the crumbling of the Compact Vacuum dynasty in North America, Goranson's brilliant success with Halley's Comet Vacuum Cleaners—imagine how brilliantly he would have done in 1986—followed by the master distributor's loss of the Canadian franchise in 1970.

Suffice it to say that when Gary Goranson saw a future in color TVs and began Colorama TV in Scarborough in suburban Toronto, it was to be expected that The Man Who Cleaned the West would soon have *eight* Colorama stores in the area, equally expected that he would close down nearly all the stores in 1973, make "one last crack at a salaried job" with Magnavox for two years, and then, even more expected, find himself with wife, daughter, mortgage, unemployment, and diabetes in the closing months of 1975. Clearly, Goranson's simile of the toilet seat may be vulgar, but it is certainly valid.

The real moment of truth for Gary Goranson was really not in the hospital, reading inspirational books about business while injecting insulin, but six months earlier, when he had tried to trade in his wife's 1971 Meteor, expecting to get $1,600 for it. He was offered only $200. And why? Because the *outside* of the car had not received the care and concern of the *inside*. *Voilà*: Tidy Car—created with a $5,000 loan from the Royal Bank, some "unique" car-polishing equipment, and the loan of the automobile bays of a local Sunoco station. At first, most of it was mobile—*DIAL-A-SIMONIZE, YOU CALL, WE COME*—booking 25 to 50 jobs a day. And the grossing of $122,000 in 1976 made it clear to the salesman that he was on to something here, at last. *At last*.

Gary Goranson hadn't thought of franchising at first, but after he ran a $500 ad under "Business Opportunities" in the *Globe and Mail* ("Millions of people with cars, trucks, aircraft and boats need our business! You can get into it as well for only $500!"), and then W. Clement Stone published Goranson's letter about his early success with Tidy Car in the February 1978 issue of *Success Unlimited*, "all hell broke loose in the States and in Canada!"

The corporate profits of Tidy Car, Inc., tell of what a good idea failed/successful/failed/successful former encyclopedia/heat alarms/vacuum cleaner salesman had during the early years: $1.5 million in 1979; $3.1 million in 1980; $3.5 million in 1981; $2.9 million in 1982 (when he briefly cut off the chance for people to be *small* franchisees, at less than a $1,000 investment, and insisted that he'd franchise only full-service people who could afford to offer *everything* Tidy Car had to sell, and not merely mobile cleaning). By 1983 he was back to over $3 million in sales, and able to afford to give away free Cadillacs and Corvettes to top franchisees (one kid in Bay City, Michigan, sold 908 cleaning jobs in *three* months in 1979, for example).

But a man who could hop from job to job to job, and still have the strength to land on his feet and inspire thousands of cash-poor people around the world ("While climbing the ladder of success, I've taken many other people with me," he says), did not lack the smarts to see the flaws in his concept: "It's really a different company now," he says, in the process of moving his world headquarters to Canada's Eleventh Province, about 20 miles north of Fort Lauderdale. "It had gotten to the point where it could never grow bigger than three million dollars; it was too transient."

It was a radical move. Rather than have hundreds of mobile operations—four-fifths of his early franchisees were part-timers—Goranson began to sell his Tidy Car Total Appearance Centres, ranging in size from 2,500 to 4,500 square feet. The 150 shops across the United States and Canada average around $20,000 a month, but he has no doubt that this will double to around $500,000 a year each in the near future. They each offer "all the old services"—the rustproofing, the sunroofs ("a tremendous business since 1982!" at around $240, Canadian), the waterproofing, etc. He's also gotten out of the business of manufacturing many of the products he uses; he used to sell his various gucks to his franchisees, asking a flat $2 royalty; today it's that straight 9% of sales. But with close to 10% of his $25 million in sales in 1987 being profit, he is clearly on the right path again.

He predicts that as many as 400 of his Total Appearance Centres will dot North America by the end of this decade, at which point he expects to return to Europe and Asia, and sell his new, bigger, more costly franchises.

Then there's the windshield repairing, and the vinyl and leather repairing, and the window tinting ("that's becoming as big as the sun roof business!" he exclaims). But why the move to Florida? Goranson replies with all the facts of a market researcher: "Florida makes sense. It's a much flatter selling-curve; there aren't the peaks and valleys of the north. The U.S. automobile population increased 12% from 1978 to 1983, while during the same period in Florida that increase was 31%! Did you know that it will be the third largest state by 1990?" (No, I didn't.)

O Canada, you will be but one of five regional offices of Tidy Car, the others being in "New Jersey or Connecticut," Chicago ("which will have eight stores soon!"), Dallas, and "Los Angeles or San Francisco." And Gary Goranson still sees himself as a leader in his field: "Ziebart has rapidly changed toward what we are offering, and there are a few new firms copying us. But I see that whole 'detailing business' on cars as faddish; there's not that many Rolls-Royces in the world. Besides, we are more the Eaton's than the Nieman-Marcus of car appearance."

But why should he succeed in this far more expensive market of permanent, not mobile, and expensive, not cheap, franchises? "It's the quality of work we do, and our services and facilities. We aren't in a back alley or in a place where the wife is afraid to take the car. We compete with McDonald's for real estate across the States. We like locations with more than 30,000 cars passing by."

Beyond his "dedication to quality," Goranson remains aware that he is offering a service that is more and more necessary as cars age. "Cars average 7.4 years in the U.S.," he states, and "people have to take care of them. We make cars look better and last longer." Not to mention sticking with the same owner; he's moving heavily into a technological breakthrough in auto alarms, which he will introduce to his 100+ + + stores very soon.

Goranson feels that "Canadians make *excellent* entrepreneurs" but is still charmed that he is "continually being accused of being an American." He certainly thinks in the kind of optimistic numbers we have traditionally identified with Americans: "I think we'll be a major force in the marketplace. Our goal is one thousand stores, ten percent of them in Canada, and we could max out at fifteen hundred stores in the States.'" That, of course, would make Tidy Car a billion-dollar business, which isn't bad for Boca Raton, much less suburban Toronto. But how could a man who works "twenty-four hours a day" do any less?

For all the millions that have traded hands, because of the strange, yet highly entrepreneurial career of Gary Goranson, there is still a surprising sense of the Golden Rule in all of it. "If you help enough other people to do well, they'll help you," he declares.

He no longer shoots insulin, having been on oral doses for some time now. And the loss of his right eye in a car accident, when he was four, is nothing more than a conversation piece: "I'll bet I'm a better judge of distance than *you!*" brags Gary Goranson. And a better judge of business than most of us, as well.

## SECRETARY TO BOSS

### Barbara Rae

Call it sexism, call it tokenism, but there's something particularly satisfying about seeing a woman who began as a secretary eventually become the president of that small firm, turn it into a major Western Canadian organization, pick up an M.B.A. at night along the way (thesis: The Role Orientation of Women), sell part of the firm to an international conglomerate, and make dozens of other women lots of money along with her.

Barbara Rae was born in Prince George, B.C., in 1931, to a stay-at-home mother and a father who was a prospector. "In the north, in mining or prospecting, your need for security is terribly low," she says. "You do what intrigues you. And they have a *lot* of free spirit!" She was the firstborn, with two younger sisters, neither of them career people. At the end of the war the family moved to Edmonton, where she attended high school and got married. So when her husband was transferred to Vancouver in 1952, she came there "unwillingly." The couple had one child, born in 1960—"*He's* an entrepreneur; a building contractor in Vancouver"—and they have since been divorced. She recently remarried, in 1983, and acquired two more sons, both in their early 20s.

Rae joined Office Assistance as a temporary worker when she arrived in Vancouver—"it was a young firm then"—and was up to vice-president by the time she retired to have her son. "I like to work thirty-six hours a day, and I threw myself right into it," she says. "A male organization would have used my energy, but I would not have moved up as quickly," she claims. The founder of the company, charmed by Rae's youth, gave her the opportunity to purchase some shares in the firm. "I had no money, though, and I was new in the city." So she went to the Bank of Montreal and borrowed $3,000 to invest in the company.

Office Assistance was part of a new industry at the time; it had been founded in 1951, when businesses were still wary about strangers coming into the office. "We did direct-mail advertising only," remembers the present president. "We had to break down resistance."

Barbara Rae returned to her 36-hour days in 1966 as vice-president, and just three years later, when the head woman retired, the board elected her to the presidency. Office Assistance Canada Ltd. was at only about $1 million in sales at that time, with 40 people full time and about 300 to 400 part-time temporaries in Vancouver alone. Almost immediately the new president opened a second branch in the city.

Today—for comparison's sake only, of course—there is a full-time staff of 175, around 3,000 temporaries, with sales of $15 million in 1985, $25 million in 1986, and over $40 million in 1987, making it the largest permanent and temporary office-help placement firm in Western Canada. And that's much of the west, not just Vancouver: She moved into Alberta in 1973, and there are currently six branches in the original city, three in Calgary, three in Edmonton, and two in Toronto, the latter since 1984. An example of eastern growth: Toronto sales were $1.7 million in 1985, and $7.5 million in 1986. And in 1986, OA bought a Quebec company, Marie Felick, quickly adding $4 million to sales. She hopes to be in Manitoba in 1988. Not only that, but there are Office Automation Education Centres in each centre, teaching its temps how to use word processors and computers. (Actually, Ms. Rae managed to get sales all the way up to $14 million as early as 1981, before the Sequel to the Great Depression hit them hard. Sales crumbled to $6 million before zooming back up to today's level.) "Temporaries are bellwethers of the economy," she says today, attractive and sharp-eyed, with short-cropped brown hair, Princess-Anne-type face, and bright smile. "Permanent placement almost disappeared during that period of the recession."

She began to develop branches from Day One. "I put them where people lived, to attract workers in their area," she says. "And I began maternity leaves with the managers almost immediately." (Yes, feminist fans, it took a woman to do it: The entire staff has access to 18 months' maternity leave. Barbara Rae never forgot how they welcomed *her* back after she took off a number of years to be home with her son.) And in 1977 she established profit sharing, reacting to "a stupid incentive plan that we had, which pitted branches one against the other!"

Rae also decided, even before she was chosen to be president, that although she "didn't need the education," she would study toward an M.B.A. from Simon Fraser University. "As a woman, I needed that professional designation to be respected by my peers. And once I finished it, I was suddenly on boards with other corporate presidents!" (In September 1985 she received the Distinguished Alumnae Award from the institution; it's not only this book that recognizes her excellence.)

The profit sharing was "my own idea," as Rae says. She had worked briefly for the City of Edmonton and felt that it "never gave a share of concern and involvement in real results." Her profit sharing at OA is "pure bottom line, not branch versus branch," and she insists that "it really helps to build a company that wants to build and not win over someone else in the firm to achieve profit sharing. Most profit-sharing plans set individual against individual."

The profit sharing paid off in more ways than just creating team spirit. At the end of 1982, two major partners in OA wanted to sell, and along came Adia, the second largest company handling temporary workers in the world, out of Lausanne, Switzerland. Although OA retained 20% employee ownership, all the workers who had been profit sharing along with Barbara Rae suddenly found themselves with a lot of spending money. "It was fantastic!" exclaims Rae. "I was suddenly rich with the sale of the company, and most managers owned between twenty-five and fifty shares!" Employees owned a maximum of twenty-five, and many longer-lasting staff had up to 200. Since the shares sold for roughly $250 each, and the purchase price was nearly $1,000—Rae owned 1,400—there was a lot more money floating around Vancouver and Alberta in women's hands in 1983.

"Nothing has changed," insists Barbara Rae. She was still president of Office Assistance of Vancouver as of the end of 1987, and Adia, which is in 11 countries, including 150 branches in the United States, where it is a public company, visits OA twice a year. "The psychological ownership is still total," she says, even though 80% is owned by Adia.

Barbara Rae's policy was always to pay the top-of-the-market wages, as well as to educate as many workers as possible. She has gotten agreement from every province in Canada to get Women in Management funding. Her various schools teach Lotus 1–2–3, management accounting and data basing, and all new business software.

"I *am* an entrepreneur!" proclaims Rae. "I've created a lot of jobs, and I'm much more proud that a lot of people have made money through our profit-sharing plan. We use sophisticated tools, but a good idea is a good idea in our firm, and I can move on it within a week or two." (For example, in the spring of 1985 she was approach by some Japanese to put an executive office in the World Trade Centre in Vancouver, a new hi-tech building, all computer-connected. Rae's firm is providing the labour. And Tech Temps, for office automation, and Accountants on Call are both quickly growing babies in 1987.)

"It's a strong management style: Ready-Aim-Fire! You get an idea and act on it. As it moves forward, you improve on it. You don't leave it on paper and discuss it for a year!" Barbara Rae credits her father for many of her qualities. "He was so keenly interested in the most minor achievement in prospecting, and he was proud that he never took a paycheque from anyone. That meant something to me, and I try to make that available to everyone."

Office Assistance became the Biggest in the West, and a growing force in the East, because of Rae's *"own* need to make things develop. I'm always going on and getting better with the business: It's always building, building, *building*! I'm not *ever* content with the status quo, whether personal or business. There's almost *nothing* I can't do. I keep trying until I *get* it!" She leans across the table, making this writer thankful that he is a card-carrying feminist, and grins meaningfully: "It's the Old Boys' network, with *women coming in*!"

# BROTHER
# COPYING BROTHER

## The O'Borns

The head office of The Printing House is near an exceedingly unfashionable corner of Toronto, at Bathurst and St. Clair. Inside the modest two-storey building is an ancient mimeograph, next to the much younger receptionist, in ironic counterpoint to what the two brothers have created. An ad on the wall displays a hand rising out a flood of paper, clutching a sheet which reads, "WE'LL MAKE YOU LOOK GOOD ON PAPER. FOR PENNIES A PAGE WE'LL PICK UP, PRINT, PUT IT ALL TOGETHER AND BRING IT BACK IN HOURS, OR WE'LL DO IT WHILE YOU WAIT. GO WITH THE ORIGINAL—THE PRINTING HOUSE." And, at the bottom of the witty advertisement: "THERE'S A PRINTING HOUSE NEAR YOU, CHECK YOUR YELLOW PAGES."

That's not totally true: the 50 stores (with their 350 employees) are only in Ontario, Alberta, and British Columbia. But somehow, the rapid printing company has been labelled "the highest sales producer" in North America in 1983 and 1984 by the industry magazine *Quick Printing*. Their sales were $11.4 million in Orwell's year, and hope for $19 million in 1987. Numbers two and three were in Arlington, Virginia, and Stoughton, Massachusetts, with New York City and Kensington, Maryland, chains way behind. No wonder the Yankees fear us so much; they just can't seem to keep up.

Don—he's the older one with brown hair and glasses—was born in 1935; Earle—the blond, football-hero type with a bit of a belly offset by his blue eyes—was born three years later. They both were born in Toronto. Their father was in deliveries—ice, coal, and oil; their mother was a timekeeper in a factory, and later sold women's cosmetics.

Neither was overeducated. Don finished grade 10 in night school; Earle dropped out as of that year. What they did was to go into the printing business, both serving apprenticeships as typesetters. In 1961, long before the concept of rapid printing was even a twinkle in its mother's eye, the O'Borns began their own business, eventually called The Printing House, but operating as Don and Earle O'Born Company Ltd. "Don had tried two other businesses before," recalls Earle. "I wanted to put a press in my garage with another worker. Then Don bombed in his last one." The young men paid $550 cash and took over $1,700 in debts, buying a business that had recently gone under. "The equipment was out to lunch!" jokes Earle. "I taught Earle all that I knew!" asserts Don. Adds Earle, "*That* took *five minutes*."

But the gags abruptly stop when Earle defends what they did. "You can go into business with the *worst* of tools—a hand-fed press and a letterpress. And to print from type, we had to hand-set with lead." They made less than $25,000 in the first year, forcing Earle to stay at an earlier job, since he had two children at the time. (Don sold during the day.)

They took no money from their tiny business in the first year, and only $3,000 each for the next few, and Earle recalls that being "the hardest part, with my two young children at home. I had to drop from fourteen thousand dollars a year to three thousand! But we had fantasies," he remembers. "We used to tell ourselves, 'When we get six employees, it'll be like we died and went to heaven!'" With over 50 times that today, the O'Borns clearly have been O'born again.

At the end of four years, the brothers had $45,000 in sales. "We thought that we had made a profit," says Don, "but found out that we had made a loss." Their entire plant was one room, and the noise was so dreadful from the clackety-clacking machines that they begged Bell Canada to put a phone booth in, so they'd be able to close the door and hear their calls. "They refused, so we used to put cardboard boxes over our heads," says Don.

What's so strange is that they were actually doing a kind of rapid printing without knowing it. And it was expensive at the time: It cost $15 to $20 to make 50 copies of a page. But in 1963 Earle had seen an ad in a trade publication: "One Million Copies While You Wait." The two brothers discussed it, and Don wrote a letter to the New Yorker who was offering this miraculous service.

It was a momentous meeting, if hardly impressive at first. Earle flew down to see him and was dazzled by the long line of waiting customers. "He was providing the service, but he hadn't seen the potential!" blasts Earle O'Born. "I saw a whole marketing scheme—that we should branch out immediately." The man had a dozen machines in a row, but no real idea how to turn his spark into a blazing business.

The O'Borns of Canada did. It took them less than a week to set up their concept, and they opened up a second and a third store within a year. By 1972 their sales were up to $2½ million; by 1973 they bought their largest competitor at the time and moved up to $4 million. Today, as noted, they have pushed past $19 million in sales from their 50 stores, which are all company-owned. "The franchise business is the franchise business," scoffs Earle, "and I thought we were in a *printing* business. Sure, we could have a lot more stores if we'd taken a different tack."

But they didn't. Not that it has been a straight-upward curve. There was a gap of about half a dozen years, which ended in 1981, when they had stagnated with two dozen stores. Earle had lived out in Vancouver from 1974 to 1984, participating in the eight stores out west, and the brothers were not clear as to the direction they wanted to go.

In 1987, however, they are the largest owner-managed printshop in the world. "What was unique," says Earle, "is that price, speed, and quality created problems for companies, so some of our biggest customers in the early years were printers!" "We really created a new market," says Don. "We are doing jobs today that couldn't be *done* a few years ago." For instance, a parts specification manual that The Printing House did for Ford. Or that job for the University of Buffalo that they had to smuggle over the border (and took two years to be paid for). They've done a resumé for a guy in West Germany, and that crazy order for a man in Toronto: 500 bound manuals of 300 pages each, which were needed within 24 hours. Three local branches slaved through the night to get the manuals delivered the following morning.

Managers of each store participate in gross margins, which leads to faithfulness. "One of our strengths has been involving, and sharing with, as many as possible," says Earle. "The broader you can share the responsibility, the further you can go." The two brothers burst with pride over what they have created, underlining that "managing thirty-eight small printing plants and our three buildings is really quite unique." And Earle argues that "we were light years ahead of *In Search of Excellence*! Every one of our successful managers came up through the system; we almost never had to hire off the street."

They claim they were successful because they offered "a high-quality product at a reasonable price." And service, always service. "You can't deliver a huge job across the country, instantly, if your stores are franchised!" exclaims Earle. "But I can shift to any branch I want, whether a hundred-thousand-dollar-plus job with training manuals, or an educational program for computers. You want a thousand pages? Two thousand copies? One million impressions? I can spread that over a dozen branches and do it overnight. We do that *all* the time! Others could never consistently guarantee such service. And our deadlines on those jobs very seldom falter."

All machines are bought, not rented. The average Printing House has six employees, working in 1,400 square feet, with maybe a dozen different machines in each branch. From 1961 to 1982 each brother wanted to do a "different style of managing," and one was president and the other vice-president. Until 1986, each of them had business cards saying "President." Then, Don went off and created a real estate holding company, O'Born Capital Corporation, taking Earle's grown son and daughter with him. So Earle is now sole president of The Printing House.

"We've watched three cycles of bankruptcies in this business," says Earle O'Born. "The most successful in the industry, the leaders, have an obsession with their business. They constantly pay attention." Adds brother Don, "I couldn't see any other way of bettering ourselves. We understood that, if you *own* a business, you can make it successful."

They are now looking to the east coast—specifically Halifax, and Montreal as well. "But Montreal is such a tough nut to crack!" moans Earle. "But we'd like to dominate in our market. We *influence* now, but we don't dominate, yet." But successful? Not yet. "I don't feel successful; you are only successful if you've done everything that you want to do," says Earle, with brother Don concurring.

Copycats.

# PENCILS OVER
# SILICON CHIPS

*Shaun Minett*

There is something charming, almost disarming, in seeing someone succeed with an idea that seems to be outdated. Selling buggy whips after the car became established is one example. An old-fashioned board game like *Trivial Pursuit* taking off in a time of hi-tech electronic games might be a better one. So what of Shaun Minett of Edmonton, Vancouver, and eventually Toronto, in his 30s but looking like a plump, excited Huck Finn? In a classic personification of Marshall McLuhan's witty image of our culture, driving at 100 miles an hour with our eyes firmly fixed upon the rear-view mirror, Minett has been fighting mightily for the pencil while the computer industry has been coating the world with silicon. His rapid success tells us that, like the millions who are happy to take the train and bus instead of flying, there will always be a place in our society for those who cry "whoa" instead of slamming on the brakes.

Minett—a French name that became English in 1066—was born in Edmonton, Alberta, in 1952. His Polish mother worked in an old folks home; his English father had worked in the Middle East with the Palestine police force, then came to Canada to run part of the Leduc oil fields for Imperial, and later helped establish the west coast pipeline out of Kamloops. Young Shaun stayed in Edmonton until he was 10, then moved to Kamloops and finally to Vancouver with his parents and younger sister. There were glimmers of capitalistic frenzy when he was a child—he briefly had six other children running paper routes for him when he was 13, until the *Vancouver Sun* got annoyed and made him quit—but his teenaged reasoning is more revealing: "It made sense; why not lever yourself?"

While studying at the University of British Columbia (business, of course), he worked in logging camps, and then used to borrow money through student loans to live on, and loaned his logging earnings to dentists who were buying condos in Whistler, at 2 to 3% over prime. It should be noted that Minett originally wanted to go into engineering, but "I looked around and saw that the only thing that drove the world was sales."

He eventually moved into accounting and spent three years in that, writing the exams but never finishing the articling necessary. "I walked away from it," he says today, his eyes bright behind his glasses. "I couldn't handle auditing anymore; it was a boring exercise."

In 1979 he went into banking, working in international money management for the Bank of Montreal for two years. And while he was doing that, he began creating his own manual accounting system. "It stemmed from seeing small businesses stumble along, month after month, without a good accounting system. They had all been told to buy a good computer system, when in fact what they really needed was a good manual system, first!" (Remember the buggy whip?)

He was stunned to see reports that over 70% of people who buy accounting software never get it working, and he was aware that they lacked the training to use the new-fangled machine. "They would read an ad, buy an IBM or an MS DOS, and think that it was the salvation of their accounting problems! All it did was to capture all the crap and speed up the addition!"

And so, Shaun Minett sat down and, over a two-year period, created MIBAR (Management Information Bookkeeping Accounting and Reporting System, "The Unique Business System that saves your time, saves your money, and saves your sanity"). It's a manual accounting system which is based on computer logic; "it's like having computer logic printed on paper," he declares. "I *had* to do it," he explains unapologetically; "Every time I visited a small business, all their books were garbage!"

It's actually a combination of several accounting systems, combined with Minett's "hands-on knowledge of how to produce a financial system quickly for a bank or an owner." He copyrighted it in 1982 and went into business for himself soon after.

All businesses have three things to worry about, as we all know: They want to produce an income statement, what their assets are, and what their liabilities are. "Most people think that their accountant should do it," says Minett, "but *I* say that a small business should be able to produce its *own* monthly financial statement themselves, and not at the huge expense of a computer." Lotus and other systems are too expensive, too difficult to train for, he insists. "Entrepreneurs lack the time and the tremendous ongoing costs. It's simply *not* cost-effective to do it."

MIBAR, Minett's system, costs a mere $70 a month and can produce financial statements and cash flows, as needed. "It's like the genius behind the McDonald's hamburger," he says. "Keep it simple."

Previous accounting systems tended to segregate sales and cash receipts journals, but MIBAR took the simple approach: If you've made a sale, then you've got a receivable or a bank deposit. He placed it all on one integrated line. "At the end of the month, the mystique of balancing is all gone," he states eagerly, "since day by day they have used a fully integrated, line-by-line balancing system!"

Computers, of course, do these things automatically, but the business person doesn't get to see how it's all done. With MIBAR, the separation of the general ledger, trial balance, and financial statements is eliminated, giving the entrepreneur a better understanding of the business, and how it is doing every day. "So the business owner *knows* what he's collected in sales, and how much he's made on each item!" rejoices Minett.

Minett wisely doesn't simply dump his manual package on the poor, abused store owner; he sells MIBAR with a full one-day training course. The system costs $800 for the first year; if you are only buying the forms, after that year the price falls to $400. "The retention rate is ninety-five percent," he states. "It's not worth it for anyone to try to photocopy my forms; the pages are huge!"

Just as any good buggy whip salesman should hedge his bets or diversify, so too with Minett, who sees the computer not as an enemy but as an eventual ally. "When a business *does* get big enough to go on a computer, after a few years, I've developed software with which I can upgrade them quickly to a computerized version of MIBAR. It allows them to do the same as they did manually." And he adds—underlining his basic belief in the cries of small businessmen who have wept, "The computer has not solved my problems!"—"It's a clean jump, since they have already been using a good manual financial system." (His.)

The growth of sales of the MIBAR system gives testament to Minett's argument: His sales during 1982, the first year he started pushing the programme: $100,000. In 1983 sales were up to $400,000; in 1984, $600,000. In 1986, with four employees, MIBAR and President Minett have sales of "close to a million dollars," and profits are well over a walloping 30%. By spring, 1987, there were seven employees, with projections of $2 million.

When he began to introduce his system, Minett went about knocking on the doors of chartered accountants, but "they perceived it as a threat." This forced him to create a market which has served him very well: the franchise people. "I had to hit that market, since I knew I would get ten to twenty at a time." What Shaun Minett did was quite intelligent; he began to create systems which were industry-specific, now totalling over a dozen: RESTAURANTS. TRAVEL

AGENCIES. DOCTORS. DENTISTS. HARDWARE STORES. PAINT STORES. MUFFLER STORES. TIRE STORES. CAMERA STORES. PRINTING SHOPS. By customizing MIBAR to particular reporting systems of each kind of franchise operation, he's been able to land dozens upon dozens of franchisees of such firms as Mother's, Pizza Delight, Mr. Grocery, Benjamin Moore, Triex, and many others.

Most of Minett's time over the past few years of his young business has been spent lining up appointments with franchisees, designing specific systems, and giving seminars, up to four a month of the latter, with 20 in a class. His problem flows out of his success: It's been easier to hit a finite target, like the franchise market, rather than hit the endless number of individual business people to whom he longs to sell MIBAR. "Small businessmen don't know what they're missing until it's too late!"

It cost Minett $100,000 to set up his old-fashioned system of manual accounting, building it as it grew, using his own cash flow. His five-year plan is optimistic: he hopes to be up to $6–7 million in sales by 1990. Two things have become clear, according to Minett: "MIBAR is more and more well known, and I'm retaining most of my customers. Furthermore, we're providing an intelligent alternative to the computer." The joke is, Minett has learned to work with the enemy, as well. By the fall of 1987, MIBAR software—to "demystify and complement computers"—reached the market.

Minett's complaint today recalls that zany T-shirt which reads "So many women/so little time!" "I have such a huge market, I haven't *begun* to get to it! My biggest difficulty now is to find someone with a good accounting background who can *sell*!" (In other words, Shaun Minett can't run a potentially $6 million a year business with himself doing all the systems designing, teaching, *and* marketing.)

Part of the answer to his complaint he has found already: He has hooked up with Campbell Sharp, who have offered to help support his system in every province west of Toronto, and with Doane Raymond, to handle the east. And although he's begun to sell to the States, the size of that market scares him somewhat, like Free Trade to an Ontarian: "Once you crack the U.S., a lot of volume comes at you!" (i.e., can Shaun Minett handle it all?)

Minett puts a good 60 hours a week into his new business, but he's aware that he is going up against the $2 billion a year spent by the computer companies on ads every year. "Computers are great tools if they're used properly," he admits, "but in most cases, they're *not*." His hope lies in the fact that the computer companies have had trouble penetrating the world of small businesses. "And how can a small business making, say, $100,000 a year, pay up to $20,000 for a good computer, plus another $25,000 annually for a person to run it?" Minett asks rhetorically. He claims that 10 to 15% of his clients own computers costing in the range of $12,000, which they do not use for accounting.

He still hopes to get the wary C.A.s on his side. "As I get my product exposed to more good accountants, they'll work along with me. Rather than C.A.s charging four or five grand a year to a small business to do their books—and losing money on it—they could do the job for three thousand dollars, while the client gives the C.A. all the info he needs from MIBAR! This way, the client has good monthly information, and the C.A. can be a better business advisor to his client, rather than merely a high-priced bookkeeper."

Newly married, Shaun Minett feels he is sitting on a fabulous system which will make him and his bride wealthy, and tens of thousands of Canadian (and American?) businesses a lot better run. There is even strong interest from China, to use MIBAR as a training system to help their accountants deal with North American companies. "My goal is to have a maximum of twenty systems to hit different areas of industries," says Shaun Minett, adding, "I hope that one day all the dentists and doctors will be given a concept like MIBAR before they go into business!"

A legitimate hope, from a man who has increased his business over tenfold in three years, with hopes of another 600% increase within the next five. But it's never easy when you are a pencil-and-paper man in a silicon-chip world.

# WRITING EVERYONE ELSE'S CHEQUES

### *Bill Loewen*

If there is anything which lacks sex appeal in the world of business, it is having to write cheques, prepare T4s, figure out deductions, and other such depressing aspects of making a living, and helping (or hurting) others in making theirs. Which is why the way Bill Loewen, president and CEO of Comcheq Services Limited, Winnipeg, turned a business earning less than $1,500 in 1968 into a countrywide payroll firm with sales of nearly $11 million, issuing 500,000+ cheques per month, has a romance all its own. And by the end of 1987, that should be $13 million.

Serious-looking but with a ready smile, blue eyes, and greying hair, William Loewen was the third of seven children born to a grain elevator operator and his wife in Elkhorn, Manitoba, a town of about 250 people, in 1930. (The name is pronounced "*lay*-van"). His early ambition was in the direction of scientific research, but "circumstances or fate took me into accounting." Although he taught in a one-room schoolhouse right after high school, Loewen took a five-year C.A. program through the Institute of Chartered Accountants in Winnipeg, which consisted of articling and taking courses along the way. He graduated in 1954 and worked as secretary-treasurer or comptroller for several firms, with a growing sense of what most entrepreneurs eventually start to experience: "I had the audacity to feel that I could do as well as the people I was working for!"

Over the years Loewen had a growing realization that it was difficult to get a payroll system which he felt comfortable with. Every company he saw in Winnipeg was running payrolls on cheques drawn on the individual firm's bank account, and this was a deterrent to setting up a payroll. An example: A hotel with between 200 and 500 employees had to buy cheques, get a computer program written to suit their particular situation, and pay a fairly sizeable up-front fee. And from a data-processing point of view, there were further deterrents: They had to stock separate cheque forms for every customer.

The origin of Loewen's brainstorm was simple: "I heard about a company that was franchising people who offered computing service that included everything but payroll. I began to think about it. Quite literally in the middle of the night, I realized that if you ran payroll on a single cheque form, drawn on a single bank account for *all* employees, then *all* the problems suddenly disappeared!"

Not that Loewen's future suddenly appeared. True, he had been involved with the setting up of computer systems since 1959, and by 1965 the IBM 360 series was out, with hardware that, combined with the business language of CO-BOL, provided the technological atmosphere in which the idea could grow. ("Had I had this idea ten years earlier, it wouldn't have worked technologically," he states today.) But it would be a number of difficult years before the concept would bear any real financial fruit.

Loewen was married by this time and had three of his eventual five children. Still, he'd managed to save some money, and he quickly made a deal with Fidelity Trust, in a 50–50 partnership. The trust company put up $10,000, and Loewen put up $5,000, plus lots and lots of legwork. (He bought them out in 1973, by which time they had jointly spent $50,000 on the business. And he had to borrow money in order to buy them out, too.)

He called the new business Comcheq, and it did "very meagerly" that first year. To be exact, for the year ending May 31, 1969, Loewen's baby brought in $1,454 for its two employees. He lived frugally, drawing $500 a month from the company, managing to keep up his mortgage, his wife "somehow supplying us with food." (He jokes that the family likes to kid his wife that they wish they were once again as poor as they were in those days; then she'd have to bake that great bread of hers.)

Much of the first year was spent developing the system from scratch, as well as drumming—or should we say scraping—up new business. "We considered any company with over fifty people on its payroll a prospect," he recollects. "I used to drive down the streets of Winnipeg, and if I saw a parking lot big enough, I'd go in." They calculated what to charge on the basis of what it would cost each company to do it themselves. "There had to be a reasonable margin of saving." The big question was: What would it cost Comcheq to produce those paycheques? "I was pleasantly surprised that the computer cost would leave quite a reasonable margin for selling costs."

The selling price back in 1969 was $7.50 per payroll, plus 25¢ per cheque for salaried employees and 35¢ for hourly ones. "There was no doubt that there was a saving for employers."

But try to tell that to Winnipegers. As Loewen remembers, "The way it evolved was kind of funny: It was easy to get people interested, but difficult to get them to take the system." There're Canadians for you. It wasn't until early December 1968 that Comcheq landed its first two customers, who had a total of 135 employees. And late that same month, the president of the struggling firm got a promise that "if we were still in business, we'd get the account of the Airline Hotel in April of 1970." They had 100 employees.

That same cold and dreary month, Loewen had to make a crucial decision: Was he going to devote a full year to those two customers? He made the commitment, and "it was a long winter." He didn't pick up another firm until April, and in June 350 employees with Federal Pioneer Electric climbed on board. Loewen's anecdote is hilarious: "Prospective customers would always ask me who was already on the system, and I'd start listing them, very slowly, hoping that they'd interrupt me."

By late 1969 he could talk a little faster. When Computer Sciences Canada tried to get him to move the business to Calgary, he opened a branch office there instead. And in retrospect, at least from the mid-'80s, "I knew the system would work well within a year. I never had anything but full confidence in it." One of the most significant clients was the Westin Hotel chain, which wanted a payroll service in Calgary. As the hotels spread across the country, Comcheq moved with them. Indeed, Westin was the first client in both Vancouver and Montreal.

To give a sense of Comcheq's growth (and, with the exception of banks, who are Loewen's strongest competitors, his is the largest payroll-processing company in Canada), here are some key years:

1970—Up to $28,672 in sales, and three employees.
1975—$614,853, with nearly two dozen employ-

ees, spread out in Montreal, Toronto, Calgary, Edmonton, and Vancouver, as well as Winnipeg.

1980—$2.7 million in sales, and about 75 employees.

1985—$8.7 million, with 180 employees in 11 cities across Canada, including Halifax, Quebec City, Ottawa, London, and Regina.

1986—$10.8 million, with over 200 employees in 16 cities, including Banff, Victoria, and Saskatoon.

The largest company that Comcheq signs cheques for is Scott's, a/k/a Kentucky Fried Chicken; the largest Top 500 is Molson's payroll, numbering in the thousands. Altogether, over 3,500 clients, with about 300,000 employees, use the services of Bill Loewen. Every branch of Comcheq does its own processing, using the computers located in Winnipeg, and all cheques are drawn from one bank account in that city.

Interestingly, Comcheq has never owned a computer! "We buy time from computer utilities," Loewen says. "Payroll requires a large and powerful computer, and most processing is done at night. And it's always less expensive to buy nonprime from a large computer."

Bill Loewen is the largest shareholder, with his wife the second largest; there are ten others who own a small amount of shares. And they are quite profit-sharing-oriented. There is a plan for all employees who stay with the firm for over a year; after four years, there is over $500,000 in the fund. Much of the staff also gets profit bonuses on top of their regular salary.

Loewen, a man who once counted cars' spaces in Winnipeg lots, thinks that Comcheq will "easily hit fifteen to twenty million dollars by 1990," recognizing that his growth is somewhat dependent upon the economy. "If the unemployment figure falls, we'll grow faster than that," he declares confidently.

But he hasn't stopped creating other ideas, other products. Such as his Electronic Time Card, which "evolved out of our exposure to collecting data and helping clients run their businesses." A number of electronics people, including Loewen's son, developed it. Having installed it in three factories, he expects it to "break out into the market next year."

The ETC is an "on-line" terminal which is used in factories where time and production information must be collected for costing purposes. They can be located throughout the factory, wired to a microcomputer, allowing managers to obtain instantaneous information on employees, expenses, and productivity.

Comcheq has also developed a front-end processor for microcomputers, which creates data collection for clients who have offices across the country. Now, a chain store can collect payroll information into a central location. Still in the works: a way of dispersing payroll funds to employees from a terminal on location, making it more convenient for bosses to zap their cheques to their workers. "We've already designed and built these terminals," Loewen says.

Loewen has had a number of disappointments, captured in his brisk declaration that "it would be a great coup for the taxpayers if we handled government cheques!" but he notes rather bitterly, "empire building interfered, and the Manitoba government ended up buying a U.S. system. The installation alone cost $500,000 more than we would have charged for the first year!" Who's surprised? And, natch, "the system they're using is expensive in terms of staff and computer time."

Profits before taxes are considerably better than 10% at Comcheq, which meant well above $1 million a year by 1985. The key to the bucks is soon clear: Part of Loewen's arrangement with his clients is that by handling their payroll banking, they earn interest on the money sitting in the bank each month. And interest on all those millions quickly adds up.

The latest breakthrough is Loewen's recent agreement with the Great-West Life Assurance Co., of his chosen city, and the Principal Savings and Trust Co., of Edmonton, to provide for RRSP payments through payroll, which could well add to his ever-growing market. And what about their new Cashex Financial Terminal, providing paycheques at work or in shopping centres? There were 20 across Winnipeg by late 1987, with plans for all of Canada. Bill Loewen has gone a long way since his first two customers in Winnipeg, and the potential seems open-ended, in spite of a never-ending head-on battle with the chartered banks, who followed him into the field less than a year after he began.

"It's a great privilege to be able to build and run your own business," says Loewen. "I see myself as being fortunate to be able to practise my profession to the ultimate. Initially, you know, I was an accountant." And secondarily, clearly, a successful entrepreneur.

## MERRY TIMES IN THE MARITIMES

*Phil Robinson*

There are self-made men, and there are SELF-MADE MEN!! Then again, there are men like Phillip M. Robinson, high school dropout, drifter, Canadian equivalent of wrong-way Corrigan (from Edmonton to Halifax, rather than vice versa), who is currently president of Eastland Capital Limited, Eastland Realty Services Limited, Eastland Properties Limited, Eastland Leasing and Brokerage Limited, and Canadian Property Investors' Trust—and Lord knows how much more by the time this sees print.

Phil Robinson was born in Edmonton in 1949 to a draftsman father who had arrived from England with $100, worked for the city, and eventually "clawed through the engineering department at Interprovincial Pipeline." It was a large family, consisting of three sisters and three brothers, and Phil showed some leadership: He won the Queen's Scout of the Year Award in Alberta, and was quarterback of the football team, before dropping out of school. As he explains it, "I moved out on my sixteenth birthday. My mother was regimented about what time dinner was, and football practice always ended an hour after dinnertime."

From then on, he was always working: Fighting forest fires in northern Alberta. Digging ditches in the cotton fields of Alabama. Running a Ramada Inn in Phoenix (until they discovered that he lacked a green card). Working as a bellboy and pool cleaner at a hotel in Miami, until he was eventually made night manager, since he "could deal with people." After wintering in Miami like a good Canadian, Robinson caught the cheapest plane back to Canada, and it happened that that one landed in Montreal. So then it was jobs at Simpson's, selling clothes, and eventually tires in the auto shop.

Then—Glorious Meeting—Phil Robinson sold five tires to the head of a branch plant of a life insurance company. "If you can sell five tires that I don't need to *me*, you can sell life insurance, young man!" said the older man. It was to be his first exposure to saving money, and why people did that. He began working at Prudential of England, winning the Rookie of the Year Award and making $250 a week. "They published me in the Life Underwriters Book as a hotshot salesman!" he says with a smile, lighting up another Camel. Six other companies began calling him to join *them*, and he chose Westmount Life.

There, another Great Meeting, this time with the vice-president of the firm, who made an "an indelible impression" on the youth. "He was a Czech, who taught me the power of questions; how to control thought processes in other minds. That was the beginning of power. If I can make you see visions, you become a listener. You know no bounds, you ask questions, and you get new information all the time."

Robinson's income tripled, and was up to $80,000 by 1970, which a single man could live on back then. "Those were the good old days," he kids. Then, his idol quit the company, and John Hancock Life bought Maritime Life. His former boss was brought in to be VP in charge of the conversion, and he needed a hatchet man. Phil Robinson, Hatchet Man, was brought to Halifax in 1970, where he remains today. "I ran the marketing operation from Montreal to Vancouver, had apartments in Montreal and Toronto, and lived on planes," he recalls. They put him on a much lower salary—$35,000—but it gave him head-office exposure. Still, he was aware that his lack of formal education, among all those actuaries and M.B.A.s, would be a drawback.

Then, another striking moment: His mentor quit and moved to Toronto, and Robinson found himself important "because I had certain information." He had a decision to make: "If I wasn't going to go for president of this firm, then who would?" It wouldn't be Phil Robinson; after nine months, he quit and started his own company. It was 1972, he was newly married, and he founded P. M. Robinson & Associates Ltd., which became the Eastland Group Limited in December 1984. Another blow on behalf of high school dropouts everywhere.

"I had learned from the life insurance business that you

make money if you sell a policy. But how do you know if someone *needs* that policy?" So Robinson came up with "a simple programme": For $35 an hour, he would look into someone's "whole situation and examine their estate."

So he did estate planning, writing reports, and, in Robinson's carefully chosen words, "boring shit." He also continued to sell insurance, "getting lucky" when he managed to persuade the Nova Scotia Medical Society to have a group insurance plan. He enrolled all the doctors and made a pretty penny. In 1974 his earnings totalled $140,000.

It was the following year that "*the fun* started!" While on holiday in the Bahamas that November, he ran into a number of players from the Canadian Football League who were not in the Grey Cup. One mentioned that Johnny Rogers's contract had been rejected, meaning that Sam Berger, the owner of his team, would still have to pay Rogers, but he'd not be able to play. "I decided to help Berger," says Robinson, who dreamt up a scheme that the owner would buy an annuity through the Haligonian's company, which could save Berger a lot of money.

Robinson phoned Berger in Montreal and flew up to see him with a contract. Berger heard his story and threw him out of his office. (Wouldn't you?) So he called Johnny "Ordinary Superstar" Rogers and talked *him* into the idea. He soon developed a whole stable of athletes from the Maritimes— "all black guys"—which exposed the Mad Salesman to negotiations. "People were amazed that someone from Halifax with no background was doing such a credible job." He became Rogers's agent and set up a company in Montreal to manage his promotions.

If all this wasn't enough to *make* Phil Robinson (and confuse the reader), the *wunderkind* then moved into real estate. "It was a middle-man function," he admits. MURBs were getting popular, and Robinson quickly made himself MURB king of Atlantic Canada. "From 1974 to today, no one would do bigger business in tax shelter syndication," he says. Since then, Robinson has done $325,000 in tax shelter syndication involving $110 million in equity.

As always, there was a concept behind Robinson's thinking: "I saw how people tried to save tax money. So I made a simple equation: If I can get a doctor who earns $100,000 to save $40,000 in his taxes. . . ." He set up a group of tax lawyers, experts, accountants—a dozen in all, plus another five dozen on a "maintenance basis" in the Eastland Group—and he was on his way to fame and fortune for the umpteenth time.

They were consultants. "What are your objectives?" they would ask their clients. "Do you *want* to pay for Trudeau's airplane?" "Do you want to retire at sixty?" "At fifty?"

So Robinson *et al.* "would develop game plans for these guys. We were pretty high-profile, and I'd enroll them all in a group insurance plan." Doctors then made up 100% of his business; today they are down to one-half that.

You'll not be surprised to hear that one tax shelter Robinson dug up was Canadian films. He flew to Los Angeles and sat down with major distributors. "I can do film financing," he told them. "What's the formula? And I want the films to get played! It's embarrassing when they don't!" His first picture was called *Siege*. Don't look for it in Pauline Kael's collected reviews, but it was, according to Robinson, "an international hit." It cost $350,000 to make, probably looked every penny, and did over $1 million in foreign sales. (Remember, the French think that Jerry Lewis is a *genius*.) Robinson was the production financier; he simply borrowed the 350 Gs from a bank and syndicated it to a group. He expects the film to do another half million in pay TV and syndication, and maybe another $200,000 in Canada and another $500,000 in the United States. "All will get a hundred and fifty percent return on their money," says Robinson, lighting another Camel. In 1985 *DEF-CON 4* opened "at a theatre near you," often closing soon afterward. (It stands for DEFENSE CONDITION 4; we thought you'd never ask. "THE LAST DEFENSE. THE LAST HOPE. THE BATTLE FOR THE FUTURE OF THE WORLD HAS BEGUN." And, one might add, the battle of doctors to avoid paying excessively high taxes to Ottawa is never over, either.) At the bottom of the rather obscure, but still hopefully futuristic, advertisement, it says, "EXECUTIVE PRODUCER, PHILLIP M. ROBINSON."

"The critics hated it," admits Robinson. "It cost $1.1 million, and it's grossing $600,000 a week. I hyped it big at Cannes. It'll do five or ten million." Then, *la pièce de résistance*: "I got a script delivered today called *Nuns with Guns!*" Phil Robinson laughs out loud, but the author glances across his desk to see if he has Mother Teresa's phone number scrawled anywhere.

"In any six months, I get fifty scripts and read ten," says Robinson. "But we've been *successful*: that's the real key! Our job is to build our clients' net worth, through tax shelter and investments. No more selling insurance!"

Robinson has only about a dozen clients now, but it's by choice. They are, as he puts it "one-million-dollar-a-year players. I charge them about two hundred fifty dollars an hour, but I waive the fee when I do the placement of their money. We make *good* investments first, and shelters later; we're not into stocks and bonds." Nor, for that matter, are they into making The Great Canadian Film.

Recent projects are more impressive. Phil Robinson purchased an old furniture factory in 1981 for $1.95 million and "turned it into the most attractive real estate development east of Montreal." It's called Spring Garden Place, it's in Halifax, and it's a beauty. "I sold forty percent of it to a partnership of people," he says, adding, "Doctors are *terrible* money-managers and whiners." The development opened on the first day of spring, 1984, and was 94% occupied within 12 months. "The sales per square foot blows people's minds," preparing them to go and see *Siege* or *Def-Con 4*. In 1987, Robinson began a $24 million second phase.

Robinson's "single most difficult achievement" was the establishing of the Canadian Property Investors' Trust, which was the leading mutual fund in Canada in 1984. It invests in real estate, shopping centres, and mixed retail offices. He put zero money into it; it was an RRSP fund, which hit the street and raised $6 million overnight. Its assets are now over $27 million. The trust buys and sells buildings, and the fund increased 32% during 1984.

He is now becoming a consultant to pension funds and life insurance companies, having sold all his buildings to a limited partnership. "I converted all my equity to cash, so there would be no conflict of interest with my clients. I've got enough money now and don't want to risk the farm everytime I go to the plate." By his 45th birthday Robinson expects his fund to be worth half a billion dollars. He is 38 this year. And of course the management payment for the fund advisor will be "a multi-million-dollar retainer." Not that it really matters; Phil Robinson had vowed when he was

25 that he would be a millionaire by the age of 30; he missed it by eight months.

Robinson has hired a new president for the Eastland Group, so he's now chairman and CEO, and "basically is a salesman again." He's still "the key player, but not on the accounting side, where I'm not an expert; I defer to experts." His empire tottered during the early 1980s, and he found that he had to stop paying tradesmen. He called everyone in and told them, "You'll be paid *after* the banks get theirs." Then he paid off the banks, and finally the tradesmen. He's not too fond of banks, saying that they should be "in the trunk. When they get into a car, and into the front seat, it's a hard struggle to stay on the road. I call them the Fairweather Umbrella Company; the first sign of rain, they want the umbrella back." He has since "made peace with the banks."

There's a farm with horses near Annapolis, three children under the age of ten, and a beautiful wife. Which is why Phil Robinson is "not into empire building; I'm more into the farm and the family." But he knew how to keep making people money, "so they'll be back. Money is stupid. It doesn't do anything. It has to be invested. I'm into the *fun* of it now." (The fun includes good deeds, such as supplying the ballet school in Halifax with a free studio in one of his buildings, and giving money to the Children's Hospital.)

The goal is clear: "To make every deal work. *Every one.*" And the philosophy is clear as well: "Don't cheat. You can be late, but you don't cheat. I didn't fuck around the tradesmen. Find out what the other guy wants before you shoot. Ask questions, control the meeting, and control negotiations. People appreciate people who listen."

He's gone a long way since hitchhiking across North America, and he now has $5 million in personal equity. "I've made *all* my money in fees, and in giving advice," he says. Phillip M. Robinson lights up another Camel, swivels in his chair, and turns to the huge steel engraving behind him. It is the battle of Waterloo, guns blazing, men on horseback shooting, swinging swords, falling on all sides. "Can you pick out the bankers and developers in this picture?" Phil Robinson asks with a grin. "The bankers are in the saddle, and all on salary."

# THE LITTLE
# AIRLINE THAT COULD

*Victor Pappalardo*

Everything about Victor Pappalardo is bigger than life: his name, for one thing; his huge belly and double chin; his long cigar, his large sunglasses; the excessive roar of the traffic from Front Street outside his oversized office window; the giant unframed map of the Toronto Island airport on the wall behind him; the blowups of newspaper advertisements pinned up on all sides, screaming, FLY CITY EXPRESS! THE TIME & MONEY SAVER! MONTREAL, $59! OTTAWA, $59! It seems only right when he orders a double cappuchino.

There is another ad, mixed in with his own, which gives a further clue to the glorious success of V.P.: FLYING THAT COSTS LESS THAN DRIVING. $39, MONTREAL TO NEWARK! PEOPLE EXPRESS—FLY SMART! Yes, indeed, Pappalardo's City Express (Cité Express *en francais*; it's a wondrously bilingual name for a company that is flying in and out of Montreal and Ottawa all the time) is not only Canada's fastest-growing commuter airline, but one that could well become this nation's version of People Express in the United States: Surprisingly cheap, surprisingly convenient, and with a much happier ending.

Pappalardo was born in April 1943, in Montreal. His mother was Tunisian of Italian parentage. His father had emigrated to Buenos Aires at the age of 17 for a year, then to Rio for two, then to New York City for seven, and finally ended up in Montreal in 1928. "He's a *real* Sicilian!" declares his very successful son. "That's what makes the country; the inspiration of the School of Hard Knocks that our parents attended."

V.P. was the third of three children, and the first boy. The first child, a daughter, died at the age of six months, and a second daughter, nearly a decade older than Victor, the president and 100% owner of City Express, is married, with three grown children.

Victor's father washed dishes, worked in construction and as a plasterer, tradesman, and contractor, and retired 25 years ago. Now nearly 80, he "travels around with my mother. They're like two youngsters!" The family lived in the west end, in the Côte de Neige and Côte St. Luc areas, although there is a community of nearly a quarter million Italians in Montreal. "We never ghettoized ourselves—that was important, and stayed with me throughout my life." Indeed, Pappalardo even turned down the chance to be the president of the Italian Student Council, insisting that "I'm not interested in Italians alone; I want to get out and blend in!" (He speaks English and French fluently, as well as Italian. He spoke French and Italian at home.)

Pappalardo used to be taken out to the construction sites by his father, and "it really exposed me! I saw how things got mechanized and organized, and I've always been good at both, myself." When in high school, he always handled the business activities for the various clubs. When in college, earning his B.A. in political science and economics at Loyola, he began to buy and sell rooming houses, even in the middle of final exams.

He recalls borrowing money to buy a Volkswagen for $600, quickly paying back the loan to the bank. A year later, he went and asked for $1,500 to buy a house. When the bank manager said that it was impossible—he was only 22, after all—Pappalardo reminded the man that he had been loaned money for a car, and "*I've got a business proposition here!* If you won't loan me the money for a revenue property, then there's something wrong with this bank!" He threatened to go to the general manager of the bank if he didn't have the cash by 11:00 the following morning. The next day, he had his money.

Pappalardo bought and sold "a good dozen properties" over the space of a half a dozen years, and "made a respectable income." He had started off as a medical student but lacked the "staying power academically to go through a decade of schooling. And I was surrounded by the business environment of my parents." He finally announced, to anyone who was listening, "To hell with this! My future will be in business!"

He had always been fascinated by aviation—he used to go to the airport to watch the planes, and would window-gaze as they went by when he was in school—so he loaded freight at Nordair at the age of 19. That same year, he told a buddy who wanted to be a pilot. "*You* be a pilot; *I'll* own Nordair or run my own airline." The friend is a pilot today, and you already know about Pappalardo. "It was just a feeling I had at the time."

When he graduated from Loyola with his "B.A. for Bugger-All degree," he told his father that "I've got the paper, but it's not worth a helluva lot." "You'll do what you have to do," said papa. We should mention that young Victor had close to $25,000 in the bank by the time he was in his early 20s.

Victor stayed at Nordair for five years full time, working at reservations, charter flights, even in the traffic area. He finally left the airline in 1969, when he reached a point where he had no future there. He was a senior sales rep at the time, earning $15,000 a year. But he was soon offered a job at Quebecair to start their charter division. It involved a cut in salary, but he helped take their business from nothing to $23 million, and gained invaluable experience. "Those were the years when they made money," he says, lighting his cigar. In 1970 he married a French-Canadian who was secretary to the president of Nordair, and was ribbed plenty when he jumped/flew to Quebecair. They now have four children between the ages of 14 and 7.

Victor Pappalardo was always well taken care of when he worked for others, getting a percentage of sales and profits. "I was a performer, and they knew that if they didn't pay me well, I could go somewhere else." Besides, he knew where he was heading, and money was not the primary object. In 1975 he was called back to Nordair and hired as VP, marketing and sales. He left his $40,000 position at Quebecair because he was interested in Nordair's stock options. All the while, he was still buying and selling real estate, and buying apartments as well. So he made one of the conditions of all his employment that he can be free to do what he wanted to do. Be sure to remember to ask *your* boss that.

Victor was at Nordair for another six years, leaving in 1981 as group VP, customer service. "All the areas I knew and did from way back when were under my control," he remembers. So it was only natural that he eventually left to go into the business of buying, selling, and leasing airplanes. The firm was called Aeroleasing and Sales and "didn't cost too much money" to start. He bought Viscounts and Twin Otters, which he sold to Africa. The company also trained airline personnel and provided pilots to work overseas. He owned/owns 100%, of course, and the firm continues to operate out of Montreal.

From the start, it had sales of $12 to 15 million, with "fair" profits.

There were some disappointments during this period. Also in 1981, a company called Ontario World Airlines went bankrupt, and Pappalardo bought it from the receiver for the licences and assets. But the Canadian Transport Commission turned down his right to use the licence, and he "was disgusted with the matter." It has cost $250,000, which he eventually got back. "It was political, the reason why we were turned down. I hadn't applied my poli-sci knowledge from university!" He happily mentions that, to this day, he has yet to donate one cent to any of the major federal parties, "and we've got everything we want!"

In 1983 his uncle, who owns MTV, Multilingual Television, whose second floor he uses for his City Express offices, sent him a clipping about a "little airline for sale." It was called Air Atonabee, based in Peterborough, and Pappalardo didn't want just a charter licence, he wanted "the whole company." They began negotiating in November of that year, and in March 1984 they struck their deal. The banks were ready to pull the plug on the unsuccessful firm, and Victor injected working capital into it. He bought it and took over all its debts, for around $2 million. He did not even have to use his lines of credit at the bank; he's only used the institutions since to finance the buses that now take happy passengers from downtown Toronto to the Island Airport, and the Dash 8s he has bought.

Pappalardo knew that he had just bought a potential money-making machine. "I was aware of what was going on in the industry, and in the States, too. [Deregulation, opening the way to lower fares and "deals" such as those which made People Express such a great success story until it overextended itself.] How could two hundred and fifty million people in the U.S. go on a joyride and Canadians have no advantage?" To put it another way, how much longer would Canadians tolerate watching Yankees fly from New York to Los Angeles for $199 round trip, while their fellow countrymen were paying $250 *one way*, from Winnipeg to Toronto?

Pappalardo, ever the crafty entrepreneur, said, "Look. Either we sit and wait for deregulation out of Ottawa, or we buy Air Atonabee and get a route structure which is the *core* of the market: Montreal-Toronto and Ottawa-Toronto." Those routes were in the licence structure of the airline he was purchasing. But there was a problem: Air Atonabee had restrictions on the size of the airline and the type of planes. Victor got around the restrictions by consulting with Lloyd Axworthy and Don Mazankowski first, telling them how he had "gotten jerked around by Jean-Luc Pepin once before." They told him to get going with what was there, and deregulation would come, in time. And it has.

So Pappalardo went "full steam ahead" with his plans, buying a Dash 7 from Israel, even though he lacked legal ownership of the airline at the time he did it. Numbers, as always, tell much of the astounding success story: Air Atonabee—talk about unsexy names!—was hitting $2 million in sales when Pappalardo took it over. He sold $1.3 million worth of tickets by the end of that July, and was up to $4 million by the end of that year. Sales at the end of 1985 were in the range of $14 to 15 million, and were increasing $300,000 per month. City Express was in the $22 to 23 million range at the end of 1986, and well over $35 million by late 1987.

Pappalardo changed the name of the airline to City Express, since he needed something to say "downtown-to-downtown," which is, perhaps, its second greatest attraction. His Sanders, and later Dash 7s, were flying in and out of the Toronto Island Airport, which is only ten minutes south of the heart of Toronto's business district, rather than 30 or 40 minutes by cab or limo out to Pearson International Airport, northwest of the city. "We had to add pizzazz!" he says, referring to the bright colour scheme on his planes and buses. There were 54 employees when he took over; over 180 in 1986; over 350 by late 1987.

*'We are very aggressive!'* he asserts, and you'd better believe him. He had to do all the training of his pilots, and the Island Airport is hardly luxurious, but the price has been irresistible: $59 for the Toronto-Ottawa route and $89 for Montreal-Toronto, compared with $123 one way on Air Canada. A Canadian People Express.

After only one year of flying Ottawa-Toronto, his load factor is 75%, which is remarkable. The Montreal-Toronto route, which he began only in mid-September 1985, was running 46% just six weeks later, and Victor points out quickly that, "for a new start-up, that's not bad. There are other airlines with the same route for many years, and they are only at forty-eight to fifty-two percent."

Other routes now include Toronto-London, London-Ottawa, London-Montreal, Montreal-Ottawa, Peterborough-Ottawa, Peterborough-Montreal, Toronto-Detroit, Hamilton-Ottawa, Hamilton-Montreal, and a number of Hamilton-Toronto flights that he may well drop to improve the bottom line. By late 1987, his airline was offering over 80 flights a day. But the plans for the future are as exciting as, well, as owning 100% of your own airline when just two decades earlier you were carting luggage. Pappalardo plans to expand into the London-Toronto and the Quebec City-Toronto routes, and since April 1987, was offering flights to Newark from downtown Toronto, which put 4 million residents in the southern Ontario region at the thrilling advantage of getting to the New York City area for $99, when the biggies ask up to $149 one way for the same.

"Toronto and Dorval to Newark! Those will be *real* winners!" says Victor Pappalardo, noting that "some new rules and regulations out of Ottawa are looser than they used to be." He'd also love to fly Pearson/Toronto International to other Canadian cities, just like the giants. "It's a lot of hard work," he says; "a lot of action and no talk! Just go ahead and do the jump—go right into the marketplace!" He adds that "it's not a one-man show; you need good people." But those good people sure needed the V.I.P. VP to get the whole thing off the ground literally.

## 6.
# MANUFACTURING

## I Can Make It for You Wholesale

From the traditional "drawers of water and hewers of wood," Canadians have found themselves capable of manufacturing thousands of various products. In this chapter we look at 11 men who make a variety of goods. For the household, we have Doug Freeman of A-Z Sponge of Vancouver; Rex Faithfull of Creative International of Toronto (kettles, slow cookers, *et al.*); H. Thomas Beck of Noma (Christmas lights, extension cords, lawn mowers, snow blowers, etc.); and Serge Racine of Quebec's Shermag (furniture). For cars and aerospace, respectively, there are Bill Bartels of Canparts Automotive of Cambridge, Ontario, and George Yui, of Diemaster. In the realm of safety and hygiene, there are Ernie Butler of Ruxton Water Filters; Gerald Yaffe of Safety House of Canada (first aid kits, fire extinguishers, and 10,000 other things); Steve Chepa of Dicon (smoke detectors); and Leslie Hulicsko of Regina's Rite Way Manufacturing Co. Ltd. (street sweepers and rock pickers). And—a bit of whimsy here—a man who keeps it all together, Sandy Archibald of Britex, of Bridgetown, Nova Scotia, which makes elastic for bras, girdles, and a hundred other fabrics and products.

There are some interesting patterns found in the entrepreneurs who make up this chapter on manufacturing: First, they are, on average, the oldest of any in this book. The youngest is 42, the oldest is 63, and five of them are 50 and over, three in their 60s. Also, interestingly, nearly one-half were born in countries other than this one: They come from England, Hungary, New York, and Manchuria. Also—atypical for this book as a whole—nearly half created their businesses in relatively small towns: Sherbrooke, Quebec; Cambridge, Ontario; Moose Jaw, Saskatchewan; Regina, ditto; and Bridgetown, Nova Scotia.

Why would these business people be so different from those in other chapters? The ages might suggest that setting up factories and succeeding in manufacturing products takes many years longer than, say, creating the concept for a store. The non-Canadian origin of many of them might suggest that immigrants are more at home with manufacturing than, perhaps, a service industry or a faddish fashion product or food. And as for the small towns, I am totally stumped.

But what *is* clear in this chapter is that each of these men discovered a need, a niche in the marketplace, and went after it with determination. As Serge Racine (who has a Ph.D. in economics, one of a handful of doctorates in this book) states, "We know what tastes are in furniture in each area of the country." Doug Freeman, on the other hand, the unproud owner of a "Mickey Mouse diploma" from England, creates dozen of different uses for sponges, ice packs, etc., and flogs them with wit and verve. Rex Faithfull and his partner designed a new kettle, approached Canadian Tire, and soon exported it around the globe. Tom Beck and his late mother steadily took over the Christmas light market in Canada, and then purchased failing companies, one after another, which manufactured other household products—to the point where he has broken $300 million in sales—with expectations of half a billion dollars annually, and well over 2,000 employees, by the end of this decade.

Bill Bartels specialized wisely in replacement disk parts for brakes, as did George Yui with his tool and die concern. Lousy water moved Ernie Butler to create his water filters, and a drive to "go out and build demand" is what helped make Gerald Yaffe's Safety House a nearly $50 million business. "Smoke detectors were the coming thing," understood Steve Chepa and his partner at Dicon, and a rage over incompetent street sweepers on the market is what moved Leslie Hulicsko to create his own. And a thrust "to be competitive in the world market" with his elastic firm made Sandy Archibald's Britex the amazing success story it is, in small-town Nova Scotia.

Most of these men are extremely enlightened in their labour relations, with good union relationships, or profit sharing, or a careful nurturing of employee satisfaction. (It's not by chance that at least three of these men took over bankrupt companies and led them to success—Racine, Beck, and Archibald—and a number of others took over the unsuccessful products of earlier companies and made them do a lot better in the marketplace—Freeman, Yaffe, and Chepa.)

Some of these entrepreneurs have a passionate belief in a corporate culture and employee relations (Racine, Beck, and Archibald); all have worked 60- to 80-hour weeks, taking pennies home for many years, in order to build company equity. And every one has been highly—often stunningly—creative in sales and marketing, getting the products out on the market, onto the shelves, and eventually into the home. Even around the globe.

"Lean and mean" was a common expression of these men; Serge Racine of Shermag notes his lack of a secretary, and Leslie Hulicsko of Rite Way Manufacturing adds that one "must watch costs; no fancy offices; watch every dollar." Four of these companies have gone public; a number of others would love to, to have the money to expand their businesses even further. Some are millionaires; others are still struggling and have barely begun to take a decent wage home. But always—always—the same things in common: an insistence on good service, top quality, and continual improvement of their products.

## SPONGING UP PROFITS

### Douglas Freeman

Creativity is always an important aspect of business success, but in the case of Douglas Freeman of A-Z Sponge and Foam Products Ltd. of New Westminster, British Columbia, it is at its core. The 60-plus years of Freeman have been years of almost nonstop creativity, mixed with lots of hard work, some luck, but mainly very canny marketing strategies.

Freeman was born in Tonypandy, South Wales, in 1924, to a Russian-born father who was one of 26 children. When Douglas was 3, the family moved to London, after the father's store at Pithead went bankrupt along with those deadly mines of Wales. So young Doug grew up in London, graduating high school, but not before showing some entrepreneurial flair: When he was 15, some samples came in for his father, who was sick in bed. So the teenager hopped a bus, stopped at London's biggest department store, and sold 1,000 hot water bottle covers to the place, at 11 pence and a half-penny apiece. When he returned home that evening, the father was stunned; he'd never been able to sell to department stores.

During the war Freeman was 4-F, having suffered a major back injury as a youth, but he served as a part-time volunteer fireman during the blitz. "I saw the first V-1s come over, when I was on night duty, and they scared the shit out of me." Interested in commerce, he went to the School of Economic Science in London, earning "some kind of Mickey Mouse diploma." Then his father died in 1941, meaning that Doug had to earn some money to help support his mother and younger sister. (He was the second child of three.) He trained as a projectionist at Europe's largest theatre, which had one hour of vaudeville, followed by three hours of movies, for 15¢; "Those were the days!" the charming, grey-bearded, British-accented man says today.

When the war ended, he was unsure of what to do, so he took an exam to become a schoolteacher, teaching in the slums of London for a year. But on the side, naturally, he made ten pounds a day selling war assets to Army-Navy stores. Soon, he dropped teaching and began flying to Belgium, three times a week, to buy the legal limit—as well as illegal amounts—of nylon stockings, wrapping them around his belt and later selling them on the black market. (He brought back coffee as well.) He was never caught, but when he saw how desperate England was in the late 1940s, he approached the American and Canadian embassies, and the latter said "welcome." For £33, he booked second-class passage to Halifax on a boat full of war brides.

In 1947 Freeman landed in the New World, quickly taking the train to Toronto, where he soon landed a job selling auto parts. He bought a 1938 Dodge, sent for his mother and brother, and bought a bungalow. But after one winter in Toronto, "that was enough! Everyone I spoke with told me, 'When I retire, I'm going to Vancouver.' So I figured, if Vancouver is such a Paradise, why should I start my career in Toronto?"

His first job in Paradise was with the National Biscuit Company, where he was told that there was no job, but a stock of jellies and creams in two-pound boxes, if he wanted to sell them at 15% commission. "I called on every mom-and-pop store in Vancouver!" declares the supersalesman. He made 56 calls on Monday, 50 more on Tuesday, always delivering on the next day. "The other guys would call on people every two weeks!" exclaims Freeman, still surprised at how lazy other people are. "Dummy that I was, I made every call." Sales increased over 100%, and, as you can imagine, at the next sales meeting all 22 salesmen refused to talk to him. "The boss had bawled all the others out for selling so few."

After three months he was fired, moved on to sell candy for Rowntree, and eventually sold imported candies from England. "We sold $350,000 worth of Pez in Vancouver!" he says with enjoyment, cracking the Safeway account for Morris Import Sales. He also sold iced mints, "which sold like hell in the stores!" He was at that place until 1956, before one of his greatest triumphs took place.

It was an ad for a salesman for the *Wall Street Journal,* to push subscriptions for the paper. It had never been successful in Canada before, but thank heavens, Douglas Freeman was unaware of this lousy track record. So he designed a three-minute sales pitch for Canada, selling the $20-a-year subscription, which would give $10 to the salesman up front. (Sell nine more, an extra $30; another nine, another $30.)

Freeman was soon up to three, four, five subscriptions a day, and, as he says, "I was *really* making money!" He was actually outselling every salesman in the States by two to one, and the word got out. He was called down to Chicago to meet with the national sales director. "How do you do it?" Freeman insisted on a slum area, knowing that it was virgin territory, and took him along, making five sales with his first five pitches. "I've seen enough!" cried the sales director, who offered Douglas Freeman the job of national sales manager for all of Canada. "I didn't want to do it," recalls Freeman. "I was making up to four hundred dollars a week, and he offered me only one hundred and fifty dollars a week, plus an open expense account" (adding "don't be stingy!").

So it was off to Calgary, where SuperSalesman discovered that no one had ever been canvassed by the paper. He came out of one building in the oil town with 40 subscriptions, and on it went. "I was making pretty good bucks and really loved that job," he says, and he was soon the national trainer for the States, based in Montreal. But he was now married—with a ten-month honeymoon that the *Journal* paid for—had a baby, and was leaving his family on Sunday nights and returning the following Saturday morning. "Who are you married to?" his young wife began asking.

So it was back to Vancouver with *famille* in tow, working for the *Vancouver Province* briefly, making surveys of its problems, and then a job with a chemical company, as its sales manager, for a number of years. Since the market was declining in fuel oil additives, he pushed the firm into plastics, seeing it as the future.

Then came a fateful trip to Montreal in 1960. Freeman walked around Steinberg's and saw a package of sponges. He knew from his background that they were not available in Vancouver. "You do any business out west?" he asked a nice gentleman there. "No." "We'd like to buy your product." And he purchased $1,000 worth. He went back and sold it to Safeway, Army-Navy, SuperValu, and other stores in his adopted city, buying and reselling at a good profit.

Then, one day, a man at Army-Navy needed random pieces of foam. Freeman said he would find some, and encountered a local supplier "with a mountain of it. He couldn't get rid of it! He offered to give it to me for free if I took it away, but I gave him fifteen cents a pound." He realized that the only way to merchandize the stuff was to weigh it, mark it with a retail price, and sell it. So he did that and shipped it off to the stores. "I made big bucks for the chemical company," recalls Freeman.

But one is not always appreciated, as we all know so well. One day in 1965 a new owner came in and told Freeman that he "didn't like this plastics business" and wanted to get rid of it. Freeman offered to buy the inventory for no money, giving him promissory notes. A business was born: He took a small warehouse for $25 a month, and within six months, while Freeman was raking in the business, the chemical company had gone bankrupt.

A-Z Sponge and Foam Products Ltd., incorporated in 1966, sold $70,000 in its first year, making $15,000 in profits. The second year, it was up to $200,000; the third year, $500,000; the fourth year, $900,000; the fifth year, $1.2 million. And that was only buying and selling the stuff; Freeman didn't start manufacturing until 1978. But there are lots of good stories, along with the profits, such as the carload of rejected car-seat foams that Freeman bought, selling the things to Army-Navy stores for $2 each (he had paid $1, and had

Goodrich pay for the freight). People would mill around them in the stores, grabbing for them. When Freeman asked a man what he planned to do with his, he replied, "I don't know. I'll put it in the basement and I'll eventually find a use for it." Of such lines are careers built.

Another anecdote: Army-Navy told Freeman that they wanted cut-to-size camping pads, to lay sleeping bags on. So our hero had "a brilliant idea: White was not it; *green* was it! To match the grass!" A man at Goodrich agreed to make green foam for Freeman, and "that was a real turning point; we went to $1.2 million in sales that year." The two-inch pads sold for $3.12 wholesale, and the stores sold them for $4.99. With the 12% profit on that product, Freeman was able to buy a sailboat that year. (He had already built a house in North Vancouver.)

Which leads us to that tense moment when the distributors of foam tried to cut Freeman out, so he phoned Seattle—"I didn't want to deal with Canada!"—and had railway cars ship foam up to Vancouver. Since he needed a warehouse on trackage, he found a dumpy factory on Water Street, called in high school kids, and "cleaned the filthy place up, wrapping the pipes to kill the condensation." Within three months the entire 8,000 square feet was filled with foam. He bought a small saw and a table (to cut the 54 inches down to 27 inches), and his sales were up to $1.7 million by 1971.

By early 1972 he moved "to the boonies"—Annasis Island, 18 miles southeast of Vancouver—where he bought 20,000 square feet of building with a 99-year lease, prepaid, plus a dollar a year rent. Now he could order 10-foot high, 87-inch wide, 36-inch deep slabs of foam from California. He became the largest client they had, rolling 350 railway cars in 1977 from them, with 36,000 board feet in each, paying $6,000 for each car-full, selling them for twice that.

By the late 1970s A-Z Sponge and Foam Products Ltd. was the only vertically integrated sponge manufacturer in North America, taking liquid chemicals that you couldn't pronounce the names of, making them into foam blocks, cutting them into sponges, and packaging them. And along with this comes the inspired Freeman creativity, noted above: the Rainbow Pack, of a dozen brightly coloured polyurethane sponges, which he sells to Safeways, London Drugs, Army-Navy, and Woolworth stores in the west for 72¢, who turn around and sell them to you for $1.29 or more. And what of the Eye-Full Towers, filled with assorted household sponges of all different sizes, shapes, and colours? Or the glorious Fun in the Tub, which are designs of pigs, sheep ducks, and fish of various colours which can be pulled out and put back inside square sponges? There are also the sales of foam beds to hotels and motels, which he insists is still "an immature market." Supermarkets, however, are still the biggest buyers of his wonderful sponges. (Including—did we mention it? —Absorba the Great, a car sponge, and a best-seller.)

The number of employees in A-Z is now up to 16, including 4 in the office and a lot of part-time kids. And in January 1987 he opened an office in Los Angeles, "selling the same stuff." But a mind like that of Doug Freeman would never be satisfied with only sponges. For instance, there is the tale of Cold-Ice, the ice packs that you've seen all across the country. In a February in the late 1960s, Freeman went to a packaging show, where MacMillan Bloedel was giving out little packages of ice gel. So when there was a heat wave that year and Army-Navy ran out of ice packs, the president of A-Z Sponge and Foam recalled what MacBlo had done. He picked up ten cases of little gel packs, and sold them in two days, and cleaned out a railway car over the next two months.

Which led him, understandably, to make gel packs for the fishing industry. "Airlines won't let fishing companies fly fish on ice, since the ice melts and stinks up the plane. But my gel packs keep the fish cold." So today, every pound of B.C. salmon which you have enjoyed over the years is shipped with Doug Freeman's ice packs, which sell for 40¢ each. "No one else in this part of the world makes them," says sweet-talking Freeman.

He used to work 16-hour days, 6-day weeks, but today he's slowed down and goes only from 7:00 A.M. to 6:00 P.M. each day. The three kids are already grown, but he still decided to go ahead and sell the place in early 1986 for over $2½ million, until the deal collapsed. "Emotionally, I'm not a manufacturer," he says. "The real fun is still in the selling." And what was the key to success of the British immigrant? "The ability to be rational when the world is crazy," he states, laughing. "You have to have a lot of fun in business. I'm *still* excited when I pick up a $200,000 idea." Plus the fact that "People trust me. I'd sooner lose everything than screw anyone."

He shows this in his generous wages, paying up to $14 an hour to his sponge cutters, along with loads of fringe benefits, which have included dental and medical insurance since the earliest days, as well as profit sharing. So it is a "zero defect shop. It's so rare that we get any complaint. You have to approach a block of foam like a diamond!"

And Douglas Freeman, ever bristling with creative ideas and concepts in the world of business, has somehow managed to turn what must seem like worthless cheap foam to most of us into a business which has allowed him to *buy* diamonds, if not cut them, with sales of close to $5 million in 1987. And if it weren't for those crummy winters in the east, just *imagine* how well he would have done. "If I was in Toronto with this business, I'd be doing over ten million dollars a year!" he cries. But he's really not crying at all.

# PROSPECTING
# GOLD IN KETTLES

### Rex Faithfull

It's called Tut Enterprises, or TTX on the Toronto Stock Exchange, but that's really a misnomer, and a leftover from a reverse takeover of a small mining company once traded on the Vancouver Stock Exchange. The real name of the company—and what it will soon be called everywhere—is Creative International Inc., one of Canada's most successful makers of kettles, toasters, and more. The tale of these two entrepreneurs—Rex Faithfull, chairman, and Herman Herbst, president—is one that is creative with a small *c* as well.

Faithfull was born in Toronto in 1926 and studied chemistry at the University of Toronto. "If you didn't get eighty percent, you were kicked out in the second year," he says, unchagrined at having been kicked out. So he went into business for himself, electroplating precious metals, silverware, etc. Then he branched into manufacturing marine hardware, such as boat fittings and steering wheels, under the name of Canamarine, which he founded in 1951. "It did quite well," and when he found that he had to send out a lot of parts to get them plated, he simply bought a machine that put metallic substance on anything.

Then, Faithfull got "burned badly with some acid" and was laid up for 18 months, during which time he sold his company to a firm in Belleville, Ontario. He later joined them and was made plant manager of the 100-employee outfit, but "it was very difficult to go from president to being someone else's plant manager." He "stood that" until 1960, when he returned to Toronto.

Then, Faithfull began another business with a partner, making trophies—casting parts, polishing, making awards for hockey associations, among others. He also had a woodworking plant, with 60 employees in all. He was a president once again, this time of Orillia Artcraft and Armstrong Trophies in Toronto.

In 1969 Faithfull had another accident, badly injuring his back. It took two spinal fusions to get him on his feet again, and he was laid up for another year. So he sold his company and went into consulting. He did this until 1975, setting up assembly plants, advising new owners how to operate their companies. Then he met Herman Herbst, three years younger, who was a tool-and-die maker and mechanical engineer who had immigrated from Germany in 1956 and had begun Eastern Tool and Manufacturing. Then, in 1974, there was a huge recall, due to lead soldering in the kettles that many firms had been manufacturing. A lot of companies got hurt, including Herbst's, which went under, as a result of bankruptcies of "huge companies and a supplier."

"I knew Herman and I liked him," says Faithfull. Herbst invited Faithfull and a third man to go into business with *him*. In 1976 the men began H & M Metal Stamping, with Faithfull the president and Herbst the secretary-treasurer. They made metal stamping and tool and die for Admiral and Sunbeam, making parts for freezers and refrigerators. They were doing very well when, in late 1977, Venus Electric went bankrupt, owing the men $50,000. They had to rearrange their financing, putting up all their securities, and having their wives sign as well. "We *did* survive it!" declares Faithfull, but it was clearly by the proverbial skin of their teeth.

The entrepreneurial moment soon came: While making parts for Inglis and Proctor-Silex, the men came to realize that "*they* were making the profits, while *we* were doing the work!" So they thought that they would go into kettles again, due to Herbst's history with the product.

The first thing the two men did was to learn from earlier mistakes. Herbst designed a completely new kettle with a plastic top, which eliminated a lot of the soldering, polishing, and tools needed to form a metal one. Since the men were taking so little home from the firm—only around $8,000 each—they saved enough to buy a mould. In the meantime, they made metal parts, working every night, Saturdays and Sundays, creating the tooling they would need for their Dream Kettle. A designer helped with the shape.

After they made a model of the finished product out of wood, they approached Canadian Tire and Woolco, who both liked it and said they could carry it if it was certified and ready for production by September 1979. "That gave us real incentive," recalls Faithfull. "We finished the tooling, made samples, and applied to C.S.A. for certification." After that, they applied for the patent.

In the meantime, every new entrepreneur's nightmare: Most of their customers dropped away—McGraw Edison, Proctor-Silex, and others—since they were about to become competitors! (Does Eaton's help Simpson's? Well, maybe in malls, but where else?)

In the summer of 1979 Faithfull and Herbst produced their first order of 50,000 pieces, "a tremendous order for us at that time!" There were one dozen workers on their small assembly line. They incorporated Creative Appliance that year, with Herbst owning 60%, Faithfull 40%, and delivered the order to Canadian Tire: Canadian entrepreneurship in action.

After their innovative kettle had been shown around, Proctor-Silex was suitably impressed and wanted to buy the rights, claiming that *they* could sell 40,000 a year. The two Canadians had a meeting with the head office in King-of-Prussia, and decided to remain on their own.

Canadian Tire repeated the order, and they picked up an account with Woolco. By 1980 they hit $1 million in sales, moving over 100,000 kettles into kitchens across the country. Profits were around 7½%, and then the men shot their salaries up to $300 a week at that time.

Then they were told, "You have *only one product!*" So they

sat down and designed another kettle, with a bigger handle, four-colour carton, better pouring, and more trim. Rather than sell for only $9.80 wholesale like the other, this new, improved model went for $12. It was a flop, with everyone complaining, "It's just a duplicate of the other!" (And this after all that extra chrome had done so well for Detroit's automobiles back in the '50s.)

Back to the drawing board, literally. They decided to make a kettle with a detachable cord, and began to *think export*. Eaton's quickly requested it for their Viking line, and they agreed, but only if they could also market it under their own name, the B-32 Creative Kettle.

Sales doubled every year. By 1983 they were up to $6 million; by 1985, after a slowdown in 1984, they expected to break $10 million. Other business actions took place: In 1981 Creative bought an existing company's assets in Montreal— Danby Corporation—which had made deep fryers, slow cookers, and hot plates. They paid only $180,000 for it, since it was going out of business. But they "still weren't happy," so they added to their line The Hot Pot, an import, for heating tin cans, good for people living alone or travelling. It would sell for $7 or $8 retail. They then bought the tooling and began to make a better one than those coming in from Taiwan. Their own version sold for around $15 retail.

But the biggest seller continued to be the original kettle, the B-1, which got Creative started. Then they made a little kettle, coincidentally called The Little Kettle, which was also "very successful." And the men continued to look to other markets, other lands. While 70% of their sales were to Canada, they sold to the States, Trinidad, Jamaica, Barbados, France, even Hong Kong, Singapore, and Japan. (They are currently getting certification for their kettles in England and Germany, which is about time, considering the origins of the two owners of Creative.)

Like intelligent entrepreneurs, Faithfull and Herbst have taken advantage of outside assistance whenever available. They use PEMD, help from the government to pay one-half fare and expenses for selling trips to foreign countries, on the understanding that they will give 5% of the profits from that trip back to the government. They have also gotten assistance from the Export Development Corporation to finance their invoices. "We wouldn't sell to Nigeria without government help," says Faithfull, "due to the general unrest there."

But there's no rest at Creative, either. There are at present 15 products, all of them developed by the two partners with the exception of a mixer and can-opener from Hong Kong. By 1982 they knew they needed more money, since every new product cost upwards of $500,000 to produce. So it "seemed only logical" to buy Tut Explorations, renamed Tut Enterprises, that mining company on the VSE. While still on that Exchange, they had it take over Creative and H & H Stamping, and began to have it underwritten on the TSE. By 1983 the latter had new rules, allowing small companies to go public, so they listed as TUT (TTX) and raised $1.5 million from their share offering.

Meanwhile, the boys in the back continue to develop. They've invented the first electronic toaster for Canada with a microchip timer in it, with 40,000 orders for the $29 retail product. The Creative Electronic Toaster is patented, and Faithfull is pleased to inform us that most toasters in Canada had been imported before this one. "All our boxes have a maple leaf stamped on them," he says, playing on our chauvinistic pride. They also found that they had inherited some gold mines in Ontario and Quebec when they had done that reverse takeover with Tut, and hope that they "will make history." Falconbridge is paying Creative $225,000 to work on the mines, which are still 40% owned by Faithfull and Herbst's firm.

"H & H and Creative have always made money," says the chairman of the companies, but due to the appreciation of the takeover of Tut, that cost had to be written off. Still, they expect to start showing good profits in 1987 and beyond, even if Falconbridge *doesn't* literally strike gold.

The men have added a lot of machinery and equipment since their stock offering, and are now running two shifts a day. "We have the orders lined up but can't grow that much in the Canadian market per product, so we're putting more and more effort into the U.S. and world markets." Creative has now captured over 37% of the domestic market for kettles, and 27% of our slow cookers. One-fifth of all deep fryers sold here are also made by Creative.

The latest development is a coffee machine, and Faithfull rejoices that his firm is "a real thorn in everyone else's side," with Proctor-Silex, GE, and Sunbeam all trying to buy them out. "We're making more than they are in Canada, and they're not happy," he gloats. You Canada-Firsters should know that 90% of Proctor-Silex's products are imported, and Sunbeam brings in about 70% of its machines from the Far East.

There are now 130 employees in two factories in suburban Toronto, and Faithfull and Herbst are now looking for other companies in the metal-stamping field to take over. (Since they didn't start to take home "good money" until 1984—now it's up to $60,000 each—they can do that sort of thing.) Both are married; Herbst has two children.

"It's *determination*," says Faithfull, with determination. "We had a goal—to be financially independent. And we wanted to create a company that would be recognized in the industry as a good manufacturer. We are even known for having developed parts of a precision thermostat which is used across the States and England in ovens and refrigerators!

It was a gamble to take over Tut; a calculated risk." But they feel no risk in their new whistling kettle, or in their new ozone generator, which eliminates the need for chemicals in your hot tub or pool, retailing at $850. And with Falconbridge financing 100% of the digging costs on those two crazy gold mines, they have nothing to lose in that category, and everything to gain.

"The industry had made derogatory remarks about a plastic kettle," Faithfull recalls fondly. "Since then, they've all copied our product." And Creative is "*very* automated; no one can touch us, even Japan!" Sales were $12 million in 1986; projected for 1987 is $17 million, at which point they hope to "take it easier." They still make parts for Inglis—hinges, doorframes—as well as parts for Dominion Auto and General Freezer, but they have only about a half dozen outside accounts now; they're busy putting kettles, toasters, and hot pots in kitchens from Signal Hill to Beacon Hill—and around the world as well.

"We're not entrepreneurs," scoffs Rex Faithfull at the thought. "We're just a couple of hardworking guys!"

# THE LITTLE FAMILY
# BUSINESS GROWN BIG

## *H. Thomas Beck*

When we think of family businesses in Canada, we tend to think of the Eatons, the Sobeys, the McCains; those usually begun by creative fathers and continued by often equally creative sons. Which is why the story of Noma Industries Ltd. is so extraordinary. It was founded by a mother—Teresa Beck, a Hungarian immigrant to Canada shortly after the Second World War, and her engineer son, Thomas, who joined her on these promising shores 18 months later. "I never wanted to be a businessman," admits the handsome, square-faced chief executive officer. "Back in school in England, I could never manage to sell [scalp] my soccer tickets for more than their face value! My uncle pushed me into capitalism!" An uncle, a hard-driving mother (who died in 1983), and an "extremely hardworking" son, who managed to turn a tiny extension-cord business (purchased in 1950 for $5,000 "or less") into a miniconglomerate which did over $300 million in sales in 1986. The story of Noma and the Becks is a story of capitalism in action.

H. Thomas Beck was born in Budapest in 1926, the only child of a man who dealt in produce, grain, and potatoes. But his parents divorced when Thomas was young, and "my mother essentially raised me" (although he always went to see his father with great regularity, getting around the capital city of Hungary on buses by the age of six). When the lad was sent off to a boarding school at age nine, his mother decided that she had better have a profession, since she was divorced. So she opened a small couturier shop of her own. Then, in 1939, just weeks before the war that would destroy much of the Hungarian Jewish community—most of Beck's relatives were murdered in the death camps—his mother "fortunately enrolled me in school in England," where she joined him.

Young Thomas was fluent in English within weeks, while his mother went twice a year to couturier shows in Paris, and "made enough to make a living." She was "very bright and intellectual," states her son. "Many Hungarian intellectuals would come regularly to our home in London." He mentions this, he quickly adds, because "we started the business together in Canada."

Beck went to the University of London, graduating as an engineer in 1948. "My mother felt that I should take a profession that would be easy to transfer from country to country," he notes. (On the wall of his north Toronto office, a framed sign reads: ASSOCIATION OF PROFESSIONAL ENGINEERS OF THE PROVINCE OF ONTARIO—HENRY THOMAS BECK.) As luck would have it, his mother's brother, that famous uncle mentioned above, had managed to make it to Toronto in 1939, in one of the last ships out of the doomed continent. "He paid for my education, and his aim was to get the whole family over," recalls Beck. "We were British, so it was a cinch!" Mother came to Toronto in February of 1949, with her only child joining her in July of the following year.

With them they brought significant skills. "In England, my mother learned mass production of ladies' dresses," says Beck. "She was a very capable manager of people. But couture was not considered important to the war effort." Fortunately, the capable managing of people is important at any time.

Beck's uncle bought a tiny business for his sister and nephew, Irving Lamp Sales, which made extension cords. "We bought wire, put plugs on each end, and sold it." There were three employees and a shipper at the start. But they kept going after customers and kept expanding the business, taking home $25 a week each from the firm. Then, just a few years later, in 1953, while baby-sitting for the young couple who lived below their apartment, Beck heard that the woman's late father's estate was about to be liquidated. For around $300, Beck bought the inventory and distribution rights for Parco Products—Paramount Industries—which made Christmas lights.

A decade later, the Becks already had about 15% of the market for the little bulbs and wires in Canada, and their sales were just under a million dollars a year. So when they saw *the* Christmas lights company, Noma (National Outfits Manufacturers Association), floundering, the minnow swallowed the carp. Noma's sales were about $1½ million annually, but it was losing more money than its net worth at the time. "We understood the market," declares Beck confidently. "We were appalled at their inefficiency. We were certain that we could make substantial quality improvements, and events proved us right." Slowly and surely, Noma and the Becks captured the market, and Canadian General Electric eventually quit the business in 1974. Today Noma has well over one-half the market in Christmas lights, and over 50% in artificial trees as well. In "big light sets," they also have more than half: "We're a significant market presence!" Beck says. Through quality workmanship and by pushing their name in television advertisements, Noma sells in the neighborhood of $25 million a year in Christmas-related electrical products and accessories. And by taking over Noma, they were up to 200 employees, with a plant in Owen Sound, Ontario.

Tom Beck and his mother worked from 7:00 every morning until 9:00 every night, six days a week. "But that's nothing special," pooh-poohs the owner. "*Everyone* does that when they start." But not everyone has an uncle who guarantees their bank loans, or gives them strange, but ultimately superior, advice: "My uncle told me when we began our business," recalls Beck, "that at the end of each day, we should pick up every bill and send it out with a cheque. For a year and a half we didn't have a *single* accounts payable! If we got a bill twice a week, that company got two cheques!"

The Becks finally realized, of course, that "it was a bloody nuisance!" But what they didn't mind was that they got the goods whenever they wanted. And they had earned "a reputation that people didn't have to worry about getting paid." The crazy advice displayed Beck's uncle's "tremendous perception of what was needed. The Korean War was on, and there was a shortage of supplies in the early 1950s. I would take our suppliers out to lunch more often than our customers!"

At the start of their unpromising business, the two Hungarian immigrants didn't even have a punch press; all the work was done by primitive soldering. But there was Thomas Beck to do all the selling, most of his visits being in Montreal, Ottawa, and the Toronto area. "My uncle gave me other advice: Cover the area where you can most efficiently do business; don't go running off to Vancouver. There are enough opportunities in Toronto." Indeed, although Noma products are .sold across Canada, fully two-thirds of their business is still done within a 100-mile radius of his chosen city, since such places as Woolco and K-Mart have their head offices in Toronto.

There were risks in all this expansion; Teresa and Tom had to borrow heavily from their bank and were forced to mortgage the building they had just built. But there were favourable side effects, as well: They were given 5% discount for paying off the debt to Noma's owners, and they found that they had no taxes for a few years, since their losses were so great at the start. "But it was a tremendous break for us to buy Noma!"

By the mid-1960s the Becks were the biggest extension-cord manufacturers in Canada, with over 50% of the market. The reason was simple: "The only way people will buy from us is if we are better," says Beck, "and we didn't want to be better in price. We didn't like price cutting. So we decided to put in equipment to shorten our reaction time to orders. We had to be able to deliver. Our credo to this day is 'Always be cost-conscious and service-conscious.' We would do business the way the customers wanted to do business."

It all sounds like so much motherhood, but for the Becks, it proved to be salient to survival: "Woolworth's will do business differently than Canadian Tire, and we had to understand that. And we kept innovating, and getting in new equipment, to keep inventories in a state where we could react quickly to orders and make money." (An example: In extension cords, you sell in a few basic lengths—6 feet, 9 feet, and 15 feet. The Becks expanded their equipment and got more wire into the finished state, so they could deliver incredibly promptly to their customers, just like all those accounts payable, during the first year and a half.)

"We are a customer-driven company!" declares H. Thomas Beck, and the fact that they have never had a static year except for 1969 suggests the truth of his words. By 1968 they started up their own wire company, called Cable Tech, which has been profitable every year of its operation. They started with 25,000 square feet and are now up to 300,000. "Initially, we used it almost entirely to supply ourselves, but now, forty percent of its products are sold to the outside." And in 1971 Beck, Inc., was incorporated in the state of Connecticut to manufacture Christmas light string sets for sale in the United States.

By the early 1970s it was clear that the two Becks, who owned over 90% of their booming business, should go public. "We felt that we could motivate others by giving them a piece of the action." The disadvantage, naturally, was that "we'd have to hang up all our washing for all to see." But with all the flexible insulated wire and cable pouring out of their factories, they'd have no trouble obtaining clotheslines. "And we wanted even the people on the assembly line to be rewarded," he says. "We gave shares of Noma to everyone who'd been working here for more than two years."

By 1973 the number of employees was nearly 300, and they must have been pleased to see Noma Industries Limited offer 260,000 common shares to the public at $8.75 each. They quickly sold out, and the Becks poured it all back into the company. With the splits, each share is worth over $150 now.

In the following year, Noma acquired Canadiana, which made lawn mowers and snow blowers. The company was managing around $3 million in business, but it was doing so poorly the Becks managed to pick up 70% of the firm for less than half a million. The sales of Canadiana are today over $50 million, suggesting that Tom and Mom must have been doing something right.

Two anecdotes to help explain what was right about what the Becks were doing:

1. In the late 1950s the Becks were still making Christmas lights by the hand method, and the design appeared to be faulty. They told their workers, "If your day's production has less than two percent rejections, we'll give you a twenty percent bonus. And if, at the end of the week, you've earned that twenty percent bonus every day, we'll give you an extra ten percent." By ignoring the quantity of output and stressing quality, they made everyone happy: Their workers were often earning 30% above their regular salary each week, and "most of the time they all made it, and the quality problem disappeared."

2. The Becks used to pay their foremen on the basis of the extra hours they worked each week, and they kept a rough inventory of overtime. "But we soon realized that we did not want to create a sweatshop atmosphere. So we told them that, in the new plant we were moving to, we'd pay them a higher bonus for working less hours."

They didn't believe it at first, but they did believe it when they got their first big cheques for working less. "You see," says Beck, "we wanted people to work regular hours, and stop pulling in extra people who would have to be paid overtime! It worked extremely well."

Most recently, in May 1985, Tom Beck paid in the range of $4.3 million for Danbel Industries Inc., along with the transfer of 100,000 presplit Class A nonvoting shares of Noma. Danbel, a group of companies which make and distribute lighting and hardware goods geared to the home-improvement market, was expected to add $30 million in sales to Noma's operations in the first year alone.

H. Thomas Beck has done rather well for himself over the years. He got married in 1954—but took no holiday before 1961—and has two grown daughters and a teenage son. The family owns around 5.8 million shares, which were worth in the range of $29 each as of mid-1986. And the growth of Noma Industries has been awesome: In 1983 the firm had a profit of $7 million on sales of $108.9 million, and in 1984 that leapt to a $11.4 profit on sales of $156.2 million. And not unlike the brilliant Frank Stronach of Magna, Tom Beck insists on each of his nine operating companies being directly under the control of a president or general manager, in order to give "breadth of entrepreneurial opportunity" to his employees. "We give a sense of proprietorship to our managers," says Beck. "We keep telling them that we are *not* a big company, but here to service our customers."

And the customers are growing, as implied by Noma's $8.5 million expansion program, including the construction of a plant for automobile harness manufacturing, as well as equipment upgrading in the Canadiana Outdoor Products Inc. and Cable Tech Co. Ltd. divisions. "All we've done is understand consumers' needs. We have a good understanding of when the mass market is ready for certain products, so we've done well introducing them. There are products out there all the time. We see a product, and engineer the cost at the most effective level, and bring it to customers in the most efficient way." How efficient? "I'd be *most* surprised if our sales weren't over $500 million by early 1988," due to the acquisition of such companies as Western International of Iowa, maker of lawn mowers and snow blowers, and Beacon Electric of Boston, also in the Christmas lighting business, both in 1986.

Not that the over 2,000 employees have been ignored (up from the original 3, plus shipper, please recall): "The motivation of all the employees is what's important. That they are working together happily, that's the main reason why we have small plants. We're in the top quarter of paying our workers on every level in our industry. By the 1960s we tried to find out what others in the industry were paying, as we wanted to pay as good or better."

Suddenly, Tom Beck receives a phone call, and he begins to scream in Hungarian. He runs his hands through his thinning but still rich grey hair, as he continues to yell passionately in his native tongue into the receiver. At last he finishes and plops down into the chair behind his desk at Noma Industries Limited (or perhaps Unlimited). "That was my father. He's eighty-nine, and he wants to go back and start up a business in Hungary! I told him *'no, no, no!'* "

But why not? He's not even 90, and look at how well his son and ex-wife managed with their business in Canada. And Tom Beck's mother was at work all day, the day before she died.

# SAVING QUEBEC WITH FURNITURE

### Serge Racine

There are few businessmen in Canada who are more dynamic, exciting, or passionate about their work than Serge Racine, of Shermag, a ferociously successful furniture manufacturing company. In 1977 he and some partners organized the firm; it began with a dozen employees. At the end of 1985 it had over 550 workers in six factories, with sales of over $25 million; seven factories and $32 million in sales, as of March 1987, over 10% of that profit, with 2.8 shares outstanding on the Montreal stock exchange. All this from the oldest of seven children of parents who ran a small corner grocery store in small-town Quebec.

Serge Racine was born in Farnham, a town of about 6,000 around 30 miles east of Montreal, in 1940. The town was only about 20% English, and Racine himself spoke no English until he was 20. From his earliest youth he was attracted to "the trading aspect"; he would sell comics at the corner to other children, and when he was only 8, he hired other children to pick blueberries for him, which he would sell to stores. While still in grade school, he even organized other kids to sell Christmas cards by bulk. "I was always an organizer," he says, his deep blue eyes shining, his greying hair giving him the distinguished look of a Bay Street lawyer. At the age of 15, he founded a playground organization. Although it started "as a good deal for the parish," it was eventually taken over by the city, which built a gym and a swimming pool on the site. Racine was even hired at his creation for five summers.

With a youth of such entrepreneurial gifts, it comes as a bit of a surprise to discover that Racine actually was interested in becoming a diplomat. He studied political science at Loyola College, earning an Honours B.A., and then, unsure of what he wanted to do with his life, won a major fellowship to Georgetown University in Washington, D.C., where he eventually earned his M.A. and Ph.D. in economics.

In the mid-1960s Racine taught at Georgetown, then at the University of Virginia, and finally came up to Sherbrooke, Quebec, where an economics department had recently been started. "I was interested in consulting and research, as well as teaching," he says, but he still performed the latter, from 1967 to 1969.

Then, the future furniture manufacturer got interested in the economic development of underdeveloped countries, and went off to Africa in 1969 as a visiting professor at the National University of Rwanda, in Central Africa. After returning to Canada, he founded the Centre for Economic Studies in Co-operatives at the University of Sherbrooke, working with over half a dozen French-speaking countries in Africa.

Although he returned to Africa several times, Serge Racine finally turned to his own, slightly underdeveloped, province, and stared another centre—for Regional Economic Development—in Sherbrooke. Jean Marchand had founded DREE, and as his centre's director, Racine published nearly two dozen studies over a two-year period on regional development in Quebec, in food, forests, tourism, and many other crucial areas. There were 50 researchers working under him.

After all the work on his native province, it seemed almost inevitable that Racine would be invited to some kind of civil service. And in 1972, the same year he married, he became the general city manager for the city of Sherbrooke, concerned with the duties of 1,400 employees in the hydro system, police, fire, public works, etc. He was there for five years, until one of those events which can change a person's life forever: A furniture factory burned down near Montreal, and it was considered that it be moved to Sherbrooke.

"At the last minute, the project fell through," recalls Racine, "so I decided to invest in it." (You will not be surprised to discover that he had other businesses during his years of service to the City of Sherbrooke; he had been in real estate since 1971, owning up to 200 apartments at the time of the furniture factory acquisition.)

So Racine and a friend bought the plant and machinery, but were basically passive. "We were only going to invest in it," he says. The plan was for $50,000, along with taking advantage of every grant available. They ended up putting in $400,000, and Racine had to put up his house for collateral. It was organized as Shermag Inc. in 1977, but they quickly saw that "we were going bankrupt; we didn't have the right management."

So what better leader than a man with a doctorate in economics and a lengthy teaching career, *and* a manager of a city? He quit the job at the City of Sherbrooke, where he was earning $65,000 a year, and took the position of president of Shermag for $21,000. "I didn't know furniture," he admits, and yet it took a mere six months to turn things around.

The numbers mentioned before are astonishing enough, but the growth in employees and sales over the last few years make them all the more impressive: By January 1979 his original dozen workers had become 35, with sales of $500,000. In 1980 he was up to 45 employees, with sales of $1.5 million. In 1981, 70 workers and $3 million; in 1982, 170 and $6 million; in 1983, 230 and $16 million; in 1984, 410 and "about $20 million."

With projections of $40 million by March 1988, and over 700 workers in 7 factories, it is pretty clear that Serge Racine has some kind of touch, although he would deny that it is due to any magic: "It doesn't just happen," he declares. "You must have a commitment and a philosophy. The extraordinary thing for businessmen is to do the ordinary things well. And that's what most businessmen don't do." Racine claims that the typical entrepreneur in Quebec is, by nature, dynamic, overexcited, hyperactive, stress-oriented. "The daily discipline and routine is important," he declares. "The regular, day-to-day clerical work. What's *not* exciting is extremely important to a successful business."

That's all well and good, but it must have taken more than that to turn one tiny factory into seven: one each in Lennoxville, Scotstown, Disraeli, Victoriaville, Thurso, Ascot, and even Athol, Massachusetts. And it did. Serge Racine is as much concerned with a corporate philosophy as Magna, the enormously successful auto parts manufacturer in the neighbouring province. "The philosophy must be shared by all, certainly by the top and middle levels of management," he proclaims. "There must be a love for hard work. There must be social and intellectual integrity; I won't stand for any bullshit or lies! And this is with customers as well. I insist that all women be addressed with '*vous*.'" In fact, Racine holds sessions every Monday at the head office in Sherbrooke, to talk about the last books they have read or to have seminars on the business. "I've realized over the years that what we're doing is *not* done everywhere!"

It probably should be. Racine has no secretary; a receptionist answers all calls. Every factory has its own plant manager, and "it's *his* problem until he can't handle it." He is working on profit sharing and hopes to have it within the next year or two. "We grew too fast for it, yet; it must be conditional. You can't just give money away."

With all the jokes about economists who would be lost in the world of business, Serge Racine claims quite the opposite: "You have to know the workings of the economy," he says. "At Shermag, economics has served me well. We did all our growth during the depression period of 1981 through 1983."

For example, the bankrupt factory which Racine bought in 1981. It was extremely mechanized, with $6.2 million in machinery. He paid $400,000 for it, yet discovered that he had just landed a $150,000 windfall in the lumber sitting on site, and quickly lined up $200,000 in federal and provincial subsidies. It had 200 employees when the furniture factory was purchased; there are 180 today. But it quickly doubled his sales figures.

Another reason for success is that Racine insists on paying

above the industry average of $6.30 in Quebec. His average in four of his factories is close to $10 an hour; since the fifth one in Quebec has mainly "young kids," it is lower. There are five different unions, and in the first seven years there was only one strike, in the summer of 1985, when they turned down a 12% offer.

Although it might not warm the heart of Mel Hurtig, Serge Racine is actually for free trade in his industry. "We have to be as good as the U.S. companies; that's why we brought that factory in the States in 1983." (They use it for redistribution, and make only cushions there. Yet Shermag sells over $2 million worth of its furniture to the Americans.) The furniture industry disagrees with the economist/entrepreneur, as you might well imagine; they wrote a letter to the government, saying that Serge Racine did *not* represent their views! "The Yanks won't beat me," he counters; "I'll have the best technology."

Racine has also flourished by finding his own, rather large, niche in the marketplace. His product is middle to high price, only solid-wood furniture, no veneer or conglomerates. Sixty percent of his sofas, chairs, etc., are made from solid oak, and in the few years since they began making a single item—a rocker, which sold for $75 to $600—Shermag has become the largest manufacturer of case goods (nonstuffed furniture) in Quebec, and the third largest in all of Canada.

Distribution of Racine's furniture has also been intelligent; 50% of his business is with "the majors," such as Sears, Simpson's, Woolco, Leon's, etc., and 50% is sold to buying groups. And note the distribution across the country: 33% of Canada's population lives in Ontario, and that is the exact percentage of his furniture sales to that province in 1985. Ditto with Quebec, with 31% of the population and 31% of sales. "We know what the tastes are in furniture in each area of the country," he states.

"When you almost double your figures each year, by acquiring large factories, you're gambling the shop," Racine admits. So he has set targets to avoid waste in money and man-power. For instance, he hopes to have 1 administrator per each $1 million in sales. He has about 28 today, putting him only slightly over his goal, but vastly lower than the average in Canada, which he claims is 3.4 managers per million in business. An example will suffice: In 1983 Racine purchased a factory where there were 47 in the front office and 125 in the plant. There is now only a secretary in that front office. In another factory, where there were 26 in the front office, the number is down to a mere 3.

Serge Racine's style has changed over the years, and not only because of his heart attack in 1983, after half a decade of 18-hour days. "I was an orchestra man for the first three years," he says jokingly. "I was a one-man band." Today he has moved to being a conductor, "surrounding myself with good people."

The runaway success of his business is seen by Serge Racine as part of "the awakening of entrepreneurship in Quebec, which will save our province and Canada." He is delighted to quote the recent survey which noted that 33% of Quebecois trusted businessmen the most. "In the old days, it would have been the curé," he says. "For 300 years, it was difficult to be rich and go to heaven, according to the priests."

But the priests can hardly complain about hundreds of their parishioners not flinching and turning away when the plate is passed; jobs are always welcome in Quebec, as elsewhere in Canada. And the "only constraint being human" to Shermag not growing even faster, they can only rejoice in the human output of their fellow citizens.

What of Serve Racine, as he edges into the second half of his 40s? "At this point, I'm a rich man, in terms of what I've accomplished," he says. "But we are not yet where we're *going* to be! I believe in programming, not planning. We are growing as fast as we can, and will continue as long as the market can stand it. The past belongs to me; I don't need more or want more. The future? It belongs to the sharers."

# A GOOD PART OF
# THE PARTS MARKET

### *Bill Bartels*

Bill Bartels, the president of Canparts Automotive International Ltd., has no title on his business card. He refuses to give sales figures for his booming disk brake pad manufacturing company (although he *had* to give them to the people who showered him and partner Jim Smith in 1984 with a Canadian Exports Award and a Canada Award for Excellence; they put sales at over $12 million a year then. Insiders hint at over $20 million by the end of 1987). But in a just a few short years, the men have started a multi-million-dollar company from literal scratch, made it the largest industry in Cambridge, a good-sized city about 90 minutes west of Toronto, and made that city a world centre for auto parts. No wonder his Jaguar has Y NOT on his licence plate; it is the rallying cry of the true entrepreneur.

Bill Bartels was born in Hespeler, a small town later merged with two others to become Cambridge, in 1937. (His office at Canparts is within two miles of the house he was born in; so much for any arguments that you have to get away to get started.) The oldest of three is the first in his family to have his own business; his father, who came from Russia during the Revolution as a Mennonite in search of religious freedom, had worked in various factories, including a quarter century for Ford. Even in kindergarten, Bartels recalls "always buying and selling. I sold vegetables from my mom's garden; I sold seeds in the spring; I sold Christmas trees in December."

He still sells, except it is year-round, and to 50 countries world-round. "I always heard talk about business, and I took it as the gospel truth," says Bartels. "I had this work ethic." So when he finished grade 13, he briefly "debated whether to go to university," but the work ethic won the debate; he got a job in an auto parts factory in Preston (another pre-Cambridge town), which manufactured oil filters. At the age of 20 he was a salesman, covering Western Canada. "I never went to college, as I became aware of the money you could make!"

Through his helping customers to obtain product lines, he was hired by a U.S. company as a salesman. Echlin Manufacturing Company out of Connecticut, which made ignition and brakes auto parts, was eager to hire such a crackerjack from the north. He worked seven years there as a salesman, and was the sales manager for all of Canada by the time he left.

Then it was off to Certified Brakes of Mississauga, Ontario, which made brake assemblies for the North American auto industry. There he met "a man I liked," Jimmy Smith, with whom he would grow rich and semifamous. But the rich/famous would not come until much later. He would eventually leave CB for the same reasons that he had left

Echlin: "It takes two things to make you move; you've got to be cheesed off where you are, and you've got to see an opportunity." Both would come, in spades.

Always the salesman, Bartels sold brake franchises for Certified and then "got the idea to go worldwide. They'd never gone out of Canada." So in the mid-1960s he flew off to Europe to check things out. ("I thought at the time that it would be the only time I'd go there; now we go *all the time*!") They gave him no commission, albeit generous bonuses, but, most importantly, they gave him "freedom," so he stayed with them, faithfully, for 16 years. For the last half, he was general sales manager, with "twenty guys reporting to me," and was making up to $50,000 a year, which wasn't bad back in the 1960s.

Then, in 1969, the company was sold to a conglomerate out of California, Royal Industries, which treated him "just as well," so he stayed. The company was only a few million in sales when he had joined it, and 15 years later it was in excess of $50 million, and he feels that he had a part (an auto part) in it. "I had my own philosophy, which I still have, at Canparts today: Get as close to the market as possible; don't look to giant places. I liked to call on parts distributors in different countries and sell to each. I can walk through a front door and tell what kind of guy someone is." An example he gives is "a guy I handle in Vienna today. I call him by phone, and it's like calling down the street. So it costs twenty to forty dollars for the call; what's the big deal?"

Working in a big firm, Bartels had what he describes as "an ego thing"; he enjoyed investing on the side "in a few things. A little real estate, getting stung on the stock market, some second mortgages. I'm not a real strong gambler, though." (In his private life, either; he's been married more than 28 years to the same woman he had met in high school, and has three children.)

And, as always, he had his roots sunk deep in Hespeler/Preston/Galt, a/k/a Cambridge, always commuting to his job in Toronto. "It's OK to work in Toronto, but I always wanted to live out here. I got a lot of my kicks buying old licence plates and antique cars, seeing an old car and finding a buyer for it, making money from fixing a house in Preston. But I always commuted."

During those years at the ever-growing firm in Toronto,

he became friendlier with Jimmy Smith, who had joined as a secretary-treasurer. "Jimmy's from Scotland, and been here for 30 years. HOW OLD'S SMITTY?" he suddenly yells from his room out to the hall. The answer comes back: Smith is 56. "We really liked each other. He's an accountant, but no penny-pincher. He's really different. We could disagree strongly, yet get it out together, patch it up, and not get on each other's feelings. We could sound off and get it over with." Then, the crucial decision: "Because we saw that we could do this, we desired to go out on our own."

But if you recall his earlier double reason for leaving a place, one has to get cheesed off first. And that happened when Royal Industries was swallowed by a larger fish, Lear Siegler of Santa Monica. "Again, we had new bosses! As time went on, over the first year, it became evident that we'd lost our freedom." (There's that word again.) "All was *professional*, and we didn't fit in. Or we *felt* we didn't." By 1979 they "pulled out."

Earlier that year the two had attended a meeting at the Harbour Castle in Toronto, called Opportunities Ontario, one of those one-day seminars where speakers from the provincial government urge the audience to go out there and create jobs (and—hint hint—tax revenues). One speaker was from Industry, Trade and Commerce, expounding on "government help for people in business, and we took it right to heart." Bartels met him in the john later and found him "an extremely hard worker. He wasn't just doling out government money; he showed us clearly how we could put a firm together with federal and provincial help, banks, and ourselves."

Smith and Bartels would meet in their off hours, sharing their ideas, and the day after Labour Day, 1979, they struck out on their own. "We were enthused enough, but not carried away," Bartels recalls. But they soon discovered that they had to "take that first job! It's a big step! *We* had no job any more!" They looked around and saw that Japanese cars were coming on strongly, and that there was this huge market in the United States. And they decided to specialize in replacement disk brake parts. They began with initial loans of $775,000, which were paid back by 1983. They began with 20 employees; there are now more than 260 hourly and nearly 4 dozen salaried. They began with 20 different parts numbers; there are now over 400. Canadian capitalism in action.

It wasn't cake from the start; they had attempted to rent a building, but it didn't pan out. So Bartels suggested, "Let's go to Cambridge, where I'm known. We'll build a plant with a Government of Ontario mortgage." There are now three factories.

The truly inspired move was, of course, to go for the "aftermarket." Afterbirths might not be cuddled and cared for in the labour room, but in automotive labour, aftermarket is the rage. "It's an *excellent* business," states Bartels, emphatic as always. "It's recession-proof. Auto parts are always good. In the aftermarket, the Big Three auto makers don't hold a hammer over your head. And people are always fixing their cars in bad times."

It almost snowballed, which in Canada is to be expected, although not always in the world of business. "When we first started the business, a guy I knew placed a good-sized order. Then we got a *big* order from a middle company, going into Iran. [Author's note: *Iran*? We thought that Canadians were trying to get *out* of there.] Suddenly, we had more business than we had imagined!" And this was all for *one* part number.

Sales have grown "tremendously," as Bartels and Smith surpassed their five-year plan in half that time. "We have to update every year," he says with satisfaction. Canadian Tire and Midas are the typical market in Canada, but with over four dozen countries being shipped to, they look far beyond their own country's borders. They keep a percentage of profits for their workers—profit sharing, they label it, and "a bonus that has really grown; we give so much per month." Having a union since November of 1983 hasn't hurt matters, either.

Canparts Automotive International Ltd. is already the largest in their field, but they are being "careful in branching into American cars. And we're selective in our pricing." Bartels prides himself on their being able to "react quickly" to the ever-changing market. "If you sell only in Toronto, then you're dead if someone moves in. But when you sell worldwide, if South Africa shuts down, we go somewhere else. So we don't have to always fly high in every market." And he's also proud of their "moving out of asbestos." "That's one of the *big things*," Bartels declares. "We've come up with super products which do not need asbestos in them. We're one of the leaders in asbestos-free material.

"Any customer worth getting will take you a while to get," philosophizes Bill Bartels of Canparts. "If he comes easy, beware; he'll *leave* easy." Perhaps surprisingly, Bartels leaves his office easily, each evening, maintaining only an eight-hour day. "We delegate a lot," he says. "We've got a lot of good people with us." Still, "It's a total commitment, and a wonderful life."

Smith and Bartels plan to "broaden out; maybe we'll put up a plant somewhere in Europe soon. There is assistance available in certain countries." But he's particularly pleased with having created so many jobs in his hometown. Yet with the Jaguar, the millions, all the success, Bill Bartels really hasn't changed much. "I still do selling, and I *love* it! I'm still enthused about that. I love to call on an auto parts store even today," although the parts he now pushes have his *own* company's name on them. "The bucks stops with us," states Bill Bartels with a smile. "*We* are the buck."

# THE PASSIONATE CHINESE RUSSIAN (OR RUSSIAN CHINESE)

### *George Yui*

When George Yui bursts into his board room, brushing past the Canadian Charter of Rights and Freedoms framed on the wall, defiantly proclaiming his unconventional philosophy in a torrent of words, the effect is momentarily stunning. The observer soon realizes that his ideas have more than shock value, however. "This plant has been acclaimed everywhere!" he practically shouts. "When I designed it, I was criticized. 'He can spy on his workers from the offices in the middle,' they said. I was called a cheapskate on heating. But every detail of the conceptual design was mine! Heating is only four thousand dollars a year! The electricity bill is the same as the old facility, which had half the footage and half the employees!

"There is a difference between warehouses with a roof over your head and factories. All the large industries are built for warehousing and some light manufacturing. But tool-and-die needs are different! I'm a tool-and-die maker! I wanted to make the environment more humane and create good working conditions, with light and air. Canadian factories are the worst in the world! We are so rich, and the richness is killing us! I've got separate air intakes from the outside, providing one hundred percent fresh air; it's usually only ten percent. We've set a world standard!"

So begins a long interview with the founder and owner of Diemaster Tool Inc., whose new factory was built in 1982 on land that cost him $3.2 million to purchase. The fact that he started this business, which in late 1987 had 170 employees and $9 million in sales, with an investment of $1,200 in 1972 makes Yui's story one of momentous entrepreneurship, and not merely because of his exotic origins and heritage.

George Yui was born in Harbin, Manchuria, in 1942, to a father who was a peasant but who built a sausage factory/bakery/deli. "We made the *best* German sausages!" he exclaims. His mother was Russian, from Siberia, which helps to explain the look—thick Chinese hair and Oriental features—and an almost stage-Russian accent. He was the firstborn; a younger sister is a design engineer in Toronto. He spent an apprenticeship at the National Railway Machine shop and finished high school in China, in the midst of the one-million-strong Russian colony there. (He spoke Russian at home.) The coming of communism didn't affect their lives at first, but "they cut down ownership bit by bit." When his father was jailed as a counterrevolutionary, George Yui left the country on his advice, getting help from the United Nations, who sent him to Brazil, where his godfather was living. He reached South America when he was 21 years of age. (He finally brought his father over from China in 1979.)

He worked as a gauge maker for Volkswagen in Brazil—"I learned *the most* there; it was *excellent*!"—making $200 U.S. a month, when the minimum wage was $40. "Toolmakers were the aristocracy of industry in that country!" he reveals, making it quite clear that he thinks Canadians are rather dull not to feel the same way. "I had no accent when I spoke Portuguese!" he brags, "even with my Chinese/Slavic background!" But after three and a half years on the job, he no longer wished to stay in Brazil, "always baked by the sun and that rotten greenery and insects!" He also watched the instability around him, and was concerned that Communists might come to that country; he knew what *that* was like. "I didn't want to end up in a situation like my father did."

His first choice was the United States, but the Vietnam War was going on. Canada had no embassy in São Paolo, but he somehow got a visa and came here in 1966. (He had actually managed to land a job in Cleveland, but quickly "discovered the differences between the two countries, and refused it. Canada was cleaner and less troublesome, with less racial tension and crime. It was an ideal home for me.")

Within ten days after his arrival George Yui became a toolmaker in a small company, "and I've never been unemployed *since*!" He moved from shop to shop, working for seven different companies in three years, not able to find a place he liked. "Every one was very dirty, disorganized, making poor quality goods." He was clearly spoiled by Volkswagen, Brazil. Besides, "I *knew* I would be in my own business. My father always told me to go into business, saying, 'Be like the Jews! Know everything, but manage others to do it for you.' My father was nicknamed 'the Chinese Jew' in Manchuria, because he did the deals. One thing my father did *not* tell me was how long it takes to know everything, by doing it yourself."

Yet the future owner of a major Canadian tool-and-die firm never managed to save any money. "My father would tell me, 'Money comes and goes. It's only what's in your head that they can't take away. So *learn, learn, learn*!' " After Yui worked for another company for three years, it was sold to ITT, so he went to Ryerson Polytechnic for tool design at night over the next three years. "Then I found out that to find a job as a designer was very difficult in this country! They keep telling you that you are overqualified."

So he started his own shop, to do it the way *he* wanted. For the first six months he was the only employee, then doubling to one other. First-year sales: $60,000, and no wages drawn for the first 24 months. He quickly estimated the market: There was a middle—where most people compete, and two ends—the large, capital-intensive, and the small, precision, low-capital, and high-skilled. It was obvious that he would choose the latter.

Within three years he became the top supplier for IBM and Xerox for the dies and fixtures to make their products, also supplying the same companies in the States. "I recognized that the market was too small, and I had to get into aerospace metrology, the art of measurement." It was 1979, and he began to make aircraft engine components for Avco-Lycoming, and aircraft engine tooling for Pratt & Whitney. For TRW, he was soon making valves for torpedoes. "Nice stuff." He grins. "Goes *bang*." George Yui hasn't forgotten what the Commies did to his dad all those years: "My ultimate dream would be to build a *tank* in Canada. *Then*, I'd have one of the best orgasms in my life. And to drive one across Red Square would be the *next* best orgasm!"

His biggest problem, as he relates it, was to choose a name for his firm. "I didn't want any initials to confuse people. I wanted a name with substance, like Diemaster. But I had to *live up* to it! All I had was a one-man shop and dirty hands; people laughed! This made me defend my name all the more, and live up to it."

The growth of the firm shows how he lived up plenty: By 1973 he was up to 5 employees; by the following year, 10. The year after that, 20. He was up to 60 workers in 1980, with sales of $3 million, and they have never been higher than the present $9 million and 170 employees. "I know my job!" George Yui declares confidently. "I have a rare combination of being up-to-scratch technically, having the ability to create, and being able to run a business. They are all qualities from my father; you can't learn them in school."

He built the business through "constant decision making. And on the strength of good quality. We got repeat business on our reputation as troubleshooters. If there's a problem, Diemaster can solve it!" (Sixty percent of his business is now in the field of aerospace.)

He recently wrote up a report for Ottawa, which he claims is "dynamite!" Only 1 out of every 2,000 Canadians is a toolmaker, which, according to Yui, is a disaster. "We are rarer than doctors and lawyers!" he cries. And with a mere 6,000 toolmakers in the province of Ontario, 1,400 apprentices, and only 350 new graduates each year, "that doesn't even cover the attrition rate!" The problem, in the mind of George Yui, is that blue-collar workers are too rare, and very respectable, but "you can't train them in two years, and the government thinks we can!" He has over 30 apprentices at Diemaster, but he keeps losing them to General Motors, with maybe 5 staying with him. "I have another forty in training, but we won't call them apprentices," he says. It enrages Yui—many things about Canada do—that apprentices are to be paid more than university graduates. "I paid $50,000 for each machine down there!" he shouts. "There are close to two hundred machines here. I've got assets worth eight million dollars!"

What George Yui is screaming for is what Canada got when it accepted him: "*I need skilled immigrants!*" He estimates that one toolmaker supports at least 20 direct manufacturing jobs. So if one in three Canadians is employed (the others being children or the elderly), then that one toolmaker supports the livelihoods of 420 Canadians. "Toolmakers create jobs!" he declares. And yet there are fewer than 12,000 in the entire country.

"The monkey who used leverage, putting a rock to a stick to kill a larger animal, he was the first toolmaker. And who will make robotics? *Toolmakers!*" Yui pays his beginners only $5.50 an hour, which is lower then the industry average, but his top men get $16 an hour, and with overtime can earn in excess of $40,000 a year. He claims that profit sharing is difficult, with a payroll of close to $4 million and a profit of less than $500,000, because wages are high to begin with.

But the plans for the future are gigantic: He looks to $25 million in sales in five years, and over $100 million in ten, with about 1,000 people on the staff of Diemaster. "This building is my flagship, to develop other industries in partnership," he says. "I plan to buy other companies, to provide technical support for what I'm doing here." He has begun to make noises about going public, but feels that he should be at the $25 million level in sales before he can. "I plough every cent back into the business," he insists. "My wages are not greater than my best-paid employees."

"I like playing the game," declares George Yui; "it provides great satisfaction. I work a seventy-hour week; my wife [VP, finance and administration], fifty hours." There are four children, ranging from 12 down to 7, from his blond wife. "She is from French/Irish stock!" He laughs. "Our children are French/Irish/Russian/Chinese!" The four solitudes, right there in Mississauga.

When George Yui opened his giant new Diemaster Tool Inc. factory in 1982, then-Federal Industry Trade and Commerce Minister Herb Gray unveiled the plaque to mark the event. Afterwards, he said to the owner/operator, "What we need is two hundred George Yuis in this country."

"No," disagreed the man in question. "Ninety-nine more will do."

# FROM PLUMBING DIRTY WATER TO MAKING IT CLEAN

### Ernie Butler

Almost everything about Ernie Butler suggests that he would have turned out to be a decent, solid Canadian, but hardly a successful entrepreneur—and selling water filters around the globe, to boot. Born in Haywarden, Saskatchewan, a tiny town about 100 miles north of Moose Jaw, in 1932, he was the seventh of 12 children of two farmers. Wearing black glasses and a Dr. Pepper hat, with greying hair and a bulging waistline, he sits in a nondescript office in suburban Toronto, 2,000 miles and over four decades away from where he grew up, in Moose Jaw. The way in which he has managed to move so far is one more example of how creativity and business can merge to create an impressive career.

As a child—his family had moved to the "big city" when he was nine—Butler showed a never-ending tendency to "earn as much money as possible." He had two paper routes at one time—the *Moose Jaw Times Herald* and the *Regina Leader-Post*; he had regular lemonade stands; and he recalls going down to the farmer's market and "cleaning stalls for fifty cents each." And after that, there's no way to go but up.

Ernie Butler went to grade 8 and then dropped out to work for a plumber on Vancouver Island, staying with the man for three years. Then it was back to Moose Jaw, where he worked for the railroad and got married. (He has "two of each" and seven grandchildren today, while still in his early 50s).

After six years with the CPR, he "got sick of it" and "thought that there was more money to be made than from working for the railroad." So the former brakeman moved to Calgary in 1958 and "went into the plumbing business by myself." He was in it for five years, and, as he puts it in his soft, delicate voice, "I did real well in that." He quickly had

21 plumbers and three labourers working for him, finally selling out "Alberta Plumbers" in the early 1960s. "I wanted to do something exciting," he says. "Plumbing got to be a drag."

So Butler went into the fire alarm business—direct sales—and, once again, he "did real well!" As he declares, "I made more money than I knew what to do with! I did well 'cause we hustled. We had a good product." He also had 15 salesmen working for him, probably most of them with more education and fancier Dr. Pepper hats, but few, if any, with their boss's drive. He made $13,000 the first year, and over $100,000 each year thereafter, which is the kind of growth that most of us would like to achieve. The fire alarms sold for $400 a set, and he moved them throughout Alberta and Saskatchewan. "There was a good profit in it," he says, understating the case.

But necessity is the mother of entrepreneurship, as we like to believe. Back in Moose Jaw since 1971, Ernie Butler became progressively more upset with the quality of the city's water, to use the word "quality" loosely. "By 1978 the water was so bad, we decided we should purify our own," he says. The "we" is not royal; he and his son, then around 14 years of age, sat down and built a carbon filter, designing it themselves. "We did it for our own family," he recalls, but not for long.

Several neighbours began to make requests, so Butler made 20 more, selling them for $120 each. Then, as the requests continued to grow, he built another 80 in his basement over a two-week period, and sold them all within a month. (We *told* you the water in Moose Jaw was the pits.)

"There was competition, but it wasn't that active," says Butler. Obviously, since some people out in Calgary heard about what father and son were doing in Moose Jaw, and the Butlers soon "had a big thing going in our basement." They quickly sold around 2,000 of the water filters.

By 1980 Ernie Butler began to export his filters to Germany, selling about 4,000 units there in a short period of time. He had four people working for him by then. Clearly, this basement industry was getting a bit out of hand. And then there was the name problem: "We were going to call our filter Springfresh, but it's not a strong name," says Butler, who *does* have a strong name. Then his son said, "How about something *strong*, like Ruxton?" So they called it Ruxton Water Filters, and a new prairie industry was born.

The sales figures tell part of the story. In 1978 sales were not much more than $10,000. By 1979 "that jumped to sixty to seventy thousand dollars." By 1981 it was over $120,000, and in 1982 "about two hundred thousand." (It was that year that the basement reluctantly gave up the creative ghost, and Ruxton Incorporated—"The Water Treatment"—moved to a small factory, costing $150 a month rent. This is still in Moose Jaw, as you can see.)

By 1984 sales were up to $325,000, and with a difficult move to Toronto in 1985, sales remained about the same.

Still, there must have been a lot of "word of mouth" going on, to grow so rapidly. Germany, for instance. "A German asked to distribute my filters in his country," so he agreed. By 1985 Ruxton water filters were selling in 22 different countries, including the Caribbean, United Kingdom, India, Singapore, Australia, and Chile. "We've gone on trade missions around the world," says Ernie Butler, pointing to the 12 to 14 people now on staff.

There are at least three other water filter companies in Canada, but Butler insists that his "is the only one with a unique disinfectant process. It kills the bacteria within the filter bed itself." He believes that he is already Canada's biggest manufacturer of water filters, and "we have more models than anyone!" They can clean from a half gallon to 2,000 gallons a minute.

The move to Toronto from the prairies was a must to Butler, who declares that "we had to expand, and we wanted to expand where the population is!" He has left the U.S. market alone, up to this point, since "I didn't want to touch it until I could handle it." He goes on, "If we got an order that we couldn't fill, it would hurt us more than help us." At this time he can turn out only a thousand units a day, which sure beats his basement, but couldn't handle any potential American demand.

Yet "the business moves faster than we always seem to plan. We get conservative, and there's always more." Ernie Butler has no doubt that by the end of the 1980s, his sales will be at the $2-3 million mark, since his new facility in suburban Toronto has 120,000 square feet to work in.

Like all good entrepreneurs, Ernie Butler works from 8:00 A.M. until 10:00 or 11:00 each night, seven days a week, doing all paperwork and correspondence, training people, setting up agents. (He has four dozen agents across Canada, and another two dozen around the world.) He also has a partner now, since he needed money to expand and meet the demand for his water filters.

And why the success and the multi-million-dollar future? "It's common sense and hard work," exclaims the common-sensical and hardworking Ernie Butler. "Some people are educated in different ways. I've educated myself in a me-chanical sense. Most people think that if they put in eight-hour days, that's enough. But in my work, an extra ten minutes or three hours *can* make a difference!"

Butler has never spent a penny on advertisements, insisting that "it can come *without* spending millions!" He did not take a penny out of his business until 1985, but doesn't credit that for his success so far. "Too many businesses fail because they don't know how to price their products so they can stay afloat. They don't price properly—and they don't work hard enough!"

And how can Ernie Butler lose, when "the water field is just coming into its own. There's so much pollution and water contamination that it even has the governments and health authorities concerned!" He likes to point out that it takes 250 gallons of water to make one single newspaper, washing all that pulp. "We *can't* turn the pollution around, because of the necessity of the substitute materials, like plastic. We have to learn to clean up our water."

And not only water. "We have other products in mind to clean up all the pollution," he says. Like PCBs. "I've got an idea on how to clean those PCBs up without hauling them around the country."

The goal is clear—a mixture of altruism and capitalism, and not necessarily in that order: "My whole purpose is to clean water in as many countries as I can!" proclaims Ernie Butler, quickly adding, "And to be as *successful* as I can."

But success can only come to those who love to work, according to Ernie Butler of Moose Jaw and Toronto. "I like to work. Even away on a weekend, I like to find something to do. Even shovelling dirt. I don't *like* to be idle."

---

*In early 1987, the author was told that Ernie Butler "vanished" a year earlier, after selling 49% of Ruxton to Itarb Venture Corp. Vince Lombardo of I.V.C. insists that Butler "misrepresented documents" and that the filters "did not have the quality he claimed." If this is true, Butler is the only one of the 80 entrepreneurs in this book who has not gone from strength to strength since the 1985 interviews.

# THERE'S NUMBERS (OF DOLLARS) IN SAFETY

*Gerald J. Yaffe*

There are over 500 pages in the 1987 catalogue of Safety House of Canada Limited, of Toronto, overflowing with everything from A (AFTER-BURN Burn Spray; Anti-Slip Paint; Arm Slings; Automobile Roof Lights) to G (GLOBE Airline Respirator; Gas Masks; Glove-Welders; Grounding Cables) to S (S.O.S. Safety Kit; Safety Belts; Smoke Ejector Fans; Snake Bite Kit; Stretchers) to W (WATER-JEL Fire Blankets; Warning Flags; Water Fire Extinguishers; Wooden Tongue Depressors; Wound Dressings). In short, everything that the underinsured company or overly concerned hypochondriac should have.

The story of how Gerald J. Yaffe, 42, turned a $100 investment into a company doing over $40 million a year in business is surely one of the more extraordinary studies of entrepreneurship in this country. Not that there weren't hints from early youth: "When I was a kid, all the kids were trading and collecting hockey cards," he says, sitting in shirt and tie in his crowded office in north-central Toronto, surrounded by fire extinguishers, cans of Band-Aids, pictures of the wife and kids, and—not irrelevantly— a new Rolls-Royce just outside in the parking lot. "I had memorized every president of every company from the age of seven or eight."

His mother had wanted him and his older brother to be professionals, to be doctors, and when Yaffe challenged her, she explained that they earned a good living. "Why don't I do the art that they're trying to accomplish," the boy replied, "which is to capture the most money. They've got a disguise—a smock. I can do it without that."

Yaffe's father was a tailor who used to quiz his youngest son on "who is the president of Imperial Oil?" The man had no business aspirations but felt that "you've got to be paid on Friday," and this somehow inspired Gerald. By the age of 9 he was reading the financial section of the newspapers. "I always felt changes and developments affected me. I learned from General Motors' new models, and it enriched my career." He read every book on Henry Ford that he could get hold of. At the age of 13 he worked in a clothing store over the Christmas holidays, where his father was a tailor. He was paid only 50¢ an hour, "but I really hustled," surprised and troubled that "the others were either lazy or dummies." The store manager used to mumble, "Why are there so many sales when Gerry is here?"

One year, the lad was phoned by the manager and invited back, but Gerald insisted on $1 an hour. He was offered the same 50¢ but after a few weeks the man gave in and hired him at $1. In early January, when Yaffe got his lump cheque, he discovered that all he was paid was 50¢ an hour. "It was an important point in my life. In my early teens, I recognized that I'd never let that happen to me again, and that I would always treat people fairly. To this day, I have a *real* sensitivity to employees' needs."

The beginnings, then, were hardly auspicious—"If you looked up poverty in the dictionary, our picture was there" —and the origins of what would become a multi-million-dollar safety business were equally unawesome. "At the age of 16, I sat down and tried to figure out what everyone *needed*." The rather surprising answer? Band-Aids! "I had no business training, but I had a wealth of knowledge," Yaffe declares.

The teenager made a list of all the people he and his family knew, and began with a toy manufacturer. He went to see the man and told him, "I'm in the safety equipment business: Band-Aids, fire extinguishers . . ." "I don't use Band-Aids." "Surely you use welding goggles or gloves?" "No." "How about fire extinguishers?" "Nope."

Another lesson learned. The 16-year-old high school dropout returned to his father's car and decided to scrap his list. He wouldn't go to friends, but to strangers instead.

Gerald Yaffe decided to start literally and geographically at the bottom of the city; in this case of Toronto, at King and Dufferin, near the Canadian National Exhibition site. He parked the car and started walking. In the very first establishment he entered, the owner asked the boy, "You got any salt tablets for horses? How about some alcohol?" "Of course," replied the cocky kid. "I'll have them at once."

He rushed off to a nearby drug store, purchased the salt tablets and alcohol, and took the stuff to the man. He received $11 for everything. "How long you been in business?" asked the man. "I started only today," replied Yaffe. Impressed, the man sent the boy out to the edge of Toronto, to a huge factory where they made brake shoes, to ask for Mr. Albert. When the latter met the budding entrepreneur, he told him, "My friend told me to buy all our safety equipment from you from now on."

A footnote: That summer, Gerald Yaffe volunteered to work for the PC campaign of John Bassett, the wealthy and famous communications genius. He (naturally) asked for $300 to spend, and paid people $1 each if they would put up a Bassett sign on their lawn. (Other workers gave out combs.) An old man watched the kid do all this, and he called Yaffe over to his jewellery store. "I've been watching you," he said. "You're going to be a very rich man some day. I don't know at what, but I'm going to give you a tip: Always give the customers what they need, not what they ask for." "The advice went in one ear and stayed," Yaffe recalls today.

When Yaffe began his business, it was only over Christmas and Easter, and he did not drop out of school for some months after. So while he was in school, customers—he had over 100—kept calling to his bedroom phone. His mother would call little Gerry at school, and the boy would call the businesses back from the vice-principal's office, telling them that the goods would be "on the late afternoon delivery."

A brief example of Yaffe's aggressiveness: He saw a tender for the Edmonton School Board for a vocational school in a Toronto newspaper, and saw "safety equipment" on the list of tenders. "Who better than I, who is still in school, would know about school safety?" he thought to himself, and he sent a complete proposal for their requirements to Alberta. While still in grade 11, he received a letter from the Edmonton board, ordering all that they needed from the Toronto schoolboy.

In Yaffe's first year—1960–61, he had $25,000 in sales, which is assuredly a helluva lot of Band-Aids. By the next year, finally working full time, he sold $80,000 worth of safety equipment, with nearly $30,000 of that in profit. Within his first few years of business he was able to put the jeweller's suggestion into practice: He knocked on the doors of Texas

Instruments, where he was told that they wanted a complete medical room for their 30 employees. "You only need a first aid kit," said the teenager; "only over 200 employees do you need a medical room, under the Health Act of Ontario." "But we want one here!" "No, you're throwing out money," insisted Yaffe. "A stretcher and a first aid kit are all you need."

The man finally agreed, but asked for a quotation on the cost of a medical room. Three months later, Yaffe got a call at his bedroom office: "Come quickly! A man just lost an arm!" He came and wrote an order for a medical room, and made $3,000 profit on the single order.

Gerald Yaffe worked seven days a week, 18 hours a day, typing all his letters and invoices, "always considering the business my golden egg, to be preserved." By 1964 he moved out of his bedroom into a basement of a building in suburban Toronto, where he got 400 square feet, including furniture, for $75 a month. He was barely out of his teens, and his sales were up to $130,000, with profits totalling 30% of that. It was just Yaffe and "a girl" in the office, and a few salesmen who came and went. And he still had no buying power.

So why such a success? "I gave them what they needed," he says today, chomping on a cigar. He has a fair-sized paunch and jowls that would do an ex-president of the United States proud. "I always looked older than my age, and I talked intelligently. I wasn't hustling; I legitimately matched product with application. I would come into a place and point out that it was dangerous to hang that coat on that fire extinguisher—and no one else did that. I would tell people that their aisles should be labelled properly, and they appreciated it. People started to trust me for advice."

It was just as the child had realized: He was like the doctor his parents wanted him to be, as the professional aspect of his work took over. "I just didn't have a scalpel and a blade in hand," he states.

Not that Gerald Yaffe was the only game in town; not by a long shot. There were three major competitors, two Canadian, one American, and "they could easily have put a stop to me. They had all the big accounts, but they were smug about it, and arrogant." In what way? For example, the industry tended to work on exclusives, such as a particular line of safety glasses. So the kid from Safety House would handle a number of firms, giving clients a greater choice of products.

When a client would complain to a major company about a product, he or she was often told, "No one *else* is complaining!" But young Yaffe knew exactly what the client needed, and got samples over to him on the double. "Not only did I use knowledge and general common sense, but I also offered products to solve their specific problems," he says today.

Like most successful businessmen, Gerald Yaffe took little home: In 1966 he was taking only $50 a week out of the till; the following year that leapt to $80. "My salary is still low," he insists.

But if the salary was low, the sales certainly weren't. Some numbers: In 1970, edging into his second decade with the business, sales were about $1½ million, employees numbered 6, and profits were over $100,000. Five years later, sales were up to $3½ million, with nearly 20 employees, and profits of $300,000. The year 1980 witnessed sales of over $28 million, 90 employees, and profits of over $1½ million, and 1985 saw sales of $40 million, with 165 employees and profits of over $2½ million. The federal government should do so poorly.

Some sales stand out, of course, like Yaffe's product line of mass inoculation guns, which could "do" up to 1,200 men an hour. When the swine flu epidemic was believed to be on the horizon, the federal government asked Safety House of Canada to be the official supplier of all equipment except the vaccine itself. There were no tenders, and the sales for Yaffe's firm were in excess of $10 million. "That was my first Rolls-Royce," he remembers, smiling. (Not that it was as simple as from Ottawa's pocket into Gerry's: Safety House produced training films on how to care for the inoculation guns and Yaffe maintained repairs in the field. And much more: "I locked up futures on the guns, so I was later able to sell many back to the States when they needed them.")

His building of nearly 90,000 square feet came soon after the swine flu bonanza. Yaffe's firm manufactures many products, which grew out of an early philosophy. "We establish a market and then improve the products through private branding." Yaffe asks manufacturers to make various changes and, if they refuse, he asks for parts and assembles them himself.

Not unlike the way auto parts firms boom during recessions, because people hold on to their old cars, which often need repairs, Safety House has done "extremely well" during the recent hard times. "In tight money times, accident rates increase dramatically," Yaffe declares. "People become less efficient and more careless." And because he was into wholesaling, companies which felt the slump would go to him and ask them to fill in their slump with safety products, adding Yaffe's products to their lines.

Since the early 1970s Yaffe has been printing his massive catalogue, sending it off to every major industry, institution, government, construction company, *et al.*, across Canada. The circulation is up to 100,000 now. The spread of the catalogue is echoed by the 17 branches of Safety House in Ontario and the Maritimes—with the second one coming only in 1982. When the recession hit, "that's when we got *really* aggressive!" Every one of Yaffe's competitors pulled their advertisements and trimmed their operations, firing and laying off large numbers of workers. Not Yaffe. "We were always lean and mean. So we hyped up our ads in the trade journals, and began opening branches while others closed theirs. It took a lot of balls to do it."

By the late 1980s Gerald Yaffe expects to have 45 to 50 branches across Canada: actual physical, industrial locations, with inventory, salesmen, everything but the paperwork, which will continue to flow out of Toronto. "Our aim is to get it up to $100 million in sales, through our present aggressiveness and acquisitions. We will start acquiring others. The mom-and-pop places will fall by the wayside. I'm number three in the business now, and number two is at seventy-five million dollars. We'll surpass them soon." Indeed, projections for 1987 are nearly $50 million.

Not that the future is all roses. As Yaffe puts it, "Robots don't use hard hats and safety goggles, and high unemployment is a problem. The extra dozen men on the assembly line will soon no longer be there. So twenty percent of our business is exporting to forty-five countries around the world." The States look attractive, but Yaffe recognizes that either he or his partner would have to be there to run things.

"One of the keys to success is self-discipline," says Jaffe, adding that "I should have been in the military!" Back in 1967 he realized that he needed "a good inside man." He offered one-half of the business to a man named Alan Schwartz, telling him that he could have it for free. Schwartz insisted on putting $9,000 capital into Safety House, interest-free, and a partnership was born. "I look after finance, sales, R & D; Alan looks after orders, etc. We've never had a cross word in our lives, and later became brothers-in-law." Yaffe claims that the two are "as opposite as night and day." (They must be; Yaffe drives the Rolls, Schwartz a Porsche.)

Are the men and their business admired in the industry? Not on your danger-filled life: "We're very aggressive and disliked by the other safety companies because of it. We're innovators; every product we have, we go out and build the demand! We're no me-too organization."

An example will suffice: Safety House of Canada is the largest manufacturer of first aid kits in North America, and have been number 1 in the product since the late 1970s. The reason for this is extremely revealing: Yaffe had been selling kits to Eaton's, Simpson's, The Bay for years, and had strong competition from Johnson & Johnson and Curity. "They were low value, but people gravitated to them because of the famous names." Yaffe went to Canadian Tire and suggested that they fight that with a private brand, and they did. But the brand names continued to dominate.

The decision was simple: Spend $10 million to $100 million to build up a name. But he couldn't do that. So Yaffe thought to himself. "Who's got the most respected name in first aid?" The answer came quickly to mind: St. John's Ambulance. Yaffe went to them and asked the $64,000,000 question: "Do you people believe that the first aid kits on the market are any good?" "They're all junk," was the reply. "Would you be willing to design one with me?" "St. John's in the stores? No way!"

It took seven full years of begging to get the loan of the name of St. John's Ambulance. Today, St. John's Ambulance First Aid Kits sell in the $16.95 to $18.95 range, right across the continent, hundreds of thousands of them, every year. "I kicked Johnson & Johnson right out of the stores," says Yaffe, grinning. "And Curity went right out of the business of first aid kits." The new best-seller is manufactured by Yaffe.

Gerald Yaffe has simple advice for any teenagers in the late 1980s who wish to go into business as he did: "You have to give customers what they want, and must switch immediately with the times. You must plug into a localized market, even if suppliers won't change. We won't flog a product that isn't moving. For instance, we introduced fashion safety eyewear.

People want to look good wherever they are! A game plan has to be established, and there must be a consistency to that plan. You've got to work hard and learn to understand how to finance a business well at all times."

Yaffe differs from many entrepreneurs, in that he believed very strongly in the ownership of his assets. "There is nothing leased in this place," he exclaims. "My lower-class background made me want to own everything. We owned our phones the very day that Bell Canada allowed it. You can mortgage assets, not leases. And you can depreciate assets, too."

Yaffe has lots to depreciate. His fixed assets are close to $7 million, with $4½ million worth of safety products in inventory and another $1 million in the warehouse.

Any spare time Yaffe has is spent with his wife and two teenage daughters, and the many charitable institutions he helps run and support, to the tune of hundreds of thousands a year. And how can anything go wrong when every disaster is a potential windfall? The Canadian and U.S. armies have access to Safety House of Canada on an emergency basis, and most of the supplies for the Italian earthquake relief came from his warehouse. "We're plugged into the PCB situation with protective kits as well," says Gerald Yaffe. "We look above and beyond. The growth is there."

# WHERE THERE'S SMOKE THERE'S MONEY

### Steve Chepa

One of the magical aspects of business and entrepreneurship is that new markets, new inventions are always opening. Twenty years ago—even ten years ago—which of us had a smoke detector in our home or apartment? That was the stuff of factories and hotel rooms. And today, which of us do not? (If you are one who does not, the name of the firm profiled here along with its creator is called Dicon Systems Limited. That's D-I-C-O-N.) Founded only a decade ago, back when you barely knew about the product, Dicon had sales of 16.2 million in 1986, $1½ million of that in net profit after taxes, making it one of the world's leading developers and manufacturers of ionization and photoelectric smoke alarm systems for residential use. And winning the Canadian Export Award of 1984 as this country's top exporter shows just how successful Steve Chepa and John Mallory have been.

Chepa, with a striking look caused by his prematurely grey hair and still-black eyebrows, was born in Hamilton, Ontario, in the spring of 1939. He was the second child and first boy born to a father who came from the Carpathian Mountains of Eastern Europe to the Montreal/Toronto/Hamilton hills of Canada. (His wife had lived on the other side of the mountain, and stayed at home to raise the kids while he went into the baking business.) When the future president of Dicon was in grade 3, he was "a junk dealer," picking stuff out of garbage cans and selling it. "There were rags-and-bones men, and I would bargain with them, getting one or two dollars for my loads."

As with many future entrepreneurs, Chepa never received an allowance; "If I wanted money, I had to go out and earn it." So he would buy bubble gum, chew it to death, and then use it to pick coins out of grates, just like they used to do in the movies. "I made a dollar on a good day, looking down all the cracks in Hamilton."

With such an inspired background, Steve Chepa just had to get his Bachelor of Commerce degree at McMaster University, followed by a stint at Price Waterhouse as a C.A. "I'd always wanted my own business," he says, however. "When I was in my late teens, working in a bakeshop on the night shift, I used to daydream and build empires." With smoke detectors on the ceilings to protect the emperor, one hopes.

After he wrote his final exams, he found that the going rate for C.A.s at the time was $8,500 annually, to which Chepa announced, "Whoever pays me nine thousand dollars will get me." Chubb Mosler & Taylor did, and got him. "I thought that if they'd pay that much, they would surely use me," he recalls. How wrong he was. They sent him to a converted garage filled with 15 people in a giant room. His desk was in the middle. He eventually called his boss and asked, "What's my title?" He was chief accountant. The year was 1965 and he was 26. "I put down my head and said, 'Oh, fuck, what have I *done*?'" He quickly got his title changed to controller, and within two weeks he had an office in the corner.

Chepa was at Chubb for over five years, steadily moving up the corporate ladder: secretary-treasurer, then assistant general manager, then vice-president, then vice-president and general manager. Why such upward movements? "I was in a position to be able to do things that would be seen," he says. It was a case of doing more than what was expected of him; he would quickly get everything organized and then ask for other stuff to do. He got the salesmen to do better too.

He kept getting raises, and "they were aware that I was ambitious and wanted to do things. I worked pretty hard." It was a case of "living your work," Chepa explains to you other potential entrepreneurs. "That's the difference between getting ahead and not getting ahead; between the guy at the top and the mediocrity." (He defines the latter as the one who may work 12 hours a day and be a "super-production machine," but he never improves anything—he never does anything creative. He adds to this, "There are very few positions where you can be *seen* to produce twice as much as others, but if you *produce* changes, and they're *better*, you get noticed.")

The problem was that the powers that were at Chubb "*knew* that I was chafing at the bit," so they tried to keep it challenging for Chepa. And they tried to keep him from leaving by paying him very well. "I could have ended up as a career executive," he admits, "with money piling up at the bank." But Chubb Canada moved its premises, earnings declined, and the chairman decided that he'd help Chepa "run things better. And I used to correct *his* errors at my meetings."

Eventually, Chepa was fired, since he was "not willing to let him star in the circumstances. It was my ego; I had to let everyone know that I didn't agree." Like many a man or woman pushed out, Chepa looks back and thinks, "If I hadn't been fired, I'd be nowhere near where I am today."

So in 1971 Steve Chepa found himself married, soon to be a father, and unemployed. He kicked around for a while, ending up joining with John Mallory. Chepa had hired him when at Chubb back in 1968, to start electronic manufacturing, and he was still at the firm when he called his former co-worker in 1972. The two men had heard of a division of Neeco for sale, they decided to be partners, and they bought it, putting up $5,000 each, "along with a lot of paper." By the end of the first day at the business, they realized that good will was so low they'd have to change the name of the place, which made alarm systems for high-rise towers and apartment buildings. The new name was Check Security Systems.

For two years the partners struggled against a large competitor, who kept undercutting them. Sales were low, there was only one secretary, one on the product line, a service man, and the two of them. "We tried to build a business out of that," Chepa recalls. Then, in November 1974, when Chepa "tried to steal a large account," he ended up selling the business but keeping the smoke alarm product. They took all the money they received and rolled it into that alarm, founding Dicon Systems in the summer of 1976. (The name came from their playing with words and symbols, finally contracting "digital" and "controls." And it was "the easiest to register, since Dicon really doesn't describe anything.")

They started manufacturing that same summer, their first order coming from Sunbeam, for 20,000 units. In the first year of Dicon the two men sold $1 million worth of smoke alarms, making $60,000 in profit. The second year they sold $6.6 million worth of alarms, with an awesome $2 million in profits. "It was a bonanza year!" Chepa declares, his long, wavy white hair seeming to waterfall down the back of his neck, his white teeth gleaming. "We realized that we were right: Smoke detectors were the coming thing!"

But not so fast; in the third year they lost money—the only year that they did. They had an amazing $10 million in sales, yet they *actually lost money*. How? "We weren't the *only* people who bet on smoke detectors! We discovered forty-five different manufacturers in the States making them for the North American market!" It's the old story; how long did Häagen-Dazs and Tofutti remain the only premium ice cream product and tofu derivative?

They had already grown to 240 employees, and they quickly cut back to 60. "We had to scramble to stop the hemorrhaging!" When the fourth year was complete, their sales were down to $3 million, and they began rebuilding. They made a drastic, but ultimately lifesaving, move: They pulled out of the American market. "We felt that no one could make money there, and we didn't have the resources to fight it out."

So Dicon looked to Europe, doing pioneering work there, and took the major share of Canada while they were at it.

They started in Sweden, then moved on to Norway and Finland. It wasn't until 1983 that they decided to take another shot at the U.S. market, "and we've been very successful against people who had grown tired of fighting!" As of 1986, Dicon of Weston, Ontario, in suburban Toronto, will probably have a dominant share of the smoke alarm business in every country they are in, with the exception of the States.

From that low point in 1981, Dicon Systems has grown steadily to where it is today. To get more liquidity and diversify, they went public in 1985, listing on the TSE and selling 1.1 million common shares at $4.25 each. Within weeks, the price was up 50%. Furthermore, Chepa and Mallory felt that they were at the point that "the next logical step was to get bigger." The two men still own 67% of Dicon between them, but the company is finally out of debt and has money in the bank. "Now we are free to think of more smoke detectors, more gas detectors, more burglar alarms," Chepa says. "If we're as successful as we hope, we'll need money for more parts and inventory."

Dicon looks like a solid success at last, with no domestic producers to compete with them anywhere in Europe, so they can meet the Yanks as equals. And they still manage to sell close to half their products in the States as well. "You can't buy a better smoke detector at a better price," declares Chepa. "We're equal to the others in every aspect—warranty, the completeness of our line, our delivery, our ratings in every consumer study."

The potential is indeed spectacular. The 80 million households in North America means a $100 million potential, and Europe has an equal market, making $200 million possible sales in the developed world. It is fascinating to note that when Chepa, Mallory, and Dicon went to life insurance companies, they got turned down by them all! But the *property* insurance companies supported them from the start, giving discounts on home insurance to those who had smoke detectors in their residences. And at least 20 companies in Canada have mailed out brochures to all their subscribers, recommending Dicon. How many businesses get free brochures plugging their product, mailed by *other companies?*

Dicon now has up to 30 different models of smoke detectors, along with a growing security system of alarms. "In our R & D efforts, we have a revolutionary residential burglar alarm which should change the way people buy them." They also have developed gas detectors for recreational vehicles and, soon, for the home, too.

Why such success, Steve Chepa? "It takes a lot of perserverance. You've got to want it badly. You've got to live your job, so your personal life suffers, so it's important that one's family supports you in it." But even with "intelligence, desire, and a lot of hard work," there's that All-Canadian Problem: Our market is simply too small for one to sell enough units per day to get labour costs low enough to go international. "You must take a share of the world market to succeed, if you're Canadian; in the States, they can stay home to do it. Well, we're taking on the world, and winning. Our sales could be up to $100 million by 1990." To make it in the cutthroat world of smoke alarms is to be a survivor. Margaret Atwood, meet three more Canadian survivors: Steve Chepa, John Mallory, and Dicon.

# CLEANING UP IN BUSINESS

## *Leslie Hulicsko*

Many of the women in this book created businesses out of their hobbies, so there is no reason why some Canadian men could not do the same. In the case of Leslie Hulicsko, of Hungary and Saskatchewan, the hobby was anything mechanical, and the results have meant a good living for the immigrant, and paycheques for the many Regina employees of Rite Way Manufacturing Company Ltd.

The handsome, square-faced Hulicsko was born in 1936 in Kacs, a small town about 100 miles east of Budapest. His family were "very small farmers," working about 20 acres of corn, wheat, and vineyards. "We starved for about a year after the crops were ruined during the war," he recalls. He was the fifth of six, and the only child who would eventually leave Hungary. "I was *very* industrious," he brags. By the age of three or four he was building miniairplane toys, and cars that he could drive and steer. By the age of nine he was fixing clocks and other household items "as a favour for friends. I could make parts for them. I had super skills with my hands."

It was only natural that he took four years of engineering, finishing in 1955. He had just started work, with plans to continue his studies in engineering in the evening, when the Revolution came. With great pleasure, Hulicsko recalls knocking down Russian statues and picking up a piece of marble from one and placing it in his pocket. It sits now in his home in Regina. "I saw history being made!"

But it was time to get out. After some difficulties with Russian soldiers in Budapest, he managed to get to Canada in 1957. He had hoped to emigrate to the United States, but the quota was filled by the time he got to Austria. After eight months of waiting, he decided to come to Canada. "I asked to be dropped off anyplace," he says, "and they dropped me in Regina. And I'm still here!"

Business success did not come overnight, to be sure. Although he knew no more than a few words of English, he found a job in construction within two weeks. He would go to the unemployment office every day, staying there until it closed. "They noticed that I was persistent, so I finally got work." He laid sewer pipes from August 20 until they were laid off the winter. The following spring he landed a similar construction job, building runways at the Regina airport.

But the Hungarian/Canadian had a history of a bad knee, and he reinjured it and had to put it in a cast. Since he could no longer do any "hard construction," he took a job as a window cleaner. It was to be one of those fortunate, injury-caused turning points in a person's life.

"I saw it was a business that I could get into easily!" he exclaims, over a quarter century later. "The owner of the business was *so* inefficient! He should not have survived, yet he was making money!" Sounds like federal politics. Hulicsko was struck by the fact that the prices were so good "my boss could charge whatever he wanted and make a good living from cleaning!"

He learned the lesson quickly, opening his own company in 1959—Rite-Way Cleaning Services Ltd. "I saw the name in a U.S. magazine and liked it." (Thank heavens he didn't see ads for IBM.) It cost him less than $400 to found it.

For the first while, he did most of the work himself, and when it got busy, he hired assistants. Since he specialized in window cleaning, he soon bought a stepladder, pails, sponges, and brushes. Sales the first year were around $15,000. His first breakthrough came in a rather strange way; he happened to get the contract to clean the windows of the federal buildings in Regina. "I was very, very fortunate," he says. "When it came up for tender, I didn't really want it, so I bid *very* high. Yet all the other cleaning companies bid higher! So I beat them all!"

The victory was short-lived; at the end of the following year the other companies "fought back," and Hulicsko lost his government contract. But by the third year the others "realized that I was here to stay, and they stopped undercutting me."

In 1965 Hulicsko saw himself overlooking a miniempire. Sales were up to $80,000 a year, with some ten part-time employees. (In the winter they were all laid off; this is Regina we're talking about.) And all this while, those gifted hands of Leslie Hulicsko could not be kept still. He finally incorporated Rite Way Manufacturing Co. Ltd. in 1969, and by 1973 he had created a rock picker. Within two years, he was up to $1½ million in sales, with up to 20 employees.

"The rock picker was an instant success," he says gleefully. "The need was there, and the timing was right. We projected twenty-five units in the first year, and we ended up selling over three hundred and fifty in '73–'74." (He was lucky if he sold a few dozen rock pickers in 1986, due to the economy of the prairies recently.)

But there were very good times. In 1978 he sold 600 rock pickers, which cost as much as $2,800 apiece. "I designed and built a machine that works on large *and* small rocks," he declares. "You *know* that I was trained as a designer-engineer!"

But something else occurred in the life and career of Leslie Hulicsko that could make him a very rich man. It had to do with that earlier cleaning business. "As I grew from windows to janitorial, I began to do a lot of parking lot maintenance. I purchased a sweeper to clean the parking lots and the streets around them."

The great thing was that the sweeper turned out to be "the most troublesome part of my business." It broke down continually, and guess who had to fix it? "I couldn't afford to keep doing that, and the warranty ran out! It was built *terrible*, from an engineering standpoint!" (Hulicsko used to mutter, "I will *hang* the man who designed this machine!" You can take the boy out of the country. . . .) Oh, yes: It was American-made.

"So the need was there!" enthuses the mad inventor. H
had heard of a machine in Sweden, and went there to bu
one. It was better than all the others he'd seen, but still no
satisfactory. "No one could perform parking lot maintenance!"
It was 1978 when it all began to come together: He wa
building a lot of rock pickers, but farm machinery was gettin
harder to sell, and Hulicsko was looking for diversification. S
he sat down and designed a sweeper.

It was not an instant success, but he began to sell a goo
number to small municipalities. "It was a tow-type, towed b
a tractor," selling for around $23,000. And Hulicsko centere
on that type until 1982, when he realized that he couldn't se
to larger cities unless it was self-propelled. "We knew we ha
a reliable sweeper, better than all others on the market, but
needed to design a self-propelled unit, with a tractor in it.
The first ones came off the assembly line that same year.

During the fiscal year 1985 Leslie Hulicsko sold nearly 5
units, at a cost of between $72,000 and $82,000 each, an
20% over that, in 1986. Sales from all his inventions, whic
had reached $3 million in 1980, were up to $4 million by Jun
1987, with four dozen employees. "They sky is the limit,
says Mr. Rite Way. He has sold the self-propelled models t
Regina, Prince Albert, and the Departments of National De
fence and Transport. Even the States have been impressed;
he sold five to Los Angeles, and one each to San Francisco,
Chicago, and Clearwater, Florida. He has even sold a mode
to Australia. "I'm working hard on the City of Chicago now,
he says, smiling. "I have a fair chance of selling them twenty-
five units." (We've been in the Windy City recently; it needs
them.) Pittsburgh and New York City are testing them, and
Australia and Mexico have actually bought. And the profit on
each machine is a very, very healthy 30%.

The sky—which needs to be kept clean, too—certainly *is*
the limit; Hulicsko expects to be up to 200 units annually by
1990, and with his facilities—28,000 square feet—he would
have up to 75 employees at that time. "These are the *only*
self-propelled sweepers made in Canada!" he cries, and there
are only three companies in the States who make them. (And
we already know about how good *they* are.)

Leslie Hulicsko has been married for 18 years and has a
teenaged son who he hopes will join him in the business. And
for a man who owns a multi-million-dollar manufacturing

firm, he takes home very little money: Around $55,000 a year. "I live very modestly," he says. "A nice home, new cars, a modest boat."

But there are debts, of course. He owed $2½ million to the bank when those interest rates climbed to 22%; he has managed to chop that debt down to less than $1 million. And he knows why: "You've got to watch your costs; no fancy offices; watch every dollar. And hard work; there's no substitute for hard work."

And creativity, too. "I've got *millions* of ideas, but you can only do so much! I could produce a whole *lot* of machines, and different designs!" And the fact that Rite Way Manufacturing Company Ltd. is in Regina and not Budapest is one reason he probably *will*.

# RAISING THE DEAD WITH ELASTIC

## Sandy Archibald

When someone "makes a go" of a business where someone else failed, it seems almost doubly pleasurable. And when a major reason why that "go" is going so well is due to employee ownership, it is enough to make us dance for joy. Which is why there is such a special response from all who hear of Sandy Archibald and Britex Ltd., of Bridgetown, Nova Scotia.

Archibald was born in New York City in 1943 and grew up in Westchester. His father was from Halifax and his mother from New Brunswick, so it was only natural that he attend McGill University in Montreal and, to quote from poet Leonard Cohen, renew some of his neurotic affiliations. He had planned on premeds, but ended up in chemistry.

After graduating in 1965, Archibald "decided to go out into the real world" and was a technical salesman for Allied Chemical Corporation in Morristown, New Jersey, covering New England. Then he decided "to move back to Canada," resigning his position and returning to Granville Ferry, across from Annapolis Royal, where he had visited year after year with his parents.

The future saviour of Bridgetown, N.S., had been with

his first job for five years and a day, and he found himself with a wife, two children, and no job in Canada. "But we knew that we had to move then or not at all. Maybe there is more to life than the rat race." He eventually ran into United Elastic, which he knew from his earlier job, when he used to sell to one of their American divisions. They made him a job offer as a plant chemist, and he accepted. "My goal was to stay in the Valley, although there wasn't much industry around."

He soon moved up to the role of plant production manager and ran the narrow fabric division for five years. "We made anything that stretches: trimming for bras, girdles, hockey chin-holders." They are even into dancercize suits, and have "some potential for moulding in the auto industry."

The history of United Elastic is relevant here. It was a company out of East Hampton, Massachusetts, created from a merger in the late nineteenth century of a number of New England elastic manufacturers. It evolved as a public company but was privately held by one family. After becoming the dominant elastic factory in the world, it looked at foreign markets, and had exported a lot into Canada. The branch plant in Nova Scotia was created in 1959. "They chose Bridgetown because they could get cheap, and good, labour here," says Archibald. It was not typical for the area, of course; squashed between Middletown and Annapolis, about 15 miles above the tidal basin, the area is basically agricultural.

The Bridgetown plant grew and prospered, with three expansions over the years. At its peak, 300 people worked for United Elastic, which made it the largest employee in the Valley. Then, in 1967, the plant was acquired by J.P. Stevens of the U.S., "a billion-dollar textile company of *Norma Rae* fame," says Archibald. Stevens went on to pick up Mexican and Belgian operations, but the Canadian plant did not fare too well as the years went on. It became out-of-date and unprofitable, which is not, traditionally, the way that multinationals like their branch plants to be.

Meanwhile, Sandy Archibald had left United Elastic in 1975 as manager of its narrow fabric operations. He went with one of the many Irving companies, which manufactures mobile homes. Then, in 1977, he got a call from Stevens, asking him to come back as managing director of the Bridgetown plant. He was basically in charge of Canadian operations, whereas before, "I had run a half-plant, from the manufacturing point of view."

The problem was that the old plant really "required a turnaround. They used to be able to mint money on that place, but no longer." From 1977 to 1980 Archibald tried to clean up operations there, but the management group recognized the need for major investment—an infusion of capital and state-of-the-art equipment. Stevens decided that it could not justify the risk and cost of modernization, and considered, in 1979, either closing it or selling it. Which is where Sandy Archibald, Entrepreneur, comes to the forefront of our tale.

When our hero was advised of Stevens' decision in early 1980, he asked if they would be willing to look at an offer from the present management group. As Archibald says it, "We located a damned fine accountant, and a good lawyer, and made an offer to the mother company." The offer was craftily based on how much it would cost Stevens to close the place down.

The structure of Archibald's plan was simple: DREE (the federal Department of Regional Economic Expansion) was in place in the Maritimes, and he managed to get its approval for a close-down and start-up. He got money for job creation and modernization, along with the recognition that the factory would close if Archibald and its crew did not take it over. The DREE grant was $1.4 million for the acquisition, and to finance the purchase he went to the Industrial Estates Ltd., a provincial organization, for the mortgage. "We had to come up with $500,000 for equity level; eventually, it was $750,000."

The only catch was that Archibald didn't have the cash. He went to the six in his management group and told them about the dilemma, and they began to scurry around for money. They ended up buying the whole corporation for a mere $100,000 in cash, after convincing Stevens that they needed loan-backs. "We wanted to ensure employee participation, but did not tell them yet. So we borrowed $100,000 on behalf of them."

In other words, the deal was extremely high-leveraged. All seven in the group went out and borrowed money, and, fortunately, the package satisfied Stevens's needs and gave the new company a healthy let-up. Next came the business equivalent of the cavalry coming around the bend at the last minute: Stevens announced the shutdown of the Nova Scotia plant in July, since DREE was late with the funds. Archibald had to notify the employees of their anticipation of DREE funding, which came through on August 1, 1980. "We quickly reopened under new ownership," says Archibald. "There wasn't even any interruption in supplies to customers."

That's all very nice, but Sandy Archibald and his employees had a slight problem. In his own words: "How the hell would *we* be able to make a viable company when a billion-dollar firm could not? And why buy it if we couldn't do it?"

Fortunately, they had answers to those bothersome questions. For one thing, they knew that there was genuine opportunity for market growth. For another, they had all that new technology. "The only real competitive advantage we had," says Archibald, "is that we had local people and talent in Nova Scotia. And the concept of employee participation and profit sharing was the *key* thrust."

There were credibility problems, naturally: "You were the guys who ran that firm into the ground!" To which Archibald would reply, "It's a different ballgame now! We've got profit sharing!" They set up a management-employee committee, and wrote a new company policy manual. Archibald announced that 10% of pretax profits would go to employees. (There were 175 workers then, and now.) "The employee committee has evolved to the point where they kicked the management off, and did a fantastic job!" declares the then-president, now chairman, of Britex Ltd.

Archibald was thrilled to discover that the employees were often harder on themselves than his management team would ever have dared to be. They even hired a stockbroker to help them on how worthwhile it would be to invest in the company's stock. "One thing I noticed," says Archibald gleefully, his youthful countenance all smiles beneath his thick moustache: "The attitude before was 'If that machine comes in, there goes my job!' Now, it's 'When you gonna get rid of that old machine and get some new ones in?' "

Under Stevens, when the factory briefly closed in the summer of 1980, sales were between $5 and $6 million a year. Today, they are edging up to $10 million annually. "The same number of employees, with three times the sales!" rejoices Archibald. In the very first year of the revolution, they distributed money through the profit-sharing plan, as they have continued to do for every year except one. "It *is* viable and profitable!" says the chairman. "Being totally employee-owned, the concern is the return to the shareholders over the *long* term. We are committed to a state-of-the-art shop, with a lot of reinvestment here. We are willing to forego profits today to be in better shape ten to fifteen years down the road." After "a year of adjustment" in 1986, which included "major capital infusion," Britex is running at a 25–30% growth rate in 1987 over last year.

The money explosion has been modest for the workers; they have averaged one to three weeks' extra pay, per employee, in profit sharing. But it has paid off in other ways: Those who bought shares in 1981 paid around $1.25; those same shares are worth close to $6 each now, plus some $1 in dividends over the years.

Archibald is also pleased with the way his company has broadened and diversified itself. Before the 1980 takeover, 80% of their business was with the bra and girdle trade; today, there is no single market which takes more than 25% of Britex's products. There are up to ten different markets which buy their goods.

The "boss" is still not satisfied with the hourly rate at Britex (which is a contraction of Bridgetown Textile, by the way). They were 77% of the average wage in knitting mills when they took over the factory; currently they are 93% of the average. "But we've sweetened the benefit package, and there are productivity bonuses as well. Still, our average hourly rate is between $6 and $6.50, which is *not* very high."

But the five-year plan hints at a bright figure for the lunatics who took over the asylum. Archibald predicts sales to be over $20 million annually by the end of this decade, and he adds quietly, "It should be higher than that, actually. We want to stay small, and not go over two hundred employees."

The "basic thrust" of Archibald and his employees *cum* partners could not be more simple (or more un-Canadian, to be nasty for a moment): to be competitive in world markets. The direct labour costs of Britex were 22 to 23% of expenses in 1980; today they are down to under 12%. His goal is to get them down to 8%.

And he is cognizant of the fact that the future growth of Britex will not be in the Canadian marketplace, since their base in this country is diminishing with all the foreign imports. "We'll stick with Bridgetown, and we'll ship to the

Philippines," declares Archibald, giving what one must consider the elastic and textiles equivalent of coals to Newcastle. "We will produce specialties in small volume, cheaper and of higher quality than anywhere else. Flexible manufacturing is the whole structure here, while the U.S. and the Far East are into volume. We can do some runs as small as two to three days." Already he is selling to Australia, New Zealand, Europe, the Caribbean, the United States, even Hong Kong.

Like many a successful businessman, Sandy Archibald denies his importance in the matter of the saving of Britex from a fate equal to death (and it remains the town's largest single employer). "I don't have the skills, talent, and ability to pull off what happened," he insists. "I found resources and people. It was salesmanship, I'll agree: I convinced people at United Elastic and at Britex to believe in it. I had the role of the coach." He also credits his commitment to principles like employee participation as being important. "Many in our management group didn't believe in it," he notes, "but they sure as hell do today!"

Ultimately, Archibald rejects the title of entrepreneur. "I think of myself as being a fairly good businessman who can keep things in perspective, and have a good overview. And one who can convince people which way to go. But I get my ideas for the right direction from *them*!"

In a way, he is correct. It was the employees themselves who agreed to switch from a five-day week to a seven-day week, running the plant around the clock and thus increasing productivity enormously. And it was the employees who instituted a sickness insurance plan which Archibald feared would lead to increased absenteeism; instead, the problem dropped to a quarter of previous levels, due to a new moral obligation to come to the factory.

But only an entrepreneur could declare that the billion-dollar Stevens textile company "has learned a lot from Britex. They are tremendously happy that we're successful." Norma Rae, move to Nova Scotia; you'd be delighted to see what Canadians can do with the textile industry. But not half as delighted as 175 employees, and another thousand spouses, children, grandchildren, and relatives, who rejoice every day that Sandy Archibald* managed to make a go of Britex Ltd. in Bridgetown, N.S.

* * *

*Archibald completed his five years as President of Britex, in the summer of 1985, and was "bumped up" to Chairman, which involves him once a week. He is now also the President of a venture capital firm, Fundy Ventures Ltd., of Nova Scotia, which is involved in biological products, precise machinery electronics, and even a riverboat for the tourist industry. Indeed, as a result of all this, he's now the head of the Venture Capital Association of Nova Scotia. What an elastic career!

**7.**

# FITNESS, SPORTS, AND OUTDOOR RECREATION

### *"Health, Anyone?"*

One can hardly build a business based on statistics. But numbers, like calories, do count, as can be seen in the following Canada Fitness Survey, "Participation in recreational activities," for 1981: 57% of all Canadians aged 10 and over walked (they need shoes!), 38% biked (they need bikes!), 36% swam (they need swimsuits!), 31% jogged or ran (more shoes!), 21% ice skated (skates!), 18% cross-country skied (equipment!), 15% played tennis (more equipment!), 13% golfed (ditto), 11% Alpine skied (ditto), 9% played ice hockey (ditto), 8% attended exercise classes (they are more than welcome to join!), and 6% played racquetball (still more equipment).

Other statistics from StatsCan suggest the excellent business possibilities in the world of fitness, sports, and outdoor recreation: Between 1978 and 1980 there was a striking increase of 44% in Canadian households owning one or more pairs of cross-country skis. And between 1971 and 1980 the number of households owning adult-sized bikes more than doubled, until 44% of households owned them. Households owning some type of overnight camping equipment increased by one-half, from 18% in 1971 to 27% in 1980. (Alberta, with all those mountains just going to waste, had 42% of its households owning camping equipment as of 1980.) Even boat ownerships moved up 33%, from 12% of households in 1971 to 16% in 1980.

In a sentence: A Canadian time-use pilot study in 1981 showed that our average citizen spent 5.3 hours a day on leisure activities, second only to sleeping, which is traditionally more restful and less expensive, once you've purchased the mattresses.

As one can readily see, all these hours away from the office—combined with a growing amount of disposable income on the part of a large number of Canadians, joined with an even more rapidly growing desire for physical fitness and health—has led to extraordinary business potential in the realms of sports and recreation.

In this chapter we shall look at two women and five men who have thrived in the field of fitness (Barbara Crompton of The Fitness Group of Vancouver and Michael Levy of the Racquet Sports Group of Toronto), sports clothes and equipment (Sylvia Rempel of Sun Ice of Calgary, Mike Dyon of Brooks Shoes, Alex Tilley of Tilley Endurables, and the Kent family of Bloor Cycle, all of Toronto), and outdoor recreation (Harry Bondar of Hunter's, of North Battleford, Saskatchewan, and Dave Steele of Three Buoys Houseboats of Calgary and Toronto).

These men and women range from their 20s to their 60s, but their average age is barely 40, since it is a highly energetic, physically active field. (The two oldest manufacture sports clothes and sell boats and RVs, which involve less running about in gym shoes than the rest, but no fewer hours.)

More than any other interviewees in this book, the vast majority of these entrepreneurs were attracted to their chosen business due to their passionate physical involvement in the sport: Crompton had run a summer gym programme, loved to work out, and "saw a trend with exercise in the market." Michael Levy loved racquet sports, "noticed the growth of tennis clubs in Detroit," and wondered who could afford all those private clubs. Sylvia Rempel had always sewn her family's clothes, and when they all began to ski, she sewed for that as well. Mike Dyon is a competitive runner who had/has a love affair with a certain kind of shoe, which he eventually brought up to Canada. Alex Tilley was a sailor who "set out to make the ideal hat" for boating. The Kents were bikers, and in the biking business for three generations. Only Harry Bondar of Hunter's and Dave Steele of houseboat fame could be described as businessmen first and sportsmen later—and even Steele is a dedicated skier, if not a lifelong houseboat advocate.

Does this mean that one can easily turn one's leisure activity into a thriving business? Not on your sweatband, it doesn't. For these people approached their chosen businesses with a thoughtfulness that belies their hobby-into-profession ease. Crompton did "demographic research to find out the needs of the community" for fitness clubs; Levy is doing the same today, except in the States, to see the potential of his Racquet Sports Group south of de bordah. Rempel deliberately avoided department stores which wanted her ski outfits "cheap and in volume" and aimed for "fashion-conscious" ski shoppes, and she is forever "changing fabric and colours to reflect trends."

Dyon of Brooks notes how he listens to customers; Tilley created wonderfully witty advertisements, and even produced an "owner's manual" for his hats and shorts, to grab the public's attention. The Kent family "broke all the rules" with their giant bike store but have continually innovated since 1960, with literate ads, an avoidance of sales (until 1986), videos showing how to care for one's bike, good pay for employees, and a "respect for customers."

Bondar also made service his "backbone" at Hunter's; bought boats and RVs in volume and paid cash for them, so he could lower his prices (and selling $60 million worth of product in the middle of the prairies is nothing less than miraculous). And Dave Steele—well, to go from two boats and one employee in 1982 to 625 boats and 350 employees just five years later, with sales breaking $25 million, is a story worthy of Apple's Steve Jobs.

"We're in the life-style business," says Levy; so is everyone in this chapter. For some, it's a mission ("My calling in life is to change the life-style of thousands," says Vancouver's Crompton); for others, it's even aesthetic ("These [hats and clothes] are works of art," declares Tilley). But all would agree with supersalesman Bondar of small-town Saskatchewan: "People are getting away more; there's more disposable income, more time to relax." And much more time to spend money on clubs, clothes, equipment, boats, RVs, and houseboat vacations. Which is why these men and women are very successful and even wealthy. And they will get even more so—as if your life depended on it. And it probably does.

## GETTING YOUR BUSINESS IN SHAPE

### *Barbara Crompton*

As we all know only too well, the '60s were hippie-ish, the '70s were selfish, and the '80s are lose-your-hips-ish. And if sex was the last decade's big best-seller, business and health are the big sellers in this one. That is why Barbara Crompton of Vancouver—with her perfect body, shoulder-length blond hair, Joni-Mitchell-like face, and radiant smile—is so impressive: Not only has she built up an ever-expanding chain of fitness centres across Vancouver, but she began it all back in 1976, when, to paraphrase one witty commentator, Richard Simmons was still fat and Jane Fonda was known only as a left-wing actress.

Crompton was born in Vancouver in 1950, to parents who had, and still have, a contractor business, carpeting apartments. She was the lastborn of three, with two older brothers also now in business. "The role modelling was big to follow," she says, since her mother was "very wrapped up in the business." From grade 8 on, she "always had some skill going." For instance, she began a summer exercise gym program called Playin', combining working out with arts and crafts, and ran it for three years.

She went to U.B.C., graduating in 1972 from the Faculty of Education, but she "was burnt out by the time I got out of school. I O.D.-ed on children!" She substitute-taught but didn't want a full-time job, even though she was offered a number of them. In 1976 she married a lawyer who has a contracting company, but who has been active 40% of his time in his wife's business since 1981. They have two daughters under the age of seven.

Between those years, Barbara Crompton did waitressing jobs, "did nothing," travelled to Europe, Mexico, and Guatemala for two years, came home, worked, left, worked. "I was going to go back to graduate school, but never did," she says. She sold advertising for a newspaper for two years, and—*nota bene*—she "saw a trend with exercise in the market."

So, in 1976 she began The Fitness Group, with the concept "Fitness for Everybody!" There was a wide range of pupils, from 18 to 64, with the bulk from 25 to 40. "We followed the baby-boomers as they grew up," she says, going after the middle- to upper-income people, who, fortunately, have more time and money to spend on keeping themselves in shape. From the start, it was "sophisticated. The classes and activities are safe."

When she first began, Crompton rented spaces around town on an hourly basis, with maybe a $1,000 initial investment. "I knew the media, due to my advertising background," she notes. For instance, she approached a friend who wrote for the papers, and told her, "Why not write about *me?*" Why not, indeed.

Back in the mid-1970s, no one in Vancouver had done "en masse exercise," with from 30 to 100 people working out at one time. People paid $35 for three months for exercise and aerobic classes. It's now up to $80 for three months, $135 for half a year. (She has had weight rooms available since 1983 for an extra $15 a session.)

Sales in 1976? Hold your breath and jump up and down; she doesn't give out figures (although hers is gorgeous; pick up *Fitness and Fashion*, Vancouver's fitness magazine, December 1983; she's on the cover, and quite irresistible). "It's *my* business," she insists, saying that she doesn't tell her 8 full-time staff and 35 part-time, so why should she tell *me?* And she could easily physically hurt me, if I pressed further.

But it's clearly been a huge success. The first store-front location opened in 1980, with the second following nine months later. Other facilities are rented, with contracts. They put on programmes for facilities, such as the Insurance Corporation of British Columbia, managing their facilities for them. As of the end of 1987 Crompton had two stores, three rented facilities, and nine contracts with major corporations. "We do demographic research and find out needs of the community," she says. There are healthy-back programs, weight-loss programs, ski-fit programs, weight training, fitness assessment, nutritional analysis.

Crompton has also craftily taken "issues," such as *Eating to Win*, and has utilized her credibility to challenge them. She presents open lectures and gives Vancouverites a chance to hear experts on the various fields. In late 1985 she had about 6,000 people a week working out in her various stores, with the number ranging down to 4,000 per week in the summer and up to 7,000 in the winter. For the past four years she has been hired by her alma mater to do all student and staff programmes in fitness, with up to 18 exercise classes a week at the University of British Columbia. "There are probably another fifteen hundred in other programs."

With her wonderful combination of fitness awareness and business sense, Barbara Crompton is unbeatable. "I'm working toward the employee fitness end," she says. "Fitness in the workplace is the future. I see tax and insurance benefits as they see health programmes growing in companies. In the future, I see my Fitness Group playing a role in all this."

Yet Crompton is not about to be Canada's or North America's Colonel Sanders of Exercise. "I have no delusions of grandeur about one hundred stores across Canada," she says. "I decided years ago that I'm trying to teach people new life-styles and quality living, and if I am striving for a good, tight-run ship, there is no way that I can maintain my *own* quality living if I'm travelling all the time." In other words, she's staying home. "Vancouver is the fitness capital of the world, due to the life-style here. It's conducive to getting out and doing things. I had seen it but didn't recognize the magnitude of it!"

But she admits that The Fitness Group has "grown as I had expected it to over the past five years." She spent hundreds of thousands on the two stores, which include a huge, 5,000-square-foot aerobics room which can hold up to 130 balls of sweat, and a small weight room, holding up to 20, a small "stretch room," and a lot of pre- and post-natal classes, at $27 a month. There are 110 classes a week in one of her stores, and 55 in the other. "The marketing is for a specific kind of person," she declares. "We go after the bright, intellectual, baby-boomer type."

Barbara Crompton is a True Believer, and actually speaks of "my calling in life is to sincerely change the life-styles of thousands of people." Money is "no big deal" to her, although she admits that "I'll probably be extremely wealthy. But I live how I want *now*!"

Like most successful entrepreneurs, Crompton feels that her commodity is "service and the people who instruct for me." That quality is maintained through continual working with the staff. Once a week, she meets with all 40 employees

from 6:30 to 8:30 A.M., when most Vancouverites—the fools!
—are just crawling out of bed and having their first coffee
with a donut. It's a mandatory meeting to "upgrade them
constantly. I also have a great motivational technique with my
staff," she claims. "I give them energy."

She admits to "delegating very well," giving her workers
"a lot of responsibility." And she is "quite strict in my control
of how I run the business; I always cross-check. If anything
goes wrong in The Fitness Group, it's ultimately *my* fault."

Crompton admits that, in the fitness market, most workers are "poorly paid," although she pays better than most,
even "the top in the city." But "life is really exciting, working for us; we're always doing exciting new things." She sets
the example, working from 7:00 to 7:00 most days, one day
until 9:00 and 10:00 at night. "I have an unbelievable husband! He takes sixty percent of the parenting; I take forty
percent."

Advertisements for The Fitness Group consciously avoid
the sex push. "No skimpy outfits in our pictures," she declares proudly. "We'll have photos of groups of people smiling, and take pictures of famous Vancouver personalities with
our staff." (The image of Jack Webster in tights could set the
business back a century.)

It is interesting that the president of The Fitness Group
has yet to encounter anything close to what she is doing in
(and for) Vancouver. She hit 52 fitness centres across California during one frenetic week, having gone down "to be
invigorated and steal new ideas." Unfortunately, there was
nothing new at all!

"My timing was very good," Crompton explains. "I was
there at the very beginning of it all. I'm fairly astute in my
business efforts, and I've combined business with philan-
thropic activities [such as a run to raise money to Save the
Salmon, chairing a Fitness Festival on the beaches with the
B.C. Lung Association, and involvement with many community events]. I keep people in mind, and hire quality people
and put on quality programmes. I love my staff and think
they're first-rate. We have *no* turnover in our company, which
*shows* that we're successful. That's why I'm on top and will
continue to be. And the money keeps rolling in. I work hard
at it, and I deserve it."

Barbara Crompton admits that she will have "many professions to pursue over the next few decades." She had gotten quite involved with her husband's construction business, refurbishing old houses, and hopes to do it again. And fitness? "It'll be much different in twenty years," she says. "Maybe I'll go into old folks homes in the future." With all that exercising going around in Vancouver, they should have the healthiest elderly since the inhabitants of Shangri-La in *Lost Horizon*.

# IN THE SPORTS RACQUET

*Michael Levy*

In his late teens, in the early 1960s, Michael Levy came to a decision which he had never expected to confront: "A desire I had could not be fulfilled." The desire was to be an architect—something he had always wanted to be. At the end of his first year at the University of Toronto he stood in the top few academically, but third from the bottom in design. "I *knew* I had a problem when I kept leafing through *Better Homes and Gardens* for ideas!" he jokes today. But two decades ago there was no joking; he had flunked out of architecture. And today, as president and C.O.B. ("and S.O.B.," he adds) of the Racquet Sports Group of Canada, Inc., he is designing clubs across Eastern Canada—8 today, and possibly double that by 1990, grossing $10 million in 1986, with over 330 employees. So maybe nothing goes to waste, after all.

There had been hints of business acumen in his genes, of course: Levy's father had been a most successful merchant, building up a string of women's retail stores across Canada— Darling Hat Shops, they were called. But Levy senior had died when Michael was only 14, so he never picked up a single pointer from the man, and the stores were sold soon after. (To be fair, there may have been some influence: As a kid, Michael used to go with his father on Saturdays and work the cash register. His dad also liked him to open the door and greet the customers. "We do that today, with the sports clubs!" And as a teenager, Levy worked in a department store, where he was paid $1 an hour plus 10¢ commission for each pair of jockey shorts he sold. "I used to make an extra sixty or seventy dollars a month, so I must have been selling hundreds of shorts every week! I guess I learned about *servicing* customers back then.")

So the Winnipeg-born Levy (the family moved to Toronto when Michael was only four months old) went into economics, finishing a B.A. in Canada's Centennial year, and an M.B.A. in 1969. But he still did not know what he wanted to do with the next half century of his life. True, it was flattering to win a Ford Fellowship, which led to a summer's research at the company's head office in Oakville—but even that was unsatisfying. "I *loved* the car business, but I *hated* Ford. I felt they didn't know how to design or market automobiles."

In a rather iconoclastic fashion, Michael Levy took his fellowship money and bought a TR-250 with it, proudly driving the Triumph into the Ford lot each morning, and invariably fighting with his co-workers each afternoon. Already in his mid-20s, he still did not know what he wanted to be when he grew up—but at least he knew what he *didn't* want to be, which is still more than most: "I found that major corporate life was not for me, the restrictions and rigidity of it. And I *knew* that it would never become the Ford-Levy Company!"

And so the Eternal Student returned once again to the ivy-covered walls of the University of Toronto, this time taking a degree in chartered accountancy, recognizing, as more and more men and women have done over the past decade, that a few years' study as a C.A. "would give me a varied view of different businesses."

That it did. Working and studying over the same three years (1969–1972), Levy had the good fortune of viewing "lots of big businesses, huge clients, major industrial companies," while on the payroll of Peat, Marwick, Mitchell & Co. This all led to the thought which comes so often to people who eventually go into their own businesses: "I kept saying, 'I'm so much smarter than these people! So if I *am*, why don't I try it *myself*?' "

Which Levy promptly did, leaving PMM in 1973, opening his own accountancy office with $250 worth of furniture, sitting on the 16th floor of the Richmond-Adelaide Centre in downtown Toronto, reading the *Globe* day after day, and looking more and more like the loser who dropped out of architecture and quarreled with Ford Motor executives. His gross billings the first few months averaged $50 a week, but with a monthly rent of only $75—he shared office space with an established C.A. firm—"I could afford to fail. It never occurred to me that I would, however. I was too arrogant."

Arrogant? Perhaps. But bright, definitely. After putting together a couple of land syndicates, Michael Levy noticed, while visiting his mother's family in Detroit, that tennis clubs kept being created down there. He just *knew* that they would soon come to Canada. "I had always been interested in the recreational business," says Levy today, tall, lean, and in quite good shape himself. "And I wanted to develop along the line of the fancy clubs. But who could afford to belong to the Toronto Lawn and Tennis, or other private clubs?" (Perhaps the same people who can't afford Cadillacs and Lincolns, but still can afford, and buy, Fords and Chevys in far greater numbers?)

At this point—only a dozen years ago, when he was still not yet 30—we can begin to trace the astonishing success of one Michael Levy, Sports Entrepreneur. In 1973, with a total capital base of a mere $50,000 ("I needed a million and a half to do it"), he joined with a partner and a business client and opened Cobblestone Courts in Mississauga. In the first 16 months they had 1,200 members who were delighted to shell out $150 in annual dues and pay as they played. He soon sold out, but was then invited by Fidinam Realties to build a club in the Hudson's Bay Centre at the corner of Yonge and Bloor, the heart of downtown Toronto. It became the Bloor Park Club, which opened in 1975, and is the "oldest" club still in his control.

By 1981 there were four members of the Racquet Sports Group of Canada, Inc. ("YOUR FIRST CHOICE IN FITNESS"), all of them in Toronto. Sales were in the area of $3 million annually. Then, in 1983, things really began to take off: They opened The International Club, behind the Toronto airport, their first suburban club. In 1984 they took over a club in Saint John, New Brunswick—"We're paid to run it, and we've redeveloped it; it's a *very* strange market, and a gamble"—and took over another club, The Cavendish, in Montreal, which they manage, with an option to buy. By the end of 1986 there were 16,000 current, active members, paying a minimum of $500 a year to belong to the group, enjoying such amenities as squash courts, racquet ball courts, gyms, dining rooms and lounges, complete locker rooms with whirlpools and saunas, and (often but not always) a swimming pool. "We just continue to reinvest, always trying to consolidate our position. We really believe that we're the best in the business, and that we provide the best services possible."

But what makes Levy's Racquet Sports Group "the best"? They *do* charge a bit more than the others in his league. "Because we believe in the club philosophy: that we're the third home. The first home is where you live, and the second, your business. Our clubs are places to spend recreational time, whether to swim, eat, or meet friends." (One almost wishes to challenge Levy on which home is *his* first; although he has a lovely wife and two young daughters, until two years ago he was regularly working a 7-day, 70-hour week.)

"We are in the life-style business," declares Levy, ever aware that health and fitness *are* life and style for the average man and woman in the 1980s. But if Michael Levy has shown prescience, he has also shown the common sense which far too many business people lack—the ability to hire the strongest where he is weakest. "My basic expertise is to create a concept, find a location, work out the financial structure, and develop marketing; I'm *not* an administrator. I soon realized that the biggest flaw in entrepreneurs is not knowing when to get out of day-to-day operations and do what they're best at: developing the business." So Levy plays his role as president and chairman (and S.O.B.), and brought in Jay Kell to be his organization man and run the booming thing. And, do note, he has hired only women as his club managers, heads of fitness, and comptroller, arguing that "we've never found a man yet between the ages of twenty-three and twenty-six with the maturity and drive that our female personnel display." Better shape up, Charlie, and not just on the court.

A mind like Levy's could not possibly ignore 250 million souls, many of whom are dreadfully out of shape, with money (and calories) to burn, just south of the border. But he is well aware of some crucial differences between our two countries which Pierre Berton and Richard Gwyn never discussed: "Travel patterns are different in Canada; we stay *put*. I live fifteen blocks from where I grew up. In the States, the neighbourhood is always changing. And we don't want to put three million dollars into a building and have the area fall apart." Naturally, he has a major market research team checking out various states among the 50, just in case.

The five-year goal, then, is 20 clubs, 17 in Eastern Canada, and up to 3 in the States, if they'll only *stay put*. Yes, they considered Vancouver, but found that too many clubs are in receivership there, along with everywhere else. "But we will expand and become an all-Canadian company, represented in most of the provinces. We could even be up to thirty million dollars a year by the early 1990s."

And why? "Because I'm tough," Levy exclaims. "We have certain principles, and we structure our deals in a certain way. The developers must put up seventy-five percent of the cost, and we'll pay the rent." What do they gain for all that money invested? "They gain *us*! They get a company in a business for over thirteen years that's made every single payment since 1972!"

The Racquet Sports Group does little advertising—less than 4½% of revenues—since "we'd rather put the money into the clubs." And they do, too; they are constantly reviewing and upgrading the existing ones. "It's like running hotels," he says. Which is how they became "the biggest in Canada, in the field of high-quality, multirecreational clubs. There are chains of small health clubs that are bigger, but not like us."

Levy prides himself that he's managed to do all this "with *no* help from any government. I feel it's hypocritical; they *don't* provide financing for small businesses who really need it." So Racquet Sports has mortgages and some long-term financing, but no current debts. "Each club requires a significant capital investment, which we attempt to fund out of our own cash flow."

One reason for that cash flow is that, for the first ten years of his business, Michael Levy never took out more than $35,000 a year. Of course, owning 40% of it all makes him fairly well off, and the new owner of a Nonesuch in the Toronto harbour. And it's clear to him why: "I think that most entrepreneurs have one overriding common element: a stubbornness when they think they're right. This can go both ways, and I see it in myself. There were a lot of years when we should have gone bankrupt; we were badly managed and underfinanced. But there was my faith in it and my partners' faith in it. We keep putting money back in. It was a vision:

sticking to the vision of what you see that your business can be. And it was teamwork: No *one* man can run a business, although there is a psychological need to see it as a one-man show. We did a complete reorganization back in 1981, buying out most of the existing partners and taking it under my own control. The two left with me both agreed with my vision: to provide really good service."

Michael Levy has been in the health club business for 15 years—he got in at 27; he's now 42. And, perhaps not so surprisingly, he doesn't see himself in it in 1990. "I'm strictly into development, marketing, and strategy," he says. "This is a young person's business; it's not like selling TVs. You need young, aggressive, active people running it."

Levy *isn't* young, aggressive, active? Well, he'll soon surpass the number of hat stores which his late father managed to build up—16—and it seems that his is a healthier racquet to be in. Healthier for himself, and for what will eventually be tens and tens of thousands of others, across Canada and (maybe) the United States. Perhaps it was to the benefit of us all that Michael Levy couldn't pass architecture.

# FROM (MANUAL) LABOUR TO MANAGEMENT

## Sylvia Rempel

There are rare times when a company's PR blurb says it better than anyone else could: "From dirty, calloused hands of an immigrant manual laborer on a Taber sugar beet farm to an internationally known designer of ski clothing and president of the multi-million-dollar Sun Ice Company, Sylvia Rempel's success story reflects the dedication, determination, patience, persistence and creative genius of an exceptional individual." Well, most writers might not use *five* descriptive nouns and adjectives in one line, but all else stays. As husband, and general manager of Sun Ice, Victor Rempel says, "She's a doer, not a talker", "Sylvia is the basic entrepreneur who made this fly. She's the genius."

Indeed she is, and the way this woman, this family, has moved from a basement seamstress situation in 1978 (sales under $40,000) to a total staff of over 175 with $14.4 million in sales of skiwear and fashionable outerwear by January 1987, shows—yes, yes—dedication, determination, patience, persistence, and creative genius.

Sylvia was born in 1936 in East Germany, on the Polish border; her husband, Victor, the previous year in the Ukraine, of Mennonite background. The latter arrived in 1948, at the age of 13, settled in Calgary, and studied education at the University of Alberta, receiving a B.Ed. and an M.A. in administration, serving as a school principal. His future wife, whom he met while both were in their teens and whom he married in 1956, was educated in Europe, while working there as a seamstress. "Her formal schooling did *not* take her to her level of expertise," exclaims her proud husband. "She has a knack—golden hands and a drive—to finish her task!" Her uncle had sponsored her family to come to a farming community near Calgary, where she worked in those now-famous beet fields with the same hands that would make her fortune.

While her new husband continued his academic training, Sylvia Rempel took garment manufacturing and pattern making at the Southern Alberta Institute of Technology, taking "all courses in garments and apparel." She was immediately hired as an instructor; she was in her early 30s.

"Sylvia had this dream, and the rest of us followed her!" enthuses her husband again. She began to sew her husband's and children's garments, even tailoring formal dresses, suits, and pants. As early as the mid-1960s she showed signs of wanting to start her own business. From 1969 she showed signs of wanting to teach sewing at her alma mater, SAIT, in large department stores, and in many fabric shops, in such skills as swimwear, men's and ladies' wear, and lingerie.

The major breakthrough came as the Rempel son—there are three daughters as well—pursued skiing interests, and the father drove him regularly for lessons. The entire family was soon skiing in Banff and the surrounding areas, and Sylvia, ever fashion-conscious, "saw a need for ski garments." She looked around and saw that in that field her chosen country was far behind the Europe she had left. The first step was obvious. She sewed ski outfits for the children. Then, in 1975, she sewed 16 suits for her kids' friends one winter. Then the technical school asked her to teach a course specifically on ski clothing, which drove her to go down to Portland, Oregon, to take a course herself first.

By this time Sylvia Rempel had a line of ski clothing. "Okay," she said in her Eastern European accent, "Let's see if the ski shops of Calgary will sell them." Her first stop was the Ski Cellar, and they moved well. By late 1978 a half dozen retailers in Calgary were carrying them, with "roughly $35,000 in sales." She hired a seamstress to work in the basement of her house with her, and the two began a small cottage craft there. They had literally nowhere to go but up.

So, in the winter of 1979 Sylvia Rempel made that often-scarey move which nearly all entrepreneurs have to make if they are going to make it big: She found an "outside" location—in her case "an old pool hall in disrepair"—which she rented and refurbished. Used machines were brought in from Montreal, and by the end of 1979 there were 12 seamstresses, Sylvia, and her oldest daughter, Angela. Sales were up to $350,000 a year across Alberta and British Columbia.

In 1980 she was up to two dozen seamstresses, with sales of close to $800,000, and by 1985, 75 seamstresses and more than another 25 staff, pushing toward $4 million in sales. The rather ingenious name Sun Ice came during a brainstorming session with a group of friends in 1978, but the designs are "strictly Sylvia's creations," all showing her gift for sizing and colour combinations. Sales to Eastern Canada began to grow in 1981–82, with exports to Ontario and a tiny beginning in Quebec; by 1983–84 Sun Ice was into the Maritimes. In the winter of 1984–85 the Rempels—Victor left school administration to join his wife and children at Sun Ice in 1983—made their beachhead in the States at the Ski Industries of America trade show in Las Vegas, which is about as far from the beet fields of Alberta (and the burnt fields of Poland) as one can get. Sun Ice products were available on the west coast of the United States from the winter of 1985–86.

"We expect to cap at fifteen million dollars in sales in Canada by 1988," says Victor Rempel. "The U.S.A. will be as good as we want to be; it depends on personnel, drive, and commitment. But we will probably hook up with a western distributor there, and should be up to five million dollars by 1988 as well." And with profits of "more than ten percent," wealth for the Rempels seems assured.

As in most small businesses, the Sun Ice management took

no salary at the start, leaving their home at 6:00 in the morning and not returning until 8:00 or 9:00 at night. "Six and a half days a week," which includes three hours on the Lord's day. There are 170 sewing machines, and 45,000 square feet in total, 30,000 dedicated to sewing and cutting, and the remaining 15,000 to raw goods and warehousing. And by summer, 1987, there was an additional 70,000-square-foot addition, thanks to 2 million shares offered on the TSE, at $8 a share.

Sun Ice has taken its own special route into ski fashion. They try to avoid selling to department stores, since "they want exceedingly cheap, and in volume." Instead, the move is primarily to "fashion-conscious ski shops," since the jackets will sell from $200 to $800 each. Recently, they signed championship skier Steve Podborski to The Pod Line for the Bay and specialty shops, with a "mid-price" cost.

The latter gives further insight into the creativity of the Rempels. When they saw the Canadian ski team wearing garments made by European manufacturers, they didn't take it lying down at the sewing machines. They phoned the team up and offered their product, the team asked for $50,000 for the opportunity, and the Rempels now spend upwards of $175,000 a year in expenditures to provide Sun Ice garments which can now say, "OFFICIAL SUPPLIER/*FOURNISSEUR OFFICIEL*, SKI CANADA."

"The promotion has been worth it," says Victor Rempel. "When Reed, Podborski, and Hunter won the gold medal, and when Gerry Sorenson wore Sun Ice clothes, we plastered their names and faces all over the country!" And who doesn't want to be identified with winners? "We custom-make two hundred garments, from the coach to administration! They can't take them off a rack! They've got special bodies! They *must* be tailor-made!"

In 1983–84 and 1984–85, Sun Ice received recognition as "the foremost clothing supplier" in the independent vote of 450 ski retailers across Canada, for "quality, product, fashion, and service," and another 150 in the U.S. The secret, the Rempels insist, is they have always been "natural" in terms of design—in styling, fit, fashion, colour combinations, and quality sewing. They make over 70,000 garments a year, and, notes the general manager, "an insulated garment is the *most complicated* in the world to make!"

They continue to promote high-profile athletes, such as the Canadian swim teams and the kayak team, and eight medalists at the 1984 Summer Olympics at Los Angeles had their bodies draped by Sun Ice garments. A Sun Ice balloon flies over countless ski races, and 80% of ski staffs across Canada wear Sun Ice. "We have eighty-eight ski teams nailed down!" rejoices Victor Rempel. "Gaetan Bouchard will wear our speed skating outfit!" In 1987, Sun Ice was chosen the official supplier to Vail, Colorado, and over 50,000 coaches, athletes, administrators, and staff of the Calgary Winter Olympics will be sporting Sun Ice before 1.6 billion TV viewers.

More recently, Sun Ice has moved into swim suits and "active wear" made of fleece, and their summer line is nearly as strong as their winter one. Or, to put it another way, the Sun is sliding closer to the Ice. A company in Montreal has been contracted to make the summer line of clothes—er, fashions. "If people wear us in the winter, they'll want to wear the same brand in the summer," claims Victor Rempel.

Is there a downside to such ski-away success? "We've had no holiday in six years!" moans Rempel. "We take business trips and half days here and there, but that's it!" The relaxation is that half day on Sunday, when they escape to the lake with their four grandchildren. "Sylvia is like a Mother Hen!" he says with a chuckle.

A Mother Hen *cum* Henry Ford. Sylvia Rempel finds it difficult to find seamstresses in Calgary and must constantly train them, since the city lacks a large working-class and ethnic influx. They may have to set up a factory in the east. There's no union yet, but the Rempels swear that they "*don't* run a sweatshop! We are *not* garment people by tradition, and we give a fair wage for a day's work." They don't pay by piecework; only by the hour, which runs between $5 and $7 for seamstresses.

"To succeed in the garment trade, you must be *instantaneously* responsive to fashions," says Victor Rempel. "You have to be on the button—and massive factories can't do that." So there are limits to growth. But from the very start, in their basement less than a decade ago, they have had the key: "It's Sylvia's ability to come up with the right product at the right time. She keeps changing fabrics and colours to reflect trends, and keeps producing a quality garment in our shop. Every one is guaranteed; if anything goes wrong, we fix it."

As with most successful businesses in Canada, the answer is always Service, Marketing, Promotions, combined with Quality. Every retailer across the country has videos of the Everest Climb—another of Sun Ice's tie-ins—and of members of the ski team at the Olympics, etc. And they are shown endlessly at the half dozen trade shows each year.

And—pleasant surprise: Starting in Canada has been an advantage, since the United States had all the established companies, but Canadian ski shops started looking to their own as our dollar dropped so precipitously. "We got a better toehold during the recession," says Victor Rempel. "They soon recognized that our product was as good as, or better than, any other." As was his wife, Sylvia. And with the U.S., Japan, Austria, Switzerland, Germany, France, and hundreds of Canadian stores clamouring for Sun Ice products, the Rempels see over $20 million sales by January 1988—nearly quadruple what they sold three years earlier—and $50 million by 1992.

## RUNNING A BUSINESS, OR RUNNING—A BUSINESS

### Mike Dyon

"Mike's not here," the writer is told when he arrives to speak with the 33-year-old president of Brooks Canada. "He's out running." Indeed he is, and in more ways than one. In a few short years Mike Dyon took his own personal love affair with a pair of running shoes from selling them out of the trunk of his car (after he ran races) to moving hundreds of thousands of pairs out of every Eaton's, Simpson's, sporting goods, and specialty athletic store from Newfoundland to British Columbia. Running is *right*.

Mike Dyon eventually arrives and showers. (He runs about 110 miles a week, won the Canadian Championship in Montreal in 1982, and came in ninth place in the Marathon at the 1982 Commonwealth Games. He was injured during the trials for the 1984 Olympics, but showed his determination by running at the World Cup Marathon in Hiroshima in the spring of 1985, although he had mononucleosis at the time. The 26 miles took him 2 hours and 19 minutes.) And, like any young man who often enjoys the 15-mile run from his home in southwestern Toronto to his office out near the airport, he quickly tells his Cinderella business story—except, in this version, Dyon is the prince and the princess is a *shoe*. (Talk about fetishes.)

Mike Dyon was born in Toronto in 1955; his brother Paul was born two years later. His father, now an equal partner with his boys in Brooks Canada, was the president of an aluminum products company, and their mother was a registered nurse. The firstborn went to the University of Toronto, earning a bachelor's in physical and health education. (He had begun running in grade 9 and "was serious within six months of starting it." Within a year, he came in third in the Toronto high schools championship, with a 2½-mile run. He was 13, and, he confesses reluctantly, he used Adidas.) "I wanted to be a phys. ed. teacher," the handsome, blond, tall, and beanpoley runner says. "I never entertained a thought of going into business."

But we're not talking business here, as noted above; we're talking *love*. At the age of 22 the young athlete was down in Florida, visiting mom and dad—and running, of course—when he happened to purchase a pair of Brooks shoes, and it was love at first run. He purchased six pair for himself and his brother (now vice-president) and took them up to Canada.

Over the following months, Dyon would drive down to the States, loading up his car with sizes 8½ and 9, so even if he couldn't sell them, the brothers would have shoes for the rest of their lives. And, yes, during many of the races over those months, Mike Dyon would finish before many others (natch), stand at the finish line, and sell Brooks running shoes out of his car.

Now, capitalism is a very exciting form of economic system, but one cannot run a business on a (literal) shoestring forever. So it was, in mid-1977, that the brothers Dyon met with the Brooks people in the United States and negotiated the rights to be the distributor for Eastern Canada. Mike Dyon recalls feeling that "the Americans were fearful that these young runners from Canada would louse it up."

Well, they didn't. With a $5,000 loan from their father, the "young runners" bought a van, which they would regularly drive down to Hanover, Pennsylvania, where the Brooks factory was located, and bring up all different sizes. Between the two, they covered all of the country east of Manitoba, selling to sports and specialty stores. Interestingly, the distributor for Western Canada did not do as well as the Dyons, so the brothers eventually took over the entire country for Brooks. And when countless runners from coast to coast discovered that they could obtain their beloved Brooks shoes *in Canada*—and not only in 8½ and 9—the sales took off.

Then, in 1981, near-disaster struck. Disaster, really, but a combination of luck and reliability on the part of the Dyons kept it only "near." Brooks went bankrupt in the States, leaving hundreds of stores across North America with no shoes to sell. Mike Dyon had wisely moved into clothing as well, but it was a scarey time to be representing Brooks. Dozens of stores to whom Brooks owed money went under; the Dyons were fortunate enough to owe the American company money at the time, so they weathered the storm.

The storm was well worth weathering. In December 1981 Wolverine Worldwide bought Brooks Shoes—you've heard of Hush Puppies, we assume—and in January 1982 the giant complex signed an agreement with R.M.P. Athletic Locker Ltd. of Canada for the sole right to distribute Brooks shoes across this country. (The R stands for Robert Dyon, the father; M and P for Michael and Paul, the two sons.) Mike Dyon wittily comments that his father now looks after the Florida office in the winter (in Key Largo) and the Orillia office (in Toronto's cottage country) in the summer. In other words, unlike his continually working sons, he has thrown in his shoes, if not his one-third ownership.

Sales have been nothing less than spectacular—one could say off and running, but one won't—since that time. From 1982 to 1983 sales shot up from less than $3 million to "well over ten million dollars," probably due to their introduction of the Chariot, a $90 shoe which has become the number 1 seller in the States ever since ("according to a *Running World* survey!" declares Mike Dyon, as if quoting the Bible). And it has become the cornerstone of the running shoe industry in Canada as well.

They continued to grow over 1984 and 1985, levelling off in the latter at around 15% increase. Sales at the end of 1985 were over $15 million, and Dyon expects to break $20 million by the end of 1987. "It should be our biggest year ever!" enthuses Dyon, whose beard and lankiness—he is 5'8" and weighs a mere 128 pounds—make him look as if he's stepped out of an Ingmar Bergman film. Well, *run* out of an Ingmar Bergman film.

But it hasn't been only shoes, as we've mentioned; the Dyons took an enormous risk by beginning to manufacture clothing with the Brooks insignia, eventually opening a clothing factory in suburban Toronto in the spring of 1984. (There are now 100 different styles in shoes, but over 150 different pieces and colours of clothes, and the latter makes up 40% of his business.)

The Dyons manufacture nylon shorts, T-shirts, sweat suits, nylon suits, casual shorts, bathing suits, etc., etc. "It *was* a big risk," insists Dyon. "We had to buy all the machines, and make as well as sell. But we sell to every independent and major department store across Canada."

There are a lot of Canadians who are happy that Mike Dyon had this strange love affair with that pair of shoes back in the late '70s, and not because they are runners. Some four dozen work in the Brooks warehouse, another hundred sewers and clothing makers work exclusively on Brooks clothing, and perhaps another hundred work in various aspects of the marketing and sales of the products the Dyons are responsible for. Since January 1985 Dyon has had it "all under one roof"—in a factory of 38,000 square feet in Toronto.

It's true that Mike Dyon didn't create Brooks shoes, but could anyone else make such a go of Brooks Canada? (He branched into a hiking boot line which Wolverine is developing in the States, which came to Canada in 1986. "It's going to broaden our shoe line," he says, hopefully.) No, a man who only takes vacations that allow him to run in marathons is a man who feels passionately about his business.

"We are successful because we are able to feel how the market is going, and react quickly," he says. "Because we are runners, *we listen to customers*! We fit our selling to what they want. And we took chances with shoes that we simply had a good feeling for, like the Chariot, and others that were far more risky."

Not that Brooks and its lover are number 1 in Canada; not by a long shot. Reebok is the new monster with $50 million; Adidas and Nike are numbers 2 and 3. "But we're a strong fourth," declares Dyon. "And," he adds, "we were *nothing* when we entered Canada; the big jump came in 1982. Before that, we were maybe fifth or sixth."

Mike Dyon and brother Paul, both now married, continue to work 50-hour weeks, and keep "ploughing all our profits back into the business, and keeping in the area where we have expertise."

Expertise? Love. The president of Commodore may secretly lust after an IBM PC, and the president of Ford may long for a Mercedes. But Mike Dyon, president of Brooks Canada, is perfectly happy with his $90 Brooks Chariot running shoe. And when Dyon spouts a simile, you'd better believe it: "Business is like running," he says with a knowing look. "If you train hard, it pays off." Indeed it does; Dyon ran as part of the Canadian team in the World Cup Marathon in Seoul, Korea, in April 1987—where he visited his main factory.

# BUILDING THE BETTER HAT

### *Alex Tilley*

Alex Tilley is *not* your average capitalist. Alex Tilley is not even much of a capitalist. Indeed, Alex Tilley is not even average. He is inspired, charming, irresistible, driven, gifted, and, most important, utterly creative. Endowed also with a growing—if still underdeveloped—entrepreneurial flair, he is becoming a fascinating gem in the world of Canadian business.

Like Alexander Graham Bell (the telephone), Thomas Alva Edison (the light bulb), and Wozniak and Jobs (the Apple), Alex Tilley of Toronto focused on something which he felt was missing, or imperfect, in society—a hat; then shorts and pants, and now clothing of all kind—and strove for perfection. But Tilley has appeared to reach his goal of excellence in less than half a decade, while Bell, Edison, and Wozniak and Jobs would all surely agree that *their* creations, in their original forms, all had a very long way to go.

No, Alex Tilley is not rich. Yet. Sales in 1986 were about $3 million, "as predicted," and profits were close to 10% of that ("where it's all gone, I have *no* idea!" he grumps). As he admitted ruefully during an interview in his modest office in suburban Toronto, "I just discovered that a new part-time

worker I recently hired is making more money than *I* am!"
But because the sales of his rapidly growing number of clothing products are more than doubling every year (around $25,000
in 1980, $75,000 the following year, and over $400,000 in
1984), it shouldn't be long now. As Tilley puts it, "My profits
should be substantial in the near future; they should be
WOW!"

WOW? Try putting *that* on your income tax form. But
then, as we noted earlier, Alex Tilley is not a capitalist. He is
merely after perfection.

The origins, and even the first four decades, of Alex
Tilley are hardly auspicious. He was born 49 years ago in Mt.
Albert, a tiny village of less than a thousand souls, not far
north of Toronto. His mother was a schoolteacher, his father
a bank manager. (His only sibling, Johnny, is today out in
Vancouver, married with children, and at present moving out
of the basement with his Tilley products and opening a
store.) Even the family name did not bode wealth or fame:
"Tilley is old and aristocratic," jokes the hat man. "It means
'tiller of the soil.' And if you want further aristocracy, I've got
a Smith on my mother's side."

Because bank managers are wont to be moved about, the
Tilleys lived in Kitchener, Sudbury, and Vancouver, where
Alex graduated from U.B.C. with a B.A. and headed east. "I
was known in university as 8460592," he sneers, as if to
underline the pleasure it now gives him to have his name,
products, and even *face* and *body* in advertisements across
North America and even the world, less than a quarter century later.

Not that the 1960s and 1970s were particularly WOW
either. Tilley set up a tutoring school in Montreal ("because I
had hated school so much") and it folded less than two years
later. He later tried to obtain a master's degree in business at
York University and flunked out.

Then he read an article in the *Financial Post* about people
renting paintings out in Edmonton. "For the next fourteen
years, I dubbed myself an art consultant," he says today, tall,
prematurely grey-bearded, trim, soft-spoken, and still not
rich. The business was entitled Fine Art Consultants of Canada Ltd., and it provided "quality works of art for businesses." As one might expect of a man like Alex Tilley, there
were never any contracts, "only handshakes," as business

people would rent paintings which Tilley had taken on consignment from galleries, often putting that rental toward the eventual purchase. Also Tilley-like he refuses to mention the names of the artists whom he assisted; "it might offend some of the gallery owners."

There were eventually Artmobiles and employees with fine arts degrees, and Tilley admits to doing "very well with the business." But in 1984 he decided to "let it die," and the reason for that is the reason he is included in this book: Alex Tilley had sat down in the first few weeks of this decade and decided to create the Ideal Sailor's Hat.

You do not have to be a committed sailor (as is Alex Tilley) to be irritated when your hats keep blowing off. And when your hats sink all the time (as traditionally happens to sailors), it can be enraging. Furthermore, "A good hat should not shrink! It should be a rain hat! It should *not* fly off in the wind! It should be attractive and comfortable!"

Thus began many months of research in the winter and spring of 1980. "I plagiarize from only the best sources," says Alex Tilley. His first stop was Genco Sails, in downtown Toronto, which gave him guidance on materials; then came Elsie Millinery, for help on the design. Then to Park Town Hats to make them. Remember the old Wright Brothers gag? ("It'll never fly, Orville!") People kept telling Tilley that "it's *impossible* to make a hat with these qualifications!"

There must have been moments when Tilley almost believed the naysayers. "Making a hat that would not shrink— that was a *real* bitch," he admits. But the problem was soon solved. They just put the fabric in hot water which has steam injected into it to raise the temperature. "It shrinks the hell out of it before we even make the hat," says the genius.

All this quality ("IT'S MADE OF NATURAL COLOURED 10 OZ. U.S. COTTON, SOLID BRITISH BRASS GROMMETS AND THIS CANADIAN'S PERSNICKETINESS," read his hilarious ads) ran up the price, of course, which led to an immediate problem: pricing the damned thing right out of the market. With a hat costing $13 to make, a manufacturer needs to add at least 50% above that, which *already* brings the price to $20. If sold in a store (which has employees, heat, rent, overhead, etc.), items tend to be doubled in price. And who on earth—or on sailboat—would pay over $40 for a hat, no matter *how* inspired its design?

Which is why Tilley decided immediately to go almost entirely mail order, primarily from a friend's basement. There have been some minor exceptions, such as Tom Taylor, the largest chandlery in Canada (that's a seller of nautical gear), which sells the Tilley hat at the same price, approximately $32.95. And Simpson's Department Stores approached Tilley back in the summer of 1984 to sell some—they sold out quickly—and have discussed the idea of developing a special Tilley section.

As has been hinted before, Alex Tilley is no Conrad Black (nor *in* the black, for that matter; loans from his parents—his mom wears the hat all the time at the cottage; his dad won't touch it—have kept him alive over the past few years. "Thank heavens my father won a lot at poker and saved the money"). Rather than dream castles and Rolls-Royces, Tilley's intention was to make perhaps $5,000 a year profit from his hat hobby. "I expected it to be a little business on the side" of the art rental.

But the bug soon bit. No, not the money bug ("I never understood why anyone would want *more* than two million dollars and I have no desire for power—I don't see the point of it all"); the Pride in Workmanship and Creativity bug. "In my second year of operations, I began to realize that I was making the best in the world of something."

The advertisements in the *Globe* and *Mail* certainly helped ("THE NOT-YET-FAMOUS TILLEY HAT. IT FLOATS, TIES ON, REPELS RAIN, WON'T SHRINK, LASTS, AND COMES WITH A FOUR-PAGE OWNER'S MANUAL"), as did the six students from Ryerson Polytechnical Institute who began to study him as a marketing project. They promptly informed him that he was pushing sales at the wrong times of the year ("they saved me money right off!"), and Tilley immediately hired one of the students to assist him in the rapidly growing business. ("He's twenty-two; he'll learn everything and I can relax," Tilley says comfortably.)

There were name changes—ALEX TILLEY AND FAMILY'S NAUTICAL GEAR became ALEX TILLEY AND FAMILY'S ENDURABLES and, finally, TILLEY ENDURABLES INC. But most important were the rapidly expanding sales and the frequent letters of praise. "The Tilley Hat has given me a subtle air of insouciance and elan which had hitherto eluded me" (Connecticut). "Damn fine hat" (Bruce

Kirby, designer of the Laser sailboat). "Your hat is too much the rage at our Waikiki yacht club. Send catalogue that I can leave for the sailors as a hint! Aloha" (Guess).

And the stories! What of the Tilley hat which was knocked off by a boom on a sailboat off the coast of Florida? If he had tied it on, it wouldn't have happened.) A group of dolphins dragged it under with them, and two minutes later the hat popped up. "That *proves* it floats!" exclaims Tilley, although a cynic might say that the dolphins probably disliked the style. And, best of all: A man lost his Tilley hat overboard while sailing in Bermuda, and later had it mailed back to his home in New York by a fellow Tilley hat owner, who had spotted it floating, found the name and address inside, and sent it back "in the hope that someday someone would do the same" for him.

Tilley hats have been purchased across North America, as well as Papua New Guinea, Guam, Norway, Saudi Arabia ("mostly American engineers")—even a lifer in the Kingston Penitentiary bought one. Over 10,000 hats sold in 1984, and well over triple that since the humble beginnings in 1980.

But just as Canadian Tire is more than tires, to coin a phrase, Tilley Endurables Inc. is far more than hats. By 1981 he began to develop the someday famous Tilley shorts, for the same awesomely simple and astonishingly logical reason: "I couldn't find any strong and practical shorts!" They are wash and wear, preshrunk, double-seamed and lock-stitched, even double-thick-seated. (Washing instruction: "Give 'em hell.")

Some comments over the years: "Without any qualification whatsoever, they are the best shorts I've ever worn—and I am a dedicated wearer of shorts" (Peter Worthington, journalist, who attempted to climb Mr. Gongga in the Himalayas in Tilley's masterwork). "The shorts lasted longer than my boat did!" (Tony Lush, who went off on a single-handed sailboat race around the world). As Tilley says in one of his later ads (which now appear in such magazines, as *Sail, Cruising World,* and the exceedingly costly *New Yorker* and *Smithsonian,* "MY LIFE OR YOURS! OUR TILLEY 'ENDURABLES' NOW HAVE A LIFETIME (MINE* OR YOURS) GUARANTEE." (A footnote declares that you are pretty safe with going with *his* lifetime: "ALEX TILLEY, 49, HEALTHY, HAPPY . . .")

Much like Alex Tilley's up-and-down career, the success of his shorts was up and down as well. (No pun intended.) The costs of making the inspired things were so high, he briefly stopped manufacturing them. Then came such complaints from people who wanted more that he eventually returned "full steam ahead" with their manufacture, using Sara Work Uniforms in nearby Agincourt, Ontario, to put them together.

In 1984 came the Trekker Pants, which include similar Velcro closures in the patch pockets, and even have a secret pocket inside the pants to hide one's passport or large-denomination bills. And at $58 for the long pants (plus $3 shipping; $5 extra if you are a size 42 through 50 waist) and $45 for the shorts, he has still managed to keep the prices within eyesight. From the very start, Tilley accepted straight cheques as well as charge card numbers, and early "owner's manuals" used to brag that not a single cheque bounced, out of thousands received. Alas, nearly a dozen bounced during 1984, which is still amazingly low; perhaps the warm and witty advertisements and brochures create the kind of close feeling that prevents people from ripping Tilley off.

And as of mid-1985 Alex Tilley expanded in a direction that could well make him wealthy at last, and make his "not-yet-famous Tilley Hat" finally famous. He began Tilley Cottons, which are shirts, pants, rompers, and jumpers made from cotton that *will not shrink*. "We stole the design from an American company," he sweetly confesses, but improving on it, of course. "Ask your *wife* if you can get one hundred percent cotton clothes that won't shrink, are machine-washable, and need no ironing!" he cries. I did, and she's buying Tilley's.

The Tilley Cottons are a delight, as are all of Alex Tilley's creations. But when Eaton's placed a massive order to put his clothes in major stores across Canada—"a *very* large trial order" for hats, pants, and the cottons—Tilley was not able to fill it. "I didn't want to grow too fast; I'm barely holding on; I'm overworked; I'm tired."

What Tilley really wants to do most is go canoeing with his beloved Susan, a nurse whom he met during a brief stay at a Toronto hospital ("Within two minutes she had me half undressed and in bed!"), and whose lovely face and features appear, along with his own, in many of his ads for hats, shorts, pants, and cottons. "I'd like to have total financial freedom. Freedom is the ability to travel anywhere, and I've only got twenty-five to thirty years left."

But at least some of those years will have to be spent flogging his Tilley products, whether in his showroom in Don Mills, in suburban Toronto, or down at the Queen's Quay Terminal, where he made four expansions in 14 months, up to nearly 1,500 square feet from an original 70. "I told the designer, 'Make this the most interesting store in Canada!' " It may have audio-visual ads, or adventure themes, and he hopes to have Sir Edmund Hillary drop in. "We hope to get involved with adventurers, and advertise 'Come down and meet them.' "

Then there is his recent licensing of a man in London, Ontario, to open a store called Tilley Endurables. And his brother- and sister-in-law's new store in Vancouver. But he still wants to "keep it moderately exclusive; we don't want to mass market across the country. Our clients are too special." As of 1987, 30 stores handle Tilley products across Canada. And sales are closing in on $5 million.

There will soon be up to ten Tilley cottons, about which Alex Tilley brags, "We make more sizes than anyone else! Others make twenty-eight to thirty-six waists; some make thirty-three and thirty-five. But we go every inch to thirty-eight, and then every two inches, until fifty-two! We even fit big men! Soon I'll have tall for women and men as well!" But why? "I want to do it because it's my *pleasure* to do that!!" And since 1986, he's been doing well with "the world's best bomber's jacket," which costs $900, but $100 less to veterans.

It was pleasure which brought him to Ireland in the summer of 1985, where he discovered that there are no taxes there on manufacturing textiles, and it would be cheaper to make most of his products there, to sell to Europe. So he soon plans to make "nearly everything" in Ireland, for the European Economic Community, and will also set up an American subsidary company to sell Yankee distribution.

Not that he'd ever give up his delightful demo at over a dozen boat shows across North America every year. "May I show you a *new way* to keep a hat on?" he asks every few minutes, showing off the unique features of the great Tilley Hat. After they buy, he happily writes their name and phone number in indelible ink inside the crown, and then "the designer condescends to sign and date the hats!" Then he hands each lucky customer the four-page owner's manual, along with a spare lace (to tie it around the head). "This is a symbol of you getting more than you anticipated!" he tells the happy new owners. "Our hats are held on by gravity, and not by pressure!"

With his "five-foot-twelve" gorgeous 22-year-old daughter Karen off at the University of Western Ontario, and his exquisite 18-year-old daughter Alison beginning a modelling career, Alex Tilley has never been happier. "Business is lovely, and I'm delighted! I bore Susan no end with it!" (And why not? How many men get to sign the inside of hundreds of women's shorts, "Alex Tilley was here"?)

But don't ask him too much about the future, or when Eaton's will finally get that order filled. "I don't work long-term; everything I do can change in a month. We have new products today which I never would have guessed a short while ago." After all, this isn't just commerce; this is *art*. "These *are* works of art!" he insists. "I've put my honour on your head and body." And no one ever rushed Picasso, or Alex Colville, for that matter, to finish that painting and get it to market.

"After fourteen years as an art dealer, I can decorate a man's office well, and I can dress him, too," says Tilley. "I make products for me, and hope that people will like them, too. But I never set out to please customers first." Since November 1986, a new grandchild is pleasing *him*.

Yet it is clear that Alex Tilley is thrilled with the success which has come with his demand for excellence. "When I have a meeting with business people, I can't *believe* that it's all for real! I still feel it's pretend."

But it's no pretend world when York University begins to do a study of Alex Tilley and his fascinating business concept and success. "And I have *such respect* for York University." He smiles. "After all, they *did* kick me out of their business school."

# WHEELING AND DEALING

### The Kent Family

In 1934, in Toronto, a city about to grow in population and importance, Bloor Cycle and Sports was established. A few months later, in Satoraljaujhely, Hungary, a town about to be destroyed by war, a young boy barely into his teens was told that his father was dying, and that he'd have to take over the family bicycle shop. The story of how that Hungarian lad was to eventually become the owner of the Toronto store and, with the help of his wife and two sons, turn it into the largest independent bicycle shop in North America is a story of successful capitalism, sharp business acumen, and just plain common sense.

There is still only one store, although its products are sold across Canada, due to its brilliantly innovative catalogue. But there is something special about it, and not merely because Paul Kent, now 66, barely escaped murder by Hitler's henchmen, and had to literally start over in business on three separate occasions. Look at 1982, for example: a recession year, the bike business in the United States dropped 24%; in Canada, an average of 13%. Bloor Cycle? A 17% growth rate. In 1983, a 22% increase; in 1984, a 20% increase; in 1985, another 22% increase, with catalogue sales doubling in each of those years. In 1986 and 1987, two more increases of 13%. There is something *very* special about Bloor Cycle and the Kents who run it. It is living entrepreneurship.

"I was practically born in a bicycle repair shop," recalls Paul Kent, whose father had opened one the year before his birth in 1919. When the sickly man entered the hospital which he would never leave, his young child went to school in the morning, worked in the shop through the afternoon, and studied until midnight. He inherited more than the bike shop, of course; he also inherited his father's debts left over from Hungary's terrible depression.

Then came the Nazi occupation, the expropriations by the German army, the death camps, the Russian occupation. "I had to start again from scratch," Kent says. "There weren't even any shelves still up; everything had been looted."

But Paul Kent started anew after the war, only to see nearly all private enterprise nationalized by the new Communist government of Hungary, including his family bicycle shop. Still, he was soon president of his community cooperative—which included bicycle repair and sales—and thriving as much as any could thrive under the heavy hand of East European communism. When the Hungarian uprising broke out in the fall of 1956, the Kent family broke out as well—for the West, along with tens of thousands of others.

Stopping briefly in Holland in early 1957, with his wife,

Judy, 10-year-old Peter, and 2-year-old Andrew, Paul Kent received a helpful note from a friend who had made it to Canada: "Forget about your bike business that you know so well, because in this country, the only bicycles are found in museums. *Nobody* rides bikes in Canada!" (Notes Andrew Kent, bearded and charming, as he hears the ancient tale of The Letter: "I've been selling new museum pieces since I was in high school.")

And so, at the not-so-tender age of 37, Paul Kent found himself in cold, forbidding Canada—"a completely strange country to me"—where only children rode bikes, and even then, for only six months a year; and knowing only three words of the English language (which would serve him well): "Hello." "Thank you."

A thumbnail sketch of Paul Kent's first 30 months in this country provides almost a dictionary definition of entrepreneurship:

—June 1957. Paul Kent sees a sign in a window in downtown Toronto: SEWING MACHINE MECHANIC WANTED. He is sent to clean the basement, during which time he takes apart a sewing machine and puts it back together, so he can qualify for the job. The pay: $39.50 a week.

—Fall 1957. Paul Kent goes to Singer's and meets a manager "who likes DPs." Two weeks later he is earning $55 a week selling sewing machines.

—1958. Tired of carting heavy sewing machines up and down three-floor walk-ups, Paul Kent realizes that if you sell insurance, you don't have to carry anything but a briefcase. Mutual of New York hires him—no commission—at a salary of $240 a month, "which was $5 more a week than with Singer."

—1959. While picking up a shirt at a laundry depot, Kent is asked by the woman there if he could find someone to buy the place. He goes home and declares, "Judy, I'm going to buy a laundry." "Are you crazy? What do you know about laundry?"

—Summer 1959. After three months of making little money, Paul Kent visits all his previous customers and tells them, "I sold you sewing machines and insurance. Now I can wash your sheets and shirts." Soon, he is making $100–120 a week, "which was pretty good money in 1959."

—January 1960. Having bought the laundry for $1,000 a

year earlier, Kent sells it for $3,000, and with some loans from family and friends, he buys an ailing, 1,200-square-foot bicycle shop on Bloor Street, just west of Dufferin, in Toronto. After some unpleasant interruptions by Hitler and Stalin, the Hungarian bike-seller and the Toronto bike store are united at last.

Hardly the stuff of dreams. In 1960 the average bike sale ranged from $39.95 to $60.00. In 1970 the range would be $130 to $150; in 1980, around $300; today, between $400 and $500. That is barely keeping up with inflation. And as Peter Kent, now 41 and the father of two children, notes, "Everyone must eat; *not* everyone needs a bike."

Needs? Even *thinks* about a bike. When the Kents took over Bloor Cycle & Sports in 1960, only 5% of their bikes were sold to adults. Big people now make up 85% of their sales, and there lies much—but hardly all—of the success of Canada's largest bicycle store. Andrew Kent, 32, married, who studied business at Ryerson "and at the Bloor Cycle School of Finance," admits that "bikes are the businessman's nightmare: high cost and low margin." He is right; your $1,000 sofa probably cost the furniture store half that, but the usual mark-up on bicycles is closer to $35. "Buying a bike for $100 and selling it for $135 is very common," he says.

There are further problems to daunt the wiliest business mind: Bikes are continually used as loss leaders. Ever since World War II, Canadian Tire ("the biggest volume seller of bikes in Canada") has been buying bikes for $120 and dumping them for $129. And danger signs galore: One Toronto-area chain with seven stores went bankrupt in the late 1970s, owing the *Toronto Star* over $20,000 for advertisements, and a million bucks to many others. "They ignored basic principles," says Papa Kent. "They were more interested in hype. They didn't sell good quality, consistently." Another bicycle seller had six shops in the 1970s—purportedly the boom years—and went down to one, and then one-half, taking on a partner. Still another dropped from four stores to one.

So why did the Kent four expand while others shrank? Boom while others busted? Rise while others fell? Especially when, in Andrew Kent's words, "We have too many bikes, too many parts. We break all the rules."

A lot of the success of Bloor Cycle can be traced to a gut respect for the buyer, a refusal to underestimate his/her intelligence, an almost maddening self-respect and pride in their name and business ("I don't want to hide behind a bush when I see a customer," confesses Peter Kent).

From the first day he opened his tiny shop, Paul Kent gave six months' free service, when most other stores were giving 90 days. (There are risks in this, of course. One woman requested free service on her damaged bike. "Sure, what's wrong?" "I backed my car over it." It was then that the Kents began defining the store's responsibility very clearly regarding that free servicing.)

Almost immediately, Bloor Cycle moved beyond the local bicycle market and "went Italian, dealing with Cinelli and Legnano." Later in the 1960s came the French Mercier; Japan's sun rose in the 1970s. "We opened Canada in 1978 for Panasonic," says Andrew, proudly. Bloor Cycle (the "& Sports" is a misnomer now; the Kents dumped hockey sticks and fishing tackle within the first half dozen years) was also the first, aside from Ford dealers, to introduce closed-circuit TV in their store. Since 1972 videotapes have been showing customers how to maintain their bikes, shift gears, determine their biking needs.

There were many other industry firsts: the first store to introduce folding bikes to the area, the bringing of Carnielli (Bottecchia) to North America, and more. But what really helps one understand what gives Bloor Cycle such clout, and respect, in the industry, are their inspired ad campaigns. Before the early 1970s the Kents relied upon word of mouth, until Peter pushed for modern modes of letting people know what they were about. From an initial $3,000 spent in 1971, Bloor Cycle now spends over $250,000 in ads, including the sponsoring of a racing team.

The 7½ by 10½-inch ads in the papers stay in the mind many years after they have appeared: BLOOR CYCLE HAS NEVER HAD A SALE, reads one, followed by such copy as "The price you pay in May is the same price you'll pay in November. We don't have any fall clearances or Boxing Day sales simply because our prices are carefully arrived at and can't go any lower." Father Paul Kent remembers a Hamilton businessman who came in and exclaimed, "I want to deal with a store that has never had a sale!" Alas, in 1986, they finally had their first one. And since it brought in 1,000 people a day, it will now be an annual event.

From 1960 until 1968 the Kents lived above the original, 1,200-square-foot store (a newspaper at the time wrote that Paul and Judy Kent "ride to work on a tandem each day," which still has the family stumped). Then they bought a furniture showroom next door, providing them with a three-level retail operation covering 20,000 square feet—well over ten times the size of the average bike shop. Now there was room for the cornucopia of bicycles. "Without taking into account colour and size, or speciality bikes for ladies, kids, etc., we have approximately eighty different models, about half of them domestic. Add colour and size, and you can multiply that by eight. And that's ten-speeds alone!" proclaims Peter Kent.

There are always over 3,000 bikes on hand, but occasionally they've been overzealous. "Our record was five thousand, nine hundred under the roof at one time," recalls Andrew. "We could hardly move around the store." But what it meant was that Bloor Cycle is now the largest store of its kind in North America, in terms of service, selection, stock. Some stores in the states might sell more units, but it usually means that they carry a half dozen different kinds, limited to, say, Schwinn and Raleigh.

There was a bicycle boom, as we all know, related to the oil crisis, the rising cost of gasoline, the growing health consciousness. But whereas the boom began in 1972 for everyone else, it began as early as 1969 for Bloor Cycle, its store overflowing with Canadian, British, European, and eventually Asian bikes. Their single-day record: 132 bikes sold, serviced, and out the door during a single 8-hour day, a few summers ago.

The store continues to blossom, a quarter century after Paul Kent bought his Canadian Dream, and a half century after he found himself on the precipice of the East European Nightmare. Over 50 people are on staff in season, doing sales, service, repairs, administration, some there for five and even ten years. Yet there is always a human/humane quality to the place: The store closes down the entire month of January and locks its doors at 1:00 P.M. every Wednesday, all year round, while the employees, Kents included, visit suppliers, do administrative work, and "do *not* go golfing." Mom and Pop Kent are still there, as is manager Andrew; Peter practises law full time but is in the store "in body, all day Saturday; in spirit, 27 hours a day."

In the mid-1970s Peter Kent created and chaired Urban Bikeways, which pushed for a system of bike paths throughout Metro Toronto. "We recognized that we were selling a lot of bikes, and felt a responsibility to the public to help create facilities for them." Self-serving? Perhaps. And the word *responsibility* does not always ring true in the mouths of business people. Yet in the case of the Kents, one doesn't doubt it for a moment. "Our sales people are instructed *not* to knock the competition," says Andrew Kent. "If we tell our story in a straightforward way, we'll be successful. We say, 'They're good; we're better.' " Peter Kent speaks proudly of "spending as much time talking people *out* of buying bikes as we do *into* them," insisting that "the sale is not that important. When we encounter a mother demanding an adult bike for her kid, we refuse to sell it; it's unsafe."

But that doesn't put a bicycle store into the top one percent of sales on the continent." Yet they are. Perhaps it's the "much better salaries" than the industry average paid to their employees. Or maybe because it has kept those same employees *off* commissions, so no one will be tempted to rush customers into an unneeded purchase. Or—heaven forbid—to bait and switch. When employees feel well paid, and customers feel that they do not always have to keep their hands firmly clutching their wallets, a sense of trust and reliability can develop.

And an awareness that needs do not stop at the borders of Metropolitan Toronto. As with automobiles, many people want more than one bike: this one for commuting downtown every day, this one for recreation, etc. But where will people obtain those different kinds of bikes when their local store in Saskatoon, Glace Bay, or Yellowknife has such a limited selection?

Bloor Cycle to the rescue, spokes gleaming in the sun. After over two decades of expansion, and after hundreds of requests from every part of Canada for this bike or that part, they "went national" in 1982, distributing 5,000 catalogues. By 1985 the number was up to 45,000 nationwide, to their mailing list. By 1987, 65,000 received copies. "Our catalogue has greater circulation than the *combined* circulation of every cycling magazine sold in Canada," exclaims Peter Kent. From the first year there was a special mail-order phone line. Everything in the store was offered, often at the same price to the penny: parts, accessories, complete bikes, frames, custom wheels, bags to flop over the bike or even you. All bikes were "prepped" before being shipped, rather than in the "knocked-down" form, the way Bloor Cycle receives them from Europe or Asia, so that it is simple for Mr. Peace River or Ms. Trois Rivières to put it together. And there was a low flat charge to ship a bike anywhere in Canada.

Can a neighbourhood bike shoppe become The Bike Store of Canada? It seems to have done so. Catalogue sales have doubled every year, as noted before. The Kents are reluctant to discuss sales figures, but they admit to "well over five thousand bikes sold a year," which, at an average price of $300–400 means sales into the millions, considering the many other products they sell—including over two dozen, such as clothes, exclusively made for Bloor Cycle. "Nearly one-half our sales are in parts, accessories, and clothing," declares Peter Kent.

"But I don't care *how* big we get," adds father Paul Kent [in his Hungarian-Toronto accent]. "We'll *always* be the neighbourhood bike shop. We treat orders from across the country as quickly as if they came into the store themselves." Peter agrees: "We've been so successful because we try to do it in an old-fashioned way for customers, regardless of modern efficiencies. We see our function as educating people. The more information they have, the better informed they are. And that's good for us at Bloor Cycle, with our phenomenal selection available."

The Kents love to tell the story of an extremely wealthy businessman who came in and bought a Cinelli—the Rolls-Royce of bicycles. (One could hardly call it just "a bike.") After his *real* Rolls-Royce, Mercedes, and yacht, the man had to taste perfection in another mode. A short while later, he bought another one, for another $2,250, in case he got a flat on the first and couldn't ride it for a day. "I've never enjoyed anything as much," the man told the Kents, "except maybe sex."

It's a good analogy. Like sex, the Kent family have defeated death, gained pleasure, attempted innovation, grown passionately. And like good sex, Bloor Cycle has always included honesty, faithfulness, and love in the bargain.

# A NEAR TOP-500 IN NORTH BATTLEFORD

*Harry Bondar*

---

North Battleford, Saskatchewan, is a town of about 16,000 souls, about 80 miles north of Saskatoon. Like all Canadian towns, it has its share of tiny restaurants, milk stores, movie theatres, car dealerships. What makes the place so extraordinary is that it has a business there—Harry Bondar's Hunter's Sport Shop Ltd.—which had sales of over $60 million in early 1987. And that was in boats and RVs (recreational vehicles), not illegal drugs. Every country has its legends, whether in politics, athletics, or business. But in North Battleford?

Harry Bondar was born in Prince Albert, Saskatchewan, in 1922, the first child of two. He went to high school in Regina, but never beyond, since "I was never smart enough for college!" (If the college kids are so smart, why ain't *they* rich?) Then it was off to the navy, at 17½, and eventually back to the prairies, when "a situation happened."

It was hardly a promising one. A sports store was available for purchase, and "a small one" at that. So Bondar took a $3,000 veteran's loan in 1946 "and a few thousand more," perhaps $8,000 altogether, and bought the place. "It was a little business, selling tricycles and the odd gun." Sales in the first year of operation were $36,000, and that was that.

But, in the revered tradition of Topsy, "it just grew." The major change was sometime in the mid-1960s—"I can't remember; probably eighteen to twenty years ago," Bondar says, in that gruff but warm voice of his which has satisfied a hundred thousand westerners in search of a decent deal in sporting goods and products. That was when Harry Bondar decided to carry boats and RVs at Hunter's Sport Shop. By 1970 sales began to take off, and since the early 1970s "it's been a way of life. People are getting away more; there's more disposable income, more time to relax."

It meant less time for Bondar to relax, but when you build a business up from $36,000 to 60,000,000 in four decades, you can't sit around. The original store was only about 3,000 square feet, in the heart of beautiful, downtown North Battleford. (It's now used for storage.) One of his smartest moves was when he began to collect his war pension cheques—around two dozen of them, worth $127 each month—and bought many acres of land on the outskirts of town. "That became the basis of my growth,' he says today, "since I had low property costs. The land was almost free!"

So now there is a gigantic new sporting goods store at the city limits, of about 100,000 square feet, built in 1983, added on to the existing marine and RV business. "That was the biggest advantage, being in North Battleford," he declares. "In a city, all that land would have cost me a fortune."

But cheap land is no guarantee of success in a retail business, as thousands of struggling men and women in small and even big towns across this country will tell you. Harry Bondar, on the contrary, will tell you little: "When you start with nothing and go through the years, all you want to do is pay your bills and not worry about paying the bank back," he says.

Furthermore, "everyone wonders how many boats and RVs I sell, and I don't want to tell." (An average boat runs $9,000 to $15,000, and RVs can cost anywhere from $12,000 up to $70,000, which means he's got to sell quite a few to get into the tens of millions of dollars.) He will admit to buying up to 40 boats at a time from one company, and once buying 200 boats from another. "You book and commit yourself," he says, noncommittally. "Others have higher overhead and their sales don't warrant such buying power." As for telling too much about his success, he notes that "when you're the big gun on the hill, everyone shoots at you." (Yes, guns are still available at Hunter's Sport Shop.)

But there are still reasons for such humongous sales figures, and Harry Bondar, looking more like a guy on your company's bowling league than one of Canada's best salesmen, is willing to share some of them. Hard work is one. His hours were seven days a week in the old days, although he's closed on Sundays now. "I used to leave the lot open on Sundays, but not for the last few years," he confesses. "My body is slowing down, but my mind sure isn't."

The mind is an awesome one, and the computer businesses of the world would have done even better had they studied Bondar's. People in North Battleford still talk of how he will buy back an RV from a man, many years after he sold it to him. No need to look at the thing, or to look up any records. Harry knew exactly what he sold it for and what he would allow on any trade-in. As he states it, "I can remember everything," even the colour of the boat I sold you a half decade ago."

Service, of course, is, in Bondar's words, "the backbone of the business. You've *got* to take care of the people you sell to." Since his store first opened in 1946, he has had a gunsmith on hand during hunting season, and bicycle repairs as well.

The response to such servicing has been clear. It's almost touching to hear it, but when Bondar bellows it out, it becomes merely another fact of (successful business) life: "We've been here a long time. The father dealt with me, then his son, and now his grandson. I've got a forty-year track record."

Bondar denies that he always gives a better deal, claiming only that "we've got a lot of credibility." History suggests otherwise: He has traditionally bought in volume and paid in cash. In an interview over five years ago, he told a reporter, "We're always looking for an off-season deal to give our customers a good buy. That's what merchandising is all about." (A famous deal was when he bought hundreds of men's ski jackets in a horrendous shade of pink from a manufacturer in the east for three-quarters off the wholesale price; they were all gone in less than a week, scaring rabbits, foxes, and horses across the prairies for the following few winters.)

We've noted, throughout this book, how much most business people suffered during the early 1980s, due to the high interest rates. Not Harry Bondar of North Battleford, who had no mortgage payments at the time, and sold $20 million in goods in 1980, more than tripling that seven years later. "A lot of our inventory was paid for, so we still had good years during the recession," he states with a smile.

And the good years keep rolling on, as Harry Bondar's amazing business enters its fifth decade. In season, he gets an average of 300 calls a day—"What you got?" "What you showing?"—and he has never found it necessary even to have a catalogue. Customers still pour it in from across Alberta and Manitoba, as well as Saskatchewan.

One would almost expect such a success to be franchised across Canada by now, but not if you know Harry. "You can't just open a store like mine in a nice shopping centre! Everything is so trendy today that if you don't have enough capital, and make mistakes, you're *dead*. In our business, you need to know trade-ins, and what things are worth." (He admits that no one could start nowadays like he could four decades ago; "It's a tougher ballgame in the 'eighties; today, you'd need twenty times more money than I began with." But he *did* open a second store in Edmonton in 1986, taking over a Canadian Tire. They expect over $15 million there, in 1987.

No, no franchises for Bondar. "I find that it's better to stay where you've got control. Some people overextend and don't have the right people to watch the other store." The right people are right there with Harry, including two sons and a daughter, and up to 100 other employees "in season." He admits—one senses almost reluctantly—that "you can do only so much as an individual; you don't win those ballgames alone; it's teamwork." He applauds the "pretty good people who work with me," and adds that he's "from the Old School—the key people have stayed."

Boats and RVs taper off by the end of August, of course, but there are always the Honda bikes and four-wheelers. And when the weather gets cooler, there's ski equipment, hunting, and hockey, hockey, hockey. But the crux of the matter is that Harry Bondar of North Battleford, Saskatchewan, loves his work. ("I don't find it too easy to enjoy myself away from the store," he declares.) "I like people; I relate to everybody. I enjoy them, and most people are nice people. If they are unhappy, we can sit down and talk." And, he adds, "I've never had *time* to dislike people!"

Bondar knows that he has created an institution out on the prairies, as eccentric and as renowned and as controversial as a certain prime minister who came from his hometown of Prince Albert. "We got lucky; our type of business became a way of life out here. Nobody knew what would happen forty years ago! You wake up forty years later, and you're really surprised."

But that implies that Bondar has been sleeping, and everyone know that's not true. "It's been a helluva challenge. And I'd never retire." (He is edging into his mid-60s.) "It's not even a question in my mind!

"It was a combination of things that made it work," he sums up. "I was in the right place at the right time, and I love people. . . ."

Yes, yes, Harry. But tell us, on sales of $60 million a year, just how much are you making?"

"I'm making a living." And he grins. And he has good cause to grin. In 1986, Bondar purchased the largest RV manufacturer in Canada, in Kelowna, B.C., for over $10 million, and moved it to North Battleford! The 400 employees will build over 2,000 units a year—selling for $15,000–$80,000 each—a prairie miracle which began in February 1987.

# THE TWO BOYS FROM CALGARY

## Dave Steele

The Canadian newspapers and magazines have been full of it—in more ways than one. But in this case, full of major articles on the utterly brilliant concept of the three boys from Calgary (later two, since the third "dropped out the day we started; he never wanted it to be big") who saw houseboats as the future of Canadian vacation holidays. Young men from the west, in their early 20s, who grew from 2 houseboats and 1 employee in 1982 to over 200 houseboats and 250 employees three years later, with sales revenues closing in on $10 million. By early 1987, it was 625 houseboats, 350 employees, and $25 million. But never before now—we think—have the specifics of their lives and business acumen been laid out as they will be here, compliments of Dave Steele, the president of Three Buoys Houseboat Charters Ltd., which could well be the Club Med of the 1990s and beyond.

Phil Carroll and Dave Steele were both born in 1959, the former in January, the latter in October. Both are Albertans, with Steele born in Banff but raised in Calgary, as was Carroll. Steele's father was an engineer for Bechtel, leading the family to move to Labrador for seven years, where the thirdborn spent grades 4 through 9 in a tiny school of 100 children. Steele, with his thick glasses and even thicker biceps, overflowing with good health and Hollywood-leading-man attractiveness, was in sports, but there was always a sense of entrepreneurship as well.

At the age of 14, for instance, Steele had a little catering company, in which he sold orange juice and sandwiches in Churchill Falls for pocket money. Phil Carroll's parents, according to Steele, were entrepreneurs "from the word *go*," with his mother running a gift store in Banff, and his father operating a successful restaurant there. Yet the two who would make such creative magic in business did not meet until their last year in university. If they'd met before, Trudeau could have used them to vanquish the budget deficit.

Between the end of high school and the start of college, Steele worked at Fort McMurray, as a time clerk in a men's camp to earn money for his studies. His older brother currently has an advertising business in Tokyo, and a sister is a secretary with Esso. Phil Carroll's older brother recently joined Three Buoys in Calgary, where Phil maintains the western office.

The years of Dave Steele at the University of Calgary radiate the kind of mentality and actions which would serve him in very good stead in his later entrepreneurship. He studied marketing and finance from 1978 to 1982, with his "emotional interest in a psychology degree" but his "common sense telling me that I should get a business degree, since I *knew* I'd be good at it."

But how did he know he'd be good at business? Well, he had lived in California for two years while in high school, when his father was transferred there, and he travelled a lot to Europe. "Travelling *opened my eyes*," he exclaims, in a voice filled with excitement and drive. "I've met presidents and senior executives of major companies, and I've never been impressed with them. They weren't that successful and had no dynamic qualities. They made me feel that I should do things for myself."

Which he did, while still in university. For instance, when Steele became president of the Ski Club—this is Calgary, remember—the membership shot up from 250 to over 1,000, almost overnight. "I just started marketing," he says. "I got people excited about belonging to a good organization. The ski trips, the parties, the energy—I felt that it hadn't really been *sold* before." (You can already see why Three Buoys would take off.)

Then came the moment in Canadian business history which should rank next to that of Adam being formally introduced to Eve in an earlier history: Phil Carroll and Dave Steele were chosen by the province to represent Alberta at a Student Youth Energy Conference in Montreal in 1982. "Before that, I didn't know Phil from Adam," says Steele, proving the validity of the metaphor above. There were seven sent from the province, and each student had to persuade an oil company to put up the money for his or her trip east, for which the youths would "represent their views at the conference." They managed to persuade some.

The two students met on the plane to Montreal, and all heaven broke loose. "Phil has an incredible energy about him!" cries Dave Steele, incredibly energetically. "It was amazing how much business wisdom and go-go-go we had in common!" Every night in Montreal, they would party until 5:00 A.M., talking.

When they returned west in March 1982, Phil told Dave at the Ski Club that he "wanted to throw a party to leave university with a bang!" What resulted was, in the memory of Dave Steele, at least, "the largest party in the history of the University of Calgary!" Over 1,200 showed up at a ranch, at the cost of $10 a head (per student, not cattle), with all profits going to the Ski Club. The party began at 3:00 P.M. on the last day of classes, and 15 school buses were shuttled back and forth. "We had posters and brochures about the event," says Steele, with fond reverie, but tickets were sold out in four hours, even before the brochures were delivered. "We created an unbelievable word-of-mouth!"

After that May 1st party, the two young men "realized a real synergy working together." They briefly considered T-shirt distributing, but, as Steele quotes Peter Pocklington, "If you can't do it *big*, don't do it at all." They also looked at lawn maintenance, a permastamp business, and "twenty different business ideas in all."

In the meantime, Steele took a job as a commercial mortgage broker, and Carroll as a financial consultant. (The latter, on straight commission, won a diamond ring award for setting a company record in selling mutual funds. We told you these guys were something.) Steele was on salary as well as commission, raising financing for large development projects. They worked at their respective jobs from May 1982 to January 1983, when IT HAPPENED.

The origins of Three Buoys could not be more inauspicious, or more ingenious. Steele had gone to South Africa for five weeks, visiting relatives, and at 5:00 A.M. on the day he returned, his buddy Phil Carroll called him: "Pack up your stuff; we're going skiing." Steele had missed three weeks' work, but his friend insisted that he "phone and say you won't be in." It was as if they each KNEW SOMETHING WOULD HAPPEN.

It did. They drove west, on their way out to Vernon, B.C., to ski, which is a six-hour trip by car. As they passed through a tiny town called Sicamous, they saw houseboats docked in the distance. "What a howl to have a week on one of these boats!" one said to the other. When they got closer, they "couldn't believe how run-down and shoddy they were," but they still asked for a rental. *Every single one was booked up through August, and this was only January!!!* They looked up and down the Shuswap River and saw all these poor-quality houseboats, all owned by little mom-and-pop firms, and *they were all booked.*

Phil Carroll turns to Dave Steele: "This would be a *fantastic* business to be in!" Rob Jensen, a carpenter friend who had come along for the vacation: "I can build boats." The car screeches to a halt. "If you can build them," cry Carroll and Steele to the third boy/buoy, "then we can *rent* them!"

They continued on their way to the skiing vacation, but, says Steele, in his Toronto office today, "Our minds were racing." Suddenly, less than a half hour from the lake where they had had their Big Moment of Truth, Phil Carroll turns the car into a farmer's yard and marches up to his front door. "How much to rent your barn?" he asks. "Fifty bucks a month," replies the farmer. "We'll *take* it," says Carroll, who returns to the car and wakes up the sleeping carpenter-partner-friend, Rob. "What do you think of your new factory?" "*Fantastic!*" replies Rob Jensen. A major new Canadian industry had just been born. Or at least conceived. As any woman who has ever been pregnant will tell you, they are not the same thing.

The three buddies went skiing, and later met with the largest boat people on the lake, who all agreed that "more business would be good for Shuswap," and gave them a helping hand. It was now Sunday; they had been on their vacation for 48 hours. As they began to drive back to Calgary, they saw a marina for sale. It had been foreclosed, and they offered $125,000 for the acre, having been told it was worth $165,000. But they needed a $5,000 deposit. They returned to the car and came back with a cheque for $3,000, "which was all we could raise at the time." They had 30 days to find the remaining $122,000.

Carroll and Steele were "naïve. What banker would loan us that kind of money?" They were both 22 and certainly damp behind the ears, if not actually wet. Back in Calgary, they arranged for the factory, purchased the marina—with 30 days to wrap it all up—all within another 48 hours. Rob Jensen returned to Sicamous and ordered machinery, pontoons, engines, aluminum, fibreglas, with all bills sent to the Calgary house of Phil, who must have dreaded each visit from the postman.

Meanwhile, every single day, Dave Steele talked to a different banker, with 15 "NO!"s in a row. On the 25th day, he came to a bank in Kamloops and told his story. The banker looked at the kid and declared, "This is the best idea I've heard in years!" The prescient banker loaned the Three Buoys/boys $170,000. And you will rejoice to read that the man has since been promoted to the senior level of management at a western bank, and *not* one of those that went under in 1985.

The three young men, among them, managed to put up $25,000 of their own money. In March 1982 things were moving along; on May 23 the second boat was finished and was rented out that very night to "eight girls from a sorority in Calgary." The toughest period was the initial six months in the first half of 1982, when each of the men still worked at his original job, while "dreaming, eating, sleeping the boats." When people would ask Steele what he did for a living, he'd reply, "I'm in the mortgage business, but I'm in houseboats on the side!"

The side was growing larger. The two men would get together every day before work, at lunch, and after work, discussing their market plans and ordering parts for the original two boats. And every Friday afternoon they would drive the six hours to Shuswap. Saturday mornings, it was up at 6:00 A.M., doing "all the shitty jobs," handling fibreglas, driving pickup trucks, installing windows.

But the idea was to be first class: These were the first

houseboats in history—unless there were some lost in the midst of time, owned by emperors and kings—which had a stereo built in. Private sleeping areas. Ship-to-shore communications systems. "At the time, they were the most luxurious boats that could be imagined!" Steele points out. "Now, they wouldn't even rate with us, due to the technology developed since then. But at the time, they were the cat's ass." On Sundays the men would do the books, all accounts payable, making sure they were still on budget. They would leave at midnight that night, often arriving in Calgary just in time to shower and get to work.

The boats were booked so solidly and quickly "you wouldn't believe it!" Yes, we would. They were rented out in October, when no one ever did. They were even rented out in April and May, when people might have to chop ice from the Shuswap. "No one had ever heard of an idea like this before!" Steele says. "It was a mass education for the public, and for us, as we knew nothing about boats. Hell, neither Phil nor I had ever *seen* a houseboat before that day in January!"

Then, on June 1, Dave Steele was told by his bosses, who must have known that something was up, "You want to be in the mortgage business or the houseboat business?" They gave him four days to decide. Steele proposed his feelings to Rob Jensen, who replied, "I was thinking of getting out, too." The decision was made that Phil Carroll would keep working and put every penny into the company, while the other two would go full time into boats.

Now, the other stroke of brilliance: Since no bankers would loan them any more money, they came up with the idea that a lot of real estate deals involved MURBS. What if they were to sell the boats, manage them, and get 75% of the tax revenue and tax benefits? The boats cost $55,000 to buy new, so they'd make money on that. So they put a package together with their accountant and lawyer, telling them, "if it goes, you'll get paid." They began to make hundreds of "cold calls" to people across Calgary, to tell them of their wonderful plan. Through July, August, and September 1982 they did not receive one positive response.

On September 30, 1982, they finally persuaded seven possible investors and their wives to fly out to Shuswap, chartering a plane. Naturally, the weather conditions were so bad that they couldn't take off. And they had borrowed "the last fifteen hundred dollars" from Phil's mother to charter that flight, and they had a mortgage payment to meet. So they quickly booked another flight, but all seven of the original prospective investors said "no."

On Superbowl Sunday, they didn't say a word while watching TV. That Monday they considered quitting, and called the pilot to ask for their money back. He offered, instead, another flight for the next weekend. So they had to find another seven people, and were back to square one. By that Thursday, they had four persuaded to come; Friday, another; Saturday, another; Sunday, they had to shake a business man out of bed. None was one of the original seven hopefuls. There wasn't a cloud in the sky; the pilot told them that he'd never been able to see the TransCanada Highway along the way before. Girlfriends made a big barbeque for the angels, and that Monday they started calling. Steele and Carroll quickly were given cheques for a total of $400,000, averaging $50,000 each. "From then on, it went wild," says Steele.

Phil Carroll called a TV man, who called it "the hottest story he'd ever heard in this business." They made a deal on a 12,000-square-foot factory near Calgary, where they built their first 20 boats following the original 2. The media began to converge on the factory. "PRAIRIE BOYS BUILD HOUSE-BOATS! NEAREST WATER SIX HOURS AWAY!" The CTV National News looked at these two crazies out in Alberta who dared to build boats on the prairies. But then, they laughed at Noah. And, most important, the investors began saying, "Wow!".

During that first year they often came close to collapsing over $500. And now? Let's look at the statistics. In 1982 they were in a farmer's barn; in 1983, a plant in Airdrie, Alberta; in 1984 and 1985, a new, 70,000-square-foot plant in Kelowna. Production? In 1982, 2 boats in four months; in 1983, 20 houseboats, 1 per week; in 1984, 40 boats, 1 per day; in 1985, 132 houseboats, 5 per day. By early 1987, it was back down to 2 boats a day, but these were $100,000 near-cruisers.

Marinas? In 1982, two at Shuswap Bay. B.C.; in 1983, an expanded marina there, for 20 boats; in 1984, a 7-acre marina and entertainment deck at Shuswap for 60 boats; in 1985, a new 57-acre resort on the Trent-Severn System in Ontario.

Booking revenue: 1982, $30,000; 1983, $280,000; 1984, $800,000; 1985, $2,300,000; 1986, $10,000,000.

Sales revenue: 1982, zip; 1983, $800,000; 1984, $2,700,000; 1985, $8,750,000; 1986, $25,000,000.

Employees: 1982, 1; 1983, 15; 1984, 60; 1985, 250; 1986, 350.

Now that they had the funding and the media, there was still a lot of marketing to be done. Their 20 boats made Steele and Carroll the owners of the largest fleet of house-boats in Canada, but they were told that they could never persuade that many people to book them. So they took a boat—Steele's idea—and parked it below the Calgary Tower, in January 1983, when the weather can be somewhat brisk. "It took off," gloats Steele, and ever since, their luxury boats have been creating a huge market that no one had ever marketed before.

They built that 150 by 50-foot marina at the cost of $150,000, all from their profits of the first 20 boats, pouring every penny back into the young business. (They still take out only about $2,000 a month each, in their 50/50 partnership; their only extravagance to this day is the new Mercedes which each now owns.)

The future? Steele and Carroll plan to take their Canadian Vacations concept right across North America. "I see it potentially as the most exciting vacation anywhere," says Steele, "and I've done a lot of groundwork on that." They are, as of 1987, on the Rideau Canal. At Lake of the Woods, near Winnipeg. On Lake Okanagan, in B.C. At Lake Havasu, California. On Oklahoma's Lake Enfaula, near Dallas. On Lake of the Ozarks, near Kansas City.

There are some little aspects which make for very warm feelings toward the concept as well. Back in 1984 an investor with a child in a wheelchair proposed an idea to them: Design a houseboat for the disabled. Phil Carroll was told to eliminate the top deck, to which he replied, "If we can't put someone on the top deck, then let's forget it." Three weeks later, they worked out the design. There are now four house-boats for the disabled, each selling quickly to investors for $75,000—the regular ones now cost $70,000.

Three Buoys—the name came up in a barroom discussion in the early days—is now in both the west and the east, in terms of its management and its boats. (Steele, in Toronto, is the president; Carroll, still in Calgary, is the CEO.) In the middle are "seven solid people, the type who stick with it, generate energy, or enjoy the energy around them." There are now a group of corporations: one for chartering, one for sales, one for building. The VP of sales, who's been on board (literally) since the summer of 1984, had bought a houseboat as an investment, and so many people asked about it that he sold 8. He once sold 23 in one day—at $70,000 each!—bringing in nearly $1.5 million in that 24-hour period. And who can blame the investors; they get to write off 100% of their investment over three years and then get 75% of the rental, of which 25% goes to direct costs, insurance, moorage, mechanical, and so on. Three Buoys takes 25% in management fees, and everyone is very, very happy. Since some people have up to nine boats, they must be thrilled with their tax write-offs, and the company has a financing method that avoids their being tied in to banks.

"There's no *question* that this will last," says Dave Steele. "It's a demand-driven business. We're overcoming the biggest misconception: that people don't want to vacation in Canada. This past summer, some Japanese filmed the boats on the Shuswap to be shown in Japan, and we're making major inroads into Germany. The market is there; we just have to get out and promote it."

The major step was developing that 57-acre resort on the Trent-Severn waterway, a $1 million project, with a full restaurant-bar and eventually 70 recreational condominiums. "It'll probably be the most elaborate marina resort in all of Canada." Recently, Phil Carroll thought up a Three Buoys Discount Package, to be offered to everyone who rents a boat, whether for a day, week, or weekend: discounts along the river systems to movies, restaurants, bars, golf courses, tennis courts. And the Trent system is 250 miles long. (Since they sell $50,000 worth of ice at each marina, there must be a growing market.)

Already they've had a profound influence on that market. They've noticed how others keep upgrading their boats; a company on the Shuswap used to spend $250 a year on marketing; it now spends $25,000.

What was the key to success of the Bright Big Buoys? "Never to succumb to the short-term way out," says Steele. "Too many make decisions on what the financial situation tells them; ours is based on *ideas*, and what will be generated in the future." When they invested that $150,000 on the hospitality deck on the Shuswap, everyone said they were crazy, since it would generate no income. "But now, it's the centre of the whole concept there!" By 1987, they were working on deals in Texas and Florida, and had become the largest exporters of boats from Canada. Over 40,000 Canadians and Americans have gone through their resorts.

"We're not emulating Americans," says Dave Steele; "We have a *leading Canadian way* of thinking!" And when he is asked when Three Buoys will stop expanding, he replies simply, "It'll stop expanding when people stop going on holidays."

## 8.
# THE ENTERTAINMENT INDUSTRY

### *Pitching an Audience*

One of the most frequently stated lines about Canadians in the world of show business and self-promotion is, "If you're *that* good, why aren't you in the States?" The question is a fairly legitimate one, for Canada is a geographically huge but demographically small country, bordering on what is the most powerful and wealthy nation on earth.

The image of the hustler, the go-getter, the kibbitzer, the fast-talker, the hard-seller, seems natural for Americans and somehow less dignified for Canadians. We have never seemed to have the pizzazz, to know how to brag, to be self-aggrandizing.

Think again: The six men and women in this chapter have each succeeded—at varying levels, of course—at pitching an audience, and they are honest-to-Doug Canadians. Some of these people are almost awesome in their success. Andrew Alexander, for example, who bought the Canadian rights to Chicago's famed Second City for $1, eventually produced a multi-million-dollar (and critically revered) television series, "SCTV," and finally purchased the original theatre in the States. John Pozer, of Good Stuff Games—1 store to 14 in less then a decade, along with a number of million-selling trivia games—is such a self-promotor that he is almost a (warm, charming) Canadian parody of the pushy Yankee. ("I'm very aggressive: I saw an advantage and took it!" he exclaims.)

Ian Fitzwilliam, of New World Marketing, still in his 20s, was a high school dropout who thought up an utterly brilliant concept of direct-selling cookbooks, and has made/lost/made millions in a few short years and made hundreds of others well-to-do along with him. The same goes for Miles Nadal, only 29 ("I always wanted to be successful; I enjoyed making money"), who was earning more cash taking photographs of cabins and campers at summer camps in his teens than 90%

of us made last year—and he did it a decade ago. And rather than being satisfied with a single photography business, he set up a whole group of companies, covering a wide range of marketing and communications. ("We are an American-style business in a Canadian environment," he asserts.)

To be sure, there are a few in this chapter who project the traditional image of the Quiet Canadian rather than the Yelling Yank: Anne Millyard and Rick Wilks of Annick Press, for example, who went into children's book publishing out of love for the field, starved for many years, and have only reached their present modest success (sales of just over $1 million in 1987) as a result of grants, tenacity, some pluck, but even more, luck—e.g., a superb, eventually best-selling author (Robert Munsch) came to them with his delightful writings. And in this same Quiet Canadian mode must be included Don McQuaig, of MICA, whose educational seminars for business people crept steadily for $8,000 in sales in 1971 to $5 million in 1987, at which time he finally began to expand with a Yankee-like frenzy. (He hopes to have eight education centres by 1995, and increase his present sales nearly tenfold, to $40 million annually.)

Nearly everyone in this shy/razzmatazz chapter has never borrowed from a bank, which is the usual way that people build up a business. No, each relied on a concept, an idea, "a vision," in the words of the two publishers of Annick Press. Nor are any of them particularly (formally) educated: Alexander kept dropping out of school; Pozer took but a few years of college; Fitzwilliam left high school at 16; Nadal dropped out of university before completing his degree. Only Millyard, Wilks, and McQuaig have any university degrees, and they gained little use from them in their eventual business careers.

Which is, perhaps, the point: While nearly everyone in this book is creative, the entrepreneurs in this chapter are pitchmen, entertainers, business people with flash and flair, who must continue selling every day, often only as good as their last show/game/sales sheet/book/lecture/job. It's a crazy form of existence, and in many ways, these are some of the roughest, yet most satisfying, business stories in the book, since the drive of the entrepreneurs in this chapter has such an edge to it. And pitching to an audience, as the Toronto Blue Jays' Dave Stieb can tell you, can be a lucrative, but often crushing, experience.

# MAKING ''THE
# SECOND COUNTRY''
# OWN SECOND CITY

*Andrew Alexander*

Second City. Chicago's self-deprecating name for itself, ever in the shadow of New York. But also the name of the most successful improvisational troupe in North American history, creating some of the best satire on earth. Second City, where Mike Nichols, Elaine May, Ed Asner, Alan Arkin, Joan Rivers got their start. When Andrew Alexander opened the Canadian branch plant of Second City in the "Second Country" to the north of the First, the opening cast included Dan Aykroyd, Gilda Radner, John Candy, Eugene Levy, and Joe Flaherty. Later additions included Dave Thomas, Andrea Martin, Catherine O'Hara, Harold Ramis, and Martin Short, making the Canadian version, even more than the original American one, responsible for shaping what would be North American humour for the last quarter of the twentieth century. And today, in the 1980s, it is that Canadian, Andrew Alexander, who owns it all—even the Chicago "branch plant." Thus are the ways of Canadian imperialism, in all their insidiousness.

Andrew Alexander—baby face on a huge head, solid good looks, and greying hair—sits stretched out on a couch below a photo of the cast of "SCTV," the inspired television version of Second City, which had received such praise in the late '70s and early '80s. Across from him is a giant painting of the "owner" of that mythical TV station, Guy Caballero (alias Flaherty). He was born in the spring of 1944 in London, England, the third of five children, and came over with his family in 1951. His father was an aeronautical engineer, his mother a homemaker. "I was a daydreamer," he recalls; "I had an imagination." His parents dreamed as well, wanting a "fresh start," and it was a "coin toss" between Australia and Canada. "There was a whole movement from England in the 1950s," remembers Alexander.

The initial move was to Caledon East, a small community north of Toronto. The children attended a one-room schoolhouse there, or rather, the other Alexander children did. "I played hookey all the time," says the future entertainment czar. "I used to sneak off and go swimming."

The family later moved to Brampton, a larger and closer suburb of Toronto, where Alexander graduated high school. "I had a real problem with schools all the way through," he confesses. "I kept being transferred, and just didn't like it." He finally spent two years in technical schools, switched to business and commercial, and went to Tri-State College in Indiana, where he took business for a year. Then it was back to Toronto's Ryerson for two more years, the first in business administration, the second in hotel management, "since I heard that there was wine tasting at ten A.M. each day." Lifelong occupations have been chosen for lesser reasons.

In 1967 Andrew Alexander left school and went to work for the Thomson Newspapers. He sold advertising in the *Port Credit Weekly* for $65 a week, and then graduated, in 1969, to Inland Publishing, which eventually started the first *Sunday Sun* newspaper. "I enjoyed the freedom," he recalls, noting that his parents were plenty worried about these rotten kids of theirs. They were right to worry: Alexander next opened the first "speakeasy" in downtown Toronto, where you could drink until 4:00 or 5:00 A.M., as well as another in Port Credit, a community just west of Toronto, "in a beautiful estate we rented for three hundred a month." There were "huge parties" in the latter each weekend; the one in Toronto was suitably open all week. Known as the Exit Clubs—since you entered them through the exit—they gave the young and still rather immature Alexander "an opportunity to party, and a way for paying for the partying and making some money." The police eventually closed them both down after two years, since this still was, at the time at least, Toronto the Good. "They were *very* successful," Alexander says, laughing, adding quickly that "they were very, very illegal, too."

But Alexander got tired of the craziness and moved on, although still in the entertainment field. He started a sports magazine, *Ski Life*, eventually becoming the editor. "I was *not* thinking about making a lot of money in my twenties," he declares. He was involved in that project for about a year and a half, when he was approached by three men to assist in the famous/infamous John Lennon Peace Festival in 1970. "That's a book in itself," he proposes, but this writer refuses the offer. It was right after Woodstock, and an "extraordinary event," with maharishis and the Ontario Provincial Police all involved. (Back at Ryerson, Alexander had done some booking of a number of entertainment acts, such as Ian Tyson and Gordon Lightfoot. He had also run for Student Council president, with David Crombie, then a teacher there, as his campaign manager. He got "womped," with Crombie going on merely to become mayor of Toronto and a federal MP and cabinet minister, while Alexander got to take over American culture.)

"I really caught the *bug* of entertainment," says Alexander, sitting up from his sprawl on his Toronto office couch. "I felt that I was starting to find an area in which I felt *comfortable*." John Lennon, of blessed memory, eventually took his name off that project, and Alexander still feels it was "a shame. Every major rock group wanted to be in it." He made a salary for eight months from the investors.

He then moved on to start Platform, a late-night comedy and jazz club, which swung from midnight to 5:00 A.M., with Gilda Radner working at the box office, and people like Dan Aykroyd and Valerie Bromfield, future Second City stars all, trying out. "It was the beginning of the growing theatre movement in Toronto," he declares. "I found that really exciting!"

Then, Alexander got the rights for the perennial stage revue, *Spring Thaw*, from Mayor Moore, and produced the 1971 version. "It was a disaster. I lost all the investors' money, about $50,000 in all." No one ever said that show biz would be easy.

Throughout the 1960s Alexander drove cabs, and would whip into a suit, have meetings with businessmen, accountants, and lawyers to raise money for his shows, and then return to the cab. Once, he picked up a businessman who had just invested in *Spring Thaw*, who was impressed by such a driven fellow who could do both, and was glad he had invested. He was only half right.

'I was dead broke," Alexander moans, referring to the early 1970s. Then he met a publicist at the new St. Lawrence Centre in Toronto who let him help her with promotion. For the next 18 months he was able to introduce an idea which moved the number of subscribers from 3,000 up to 15,000. He had hired a bunch of students to knock on doors and sell them right and left. The future entrepreneur was budding.

A further example: Alexander had "a tremendous fear of flying, but I tackled it," so he could zap around Canada, doing consultant work for theatres from coast to coast. Then he got a permit job in Chicago, working at the Ivanhoe Theater there. He would go and watch Second City all the time. Eventually, on a napkin, he made out a contract with Bernie Sahlins, its founder, for the rights to Second City in Canada, for $1—plus a percentage of the take if it was successful. He borrowed $7,000, rented space at the Firehall, at that time a discotheque and restaurant in Toronto, and began it in 1973. (An earlier Toronto Second City had gone bankrupt, due to absentee management. The owners would fly back and forth from Chicago, and the Toronto branch lacked a liquor licence as well. But most of all, Alexander feels, it was *time.* "They needed time to take off.") It should be noted here that Alexander is still not sure if he ever paid Sahlins the dollar for the Canadian rights to Second City. And back then, our dollar was worth $1.06 U.S., too.

The first Andrew Alexander-produced Toronto Second City opened in February 1974. Although the productions were usually quite brilliant, they were often in "dire straits," and in 1977 it "technically went under, and into receivership." The many doctors and lawyers who owned the Firehall had a lot of debts, and had their problems. But Andrew Alexander got the company out of certain obligations, and after he bought out some partners and brought in two new ones, it began to be more successful. (There were often good earnings over this period: In 1975 Second City had $750,000 in sales, up to $1.3 million in 1978. In 1985 it had hit $3 million, thanks to an introduction of a dinner/theater package in the late 1970s.)

Andrew Alexander was still single at this time, which was probably for the best; he would work from 9:00 A.M. to 3:00 A.M., six and even seven days a week, usually sleeping at his office in the theater complex. In the early years he "took home nothing; just enough to pay the rent." What rent?

In 1977 had come the most exciting development: Alexander and his gifted crew of performers came up with the idea of a fictional station parodying television, called SCTV. (Actually, it was first called Second City Television, but Sahlins wanted the name back, so they went with the initials.) Even with the success of the TV show on Canadian, and eventually American, television, it was in "constant deficit financing." The Toronto theater supported the TV series for over three years, and they accumulated nearly $3 million in debts. "By the time we got to network on NBC," recalls Alexander, "it cost $400,000 to produce a ninety-minute show." There were no profits seen until after the end of the run, surprisingly. "That's the function of TV," he says. "The return in investment is low until the show is stripped" —meaning until it goes into syndication, and endless repeats. But Alexander was able to get a "huge guarantee" for syndication from a major company in the United States, in "the high millions," he says, by 1985. "SCTV" is now seen and enjoyed in over three dozen markets in the States, and in Toronto, Calgary, Edmonton, and Vancouver, in Canada. With many more markets yet to come.

During these hectic years, Andrew Alexander did other things as well, opening a few restaurants (including the Flying Food Circus), eventually selling them, "making money for a while," but irritated at being "caught between the restaurant business and producing shows." It was not until 1980 that he "started getting comfortable." He finally married in 1983, and for the first time—possibly a record in show business.

"I found an affinity with Second City," says Andrew Alexander, barely into his 40s, and a multimillionaire at last. "It was something subconscious. If you believe in an idea enough—this could apply to any industry—it affects other people. *They* recognize that they are committed as well." Second City, Canadian version, taught Alexander a lesson. That "if you give something long enough, it can come together. Chemistry develops."

But on paper, at least, Andrew Alexander was bankrupt with his TV show. He could draw a decent salary, it's true—maybe $50,000—but he had major bank guarantees. And if the show hadn't gotten past 1981, he admits, "I'd have been driving a cab again!"

The future, as of the mid-1980s, looks more promising than ever. Alexander believes that the old SCTV shows will "always be in syndication," zooming around the world's airwaves much as the old "I Love Lucy"'s still do, for decades to come. "But the *real* future is the acquisition of Chicago." In January 1985 the child became the father of the man (to coin another phrase), as Andrew Alexander of Toronto took over as executive producer of the original Chicago company, with an option to buy the theater. "It cost a few million," says the Canadian. It's a "*very* profitable" company, grossing some $2½ million annually—and that's in real dollars.

As of the end of 1985 Andrew Alexander owned 50% of Second City Inc, his equal partner being Len Stuart. There are three Second Citys at this time, in Chicago, Toronto, and London, Ontario. A Second City is just opening in West Hollywood, California, in conjunction with Harold Ramis, an old alumnus of the company. "L.A. will give the opportunity of having all our people work out in, and showcase themselves," Alexander says.

But that's only four Second Citys. Some people are currently looking at real estate in London, England, the birthplace of the Canadian entrepreneur. "And I'm thinking of a live, five-night-a-week TV show out of Britain, Toronto, Chicago, and L.A.," says Alexander, his eyes ever on the Big Possibility. There are at present about 60 actors on payroll; with Los Angeles and London, England, that number will be close to 100. And even more employees if this new TV concept comes to fruition—an American studio came to him with the idea—and it could be on the air by the fall of 1987. But even today, the total employees "must be 300 people."

Alexander has a five-year plan, which is more than one might expect from a kid who used to play hookey all the time, and run illegal speakeasies. He plans to establish himself permanently in Los Angeles, "where the industry is." He expects to have an even greater effect on TV and film by 1990, as Second City's "whole philosophy of approach to work" spreads across the world. ("Harold Ramis says that most of the movies he's done and written have been improvised, in the tradition of Second City," Alexander comments, referring to one of the creative geniuses behind the hugely successful *Ghostbusters*.)

Second City, Chicago-born, is now Canadian-owned, and is worth upwards of $10 million. Alexander's sister is running the London, Ontario, branch, "doing a superb job. It's like a sports franchise, where you develop people on the farm team and bring them up to the majors." Andrew Alexander hopes to have an organization that he can "pass on," and he sees it going another quarter century, at least.

"I do see myself as an entrepreneur," he says. "I have the

ability to make things happen, and one of the priorities of the entrepreneur is to shake things up in business. And Second City has a new role in business. It can't be like it was in the 'sixties." And Alexander himself? "I don't know *what* I'd do if I ever sold the theaters."

## THE GAMES PEOPLE
## SELL (AND INVENT)

### *John Pozer*

If you told John Pozer that he thinks and acts like an American, the millionaire games-seller and inventor, who, with sons Shawn and Matt, has flooded North America with more trivia questions than a TV game show host on uppers, would probably consider it a compliment. In a country where people who are successful tend to apologize for it, and people who are *not* are told to go to the States to prove that they *can* be, Pozer stands out like a blazing torch. He might be one of the biggest self-promoters in the history of Canada, and maybe in the history of the States as well. *Everyone* seems to know about the Canadian-made monster hit Trivial Pursuit; if everyone does *not* know about the best-selling Junior Trivia, Tot Trivia, Biblical Trivia, and Teen Trivia games, it is certainly not from lack of trying on the part of Vancouver's John Pozer.

John Pozer was born in the summer of 1941, the youngest of six children. His father owned a dairy and a farm in St. Georges de Beauce, about 50 miles east of Quebec City. (He is pleased to note that this was where his great-great-grandfather was given land by the governor of Quebec and that the City Hall is on "Pozer land." His great-grandfather owned 150 homes, and used to tell those who rented from him, "Pay me when you can." John Pozer would end up a bit more businesslike, if no less likeable.)

When the youngest was nine, the family moved to Granby, in the eastern townships, where John won a bicycle in a safety essay contest, and sold the *Montreal Star* for four years. He would sell stuffed teddy bears and animals to "all" his customers at Easter and Christmas, and won sales awards from Maclean-Hunter for two years, receiving two lamps for selling the most magazine subscriptions.

At the age of 13 Pozer went to an all-French radio station and offered to do a bilingual show. "Get a sponsor and come back," he was told. He promptly returned with 7-Up in tow, and began to do radio broadcasts for CHEF from the Canadian Legion building in Granby. By the age of 14 he was the DJ of record hops across the eastern townships, making up to $800 per dance, getting a percentage of the take at the door. "I had a lot of clothes and independence," he recalls happily.

Pozer took extension courses in creative writing at Ottawa and Carleton universities in later years, and marketing at Centennial College in Toronto, but he was clearly always a fellow who *did*, rather than studied how to do. When he saw an ad in a Montreal paper from radio station owner Geoff Sterling, "looking for the most talented people in North America," he knew they were talking about him. He applied and got a job at CKGM Radio from 1959 to 1962, with the title "Special Events." He was 17 when he began. (Don't be too impressed. "If the news director wanted a milkshake, *that* was a special event!") But he did some on-air work and ended up in news and promotion, producing the Joe Pyne show for two of those years.

Then he was interviewed by a station in Smith Falls, where he "took big-city ideas to a small town." They were too big; after two weeks he was told to look for another job. He was 21, and unemployed.

So John Pozer drove to Ottawa, where he was interviewed for a teen show, "Club 13," later "Saturday Date," replacing Peter Jennings. (Jennings only made about a million or two last year from ABC-TV, so Pozer is doing better, as you'll soon read.) He was host and coproducer for most of 1962–66, interviewing the Beatles, the Rolling Stones, the Beach Boys . . . (In 1964, Pozer met his future wife, Darlyne, on a blind date at a Belafonte concert. The couple's two sons were to help make Pozer's career.) Pozer emceed dances and record hops, and eventually left radio to manage rock-and-roll bands. He formed his own record company, called Sir John A, which inevitably led to him having his picture taken with John Diefenbaker. He put out 13 records, sold many, had "local successes," and handled five bands over two years.

Then it was off to Toronto, and a one-year contract with

Johnny Bassett at CFTO-TV, taking "The Pig 'N Whistle" across Canada. Next came the position of executive assistant to the president of the Record Division of RCA in Toronto, travelling all over the world for them. And then Warner Brothers grabbed him for the next four years as director of Artists and Repertoire, until 1972.

After another year with United Artists, setting up their publishing division, he moved to Vancouver in 1974, which is where this story really begins.

Throughout this book, we've seen many "epiphanies," where entrepreneurs either see the light or get the idea for their moneymaker. Pozer took a year off and went to Los Angeles, "looking for a new and interesting business." He saw people playing backgammon in a hotel, and he stood and watched. Maybe he could do something with this back in Vancouver!

He considered setting up a game company, purchased $25,000 worth of backgammon sets, returned to Canada, and sold them out of a little retail store on Granville Island. "I'd never been in retail," he confesses. He ended up selling 175 *different kinds* of backgammon games, for from $2 to $2,000, the latter with gold and silver pieces. Chunky Woodward bought a set for $225.

Good Stuff Games opened in June 1974, in about 1,200 square feet of space. Sales for the first few months are indicative of how Pozer did. June sales, $80. July, $800. August, $1,200. September, $2,000. October, $3,000. November, $5,000. December, $53,000. It looks more like the electricity bills of a Maritime family, doesn't it?

Then John Pozer began to use the skills he had so finely honed in radio and TV: He started to promote like mad, teaching courses in backgammon at night. "I was the first in Vancouver with it," he brags. "The press was unbelievable," he says, making sure that it was very, very believable. There were full-colour photos of Pozer at an all-leather backgammon set. Then, in 1975, he put on the World's Largest Backgammon Game, for which he painted a 3,000-square-foot parking lot, making the pips 22 by 12 feet. (Garbage cans were used for dice cups.) He ended up on the front page of the *Vancouver Sun*, and the *National Enquirer* covered the event with a two-page story and six pictures.

The Vancouver police came and told him that he would

be "gambling in public, and we'll have to charge you." Pozer was upset, but wisely phoned the then-minister of justice, Ron Basford, and invited him to roll the dice. When the cops came and saw their boss doing the evil deed, they just drove off surreptitiously. "That *really* brought attention to the store!" says Pozer.

There was a second Good Stuff Games store in 1977, in downtown Vancouver, and the two were quickly bringing in $500,000 a year. People came in and wanted to buy franchises, to which our crafty businessman replied, "What is a franchise?" (He should read this book.) A third store was opened in 1978, with sales of over a million, and in 1979 number 4 opened in Victoria, a franchise, so Pozer must have found out.

By 1984 there were 14 Good Stuff Games stores—13 franchised, one company-owned—bringing in about half a million per store, all in Ontario and British Columbia. He eventually sold everything, reducing all his retail involvements over the past few years.

But until he got out, what crazy promotions! The World's Largest Othello Game, painted on a hockey rink. A Scrabble Tournament. A jigsaw puzzle contest involving 30 teams. Rubik's Cube contests. "We had a fun product, and the media liked what we were doing," he says. "They saw that I was a little guy having fun and building a business." And, he notes with some glee, "The publicity I received was worth hundreds of thousands of dollars." (Yes, he was ecstatic to give *this* interview, too.) "There was no competition," he points out. "I had the *only* adult game stores in North America." And, no nonsmoker in a tobacco store, John Pozer admits to being "addicted to the games."

We now turn to the second generation of Pozer business geniuses: Sean Pozer, now 20, and completing his first year at the University of British Columbia, and Matthew, now 11. In December 1982, while father John was working 80-hour weeks, often not coming home until 3:00 A.M. each day, Sean returned from working at the store and told his mother, "More and more people keep asking for a game for 'superintelligent nine-year-olds.' I'm going to created a kids' trivia game." So, every Monday after high school, Mum, Sean and Matt would go to the library and plough through reference books. The then-15-year-old worked for five months on his creation, and created the 2,860 questions of Junior Trivia. "I didn't encourage them," says father John. "The odds were so slim to make a hit." Only after they were done did he look at it.

A distributor friend was in town, and Pozer asked him if he was "in the market for a kids' trivia game." "I love it." In ten minutes they put a deal together. It sold over 200,000 copies over three years, and "It's had its run," says Pops. But that was only in Canada; it has sold over 1 million copies in the States, since "we were the first out for kids."

The Pozers—including the input of baby Matt—are now selling six games in seven countries, including Great Britain and Australia. Next came Teen Trivia Plus, Biblical Quiz, and Matt's greatest hit, Tot Trivia, for three- to six-year olds, which has sold over 250,000 copies and is in its seventh printing. (Matthew also invented the Perrier Popsicle at the age of five and the Tilted Toilet Seat, half-toilet, half-urinal, at the age of eight; clearly a kid to watch.) Some of the games have been invented by others and edited by the Pozers, it should be noted.

In their first full year in the United States with their games, the Pozers sold "just under ten million dollars worth," with profits of over 20% of that. The expectation for 1985 was between $12 and $15 million. And all *your* kids ever did was have a crummy paper route. "We have every state covered, with 250 salesmen in all," says John Pozer. Trivia Games Inc. is their American company; Let's Play Games is the Canadian. In the fall of 1985 a new game was released: The Money Hunt: Reward $1,000,000, in which one buys the game, reads the clues in the booklet, and tries to figure out where the million bucks (U.S.) are hidden in North America. The prize will be awarded in $50,000 chunks over 20 years, which will cost the ever-crafty Pozers much, much less than they make on the game, we can assure you.

Another game on the burner is Kids Beware, which is educational, and the project of wife Darlyne Pozer. Advertised as "fun to play," it features a kid who has to get to school without getting molested. It is the Pozers' first board game, since the trivia games were only cards, questions, and dice.

Most of the business is in the States now, with the games being made in five countries "to get enough printed." John Pozer now considers himself a "games agent," since inventors have been flocking to him with their ideas. As of spring 1987, he is helping several to market.

Millionaire Sean hopes "to get into commerce, to justify what I've done in the business world." Millionaire father John never took commerce but doesn't appear to need to justify it. "I've got a gut feeling of what the market is ready for," he says. "I was the first in Canada with backgammon. I was flying in Othello from New York, and was the first with Dungeons and Dragons and Rubik's Cube." But he eventually found it awkward to "wear two hats," selling to retailers while being a retailer himself, with his Good Stuff Games stores. "So now I'm in manufacturing."

The Pozers own their burgeoning industry equally, although Sean hasn't asked for any spending money. "He's been getting cash from skiing instruction," says his father proudly. "He does it his own way." The family owns one-half of the U.S. company and one-half of the Canadian. The rest belongs to a few other (lucky) Canucks. "As long as you don't walk into the States with your cap in hand, you can do well," Pozer claims. "I'm *very* Americanized; I'm aggressive; I'm a Toronto boy in Vancouver, in style. Now I'm looking at how to get on the Carson and Griffin shows."

Ultimately, it's having one's eye on the main chance: "I was in the game business," says John Pozer, "and I saw an advantage and took it." Adds son Sean, "Look out, Parker Brothers; here come the Pozer Brothers!"

## MAKING MILLIONS DIRECTLY

### Ian Fitzwilliam

Direct sales. The words arouse images of the brush man, pushing his wares upon the unsuspecting, lonely housewife. Of Dagwood Bumstead wrestling with the insistent door-to-door salesman. Of the foot shoved in the door, with the encyclopedia/vacuum cleaner/cosmetics seller screaming for ONE MORE CHANCE.

Wipe all those visions from your mind. There is a new world out there, the enormously successful New World Marketing Corp., which is changing the style of direct sales and making millions in the process. In the New World Marketing method of direct sales, the product does the selling. And the obnoxious salesman? He is obnoxious no more.

New World Marketing developed an astonishingly successful technique for selling a very basic commodity: books. In fact, in 1984 and 1985 its president, Ian Fitzwilliam, and his thousands of eager and fortune-hungry salespeople sold over $35 million worth of fat, glossy cookbooks, which are its specialty. By mid-1984 the 27-year-old Fitzwilliam, who dreamed up the New World Marketing novel selling concept, was indulging in four Rolls-Royces. By early 1985 everything fell apart, as you will soon read, but the tall, lanky black man has no doubt that New World will one day be swimming in riches again.

Fitzwilliam was born in England, the only child of civil servants who moved to Toronto in 1967 and worked for the Ontario government. Like many self-made millionaires, he was impatient with schooling. At the age of 16 he dropped out and went across the road to a shopping centre, where he got a job selling shoes for Maher Inc. After a year of selling at several different shoe stores, he went into direct sales—"the aggressive hard sell"—with Don-Mac Enterprises.

Fitzwilliam sold such items as garbage bags, pots and pans, and books door to door, and, although he "sold well," he was struck by the lack of incentive in the manner of payment: Everyone received the same $150-a-week salary! "If you sold more than the other rep," he recalls, still incredulous at the stupidity of the idea, "it was strictly for the competition or pleasure of it." Now that is *not* the way capitalism should work.

Fitzwilliam was still in his late teens when he decided to go into business for himself. But there would be a number of ups and downs before the Great Idea would come to the young entrepreneur. First came Fitzwilliam's "own little business," Elite Enterprises, in which he sold cookbooks directly, and it was "big if you sold ten copies a day." In other words, it went nowhere. The book was *The New World Encyclopedia of Cooking*, which he sold for $14.99. The fledgling business went under in August 1978, after only three months. "I was undercapitalized, and I had no good business sense," he recalls. "You learn from your mistakes."

That's for sure. For the following three years the kid

"hobbied around with antique automobiles" and then borrowed $500 from a friend and bought 200 copies of the same cookbook he had flopped with before. He sold 50 copies the first day.

Now, if you've been reading carefully, you'll recall that in Fitzwilliam's previous incarnation as a self-employed businessman, he could not sell more than 10 a day; suddenly, in November 1981, he sold five times that number. Which brings us to his secret, and perhaps the most inspired marketing concept since Henry Ford created his assembly line and dropped the price of cars by hundreds and hundreds of dollars. "It's never been done before," says Fitzwilliam. "I created it because I'm basically lazy. I *knew* what direct sales was all about, and I decided that I would go into it again only if there were an easier way."

Rather than describe Fitzwilliam's inspired concept, let's hear it in his own words, in the "Display Pitch" that every salesperson of New World Marketing has been giving dozens of times every day, right across North America, in offices, hospitals, and even churches: "HI, I'M JUST GOING TO LEAVE THIS WITH YOU UNTIL LATER ON THIS AFTERNOON, NO COST OR OBLIGATION WHATSOEVER. IT'S THE MOST FANTASTIC CREATIVE COOKBOOK EVER TO BE PUBLISHED BECAUSE IT'S THE ONLY ONE WITH 2,000 MOUTH-WATERING RECIPES AND 800 FULL-COLOR ILLUSTRATIONS, WHICH ENABLE YOU TO SEE EXACTLY WHAT YOU MAKE LOOKS LIKE BEFORE YOU PREPARE IT. ORIGINALLY PUBLISHED AT U.S. $49.99, WE'RE PRODUCING IT FOR A LIMITED TIME AT $19.95, NO TAX, AND WE ACCEPT CASH, CHEQUES AND POST-DATED CHEQUES UNTIL PAYDAY. OH! AND BY THE WAY, FOR EVERY 10 ORDERS YOU GET, I'LL GIVE YOU ONE FREE."

Does it work? Is the Pope Polish? By not hassling people, by not shoving the books down their throats, New World would allow the books to sell themselves. And by large, mass-scale buying, they could pass on the extraordinary savings and still make a bundle. The salespeople would specifically ask each secretary and receptionist not to "aggravate her employer," and to pass the huge cookbook around only during office breaks rather than working hours. The concept was based on the idea that large numbers of people would see the book, and by leaving it with the receptionist, one was actually deputizing her. And, to be blunt, which of us does *not* have a mother, aunt, cousin, niece, sister, brother, friend—anyone— whom we'd love to give a nice birthday/anniversary/Christmas/ Easter/unexpected gift to, that *looks like $49, says it costs $49*, but only costs $20? (And many of the cookbooks that New World flogged over its first few years even went for less than $10, making for an even greater saving.)

Sales were simply astronomical. One worker walked into an office one morning, dropped off the cookbook, and re- turned four hours later (having dropped off three dozen more in three dozen other offices) to get an order for 38 copies. He took the collection of cheques and cash—the secretary had done the money-collecting for him, of course—and happily left three freebies with his deputy, the now-ecstatic secretary. Hundreds of men and women across Canada started earning well over $1,000 a week, which meant that they were selling at least 250 books at $4 commission each.

But this did not happen overnight. Fitzwilliam was still struggling at the start, even though he'd already invented the light bulb. After he went through his initial 200 cookbooks, he kept buying more and turning over the money, until he couldn't get stock. Then he came across *The Good Housekeep- ing Illustrated Cookbook* and approached the publisher, Avon Books of Canada Ltd. He purchased 25 at $15 apiece and sold out in a couple of hours. He launched his new business with that book, which was selling for $26.95 in the stores, but only $19.99 when dropped in a receptionist's willing lap.

In October 1982 Ian Fitzwilliam incorporated his company as New World Marketing Corp., with 25 employees. "We were really fortunate that the recession was on. I got quite a few good people working for me!" he says. By the following month he and his sales crew had unloaded 65,000 copies of the *Good Housekeeping* book, a remarkable achievement in a country where *any* book that sells a total of more than 10,000 copies is considered a best-seller.

But the publishers couldn't keep up with New World Marketing, and that has been its ever-present nightmare ever since. (If Ford kept running out of cars, what good would it have done him? And unlike Henry, who could always speed up his assembly line, or open another factory and hire more people, poor-but-soon-rich Ian Fitzwilliam has always been at the mercy of book publishers, who are rarely anxious to print more than a few thousand copies of anything, and live in continual fear of being stuck with tons of worthless remainder copies if they *do* overprint.) So the company ran out of books overnight, and although Fitzwilliam "scrambled," he still lost all his salespeople. "I ended up with four salesmen and lots of carving knives." Carving knives? "We bought anything we could lay our hands on, and it took months to sell them."

But books were what Fitzwilliam really wanted to sell, and he spent hours browsing in bookstores, leafing through large cookbooks, encyclopedias, and dictionaries, looking for eye-catching products suitable for direct sales (or "display sales," as Fitzwilliam prefers to call it. With the negative connotations of the former, who could blame him?). He had been aware of the very special appeal of big colourful books since his days of going door to door for Don-Mac. "Cookbooks are collectable," he explains. "Everyone eats, so they have mass-market appeal. And they are a clean product. You can see and read what you are getting. And besides, nobody else in Canada was hitting our market."

It took Fitzwilliam until the following April to obtain a suitable product in the form of 25,000 copies of the *Creative Cooking Course*, a 1,024-page volume put out by Crown Publishers Inc. of New York City, with step-by-step instructions on how to concoct everything from Chinese stir-fried beef to Austrian Nuss pudding. And to protect himself from another shortfall, Fitzwilliam invoked the law of supply and demand; he kept his prices high, not so much to boost revenues as to slow down sales(!). His great fear was that he would run out of books and lose his sales staff once again. He sold the new product for $24.95 each, well above his other prices in the past.

But the books sold practically overnight, as did 7,500 copies of *The Encyclopedia of Creative Cooking*, another massive Crown opus for which Fitzwilliam paid $15 each. The book retailed for $49.95; Fitzwilliam's troops sold them for $24.95 each, of which the salesperson kept $5.

The supply problem continued; the books ran out. Fitzwilliam then tried calculators, but found what worked for cookbooks didn't work for silicon chips. He ordered 75,000 copies of *The Encyclopedia of Creative Cooking*, and they arrived in his suburban Toronto offices in November 1983. "That's when New World Marketing took off," says Fitzwilliam.

Took off is putting it mildly. Six months later the firm had sold more than 600,000 copies at $19.99 each. It had also sold 200,000 copies of *Cooking in Colour*, published in England. Then, in the summer of 1984, New World Marketing took a bold move aimed at putting an end to fears of supplies running out—or so they thought. It negotiated two of the largest single hardcover purchases in world history: Two million copies (really!) of *The Encyclopedia of Creative Cooking* and two million copies of *Cooking in Colour* (regularly $29.95, but for *you*, $9.99).

All this wheeling and dealing did nothing for the always-precarious Canadian book-publishing industry, unfortunately, since to keep the prices low—a crucial aspect of Fitzwilliam's concept—the books were printed in Hong Kong, Italy, Spain, and West Germany. In addition to its two blockbusters, New World continued to sell other cookbooks, a dictionary, and a medical encyclopedia. Fitzwilliam sold millions and millions of these books by early 1985, when he ran into further problems, but oh, what success he had until then!! Through 1984 he was selling 50,000 books a week across North America, then 100,000 books a week, then 150,000 books a week! His top salespeople opened offices in Ottawa, Edmonton, Calgary, and 100 American offices in such cities as Chicago, Boston, Buffalo, Minneapolis, Tampa, San Jose, Phoenix, and Kansas City, Missouri.

As of the first few weeks of 1985, it looked as if Ian Fitzwilliam would soon join the ranks of such direct sales giants as Mary Kay Cosmetics Ltd. ($65 million in Canadian sales), Avon Canada Inc. ($150 million), and Amway of Canada Ltd. ($130 million). In 1984 New World had sold $13 million worth of books in Canada and another $6 million in the United States and some $2 million in Canada. Fitzwilliam's staff began predicting $1 billion *in profit*—not bad, when one considers that General Motors of Canada Ltd. has never broken $800 million in profit, and *that* on sales of some $15 billion.

But then it all fell apart, and for the same reasons as always. "We ran out!" moans Ian Fitzwilliam, and they lost every single salesperson overnight, nearly all of them keeping the books which had so generously been given to them on consignment. They all ripped off the man who was making them well-to-do, to the tune of $1.6 million in retail value and over $900,000, wholesale. Fitzwilliam was stuck, back in suburban Toronto, with no sales force, just as he had been two years before. "Technically, we were insolvent," he says. "According to the Harvard Business School book, we should have gone under."

But not the man who gave hundreds of former pizza truck drivers and housewives the chance to earn up to $1,500 a week, when they had never earned more than $200 a week before in their lives. Not Ian Fitzwilliam. In November 1985, just a few months after dropping from *$2 million* in sales *a week* to *zero*, he placed advertisements in 50 papers across the United States, telling people of the wonderful moneymaking New World Marketing way of selling books. A big difference, though: No more consignment. No more nice guy. From now on, Fitzwilliam will only provide his cookbooks to his salespeople when they prepay. They will make even more money now—$10 on a book they sell for $20, instead of the $3, 4, or 5 of before—and the president of New World will be guaranteed his money this time.

"The drop worked," says Fitzwilliam, referring to his glorious concept of letting the cookbooks sell themselves, "but the consignment aspect didn't." Within weeks he was back up to 5,000 book sales a week—approximately $100,000 in retail sales—but he had no doubts that his 50 ads would provide many, many hundreds of new salespeople across the States, and eventually Canada again, who would leap at the chance of making big bucks with the big Canadian's big idea. "The nice thing about the prepay plan is, it's safe!" He smiles toothily. "The finale hasn't taken place yet," says Ian Fitzwilliam of New World Marketing. "You've seen the rise and the fall. The story now is *The Comeback*!" Besides, he says, "I'm the eternal optimist. And I'm lucky! I've got a good half-century to go!"

He's starting up again, as of early 1987, mainly in Manhattan and Toronto, after a "dismal" 1986. "I'm still trying to find a better way."

# CREATING KIDS' BOOKS WITH A KID'S KNOWLEDGE OF BUSINESS

## Millyard/Wilks

There is always something charming, even disarming, about a man and a woman making a career out of something they really love. But in the case of Anne Millyard and Rick Wilks, of Annick Press—a combination of their first names, if you please, just as their thriving business is a combination of their lives—it is almost a miracle. Knowing about as much about business—publishing or money—as the children they print books for, they have somehow made a go of it, even receiving the honour of their peers by being named Publisher of the Year by the Canadian Booksellers' Association in 1984. Their wonderfully quirky, creative, and often utterly magnificent books are sold in a dozen countries around the world, and they have (somehow!) managed to put out 100 different titles in the last decade. And while their gross sales barely broke $1 million for the first time in 1986, their story should be told, since it is a classic example of how a man and a woman, nearly a quarter century apart in age and a world apart in cultural and national backgrounds, can make a (dare we say it?) *business* work.

Anne Millyard was born in Frankfurt, Germany, in 1929; Rick Wilks was born in Toronto in 1952—a publishing equivalent of Neil Simon's *The Odd Couple*. Millyard came to this country in 1952 with her student-husband and a babe in arms. (She is now divorced, with a 30-year-old son and a 25-year-old daughter.) She volunteered to work in schools, "getting a feeling for children's literature" along the way. She is very pretty, with short-cropped brown hair and a lovely figure.

Rick Wilks, on the very other hand, was raised in Toronto, studied at a number of universities in his native city, Europe, and the Middle East, and "was not entrepreneurial at all! I never ever used the word *entrepreneur*!" He is excitable, with long hair and teenagerish good looks, sitting next to his partner in publishing in their tiny north Toronto offices. He was "a generalist" in university, eventually earning his B.A., but "not sure what it's in!" But, he adds, "ironically, it was the best background one needs to be a publisher."

Wilks continued to travel, working in bookstores that specialized in children's toys and books. He worked with children to help put himself through university. He and Anne Millyard knew each other because Anne was a friend of Rick's parents; she has known him since he was a preadolescent.

"It started off with a conversation," recalls Wilks. "I had always felt that Anne and I were like-minded, and her compassion and involvement with issues made her refreshing to talk to." (Millyard would often speak to schoolchildren on the subject of world peace.) Out of one of those talks came a concept: to produce books for children *written by children*, particularly with Canadian content. It may seem self-evident, but it's really not. Think of literature for children through history, and it's nearly always been written by men and women in their young adulthood or middle age. "We discussed how we could fulfill this vision," recalls Wilks. "We'd both seen wonderful stories written by kids," says Millyard. "They couldn't spell, but it was great stuff! We thought it was a waste to have them in our pockets when others might be interested." Visits to libraries showed almost nothing by kids for kids.

They were determined to "give kids a voice" and, they hoped, inspire other children to write—voluntarily, not just because the teacher asked them to. They wrote a proposal on the old LIP program, asking for $39,000 to study the question over half a year, employing nine people on a "reading attitude programme." They got the grant and discovered that 89% felt strongly about the idea of books by children, and they were quickly "flooded with stories. They tracked us down!" Millyard says with a laugh. Boy, did they. Millyard and Wilks received 700 stories in ten weeks. "It let the genie out of the bottle and it couldn't get back in," says Wilks, ever excited.

In 1975 they published *Wordsandwich* under a Books by Kids imprint, using the money they had to do that attitude study; in fact, it was their salaries. "We didn't pay ourselves." They typed it and pasted it up themselves and found a printer. "We knew nothing," Millyard admits. They printed 1,000 and sold them at $3.95 retail. Although they had failed to cost it out well and never managed to pay the printer, it did "phenomenally well," selling out in six weeks, and was reprinted three more times, selling 3,800 altogether, a very respectable number.

To paraphrase a famous TV commercial of the 1960s, "Is this any way to run a publishing house? You bet it *isn't*." An accountant visited them when they were celebrating their first printing, and informed them that they'd have to sell 20,000 copies of the book to be viable.

More reverse entrepreneurship: They then published *Making Waves*, poetry for younger children, which sold for $4.95. It won a National Design Award, but they lost 29¢ with each of the 2,500 books of their print run. And 400 of those were badly misbound. Then, thank heavens, the concept for Annick Press "began to bubble up," in the words of Wilks. "We felt we were discriminating against adults!" Annick, by the way, is not only a contraction of the names of the founding father and mother, but is Inuit for "brother," as well as the name of that famous Canadian satellite. "We didn't want it to sound like a law firm," says Wilks. Besides, law firms usually make money.

In 1976, barely a decade ago, the first Annick book came out, called *Your Own Story*, written and drawn by one of those much-discriminated-against adults. "We had zero money," bemoans Wilks, "but we kept doing more of what we were doing. We kept our overhead down by working out of Anne's house." They quickly had five books distributed by various companies, primarily in Toronto and Ottawa. A fortunate turn of events took place at this time. Macmillan of Canada, a major Canadian publishing house, wooed them, offering to put money into the tiny book industry of the two overgrown kids. But instead, Anne and Rick chose Firefly, a very small, shaky house, as their distributor. "We trusted our intuitive feelings," says Wilks, "that this small company would present our books better." Soon after, Macmillan was sold and dumped all of the smaller firms it was distributing. Annick would have been dead before it really had a chance to live.

Well into 1976, Annick continued to have no earnings, was "way into the red," and the two were paying themselves a big fat nothing. "We dug up vegetables and ate them," says Millyard. To top it all off, she separated from her husband in 1977 and was left with a young daughter at home and no independent income. "It became direr and direr," she says.

Maybe the Canadian Commercial Bank would have loaned them money, had it been around then—but who else?

In 1978, many vegetables later, Bob Munsch, a young teacher from the University of Guelph, mailed them an envelope with four "stories" in it. (One, called *The Fart*, remains unpublished. But you will be relieved to know that it is on Munsch's third record album.) The other three were simply superb—zany, comical, irresistible. One of them, which eventually was published as *The Paper Bag Princess*, tells the the tale of a young princess whose boyfriend is kidnapped by a dragon. The girl rushes off, tricks the dragon into exhausting himself, and saves her boyfriend, the prince, who promptly mocks his saviour for being so messy-looking. "Ronald," says the princess, "your clothes are really pretty and your hair is all neat. You look like a real prince, but you are a bum." The last sentence of the little book, which has now sold hundreds of thousands of copies around the world: "They didn't get married after all." (My kids are still hysterical when they read it, and my feminist friends have bought dozens for everyone they know.) There are now three best-selling record albums of Munsch reading from his Annick stories, and the second one, *Murmel Murmel Munsch*, won the Juno for Best Children's Record in November 1985.

Millyard and Wilks realized at once that they had the kids' equivalent of Stephen King knocking at their door, and it sure sounded like opportunity. They offered Munsch a 10% royalty, had to pay an up-front fee to an illustrator, and their printing bill was $33,000 for the first three books, all hard-cover and selling for $6.95 apiece. They got small grants from the Canada Council but had to publish first, so it was scarey.

Once *Paper Bag Princess* hit the bookstores, "things really spiralled," says Wilks. Sales have been up 100% a year over most of the last few years. In 1981 they were in the $80,000 range; by 1982, $170,000; 1983, $280,000; 1984, $430,000; 1985, well over $750,000; in 1987 moving well over $1 million. It ain't Random House or Knopf, but it sure beats digging vegetables.

Then Annick began to attract other fine writers, including the gifted Kathy Stinson, whose childlike and inspired *Red Is Best* (about a toddler who just *knows* that when she wears red everything feels better and looks better) is up to 100,000 copies sold in places like Denmark, France, Germany, Latin America, and, of course, across North America. "The Scandinavians just love *Paper Bag Princess*!" adds Millyard. Ever since Munsch lit a fire under Annick's collective rear, the two have been going to all the book fairs around the world, including Bologna and Frankfurt. Starting in 1982, publishers and their reps kept flocking to the Annick booth, and "we ran like crazy those first few years." They are still coming, except now it's the reps who are doing the crazy running, to try to get the rights to the Annick publications.

The first irregular cheques began in 1978, with regular, but still small, payments to each of them since 1981. They didn't move out of Millyard's basement until 1983, however, when "I couldn't find Rick among the stacks of books!" And, with their growing business awareness, Millyard adds that "it seemed wrong to have people come to someone's *house* to visit Annick Press!"

"I don't think a publishing house can be anything more than the taste of its publishers," says Rick Wilks. "We didn't look at seven businesses and choose this one. We had a vision of what to bring to young readers, and it was adamantly adhering to that which was important." (True, but having enough faith to risk larger quantities of printing in order to get the prices of the books down to affordable levels had a lot to do with their success.)

"It's publishing *for children*!" declares Wilks forcibly; "Others were publishing for adults, not children! Books *have* to connect with the world of the child! The writer, artist, and publisher must have a vision of the child's world: big versus little, the role of authority, looking at the world from the level of a kneecap. And a good, solid entertainment component; the book will work if it has that."

Echoes partner Anne Millyard, "For me, it's the component of *listening* to the child's voice. People act on the assumption of what the child needs, and don't ask them very often. Children know this, and there's a lot of anger."

There are now over 100 books with the name Annick on the back sitting in children's bedrooms around the world, with "a shockingly high percentage of them still in print"—at least 75, according to Millyard. Munsch's *Paper Bag Princess*, for instance, sold more in 1987 than it did in 1986, and more in 1986 than it did, etc. "The books sell *better* every year!"

They even have a philosophy of growth, according to Wilks. "We love being publishers, *not* business administrators! And we're growing to the point where it is taking a lot of energy just to run the business. But we refuse to lose the hands-on quality that is so important, so we'll simply publish fewer books each year." (They have imported a dozen from Europe that they distribute.)

One of their most inspired moves was borrowed from Europe: Annikins—tiny, shrunken versions of their best-sellers, which go for 99¢, instead of $4.95 and more. "It's for people who can't afford books for their children," says Millyard, and Annick has sold over a million of them, printing 75,000 at a time.

"We said in the early days," recalls Rick Wilks, " 'Thank God we've got a lot of ideas!' We haven't *begun* to exploit new projects, concepts, markets, and spin-offs, like the recordings of the books." A "school programme," begun in 1986, involves kits for schools, sheets for teachers, even laminated student activity cards recommended by provincial ministries. "There's *no end* to the approaches we can try." And partner Anne Millyard adds, "We have a basic commitment to lead, not to follow." And finally, it seems, to have a thriving business out of a lifelong love for books for children.

# MAKING MONEY BY TEACHING OTHERS TO MAKE MONEY

### Don McQuaig

"Small-business people are overwhelmed! They don't have complete control!" Thus exclaims Don McQuaig, in his early 30s but looking and sounding like a teenager. He paces back and forth like a cat in his handsome offices on the 15th floor of the Cadillac Fairview Tower, at the southern tip of Eaton Centre in downtown Toronto. The ancient Old City Hall clock glares through the window behind him, and it stands as an ironic counterpoint to what the youthful president of MICA is all about. For his leading management education firm is about making businesses, their bosses, and their employees work better, more creatively, more intelligently. If MICA had its way, the century-old clock would be digital, possibly metric, and certainly using its time a lot more efficiently.

In many ways, the history of the rapidly expanding business is a father/son story, even though the latter bought out the former some years ago. Don McQuaig is the son of an industrial psychologist, Jack McQuaig, and a mother who trained to be a child psychologist but never practised. "We felt, as kids, that we were part of an experiment!" the middle child of five jokes today. As early as his first year in high school, young Don ran ski trips to Vermont and sold them to people—"Much like seminars," he says. "I had seats, filled them, and made money." Indeed, he made more money in that than in the seminar business, as you'll soon discover. But in the case of the ski trips, he did them "only to make enough money for the trip, plus an extra two grand." A full-time business career would demand a lot more than a few hours' work through grades 9, 10, and 11.

McQuaig took three years of economics at Glendon College, York University—"but nothing to do with what I do" —and, interestingly, his highly educated parents did not press him greatly. "Going beyond a B.A. was discouraged. There was a sense of 'get out and *do* something; do something meaningful; study a bit, but take control of your own destiny.'"

The youth eventually did that, but the destiny was certainly shaped during his first few years of adulthood by his father. Jack McQuaig gave seminars through the American Management Association out of New York City, and had a "seminationalist view" which made him wonder why he had to go to the States to get his lectures. "My dad observed some entrepreneurial instincts in me and recommended that I work with him one summer."

It would last much longer than that. The two McQuaigs formed a company, Modern Information Communication Associates, alias MICA, spending $5 to file the name. "It was based on the idea that professional people needed ways to keep up-to-date," McQuaig Junior says, unaware at the time just how ahead of the times he was. The son was to be the legs to his father's mouth: "My dad's idea was 'Let's get high-powered people who talk quickly!' Too much of seminars was wasted time, spoon-feeding." McQuaig junior's job was to find people to come and hear his father give his speech, "Interviewing Job Applicants." He spent three months going door to door for that initial seminar, speaking to 2,000 business people to get the 100 who would pay $50 to hear his dad. It took place at the Royal York Hotel in late August 1971, and Don McQuaig worked all summer to earn perhaps $2,000. The father took nothing. The son was 18 years old.

Indeed, for the first eight years of MICA, during which Jack McQuaig was the only lecturer for most of them, "dad never took anything, and he gave hundreds of talks." His son, for his part, took maybe $25 a week home. A second seminar had followed on the heels of the first, in December 1971, and it was also successful. Don McQuaig phoned "every last one who came to the first," asking them what they liked and didn't like about the talk. "People were interested! They'd always have a colleague who'd want to come, too."

What may seem surprising in this info-obsessed world of the late 1980s is that the prevailing attitude toward education was rather different just a decade and half ago. "Most presidents and vice-presidents would say, 'Why should I send someone? If they can't hire the right person, I'll fire them!' " And when the second lecture, on motivation, was offered: "If my people don't know about motivation already, I'll get rid of them!" "Arrogance was the general atmosphere then," recalls McQuaig, who feels responsible for changing that feeling for tens of thousands. "And it was hard to attract the GMs and IBMs in the initial stage, since we had no credibility, and they were tied in to their American head offices." Fortunately, only around one-half had the negative attitudes; the problem was that the half who were interested often lacked the budget.

But the budgets were eventually found, as suggested by the growth of MICA. The sales for the two seminars in 1971 were under $8,000; by 1973 the "six or eight" talks brought in around $40,000. By 1976, when the McQuaigs started bringing in outsiders to talk—"all of a sudden we had to *pay* people!"—the sales shot up to $200,000. But the decision to hire others besides papa was soon justified: MICA hit $1 million in sales in 1981, double that in 1983, and 1985 witnessed 800 seminars on 66 topics, with sales of $4 million. The goal for 1987 is $5 million. And how could they not, with subjects such as ASSERTIVE MANAGEMENT, DELE-

GATING WITHOUT LOSING CONTROL, EFFECTIVE
PERSUASION, EFFECTIVENESS IN WORKING WITH
PEOPLE, MANAGING STRESS, SURVIVAL TRAINING
FOR NEW MANAGERS, TIME MANAGEMENT, etc.,
etc., etc.

The growth form $8,000 to $4 million in 14 years does not
fully express just how far MICA has gone. The initial office
was a plywood board laid across two big black seaman trunks
in a storage room in downtown Toronto. And Don McQuaig
ran the business part time until the late 1970s. What is most
impressive is that McQuaig began to truly listen to what all
his teachers were teaching: "I learned that we should stick
with what we know, and we know the educational seminar
business." More than that: McQuaig and his staff spent all of
1984 on what they were doing right and wrong, uncertain of
how to cure the errors they'd made. "We have, at our finger-
tips, the very best thinkers in how to run a business!" he
declares, implying that they were potentially like water bot-
tlers dying of thirst. "We put *ourselves* through the Strategic
Planning Program, which is painful and brutally honest: Why
do our clients come to us? How can we do it better?

Much of the problem was self-evident. They had some
success with many of the "fly-by-night self-proclaimed experts," which led to an inconsistency in the market. One
lecture might be good, another might let the audience feel
cheated. And with big-shots like Tom Peters charging $20,000
a day, U.S. funds, his talks on Searching for Excellence were
sending Don McQuaig Searching for Cash to pay him. (And
with all seminars, regardless of the cost of the speaker, costing $325 per person, those were definitely loss-leaders.)

But MICA was still building up a reputation as the best of
its kind in Canada, since its seminars were being offered
with great regularity in Montreal, Calgary, and Ottawa, as
well as in Toronto. Many other seminar institutions would
cancel if there weren't enough people; MICA never did that,
except when there were too few to interact in a seminar
which demanded it. On up to one-third of the seminars, they
make no money. "But if we can make a profit on two-thirds,
we can still come out ahead," McQuaig says. They began
getting their act together in the late 1970s, when "we were
like a restaurant with no place to serve food." MICA opened
its opulent offices in the heart of downtown Toronto in the

summer of 1981, in the middle of a mail strike, "when the whole economy was going to hell." But they survived—many did not—by offering "first-class, top-quality seminars, aimed at the informational person who deals with concepts and numbers." This meant starting a Computer Classroom in 1982, initially a joint venture with Computerland, buying out their interest a year later, giving one-day seminars with IBM PCs to up to 25 people. They've still made no profit from it, but "we see it as the core of the future."

The future has recently expanded at the speed of an IBM PC. McQuaig and his associates have mapped out a plan to open centres in major markets right across Canada. By 1990, they hope to have over $10 million in sales in Toronto and over $40 million overall, five years after that. "We'll open the first two ourselves, and after that, decide how to finance them. It will cost at least $500,000 to duplicate what we have in Toronto." (McQuaig has never borrowed money; he's financed all growth by ploughing all profits back into the business. As recently as 1984, he was taking only $35,000 a year home to his wife and three young daughters. "Our assets walk out the door every night," he admits with a smile.)

In many ways, the seminar business is like pop music: There are few Tom Peterses, just as there are few Bruce Springsteens. But McQuaig calls on many of the biggest gurus, including Ken Blanchard, of *One-Minute Manager* fame; John Naisbett, the *Megatrends* man; Tom Peters, still searching for excellence as well as cash; and, perhaps most impressive of all, Dr. Edward de Bono, author of two dozen books and the genius of lateral and creative thinking. "We learned from de Bono that solving problems only makes you more efficient at what you may be doing wrong," says McQuaig. "We've started thinking in terms of opportunities, and looking outward." And if going from $4 million to $40 million by the mid-1990s isn't looking outward, then what is?

Don McQuaig gives only a few seminars; most of his role has been programming, and working with faculty and staff. "We're just seeing the tip of what people can gain from educational seminars," he declares. "You can't give someone a job to do and have them work at a high level of effectiveness. It's like not giving a mechanic enough wrenches."

As they extend into new markets, the people at MICA have "grandiose plans" for the United States. "We want to take what we've got into the biggest marketplace of all," he says. He expects to open the first American operation by 1990. "Our mission is making knowledge workers more effective through continuous learning." (When they started out, the goal was merely to "help managers keep up-to-date with the information explosion.") "Our target is not just a narrow group of managers, but everyone who has to think," he says. "We're providing lubricant for minds." McQuaig is determined to serve his Canadian clients on a national basis—and they include Bank of Montreal, Bell Canada, Canada Packers, Canada Post, Canadian Tire, Husky Oil, Molson's, Nabisco Brands, Nestlés, Noranda Mines, Nova, Woolworth's, and, yes, GM and IBM—and then crack the international scene, including the United Kingdom. "The U.S. is three to five years ahead of Canada in terms of kicking ass and changing business patterns," says the 80% owner of MICA, "and our firm is more in tune with them."

Profits have been modest—10% or so—and their overhead is huge: upwards of $150,000 a month, including rent of nearly $20,000, catering staff, facilities staff, and the instructors, most of them major Canadian psychologists and teachers. But profits should shoot up soon, not only from the 1,000% expansion plans but from the fact that Don McQuaig has recently begun a new business, not unrelated to MICA: "I'll be managing seminar leaders internationally," he says proudly, with his first client being none other than the brilliant de Bono, stationed in England but lecturing to business people and governments worldwide. "I know the business and will be able to manage lecturers and position them so that they can become new Tom Peterses." Not only that, but he hopes that this will take him into international markets, like Japan.

Don McQuaig is hardly rich, but that looks just around the corner, considering his monster plans for MICA. "It's been more fun than going out and finding a *real* job," he jokes. "And if it weren't for this, I'd end up in some big organization like the ones we help!"

Begun as a father/son operation, MICA is rapidly spreading across North America, and possibly around the English-speaking world, as one of the major management seminar companies. And it may well spread to a third generation as well; when his oldest daughter was 2½ she looked at her youthful father and whispered, "I want to be president of MICA."

# CREATING SIX COMPANIES WHEN ONE WOULDN'T DO

### Miles Nadal

There are times when the walls of an entrepreneur tell a lot more than merely the number of windows and his or her taste in wallpaper. On the walls of the office of Miles Nadal, the president and CEO of the MDC Group of Companies are:

A photo of Miles Nadal with hockey giant Gordie Howe.

A painting of Miles Nadal with then-Prime Minister Pierre Elliott Trudeau, the former with his arms around the latter.

A photo of Miles Nadal with skier Steve Podborski.

A photo of Miles Nadal with former Expo catcher Gary Carter.

A photo of Miles Nadal with Wayne Gretzky, who needs no introduction.

A photo of Miles Nadal with Brian Mulroney, who will be pleased to make his own introduction.

A photo of Miles Nadal with American columnist and publisher William F. Buckley, Jr.

A photo of Miles Nadal with Ken Thomson, newspaper magnate.

A photo of Miles Nadal with Keith Davey, federal Liberal Party strategist and senator.

Huge framed articles on Miles Nadal from the *Calgary Sun*, the *Calgary Herald*, and the *Toronto Star*.

A gorgeous drawing of Wayne Gretzky, signed "To Miles, in Friendship, Wayne Gretzky."

But most revealing of all, a framed letter from Conrad Black, the Establishment Man of Canada and head of the Argus Group, dated January 16, 1984, which begins, "Thank you for your letter of January 10 and for your more than generous remarks about me." (Yes, Conrad *did* manage to find time to have lunch with Miles.)

Miles Nadal, it should be noted right off the top, turned 29 in February 1987. This is a kid who has been around—and is determined to get more around in the next 50 or 60 years—in the creative end of marketing and communications in North America. He was born in 1958 in Toronto, to a father who was in retail sales. His older brother is a podiatrist, but *he* never got to work on the feet of Wayne Gretzky, or even meet him.

There are plenty of clues to the future entrepreneurship of the kind of young man who would write letters to Conrad Black. He had three paper routes by the time he was 10, and he "always wanted to be successful. I enjoyed making money." By the time he was 13 he was making $400 a week, selling photos of houses for A. E. LePage and other real estate firms. (He had taken photography as a "hobby hub" at a summer camp, and immediately saw "the marketing opportunities in it." Why Miles Nadal looked at a camera and saw a business, when the vast majority see only a chance to capture the kid's school play or a candid shot of Fluffy, is a question that cannot be answered.)

While in his mid-teens, Nadal began to take photographs of the Toronto Toros, a short-lived professional hockey team in the 1970s, on a free-lance basis and, as well, sold pictures to an amateur hockey magazine. "I always had a love of sports and played hockey and tennis as a kid." Then he got involved with the Argonauts, the Blue Jays, and the National Hockey League, as their photographer. (Panasonic, Molson's, and Carling O'Keefe came later.) His earliest promotion and PR all involved sports.

Each summer, from the time he was 14 until he was 18, Nadal would take cabin photos at various camps, eventually photographing 20,000 kids across Ontario and Quebec, and grossing $50,000 during those months alone. Then it was off to university, taking his first year at the University of Toronto, his second at Western Ontario in London, and his third and fourth at York University, studying marketing and finance. But who needed to study? His firm, Action Photographics, "skyrocketed," and he just *couldn't* go back to school. "I've never been a quitter," he apologizes. "I *enjoyed* school, but my greatest love was business." (He found school "laborious" but had scholarships out of high school and a B+ average in college.)

Action Photographics was formally incorporated on April 11, 1980, when Miles Nadal was 22 years old. The concept was photography of all kinds, including public relations. "I sold it, I shot it, I processed it," he says. "No one else."

Then he hired an experienced photographer, who handled much of it. "I started looking after the business side."

Part of that business side, in the mind of young Miles Nadal, blond, immaculately dressed in a double-breasted striped suit looking almost too grown-up for him, was to let the rest of the world know that Miles Nadal Was Available for Business. So he would write Conrad Black, call Craig Eaton. "People would say, 'Where's this kid coming from?'" He was merely coming from the School of Self-Promotion, of course, a school which (most feel) too few Canadians have ever visited, much less graduated from. The owner of the Calgary Flames introduced him to many people after all the fine photos Nadal had taken of his team. George Cohon of McDonald's got Nadal involved with the charitable Ronald McDonald House, which led to further connections. Paul Godfrey, then chairman of Metropolitan Toronto and possibly the most powerful man in the city politics (and today publisher of the *Toronto Sun*), welcomed Nadal's work for the Herbie Fund, a charity which brings children in need of major medical care to Toronto from all over the world. "All these led to *tremendous* opportunities in business!" he explains. "Ours is a people business."

Within one year Action Photographics raked in $50,000, and by March of 1982 Nadal had five people working for him. At that time he founded the MDC Group of Companies, which eventually included The Marketing Design and Communications Group, MDC Promotional Services, MDC Public Relations, MDC Direct Marketing, MDC Visual Communications, MDC Graphics, and the original firm, Action Photographics. There are, today, 55 employees in the Toronto office alone, along with offices in Montreal and New York (in association with other companies there), and branch offices in Calgary and Vancouver.

Why such an explosion of services, of people, of *companies*? "What started the framework was working for Saffer, Cravit, Freedman [the highly successful advertising firm which made a fortune doing ads for primarily retail firms, such as clothing stores, etc.]. I saw a need for a full service of strategic marketing communications." He owns 75% of Branbury Explorations Ltd., an OTC stock which he took over in late 1986; it, in turn, owns the MDC Group and

MDC Corps., and more, but what he is doing with them is the impressive thing.

"The concept is unique across North America, and for sure in Canada," he declares. "No other firm has *all* services under one umbrella: a PR firm, a photographic arm, a graphics arm. You want photography alone? We can provide that. PR alone? We can do that too. Or we can provide them all, under one roof."

No more would Miles Nadal have to say no to a client who would ask him—as thousands of clients must ask their advertising agencies all the time—"Why won't you do *everything* for us?" Nadal went ahead and hired key people in each field—management people. For instance, he hired a man who was once the director of marketing at Adidas Canada (and was once a client of Nadal's). He now does marketing and sales and runs one of the companies in the MDC Group. No going to other *agencies* for Miles Nadal—he went to the clients themselves! So he hired the mature, 50ish ex-president of Laura Second Candy Shops. And the mature former director of communications for IBM Overseas. No incest here, of PR firm hiring PR people, and promotion firm hiring promo people, but a firm that does it all, hiring experts from the kind of companies he hopes to get as clients. And does.

"My idea was, if each company was to be a specialist in its field, then I needed management in each. And they've come together very well. I believe in a synergy, not the 'I'll do it for *me*' quality in many agencies." Profit sharing helps to create that synergy and all-for-one, one-for-all atmosphere as well. The average employee puts in up to 60 hours a week, and "everyone here is achievement- and success-oriented.

"I'm a catalyst, and I create some of the ideas, but the success of the organization depends on *their* dealing with clients," he says. "It's all based on incentive; their reward is greater when the company does well. There's no ceiling here. Everything is performance-oriented."

There are at present two buildings in an unfashionable part of Toronto, with 14,000 square feet in all. By being vertically integrated, Nadal went beyond the traditional ad agency approach of using existing personnel to fill roles. "You *can't* make a plumber into a carpenter!" he exclaims.

It has all seemed to work. Billings were about $600,000 in 1982, $1.2 million in 1983, $2.7 million in 1984, around $5 million in 1986, and the expectation is $11 million in 1987. "It's been unbelievable over the past year or two!" he exclaims. "Clients are thrilled with the specialization, the control from the concept to the final execution, the timing, the pricing!" His clients have included R.J.R. Macdonald Tobacco, Hillroy Stationery, the Royal Bank, Air Canada, Philips Electronics, 7-Up, Sony, Revlon, British Airways, and, of course, the National Hockey League.

And, as Nadal likes to stress, it's corporate, not merely certain products. He assists in creating corporate identities, through logos, nomenclature, annual reports, corporate brochures. "The corporate style at the MDC Group is aggressive, bringing together a group of people who believe in the cause," he declares. "We are capable of serving *all* the needs of the clients. Canada isn't used to full-service, twenty-four-hours-a-day, seven-day-a-week work like we offer." Still, while the concept is unique, the individual companies have "tremendous competition" from other firms. There may be no one else with promotion under the same roof as graphics and photography companies, but MDC's promotion company must still confront other promotion firms.

Every week, another two dozen companies are contacted, which, he admits, "people in this country don't feel comfortable with. We're an American-style business in a Canadian environment." There have been risks, as well, such as hiring two to three seminal (and expensive) people at a time, but "when you grow an average of a hundred and fifty percent per year, there is obviously going to be an element of risk." He insists that MDC is a logical company, with "no magic behind it. We're just repackaging and merchandizing the wheel."

So it's up at 5:30 A.M., out by 6:15, meetings by 7:00 (reached by the Mercedes 190E), working often until 10:30 and 11:00 at night. The hours hopefully improved after his marriage to Irene Fogler in March 1987. "When you are growing so quickly, you don't want to limit your opportunities," he declares, referring to the plan to double once again in 1987. His wild and crazy dream—which he insists is realistic—is to have $150 million in billings by 1995, which would mean $25 million in actual revenue. This would be partially achieved by acquiring companies in related areas of marketing research, direct mail, and advertising, in Canada, the United States, and even Europe.

"I want the MDC Group to be the biggest and best in North America," he proclaims, as if stabbing a flag into the soil of the New World. "We *know* there is·a generic need for the MDC concept. And we're shedding a lot of light on a concept that a lot of people knew was viable but never saw successfully executed. We are reinforcing the value of integrated service with all the capabilities we have. And the clients love it." In 1986, Nadal launched a joint venture with Flare, the largest independent sales promotion and marketing firm in North America, and they handle each other's clients, such as Dole and Hiram Walker. And plans include acquiring more companies in service, consulting, and production, so "we can be completely vertically integrated."

Oh, yes. Back in 1980 Miles Nadal had founded his initial company, Action Photographics, with a $500 cash advance from Chargex. It was quickly paid back, without interest. One just had to realize that Conrad Black and John Craig Eaton are merely a letter or a phone call away.

# 9.

# THE COMPUTER INDUSTRY

### RAMs, ROMs, and Raking It In

It comes as no surprise that the ages of the entrepreneurs in this chapter are the youngest by far in this book. Six of the eight are under 40, and three of those are under, or barely, 30. No surprise, because the world of computers is so young. Some numbers, compliments of Statistics Canada: The 500 establishments providing computer services in Canada in 1976 grew to over 1,800 by 1982. The total sales of these companies was under $400 million in 1976, and over $3.1 billion six years later. This is a very young and rapidly expanding field.

To give a cross section of Canadians who have been doing wondrous things in this wondrous industry, I have selected eight business people, dotted from Halifax to Vancouver. In the world of hardware, there is Steven Duffy, who sells, as the name of his quickly growing stores proclaims, Computers for Less. Sheldon Pollack, of Cosalco, junks the damned things and sells them for scrap. And Barclay Isherwood, of Mobile Data International of Vancouver, builds and successfully sells data bases on wheels.

In software, there is Sheldon Fulton, of Homestead Computer Services in Winnipeg, who is working to computerize the farm, and Alan Krofchick (and siblings), of Batteries Included, who went from one of the largest dealers of Commodore in Canada to one of the most profitable developers and marketers of reasonably priced, yet high-quality, word-processing programs, among others, across North America.

In the realm of computer service, there is Lois Warren, of Vancouver, who tracks down information on data bases around the world; Dan Potter, of Novatron, in Halifax, who has set up unique data-base services and is extremely "innovative in making technology into the art of the possible." Finally, and he is the perfect person with which to conclude this book, there is Abe Schwartz, only 30, who founded and built up Polaris, one of the most successful computer consulting businesses in Canada, and sold it for $10 million in 1983.

Other than their youth, what do these entrepreneurs have in common? They are more formally educated than most: While Duffy never went to university, and Schwartz and Krofchick took but a few courses (they were each too successful, too quickly, too young, to waste time at *that*), Isherwood has an M.A. in geophysics, Fulton has an M.B.A., Warren is a librarian, and Potter is a lawyer.

A number of these "computer moneymakers" showed entrepreneurship in their youth: Duffy was delivering 400 papers a day as a teen, while the best of us had a single route with a fraction of the customers. Fulton learned hard work and discipline on the family farm. Krofchick worked in flea markets as a child. And Schwartz, bored in school like most geniuses, was working part time at a McDonald's at 14 and was managing two restaurants while still in high school.

But most of all, these business people found a niche in this promising, yet fearfully rapidly changing, field, and developed it with inspiration and intelligence. Duffy, for instance, realized that U.S. prices of computers are vastly lower than Canadian, so he began to drive down and bring machines up by the hundreds, working 18-hour days and franchising stores like crazy. Pollack dropped out of college to take over his late father's scrap business and soon asked himself a wise question: "What will be the next big thing to scrap?" The one-word answer for him, and for everyone else in this chapter, was *computers*. Isherwood of MDI helped develop and market mobile data bases, "a new concept," and grew frantically along with a market that is increasing "exponentially." And to go from under $2 million in sales in 1981 to over $30 million, within five years, suggests the truth of his words.

Fulton, the son of farmers, has developed a Farm Management System, looks at the 2 million farmers in North America, and sees gold. Krofchick's bright idea was developing software and becoming "machine-independent." Warren, seeing that "everyone needs information," turned her library degree into becoming the biggest information broker in Canada. Dan Potter, "an opportunities seeker," wants to put a million products and bits of information on line, and create an electronic printing press. And Abe Schwartz began consulting "in the early years of computers"—the mid-1970s—and had a growth rate of 100% every year thereafter.

The consistent theme which runs through this chapter, no less than any other, is a desire "to prove something," "to have independence," "to control my own environment," to "like control," to "work hard . . . have an open mind . . . go against the flow." These direct quotations from these entrepreneurs may not directly relate to the computer, but that's all right, too, for it is that same passion to do it on their own which is at the centre of *all* successful businesses. In this chapter, it was *silicon* chips that they sold, melted down, developed, or used; in other chapters, it might have been *fish* and chips. The business principles and drives behind the successes of the entrepreneurs remain basically the same.

# GETTING RICH BY KEEPING IT CHEAP

### Steven Duffy

If there is one thing that drives many Canadians crazy, it is those infernal ads in *The New York Times* and other American papers. The prices for consumer products seem so cheap! Why were videotape recorders going for $250 down in the States, when they were $600 and more for the exact same ones at the neighbourhood department store in Halifax/Montreal/Toronto/Winnipeg/Calgary/Edmonton/Vancouver? Why were colour TVs down to $199 for a 19-inch one in New York, when you couldn't get a 14-inch colour TV anywhere in Canada for under $300?

One man did something about it—a kid, really—and the story of what he has accomplished in merely two years to undercut every other computer store in Canada by upwards of 30 to 50% suggests that there is money to be made in deep discounting in a country which has usually been too polite or unadventurous to try.

Steven Duffy was born in Sackville, New Brunswick, in the spring of 1963, to a mother who was a hairdresser and a father who began working for the vending division of Versa Foods in Toronto shortly after the first of his three sons was born. Like most future entrepreneurs, Duffy had a paper route, but he quickly picked up three or four in his area, sharing them with his brother, delivering up to 400 papers each day.

As early as 14, he was a "male serving person" at a neighbouring McDonald's, when men were usually at the grill and only sweet young things were at the cash registers. "We were very swift on our feet, and it was a stepping-stone for me," he recalls. Even to this day, he claims that he applies a lot of that famed working ethic in his computer stores: quality, service, and cleanliness.

While still in high school, Duffy worked in the shipping department of Dylex, sending clothes all over Canada, which he says "taught me skill in handling products." He finished high school in 1982 and soon got involved in a major charitable concept: When a little girl he knew died at Toronto's Hospital for Sick Children due to the lack of a particular machine, he decided with a friend to develop a four-man relay team to run across Canada and help raise funds.

He quickly lined up over 140 sponsors all over the country and captained the relay team himself, starting in St. John's, Newfoundland, and concluding in Vancouver, with Duffy running about one-quarter of the way. (To this day, he has "no idea how much money we raised," since, although donations shot up that year, many did not indicate whether their money was related to the run across the country.) It was, of course, a tremendous experience, in terms of getting to know corporations. He was 19 at the time, and he knocked on such doors as Eastern Provincial Airlines, CP Hotels, Adidas Shoes, and dozens and dozens of others, making contacts which would some day come in handy.

He and his friend did "tons" of media, due to the successful run, such as radio and TV interviews, an appearance on "Front Page Challenge," and so on. So it wasn't surprising that he received a number of job offers from various firms, some as far away as Calgary. He eventually joined Nesbitt-Thomson for eight months, starting out as a pager, or runner, moving quickly into the cages, and then, when an opening occurred on the Toronto Stock Exchange for a clerk, he became one of the youngest traders in the history of the TSE.

Then came that strange moment which would make Steven Duffy's fortune, and possibly his future, when he was barely out of his teens: A friend and he went running one night, and discussed how dissatisfied each was with the job he had. They decided to go away for a weekend, and ended up in Baltimore, Maryland, where they were stunned by the advertisements in the paper (see this writer's rage in the first paragraph of this profile): "The prices were so much cheaper than in Canada that we bought ten Commodore 64s, originally for our family and friends, and brought them back home." They happily paid the exchange rate—which was then only about 18¢ on the dollar—as well as the duty and taxes demanded at the Canadian border. But they were still considerably ahead of the game: The Commodore keyboards which they paid $250 U.S. for were going for $800 in Toronto.

So the two young men—Martin Pahnke was the other—ended up selling the computers for $550 each, and they still made a clear $200 profit on each. It was July 1983 when they put a classified ad in the three Toronto papers, having obtained a vendor's permit before they did. It took less than one day to clear them all out of the family garage. It didn't take long for them to realize that there was a golden goose, with a silicon chip on its shoulder, sitting right before their eyes.

"We were very surprised that it went so well, and we went down to the States lots of times," says Duffy. The two men soon quit their jobs, and in August and September of 1983 they made an average of three trips a week to Baltimore. In the first three months they sold over $50,000 in machines. By October 1 of that same year they opened their store, Computers for Less, which pretty much tells what they were offering. It cost less than $4,000 to open the place, which they paid for from the capital of their never-ending garage sales.

The modus operandi of Duffy and partner was really quite extraordinary, and the border guards must have been on a first-name basis with them rather quickly: They would drive a Volvo down to the States every few days, with roof rack above and U-Haul trailer behind, returning with 40 to 50 computer keyboards at a time. Soon they were bringing in (and selling, of course), monitors, printers, disk drives, disks.

From the moment their miniature, 250-square-foot store in the west end of Toronto opened, it was a huge success. They phoned the customers they knew from the garage days, placed ads in the papers, and were plugged like mad by all the computer clubs of the city. The two fellows sold six days a week, from 9:00 in the morning to 9:00 at night; Sunday was out, due to an Etobicoke bylaw. Sales were, quite simply, astonishing: From October 1, 1983, to the end of their first fiscal year, July 31, 1984, they sold $1.1 million in computers and accessories. "We made between twenty and thirty percent of that in profit," Duffy says happily.

As you can well understand, The Powers That Be over at Commodore were hardly dancing for joy; Duffy and partner were *retailing* their product at prices that were lower than Commodore dealers could get them for wholesale! "They sent a number of nasty letters," recalls Duffy, "but according to the Combines Investigation Act, no one can tell you to cease business." The RCMP paid frequent visits, wondering how these young whippersnappers could sell so cheap, and Duffy was forced to continually show that he *had* paid his taxes and duty on the computers.

Shortly before Christmas of 1983 there was a shortage of computers across Canada, but not for the boys at Computers for Less; Duffy simply hopped in his car and kept taking trips down to New York City, Chicago, and Cincinnati, to buy more product. Partner Martin left at the end of the first full year at the store; the pressure was simply too much.

But not for Steven Duffy, who was just shy of the $2 million mark in sales at the end of his second year, in the summer of 1985. "And all these in the smallest store of its kind in the city!" exclaims Duffy. "While here is two hundred fifty square feet of retail space, the holding area takes up one hundred fifty square feet of that!" The profit? "Substantial," he admits, not anxious to discuss it.

The next move for the 22-year-old was, of course, to start franchising. The first store outside Toronto was in Timmins, of all places. "It's in the northernmost central part of Ontario," Duffy says, "so it can service North Bay and Sudbury." The store opened in July of 1985, after a client of Computers for Less had come down south to Toronto and "loved the idea." "Do you know what these things cost in the *north*?" the man asked. We can well imagine that it is plenty. Or at least it *was*. Duffy charged merely $5,000 as a franchise fee and only 2% royalty, but by insisting that a minimum of 30% of product would be provided by the president of the firm, there was still money to be made.

While they are all in Ontario, they have something else in

common: Each has a university to support a computer store, or at least, each is "a result of urban sprawl." At the end of 1987 there were six stores in operation, and the youthful, pleasant-looking high school graduate expects $5 million in sales, which is one helluva lot of trips to and from the States. And he's moved into handling IBM clones, imported direct from Taiwan, of course.

Requests for stores have poured in from Montreal, Halifax, and Vancouver, but Duffy is a bit reluctant to travel too far from Toronto. "I'm seriously considering Montreal, though," he admits, "since some of our staff is bilingual." What Computers for Less would be in French is unknown, but it could be dozens of words.

Most tempting is the recent offer by an American interest to purchase Duffy's minichain for "close to a million and a half in U.S. dollars," which is a lot more in Canadian. The people know Duffy since they've dealt with him, and they are looking for new, international markets. "But I'm not anxious to give it up," claims Duffy. "I'm happy with what I do, and I'd feel badly if I didn't keep running the firm." Over 40 employees depend on him.

Unlike many entrepreneurs, Steven Duffy knows his own limits: "One of my traits is, I'm a perfectionist. I like to see things done well, clearly, and tightly. If they are lacking in any of those, it would be time to reorganize. Right now, it's moving quickly, but well. But I wouldn't be able to run thirty stores."

It's a problem which millions of Canadians would love to have, along with the agony of whether to sell out to the Yanks. A further problem was whether to study commerce at Cambridge, in England. "I finally decided that I wouldn't. My girlfriend pointed out to me that the skills I've learned in the last two years I *never* could have acquired with a university degree." Only in the real world, of course.

The real world holds lots of other potential new projects as well, for the boy from west Toronto. For one, his mother's business. She owns her own hairdressing salon, and Duffy recently persuaded her to buy a suntanning bed. "She doesn't have a strong sense of promoting her product and services," states Duffy, and he wants to be of assistance. He's considering opening more hairdressing salons *cum* suntanning stores with her—"plus waxing and makeup, all under one roof."

And, he notes eagerly, "I enjoy working with my mom and dad."

There's a pull from another quarter as well, from his girlfriend Gale. "She wants to open a Bargain Harold-type store," says Duffy, "and I want to help her out."

Then there's the offer to have him purchase a data-processing company with sales of $3 million annually, which Duffy could obtain for a mere $750,000. "It sounds ideal, and I just may do it," he says. "I'm looking for things to keep me occupied." Eighteen-hour days aren't enough? Or his recent foray into client training on computers in two of the stores?

There you have it: a Canadian who was willing to deal directly with American distributors, eliminate the middle-man, and pass on *part* of the huge savings to the customer. It should make everyone happy, except perhaps the Canadian wholesalers. And one other unhappy soul: the writer of this book, who hit the roof when he heard how much cheaper he could have obtained his Commodore monitor, disk drive, and accessories. *Damn!*

# BUYING JUNK AND
# SELLING ANTIQUES

### Sheldon Pollack

If the Harvard Business School isn't interested in the very brief, three-year history of Cosalco (Computer Salvage Company) of Markham, Ontario—and they should be, as you'll soon read—then maybe Sigmund Freud would have been. Let us explain: The firm is run by two young men in their mid-20s who both lost their fathers. "I think we're trying to prove something," says president Sheldon Pollack. When you go from around $80,000 in your first year of business to $1 million in the second to over $2 million in the third, and $6½ million in the fifth, you can be sure that dad would have been very proud of you.

Sheldon Pollack was born in 1961, as was his later partner-in-success, Phillip De Leon. The latter went to the University of Toronto to study commerce, and the former to Western, to study real estate development. But in the early 1980s Pollack's father died, leaving a scrap business just north of

Toronto, Stouffville Iron and Metals. The son dropped out of school and took over the business in 1982. "I hung on until prices came back, and then I sold out. I wasn't interested in the business; it wasn't my cup of tea."

What did heat up in Pollack's fertile mind was the question of WHAT NEXT?—the kind of question which most entrepreneurs have to eventually ask themselves, and why *Megatrends* sold so well. "We were scrapping hydro transformers," recalls Pollack, good-looking with his curly hair and huge grin, "and I saw people scrap planes! So I sat down and thought, 'What's the *next* big thing going to be?' " It was an inspired question, and it was "carefully thought out. I was determined to find a good concept for a successful business." Hey! How about old computers?

In April 1983 Pollack incorporated Cosalco with his friend from childhood, De Leon. "We have the same goals and objectives. We're both young, and we want to make something." And then there's that matter about their fathers. The business was begun with a rather small investment, $10,000 in all. "My dad's money from the sold scrap business all went to my mother," Pollack points out quickly. "My portion of the money came from what I earned while working there. It was my *own* money!"

The two kids opened a warehouse, and with setting up the office, gas, security deposit on the phone, and the rent, they found themselves with only $4,000 left before they began. No wonder people are afraid to go into business for themselves. That first year, as noted, "wasn't so terrific," with only about $2,000 profit for the partners and the three other employees, and they took their minuscule salaries and kept loaning them back to the little company. (Both still lived at home, so for each of them to take $20,000 out, and put back $15,000, was easier than for most of us. But in 1987 Pollack got worried.)

They began by buying old computers and selling them for the silver, copper, platinum, and, yes, gold within them. Many of the large computers of the early years were made with oodles of chemicals which can be extracted and resold. Huge companies, universities, and banks are continually replacing their systems, upgrading, improving. Pollack and De Leon would buy the mainframes, strip them for any worthwhile sections, such as printers and disk drives, and then ship off the circuit boards to Asia, where they would be melted down to get the goodies. God bless planned obsolescence!

"I thought there would be *more* gold in them than there was," says Pollack. "It's *volume* that makes the profit!" They were soon moving up to 5 million pounds of old computer equipment per year. But the big new direction was in reselling old computers. For instance, they resold some Honeywell systems, buying from one place and selling to another. "We were like used-car salesmen," he jokes. "The biggest sale we made was for $250,000 worth of computers. We cleared about $40,000 on that one deal alone." (Back in October of 1985 they did another deal buying and selling some Honeywell computers, this time making about $65,000 on a similar sale. They are clearly learning.)

What's almost funny about the strange new/old business is that these young men are "not computer freaks at all! That's why we make money on it: We don't get into what they can do, but only how much money we can get for them." It's like cars, to use Pollack's simile: You don't have to know how to build a car to sell a car, do you?

On both scrapping and reselling the computers, they average between 15 and 20% profit. But there are inherent problems, at least in the junking part of the business: "There's not a question in my mind that it will be dead in five years," says Pollack, adding that "that's very much my style, anyway; I'd get bored!" Scrapping is an easy and cheap way to *learn* about computers, though, and "a good stepping-stone into the industry." But what he wittily calls "The Information Age Equivalent of the Automobile Scrapyard Business" has that "built-in life-span."

Furthermore, the scrapping of computers has taken a lot of crafty business sense. "*You* try to convince someone that their million-dollar system is now worth only a few cents a pound!" Pollack says. "They're not prepared for how little we can offer them! So we say, 'Here's our price. It's scrap. *You* try to sell it!' We really *are* the last resort—just like that used-car dealer!"

So reselling has become the major focus of Cosalco. They manage to finance all their purchases internally, and although they have a line of credit with a bank, they've yet to draw upon it. "We have the ability to cover our asses if any difficult situation comes up," he says. Working 9:00 A.M. to 7:30 P.M., six days a week, also helps.

There are warehouses in Albany, New York, and Newark, New Jersey, in addition to the one northeast of Toronto, since they do most of their purchasing in the States. Over 70% of their buying and selling was done in the United States over the last two years. The Taiwan connection, regarding scrapping, has always been necessary, thanks to our rather expensive country. "I can get union labour in Canada to scrap the circuit boards for twelve dollars an hour, or get the same in Taiwan for seventy cents," Pollack says. "And they do a better job there, melting it down." Similarly, it costs $2.50 a pound to process gold from them thar boards in Canada; in Taiwan, less than a third of that. Still, it will be sad to see the boys drop the scrapping, when they do. There is something romantic about seeing two 24-year-old Canadians shipping over 15 tons of used computers at a time from Newark to Taiwan, at the cost of $2,000 a load. By 1986, they created a sister corporation, Onyx Computers, Inc., with De Leon its president, buying and marketing outdated computers by DEC.

Pollack and De Leon have hired over a dozen employees, and "it's going very well. Based on our previous history, we're looking at well over six million dollars in sales in 1987." Why? "We've got more knowledge of the industry, and we're picking up better clientele." Cosalco is now getting more involved in "leasing and maintaining" computers, as well as the old JUNK/BUY/SELL business. "We can put together package deals and create a leasing programme with one monthly sum for everything, including their maintenance."

Pollack sees himself and his partner as "entrepreneurs, in the true sense of that word. We're prepared to take *any* risk. I'm a little more of a shooter than Phillip, which is good; he holds me back a bit. I'm very much a dreamer." And it's "not necessarily for the money, which is only the measuring stick." They have this "*real* underlying desire to succeed, but I'm not sure *who* we're doing it for." Maybe for dad, Sheldon. Maybe for dad.

# CLUTCHING SUCCESS
# BY THE HAND

### *Barclay Isherwood*

Barclay Isherwood almost looks like his name: glasses, moustache, toothy grin, scrawny-kid-next-door looks. But what he has managed to do with a struggling firm called Mobile Data International Inc. of Vancouver in the past few years is nothing less than astronomical (which is logical; he'd once hoped to go into that eyes-up field). Sales of the mobile digital communications products were $1.9 million in 1981, $3.7 million in 1982, $7.8 million in 1983, $25.5 million in 1984. For various reasons, their 1986 sales were a "not too spectacular" $32 million plus. But with expectations of sales of $100 million by 1990 ("We'll make it," he says confidently), one realizes that Isherwood and MDI are not your average entrepreneurs and businesses, respectively. And respectfully, too.

Isherwood was born in Victoria, B.C., in the fall of 1945, the secondborn and first son in a family of three. His businessman father died when he was only seven, at which point his mother moved to Vancouver. He was not a good student but "always had a job since the age of ten—anything that turned a buck." As early as 15, he managed to land and hold a full-time summer job in a factory. "I've always had a need to feel comfortable and *have independence*," he says, his voice italicizing those last two words. "Entrepreneurs do it because they can't stand other people's bullshit." Now you know.

He was too young to be influenced by his father's career, and his mother became an alcoholic, eventually returning to Vancouver Island. "It was the classic oppressed-female situation," he says sadly, making it clear that there was "no parental supervision" for him, so he was "a lazy bastard through school."

He finally knuckled down in university, however, getting his under-graduate degree in physics at U.B.C., and a master's of science in geophysics, with some work in astronomy. "You'll have trouble finding a thread here!" He laughs aloud, referring to the eternal journalistic problem of finding where the Kid Went Right and Found His Place in the Business World. "I had *no* idea in university what I'd be doing today." He was married with two children by this time, so he left university somewhat disillusioned, since there appeared to be no work for physicists.

Fortunately, as luck and this book would have it, a friend in a company that supplied computers to labs at universities invited him to be a salesman. After "much agonizing," he went into sales for them in Vancouver, and, "to my amazement, everyone bought from me! I suppose I was different!" he acknowledges. His success came as a "revelation": *He could sell!* Like many academics, he thought that it would be "beneath" him to do such a thing, but he "discovered that selling was a fine, *fine* profession!"

Through the early and mid-1970s, Isherwood was selling minicomputers—not PCs, since these were $50,000 to $300,000 jobs—and larger businesses were buying them regularly. "I did well, compared to what I *was* making." Then a man named John MacDonald, the founder of MDA, who had taught Isherwood in university and whom he had called on to sell his computers, invited the former student to be a salesman for *his* firm. "I went there and sold around the world!" he says, as if still surprised by his good fortune. These were systems ranging from $1 to $7 million in cost—you can just imagine the commissions—which worked with satellite grid stations, weather systems, and so on. This went on from 1975 to 1981, and Isherwood "made a good living." He moved from sales to VP, marketing and sales, to VP, operations.

Then, in 1981, Isherwood and his boss and mentor "disagreed," and the former quit "with five minutes' notice." He was by then divorced, and now unemployed. But his name and selling prowess had become known across the province, and soon after, he was approached by Mobile Data International Inc. to take over as the president of the company. The firm was designing, manufacturing, selling, and servicing mobile data systems for use by taxis, courier operations, police and fire departments, boats, etc., using engineering that was done at MDA under federal contracts and R & D.

It was the perfect coming together of a mind and a business. "I use my background an *awful* lot," Isherwood claims. "Physics and math exposed me to ways of thinking which are conducive to business problems." He goes on to philosophize about this: "The people we would *think* have business minds—lawyers, C.A.'s—are *flat programmed*. But you have to be intuitive and creative in business; you can't apply a lot of history and rules to it."

That first year, as noted, sales were under $2 million, selling mobile data equipment for vehicular application. For instance, the Ottawa Police Department has MDI's equipment in their cars. The firm has been doing nothing less than taking computer data bases and putting them into moving vehicles. With a few pokes of his or her fingers, the officer can connect into federal, province, and state data bases for any kind of information required. (Is that car stolen? Isn't this fellow wanted for assault in Manitoba? If this guy is really the mayor, like he insists, maybe I should let him go?)

To this date, MDI has installed over 200 major systems around the world, averaging $500,000 each. "It's electronic mail on wheels," says the president of the firm. "You can walk down the street and talk to your data base."

But why such growth? You've already read of the $1.9 million to $32 million in under six years, with hopes to triple that again within another three. (And MDI went public in 1986 as well.) There were only 35 employees when Isherwood crawled on board, one or two salespeople, a number of technicians, a few ad men. As of the end of 1985 there were over 250 at Mobile Data.

"It's a combination of reasons," says Isherwood. "It was a new concept—wireless data terminals—and pre-1981, the world was simply not ready for it. And we're a bunch of opportunistic people here; we won't let anyone else get a piece of the market!" (Joking aside, he seems to be correct; they are the number 1 firm in mobile data equipment. "It's still early to be ripped off," he says: "it's a new market." Still, as of 1987, MDI owned 70% of the market. Furthermore, "we're doing a number of things to hold off the competition, as the market grows exponentially." Motorola in the States, for example, doesn't understand the uses and applications yet, according to Isherwood, and they're "*not* doing well in the same field. *We're* the specialists, and *the best!*" The Japanese are doing some development in it, you can be sure, but Isherwood isn't shaking in his ROMs and RAMs about it.)

It appears that MDI is a good-feelings place, too. (That happens a lot out in Vancouver.) "It's hardly a dictatorial atmosphere around here," agrees Isherwood. "People feel that working at MDI and working for me is a good thing to do—not something they *have* to do! And that can make for commitment and accomplishment!"

And why not? Every single employee at MDI is a shareholder in the company. "*Everybody*!" And since they all have a piece of the very lively action, they are all enjoying the phenomenal growth of MDI. The company is valued at $60 million now, according to Isherwood, and share values have tripled since early 1984. Employees own one-third of the firm now that they are public. "This makes them feel like they are not being exploited." MDI was listed on the TSE in late 1986, at $11 a share.

It's very much a team-oriented place, "and that's my style," states Barclay Isherwood. "There were a *few* prima donnas, and we soon got rid of them! There is a group effort and a group awareness." And there is no competition in Canada. Gandalf of Ottawa, for instance, makes mobile terminals for taxis only, and even that is "on the side" for them; mainline business is different. A full 90% of MDI's sales are into the country to the south, only partially due to the wealth and numbers. "We're respected here in Canada, but it's the standard Canadian 'If it's a Canadian supplier, it *can't* be very good!' " But MDI has made its presence extremely well known since early 1984. And with "Hill Street Blues" and "T.J. Hooker" both equipping their cop cars with MDI terminals, criminals don't stand any better chance than the legitmate competition. Offices were opened in 1987 in Los Angeles; New York City; London, England; and one in Scandinavia.

"We are *making* the industry," says Isherwood, who eagerly spends nearly 20% of his sales on R & D, always updating and innovating the technology. "It's *all ours*," he emphasizes, referring to that money, since the company did receive around $2 million in government grants in the early days, back in the late 1970s. "We've paid back the government many times over!" declares Isherwood. Their corporate income tax was nearly $6 million in 1984, so he's probably right.

Barclay Isherwood has "no personal goals to be a millionaire; merely to continue to run a company that gives good value to its customers." There's a "spectacular" new building in Richmond that was "built for employees, which has the same carpets" on the manufacturing floor as in the president's office. It cost $6 million, and Isherwood speaks of it with face glowing.

"I sure *am* an entrepreneur," says the former physicist and computer salesman. "My key to success is our understanding to motivate *all* our people. You see, I'm not pulling a bunch of employees behind me; they are *pushing me*."

# OLD MACDONALD HAD A COMPUTER (RAM ROM RAM ROM RAM)

### *Sheldon Fulton*

When you think of it, it seems only logical that computing would come to the Canadian farm, but it's nice to know that the man who is doing the most to make that a reality is the third son of farmers from Birtle, a town of less than a thousand souls, 200 miles west of Winnipeg. It hasn't been all roses, or even all growth and riches, but the story of Sheldon Fulton and Homestead Computer Services Ltd. of Winnipeg is one of tenacity and determination.

Born in Winnipeg in the fall of 1948, Sheldon Fulton did the kind of farm chores which would serve him in good stead two and three decades later. "From the age of nine, I worked around the farm. We had three thousand acres and cattle, and you learn a work discipline from that." What he also must have learned was a tremendous sense of refusing to accept defeat. For instance, the aptitude class in grade 11 in Brandon, when he was told by his principal that he "should avoid business." ("I didn't know the terminology, having been raised on a farm!" he explains.) So when he later wrote the entrance exams for law and business, and was in the 97th percentile for the latter, he decided to study it, "because of what the principal said!" This response had been echoed in his undergraduate years at the University of Manitoba, when he went into science and failed only one course—math. "So I majored in math, to prove that I could do well in a weak subject." He ultimately got his B.Sc. in the honours math programme.

Before his two years completing the M.B.A. program at U. of M., stressing the application of science to business, he spent a year working on elevators, loading and handling grain, since "I didn't get the bug to do my own things until a few years after graduation." He earned a whopping $285 a month.

While working on his M.B.A., Fulton got involved with a line elevator company, National Grain, working in economic research and doing financial analysis—where to build the new elevator, etc. "It was great—a whole new learning experience!" He also worked in futures contracts, as a commodities analyst, using the computers which would one day be the centre of his life. "We built simulated models for the grain industry." But by 1975 he moved on: "I wanted to control my own environment; I wanted to do my own thing, but I wasn't ready yet."

So he went off to Ottawa, working as a consultant with Rod Bryden, the man who is currently the chairman of the board of Systemhouse. After two years he returned to Winnipeg and founded Westburn Development Consultants Ltd. in 1977. Fulton would consult on large studies—he developed a model of the flow of grain in Canada, as well as studies of grain shipment through the St. Lawrence Seaway. It began with himself and a secretary; there were five employees by the end of the first year, and eight at the end of the second. (The company still exists.)

Then, the reason for this profile: In 1979 Sheldon Fulton began the rather poetically named Homestead—and the reasons for this are charmingly basic: He was bowled over by a speech of Adam Osborne, the once high-flying creator of the computer of the same name. "When he spoke, he said that the big future of computers was in the application area. He said that the machines were like having gold nuggets on the ground, and people keep walking past, not seeing them! He pointed out that the money would be in the harnessing of computers!"

Sheldon Fulton realized that what he knew best was grain, agriculture, elevators. "I realized that agriculture, as an industry, had *not* used computers! And it seemed as though you never could put computers on farms or in elevators; they were hostile environments." That year, 1978, was a formative one in the history of the microcomputer, of course. So the youthful, handsome young man from the farm, married to his first wife and the father of one child, noted that a computer lets one sell the same basic idea over and over. "And the selling of intelligence had a great deal of appeal to me." He had enough work in the consulting area to keep himself gainfully employed, so he began Homestead Computer Services Ltd., with an initial seed capital of "about $30,000."

The first thing he did was buy a microcomputer—it cost $8,000 of his own money back then. "Today you can buy a PC for two thousand dollars that has ten times the capacity of RAMs and disk storage!" he says ruefully. In those years he even had to "populate the printed circuit board," meaning that he had to stick those little chips into the thing to make it work. How times have changed. "It was the formulative days of operating systems, and we had to do *everything*! It was really laborious!"

But as any mother will tell you, you don't achieve creativity without pain. "I had to get my feet wet to see what it would do." He initially did a "binning program" to show where to put grain into an elevator. The purpose: "To tell where to best bin the wheat coming off the trucks, based on the moisture and protein level." You might know your breakfast cereal, but it takes a man with the background of Sheldon Fulton to be aware of how tough and damp grain can be above a certain moisture. And you can upgrade the level in an elevator by this awareness. "As far as I know, no one has integrated moisture and protein testing with grain for optimum binning," he says excitedly.

But there were problems: Fulton quickly ran into "vested interests." No one understood the technology at the time, and people thought that micros were "toys." They got nowhere in their marketing. So he moved on to another program: On Farm Micro Computer, to be used with accounting, cattle record keeping, and so on, developed by Fulton with the aid of third- and fourth-year U. of Manitoba students, on March 1, 1980. He quickly installed one on a farm for $14,000.

Fortunately, Fulton was doing $250,000 a year with Westburn, so when he had only $40,000 in sales in the first seven months of 1979, he didn't go under. (By 1980 Homestead hit over $300,000.) As he puts it, "I earned my pay to be able to run Homestead." One way he did it was by automating the Winnipeg Commodity Exchange, known as the old Grain Exchange, and charged $150,000 for it, hiring a dozen others to help him. That job was a "watershed" for Fulton, since it gave his company a public profile. In fact, until 1984 he had to keep running consulting projects to keep himself, his family, and Homestead alive.

Next, in 1982, Fulton did the Life Exchange in London, England, an international financial futures and commodities exchange, having bid $800,000 on it and won, from all the way out in Winnipeg. (Almost comically, England did not want to sign for the project with a name like Homestead—"too colonial"—so he had to use the name of Westburn for that job.) The growth spiralled: In 1981 Homestead sales were still under $400,000; by 1982, $900,000; by 1983, $1.2 million; by 1984, $2 million; by the end of February 1987, $2½ million. The projection for February 1988: $3 million.

The major product for Homestead has been the Farm Management System. He has sold over 450 of them, at prices up to $8,000. They also move in the States, where he has been selling only the software, for around $1,000. But when Sheldon Fulton talks about the Yanks, his eyes gleam with an excitement even greater than that of Brian Mulroney: "There are two million farmers in North America! It's been estimated that up to six hundred thousand of them will be on computers by the end of this decade! It's the biggest homogeneous market anywhere—more than dentists or doctors! And to this date, only around fifty thousand have computers!"

It's a dream come true, like Ronald McDonald eyeing 1 billion hamburger-hungry Chinese. But there is a Catch-22 as well: "The farmer who most needs computerization can't afford it!" There's been a dreadful financial crunch over the past few years, and a big shakeout in the number of farmers. Still, Fulton has spent, over the last three years, over $600,000 in marketing activities in the States, opening an office in Des Moines.

There are related markets as well: He has developed a Farm Financial Plan, selling for $2,500, for banks to judge the health of farms. He's sold $175,000 worth of that software. His RoyFarm Financial Assistant came out in November 1986, jointly marketed with the Royal Bank, and his Credit Analysis Package (CAP) was selected as the standard for the U.S. to judge credit for farmers. "The agricultural sector is incredible!" he booms. "But we have trouble marketing, since the farmer is in such trouble."

But not in such trouble that their saviour would turn his back on them. Fulton now has 16 different programs in the farm management area, such as keeping track of beef cattle over six years of progeny, observing 26 attributes (such as which bull to breed with to make the herd more productive. We just *knew* that computers had some sex appeal to them). "We want to harvest computers to improve productivity or enhance efficiency," claims Fulton. "Our programs are directed to do that." They vary in price, but most cost about $1,000, and the average farm sale is for $3,500 worth of product.

In just a few short years, Sheldon Fulton finds himself the number 1 company of his kind in Canada, in farm management systems, and in the top three in North America. There are five children by his second wife, although he pays himself only $50,000 a year, and there are two dozen on staff to feed as well. "I had hoped to be up to ten million dollars in sales by now, and I'm not there," he says. But with 30% ownership of Homestead (and 100% of Westburn), he is clearly a potentially wealthy man.

"You could say that I'm a dreamer," says Fulton, "but I'm not sure that one can dream in equations! The exciting part of all this is in putting the pieces together."

Like many businessmen and women, Sheldon Fulton had a goal to be a millionaire by the age of 30, missed it, reset it for 35—and now he's rapidly approaching 40. "But I don't have an end goal that I can achieve and then say I'm successful. I get awards every day. I want to make life easier by *being* successful." He also insists on a strict business philosophy: integrity. "Growing up in a farming family, I learned that you have to deal with people with honesty and fairness. I've got a driving instinct, but I won't try to perpetuate a con. I refuse to take advantage of anyone. There's only one guy you have to answer to—the guy you see in the mirror when you shave."

And Sheldon Fulton can say something about his thriving and potentially gigantic business that many others cannot about theirs. For instance, candy makers may have family that avoids sweets, or car salesmen may sell a product too expensive for their loved ones. But not Fulton: He put his parents' farm on computer back in 1982, and one of his two older brothers gleefully uses a Homestead programme for cattle records. And if that isn't success, then what is?

# SOMEONE HAD TO INCLUDE THE BATTERIES

### *Alan Krofchick*

Most entrepreneurs create something that wasn't there before, or at least something that was, or appeared to be, of higher quality: A better-tasting thingamajig, a cheaper doodad, a faster whizbang. The Krofchick siblings of Toronto at least *began* their highly successful business by *getting rid* of something—an irritation, to be exact. Which of us has not had a child in tears because there weren't any batteries included with the gift? The Krofchick brothers—Alan, 33, Robbie, 34 (and now sister Marcie, 28)—became one of the largest electronics dealers in Canada by doing an outrageously simple thing—they include batteries with each of their games. And although Batteries Included has since moved out of flogging computers, calculators, and watches, making the name quite irrelevant and even meaningless, the profits they make certainly are anything but irrelevant.

President Alan Krofchick and vice-president Robbie Krofchick were born in Toronto in the early 1950s, to a father who worked at the Ontario Food Terminal. As teenagers, they used to work at various flea markets—"we always did stuff together," says Alan—selling everything from used clothes to dill pickles. But they always worked for others. After Robbie earned his B.A. in history at Waterloo-Lutheran University, and Alan went to Erindale College, a branch of the University of Toronto, studying general science—he is still a few credits short—they tried a booth at the Canadian National Exhibition down at the waterfront. It was 1976, and they sold digital watches and electronic games. They made money each summer, and the profit motive was not lost on them.

So in 1978 they opened Batteries Included in the attractive condo/apartment/commercial/office complex, Village by the Grange, just around the corner from the Art Gallery of Ontario. They were there for about four years and "always made money." The initial concept was electronic games and calculators, but home computers were just starting to come in, and they latched onto Commodore from the very start.

When games began to crash, the calculators became the main-stay, and by 1980 it was computers that became their thrust and core. They were soon "one of the largest independent Commodore dealers in the country," selling up to $3 million of their computers and components in 1982–83.

"The company has never seen any decrease in sales," says Alan Krofchick, scoring 100% increases every year. He looked after people carefully, always able to provide information and the proper peripherals, and moved strongly into the educational market.

Early on, they moved into the volatile area of creating their own software, advertising primarily in *Compute Magazine*. Their first product, Swarmboard, was not successful. Then came the Arbiter System, developed for schools, which would allow them to hook multiple units to a disk drive. It helped teachers to instruct students on BASIC, and it was very successful across Ontario. They sold close to 5,000 pieces in that province alone, at $150 each. "One of the fellows on our staff developed it," Krofchick says.

But the monster hit was from "one of the first part-time students" they hired, an 18-year-old genius named Steve Douglas. At that time a high school student, the kid created PaperClip, a word-processing system for Commodore computers. It hit the best-selling list of *Billboard* magazine's computer software chart in January 1984, and occupied the number 1 position for many weeks in 1985, selling for around $100 in the United States and $150 in Canada. Over 100,000 of the straightforward, intelligible word-processor systems have been sold so far, with no end in sight, as Atari and Apple versions came out in the spring of 1985.

The next software created by the Krofchicks' hit factory was Consultant, a data-base package, selling for $79.95 in the States and $125 in Canada. Well over 75,000 pieces had been sold by the end of 1985, and it was way up on the charts for months. As of the last month in 1984 Batteries Included put out Home Pack, a "home productivity package," including a word-processing, data-base, and communications package for only $49.94, promptly voted "the best value of 1984" by *Infoworld*, the industry rag. Versions for Commodore, Atari, Apple, and IBM made it a good seller as well.

As one can see, Batteries Included has quickly become one of the major software producers in North America. Their product line is now about 30 pieces, with the number of different titles at over a dozen. In 1984 their sales were $10 million, and by the end of 1985 they had increased that by another 35%.

The Krofchicks have the instincts of true survivors in an industry which is riddled with those who could not keep pace with changes that came as fast as the speed of light. "Our main drive in 1984," says the president, "was to be machine-independent, and not just Commodore distributors." So they closed their retail operations in the spring of 1985 and "re-evaluated our situation."

Today, Batteries Included is a major manufacturer, with duplicating equipment and 8,000 square feet of assembly space in Richmond Hill, just north of Toronto, and nearly 60 employees. Since 1983 they have had a California office as well, handling distribution and sales. And all this phenomenal growth has been financed entirely inside, with no financing from The Banks. In their market, furthermore, they are competing against only one American company.

What's so impressive is that none of the Krofchicks have any background in computers. "Our concept from the start was to be able to market a final product—that's our specialty," says Alan Krofchick. "We're not aggressive, we're laid back," he insists. And who needs to be aggressive when "if we feel we have the right product, we feel we can sell it."

Still, there are a *lot* of good software manufacturers out there, and the bankruptcy courts are filled with them. To which we can give the real secret of the Krofchick success: "We've always gone after *value*," he declares. How right he is; the products which PaperClip, for example, was competing against were selling in the range of $300 while BI was retailing it in Canada for less than one-half that. And their major educational programme, Arbiter, was running at $3,000 for the equivalent; they got in at $1,250 and outsold them all. It's the hi-tech equivalent of building a cheaper mousetrap, and everyone lines up.

Alan Krofchick is reluctant to pin all their success on their ability to undercut others. "Price alone doesn't necessarily do the job," he argues. "We have a full organization, with eighteen salespeople covering all areas, getting paid commission. We do all our own marketing and creative work in Canada." They also have a full-time product development man, along with others contracted from the outside. And thanks to their good distribution, they can "put out a product and, at the worst, break even." They've also been licensing deals in Europe, with little financial success so far, but they're hoping.

The Krofchicks really *are* laid back, working "normal hours" of 9:00 to 5:00 today (although as recently as 1984 it was 7-day weeks). They have products planned into 1987, with no five-year plan, since things change so fast in the crazy field. But they've come a long way since 1981, when they were selling primarily by mail order, and since 1982, when they sold their pre-PaperClip programs in Baggies.

Alan and the sibs have been told by American companies that "it's an advantage to *not* be in California," away from the patting each other on the back and always worrying what the others are doing. But it's more than that, of course: standing behind their products, spending up to $1 million a year on ads, and always ready to change direction. "Our future is moving into Apple and IBM markets," says the man who had no trouble leap-frogging from games to calculators to computers to software manufacturing. "We want to be hardware-independent from now on." Sorry, Commodore, but the boys have grown too big to depend on you alone.

And our apologies to Harvard and Western Ontario business schools as well, since we have to report that the Krofchicks have "*no* business philosophy. We're in here, and we work every day," Alan Krofchick says modestly. "The key has always been a *good concept*." The president lights another cigarette and starts to ponder his words, knowing how far he and his brother have gone since they went from including batteries to including silicon chips. "Oh, we might do a *lot* of new things—eighty-column cards, and printer interfaces, and hardware accessories. . . ."

# THE LIBRARIAN
# GOES ON LINE

## *Lois Warren*

The business card of Lois Warren of Vancouver looks fairly standard at first glance: L.M. WARREN INC., Lois M. Warren, B.A., M.Sc. But the subtitle tells all: PRO-GRAMMED LIBRARY & INFORMATION SERVICES.

For Ms. Warren, a divorced mother of three, is a thrilling example of how a seemingly old-fashioned profession—that of the librarian who digs up information for you—can turn into a very profitable, very modern, new field.

Born in New York City, Lois Warren came to Canada when she was 13 and has lived here for most of her life. She has a library science background and took systems analysis in conjunction with her major in graduate school in Boston in the early 1970s. Between 1972 and 1974, as consultant to a Massachusetts data base producer, she introduced an automated Library of Congress retrieval system to libraries in the United States and Canada. After several years in two community colleges, teaching library technician courses and developing continuing education courses for librarians, Warren became the western Canadian manager of INFOMART, a data base vendor, in 1978–79.

Then, in 1979, the big leap: She incorporated her own company, bought three computer terminals, and began to hook into more data bases in more countries than almost anyone else in North America. She can now dial, through telephone systems, to communicate with 27 host computers—containing over 945 data bases—around this rapidly shrinking globe. Most people who do information retrieval, it should be noted, usually choose to subscribe to no more than three or four retrieval systems, because of the complex access procedures.

Lois Warren does no programming herself; she doesn't have to. She retrieves information which is already there, sitting patiently inside all those computers, gathering silicon dust, waiting to be drawn out by people like Warren in order to help *others* not waste their time by reinventing the wheel.

What makes Lois Warren so valuable—invaluable, in fact—is that she has access to the European Space Agency computer in Rome, Italy (with all that NASA information in it), and those excellent shipping and marine data bases in Holland and Norway and that special biotechnology data base in England and. . . . (Even though many of those data bases are in Europe, the material is in English and contains sources from everywhere—even Canada.)

All these sources are *not* the kind of thing which teenage hackers, working out of Brandon, Manitoba, can search and extract. Each computer requires special training, and all the data bases have their own special protocol required to retrieve the information. As Lois Warren puts it, "It's my business, so I've taken the time to know them. I have to study a lot."

The $75 an hour which Lois Warren used to charge has changed over the last few years. Today, instead of performing numerous one-time searches for diverse clients, she now has major clients who pay a deposit of $5,000 and draw upon that for her time and computer charges. She also does in-depth research to assist those clients with corporate planning and competitive analysis and marketing.

And what Warren often provides her clients is extraordinarily valuable. To the person who discovers that his invention has already been patented in Europe, or the scientist who can draw upon hundreds of hours of another scientist's work and build upon that, any price is a small price to pay. Warren not only charges for her time but she is (understandably) reimbursed for her costs in drawing upon the data bases in her search. She does *not* mark up those charges, however, as would your interior decorator when he/she buys your wallpaper for you.

Business has been so good—"It's a good living" is all she will say about her earnings—that Warren has had up to seven people working for her, and has even let staff take home a portable computer terminal to continue their work away from her office in Vancouver. (Alvin Toffler's predicted society of the electronic cottage has begun to come into existence.)

Some of the things Warren has done are terrifically exciting. For instance, the B.C. government has created the Innovation Office, to try and encourage R & D in the province by helping inventors market their products. Warren does patent searches on the inventions for the creators. The World Transport Institute, headquartered in Vancouver, has a contract with L.M. Warren Inc. to manage and operate its Transport Data Project. The Institute's members are dispersed from Argentina to Hong Kong, and phone requests have come to Warren's office from as far away as Milan, Italy. Lois conducted a six-month pilot project for the National Research Council of Canada using online data bases to facilitate information transfer to industry. On a standing order from the Federal Business Development Bank, L.M. Warren Inc. responds to questions submitted by regional offices nationwide.

An example of practical applications of search results related to a gold mine property on Vancouver Island. In the early 1980s the man had a problem treating gold with cyanide, which leaches the precious metal out. She tracked down information and research in Russia, in geology and technological data bases, at a grand cost of $134. She helped the man realize that too much mercury was interfering with the cyanide leaching treatment of the gold ore.

Having her computerized finger in so many data-base pies means that Lois Warren is in demand outside the office as well as in. She was invited to speak at the International ONLINE Conference in New York, and has given training courses to help all the corporate planners of BC Telephone to do their own research.

What Warren—petite, pretty, strong-willed, and bright—has done has been to created a thriving business from a brave new field. And it is one as exciting as it is lucrative. A data base with such important information on urban planning in France is affiliated with one in Quebec, for instance, so all she has to do is dial a local number in Vancouver, which is then bounced through a minicomputer in Quebec and out to the Valbonne computer in France. And the same French computer has crucial data bases listing chemicals for research and industry, and providing the immediate opportunity to place a purchase order on line.

"If a client asks me a question, I immediately know a computer in Europe or the States which has the answer," she says. "I decide which data base would be best, and go on from there." She gets calls from various places across the United States and Canada to use electronic mail to get documents for corporations, and has done research for clients from Victoria to New York to Chicago, Texas, and Whitehorse. And when data bases cover everything "from advertising to zoology," Lois Warren and her computer terminals are nothing less than an encyclopedia-by-phone.

And a great new business. "I *knew* it would be a success," she declares. "*Everyone* needs information." Most users of online data are searching for information for their own internal organizations. Others, such as libraries and information brokers, conduct online searches on behalf of others. Warren is possibly the largest information broker in Canada, in terms of access to data, offering her clients some specialized and overseas sources. Consequently, she is often hired by libraries and even by competitors, who use Warren to supplement their own online resources.

Indeed, she could be a lot larger as a business if she were to specialize in a single industry—say, food or chemistry alone. "But I like the control," she declares. "I'm a do-it-yourselfer." And since the machines run 24 hours a day, she can work out of regular hours. She has always worked seven days a week, often at her office until nearly midnight. And, as Barbara Frum, Lois Warren, and few others are aware, when she is hooked up to England and France in the afternoon in Vancouver, it's already the next day there.

"I *am* an entrepreneur," declares Lois Warren, with enthusiasm. Many individuals have attempted to set up information brokerage services based on online retrieval. Few have remained in business as long as Warren because those who have technical retrieval skills may lack the background in information sources, and those who have the knowledge of information sources may lack the ability to market.

There is no reason why Warren should expect any slowdown. As she reminds us, "Everyone needs information." So sooner or later, they might find it necessary to call on L.M. WARREN INC., PROGRAMMED LIBRARY & INFORMATION SERVICES.

## LETTING YOUR PC DO THE WALKING

### Dan Potter

Out in Halifax, Nova Scotia, there is a very exciting business that's into information brokerage. But before we ask "Halifax?" let us recall something which Dan Potter, its 35-year-old president and chief executive officer will quickly tell you: When it comes to computers, it doesn't matter *where* you are; what you're looking for will be there in a fraction of a second, whether you are in Toronto, New York, or (in the case of the world of oil and gas, in which he has often worked) Calgary or Houston. Novatron Information Corporation is a very impressive firm, as is its young, round-faced, moustachioed creator.

Dan Potter was born in Plympton, in Digby County,

Nova Scotia, a town of maybe 200 people in the southwest of that province, in the summer of 1951. His father was in business and politics—"an entrepreneurial guy who had lumber mills and up to two hundred and fifty people working for him"—who went broke a number of times. "I owned a dump truck when I went to university," Potter recalls, "and there's a lot of money in trucking. But it's hard to get it out." He got some out, since he earned enough to pay his tuition, working on highway construction near Yarmouth. He earned an honours arts degree in politics and philosophy from Acadia University in 1973, and then went to Dalhousie Law School, entering the bar in 1976.

Potter practised law for a few years and, during that time, along with a brother and one other person, invested in a fledgling computer firm, IAS Computers Corporation. They bought the previous owners out and renamed it, and he personally took one-third of the ownership. In 1982 he went in and ran it, calling it Novatron. "Usually venture capital has money to lose, but *I* didn't have any money to lose!" he says.

It was historically a time-sharing service bureau, selling access to computers and certain application software. It evolved into, and includes, software packages, accounting software, services for cable companies, and, eventually, electronic publishing, office automation, and systems integration. "We believe that's where the future of the computer industry is," he says, "to make all these different brands of computers work together."

The original concept was an intriguing one: Supplyline, a unique service, and their first product. It began as a data-based information system to help oil and gas people across Canada, as the offshore action heated up around Nova Scotia. But it soon became a total sourcing system, into computer-aided purchasing, and trade and economic development. "Supplyline is on the road to making us a leader in office automation acquisition, storage and retrieval, and communications," says Potter.

During 1981–82, Novatron had only about $300,000–400,000 in sales with up to ten workers, and it was not profitable when Dan Potter came in to save the ship. "Here's a company that we'll either lose or make something new to make it valuable," he said at the time. By 1983 Potter had devised a scheme to raise money for the project by setting up a tax-sheltered limited partnership, to help pay for the R & D of Supplyline. Over 100 people bought units in the partnership at $10,000 apiece, and the employees promptly broadened the markets to far beyond the original oil and gas data-basing. That year, the company had earnings of about $1 million, making it marginally profitable, with about 10% of that in profit and providing a good cash flow. By 1984 its sales were in the $1.5 million range; by 1987, close to 3 million, with some 20 employees in Halifax, Toronto, Calgary, and Victoria. Dan Potter's expectations are more than geometric: He hopes for $20 million in sales by 1990, and "I think it's achievable!" he declares.

The reason for such high hopes is simple: In the developing of the oil and gas information-sourcing system for Supplyline, "we found, in our process, a window of opportunity. The oil and gas is now marginal, since it's a conservative industry, slow to grow. We looked at the entire concept and declared, 'Hey! This sourcing thing is part of a much larger system!' "

There are now four basic sides to Novatron Information Corp. The first is that public-access data-base service, for which Potter sells usage and advertisements. It is still into oil and gas, but they are now creating an office sector, "moving away from vertical penetration to more horizontal." To clarify: All goods and services which are used and/or consumed in an office environment will be available: computers, ribbons, paper clips, security, typewriters, everything. Novatron is working with "key, larger manufacturers and distributors who see the timeliness of establishing an electronic link of distribution." It began as an electronic Yellow Pages; now it is an actual electronic system of distribution. The users pay for the system, at the rate of $60 an hour or $1 a minute, finding what they want and placing the order over the modem. Companies, in turn, pay to advertise on the system, as "profiled companies." There is now a whole electronic catalogue on Supplyline.

Second, Novatron is the only company in Canada doing a "Commercial and Industrial Vending System (CIVS)," which is an automated, paperless purchase concept. The keynote of their strategy is to "leverage electronic data interchange," which shifts data from one computer to another. "It's the wired world!" explains Dan Potter. Novatron has implemented a standard, easy way to go into all different computers. "If we think of it *only* as a Yellow Pages, it would limit us! It's *interactive and alive*! It can *do* things, whereas you *can't* order and fulfill that order through the Yellow Pages! Our system keeps track of *everything* that people ask for!"

An example: You wish to buy 50 desks for that uncrowded office of yours. You type in "OFFICE EQUIPMENT: DESKS." Twenty suppliers of desks—most of them have paid to advertise in this, don't forget—appear before your eyes. You like ten of them, so you search further, asking for requests for quotes on desks from each company. You can request a salesman, or do it all electronically. Let's say you buy from Johnson's furniture. You order over the computer, which prints out that you've requested 50 desks. The Novatron system sends out the confirmation, and you get an electronic mail acknowledgment of your order, for your records. "We are a utility, just like over the phone," says Dan Potter.

As of early 1987, Novatron has over 200,000 different products and services from nearly 90,000 companies on their system. Over 1,200 companies pay for their extradescriptive listing of what they have to offer, and hundreds—soon, they hope, to be thousands—are using the system.

The third aspect of Novatron is electronic publishing, or the Supplyline Electronic Publishing System (EPS). It's a further implementation of Supplyline technology for publishers of catalogues. "Like a directory," Potter says. Who uses it? Phone companies. Large publishers. Government agencies that need data bases of exporters, for example. But the main customers are those people who want the next generation of electronic marketing.

Example: Novatron goes to a major phone company. Bell Canada—for example—gives Novatron its computer printout for a major city's phone book. (The Toronto Yellow Pages brings in $50 million alone in revenue, we'll have you know.) Our Men in Halifax provide the phone company with an electronic printing press. Bell's sales force sells the usage on the data base, and Novatron licenses the technology to the publishers in each community. In 1985 they wrote to all 320 members of the National Yellow Pages Service Association across North America, and the interest has been growing. And by 1987, they were doing deals with Bell Canada, as planned.

"No one else is doing this on the continent!" declares

Potter. Singapore's General Telephone Directory Company contacted Novatron to ask if they could run *their own* Supplyline. "This made us think," says Potter. "If *they* want it, there must be a lot of *others* out there!"

The fourth aspect of Novatron is Supplyline for Trade and Economic Development. They hope to set up data bases of companies in each province whom the provincial governments want to help. Brochures describing this service have been sent across Canada.

"I'm the main idea man with a good team behind me," says Dan Potter. "I'm just a generalist, an avid person on new technologies. I'm innovative in making technology into the art of the possible."

Potter of Novatron insists that there are "oodles of opportunities" in the field of supplying information, recalling that to the Eskimo, there are 26 different names for snowflakes; to most of us, they are just snowflakes. Sure there are "variations" around—a number of data bases exist in Canada— "but none are packaged like we are at Novatron!" Over $1 million in modern computer equipment is in constant use in Halifax, making Novatron's Supplyline the largest sourcing and purchasing data base in the country.

"We see ourselves as Systems Integrator," says Potter. "Information technology *requires* generalists like us." (The VP of R & D has an arts degree; his Toronto man has a library science background.) "I haven't had a secretary in two years!" he exclaims. "I keep in touch with my agents in Calgary all the time, though"—over the computer, of course.

Dan Potter is married, with two children under the age of four, and he's far from a wealthy man, although he now owns 45% of Novatron. (He "dreamt up" the name one day, combining Nova—new, with Tron—for electronics.) It was only recently that he stopped checking his watch to see if it was 3:00 P.M. yet, when he could be sure that the banks wouldn't call to order him to cover an overdraft. As of January 1987, his company was listed on the Montreal Stock Exchange.

The future looks as bright as a new silicon chip, but as large as the horizon: "Once we sell the first phone company, more are sure to follow," Potter declares. "I didn't invent this phrase, but I like to use it," he says, followed by: "Profit is the reward you get for taking advantage of change."

If Dan Potter's grandiose plans are successful, then

"Novatron will grow quite quickly," he says. But he's no risk-taker, he insists, quoting from business writer Drucker, "I'm an opportunities seeker." He's *merely a businessman*, as he likes to describe himself, not necessarily the classic image of the entrepreneur. But if he is right—and the growth of the business over the past handful of years certainly suggests that he may be—then Novatron and Supplyline could be on the cutting edge of the information explosion that everyone's been talking about but not enough Canadian companies have been *doing* anything about. Kind of like the weather, which Potter trusts will be cloudless and warm for many, many years to come.

# MAKING MILLIONS AT THE SPEED OF LIGHT

### Abe Schwartz

The story sounds like turn-of-the-century America, except that it is post-World War II Canada: Man and woman survive war, eventually migrate to Toronto; father works as shoemaker in a factory while his son and three daughters go to school to better themselves. The one son becomes a computer whiz, forms his own company, and six years later sells it for $10 million—all thanks to the entrepreneurship of one Abe Schwartz, whose parents had the good fortune to survive the plans of Adolf Hitler.

Abe Schwartz was born in the summer of 1957 in Ramat Gan, Israel, coming to Canada with his parents and three sisters less than four years later. "It's a pretty sane family, which in this day and age is quite an accomplishment," he jokes. He is heavy-set, with short-cropped blond hair and a round, warm face. His father had fought in the Polish army, somehow ending up in the Russian, while his Cracow-born mother ended up in a labour camp in Nazi Germany. The two met in a DP camp in Europe, married, and moved to Israel immediately following the Israeli War of Independence. "I fought for the Poles and Russians; now for my own country," Schwartz senior had said back then. But times were hard in the Holy Land, and since there were already grandparents, two brothers, and one sister in Toronto, the Schwartz family came to Canada, where the father got that job as a shoemaker.

His only son had a paper route as a lad, but "nothing terribly entrepreneurial." Like many bright youngsters, he was "terribly bored in school," feeling that it wasn't applicable enough. (Although, he says wickedly, he found those math equations in physics interesting—the ones that asked when the pilot would crash from lack of fuel.) So he would get high 90s in physics and low 70s in math.

When he was only 14 Schwartz got a part-time job at a suburban McDonald's. He served customers, flipped burgers, and (one hopes), washing his hands after he did it, mopped floors. It was the Making of the Future Businessman. (He recently met George Cohon, the president of McDonald's of Canada, who told Schwartz, "It's nice to see *someone* who says nice things about my firm!") But why wouldn't he? "McDonald's was a hyped-up world. Even serving the hamburgers was made to be important. They really know excitement and vitality!"

More important, the company was so young 14 years ago that Schwartz was given authority right away; he handled the cash register the first day. No ego freak, he admits that the store "could have survived just fine" without him. But while there, the teenager learned all the various systems. Within six months, at the age of 15, he was a crew chief, the person in charge of each shift, and five months after that he was the store manager. Thank heavens it didn't serve liquor, or Schwartz would have been in trouble. "Age was no factor at McDonald's," he recalls with pleasure. "Knowledge and ability were all they cared about." Schwartz was making close to $7,000 a year by the time he was out of high school. (He eventually went to A.I.S.P., an alternate school in Toronto, where he did grade 11, got bored with grade 12, and ended up completing his high school degree in night school, and attended university classes part time as his career took off.)

After serving two years at McDonald's as a manager of two different stores, he got involved with the training system and "had input into it." All managers from Canada were to go to Chicago for further training, but Schwartz "never had the time or money to go."

His father was a workhorse, and the Wonder of Hamburgers claims that his "work ethic came from him. Anyone who could survive all those wars and support four kids. . . ." His mother died when he was 11.

Having just turned 17, Schwartz left McDonald's and went to work for the *Toronto Sun*, which had just been born out of the ashes of the earlier *Telegram*. He was soon a circulation manager for a territory, with distributors reporting to him. It didn't pay much, and he had taken a cut in earnings, but "it was time for me to leave McDonald's; I'd learned as much as I could there. It had stopped being fun."

After a year in the *Sun*—"It had the same kind of dynamism you get from a small firm with a mission from God"—he went to CPM Associates, a personnel consulting firm, hired as a junior recruiter. His job was to do initial interviews for the company. Abe Schwartz had just turned 18 and was entering his fifth straight year in the business world.

It was a "great experience" at the new company as well. He ended up being placed in their data-processing department. "I was the right person at the right time, since I'd hired many people at McDonald's. You needed intuitive judgment, and I specialized in interviewing data-processing people." He gained many contacts from the position and learned much about the computer industry in Canada and where it was beading. It was 1975, and it was "a *much* different industry back then. It was young," and Schwartz quickly got to know everyone in it. He also got to know banks, insurance companies, governments. There was a serious shortage of talent, and the teenager "read everything on computers and got a good understanding of how they worked."

By the age of 19 Abe Schwartz was itching to move into computer consulting, so he set out and founded Polaris Technology Corporation. "I recalled a photo of John Kennedy looking at a Polaris missile, and it had a futuristic name, which could give the company credibility." He took out a $10,000 loan from the Unity Bank, today the National, which was really a line of credit, since it was secured by receivables. Although he had been making $25,000 a year with the earlier company, he drew only $5,000 and paid back the bank within six months.

Schwartz began with three others, including a partner, Terry Graham, who was with him until he sold the company in 1983, getting one-half of the $10 million noted above. The office was on King Street near University in downtown Toronto, in a "trendy building" with fairly trendy rent: $700 a month. But since he took no salary for the first eight months, there was "sweat equity involved."

The target was to assist companies who required assistance in locating data-processing personnel, or who needed help on a consulting basis. The first big client was the Ontario Government, which was putting together a major computer system for vehicle registration. They had up to 15 people working on that program. Over 60% of their work was for the private sector, however, specializing in developing systems. At one point, Polaris was the largest private service that IBM used, and they assisted that giant in developing some of its own systems. Schwartz and his growing firm did "major work" for the Bank of Nova Scotia, Colgate-Palmolive, and the federal government itself.

The numbers tell it well. From an initial year of $125,000 in billings in 1975, the company was up to $400,000 by 1976, $1.4 million in 1978, $4.9 million in 1980, and close to $10 million in 1983, the year Schwartz and his partner sold the business for nearly the same sum. There were 100 employees of Polaris at the time of the sale, and the "average compounded growth rate was 100% per year."

What did Schwartz and Polaris have that led to such astonishing success? "Computer expertise is fragmented into specializations of its own," he says. "My skills were in project management and end-user systems. We had a lot of talent in programmers and analysts, but no one would/could manage them and have a *delivery date*. I knew my staff and what I could get out of them." It was Abe Schwartz who would be able to figure out that "this guy must finish this module in two months, or it will hold up the rest of the project." As he puts it strongly, "We met deadlines, which was the name of the game."

The end-user system is important: "So many company systems were poorly designed by technical systems which had a systematic view of the world, and it was impossible for secretaries or business people or salesmen to adequately describe to technicians what they needed. You had this gulf between technicians and everyday English! No one could translate, and the systems weren't designed for the end purpose."

Enter Abe Schwartz, End-User Extraordinaire: "I was

able to go to a VP, who would ask why he was getting 'screwed around.' And I was able to explain that he was sometimes asking for the technologically impossible." Schwartz and Polaris would work on a per diem rate, as low as $150 a day for some junior programmers, and up to $1,000 a day for experienced people. The boss himself rarely contracted himself out, since he was "the rover, the juggler. I couldn't keep all the clients happy." Recalling his burger days, Schwartz says that McDonald's had up to 100 staff per store, with up to three-quarters of them part time. "The success was how good you picked them," he says.

So Schwartz ran "a McDonald's version of consulting," which never would have been as profitable as it was had he milked the profits. He had a "corporate culture," handing out silver and gold service award pins that "they'd wear every day to work, and at the clients' offices." "Oh, there come the Polaris people with their pins" would ring across Canada. "They were *real* gold and diamonds," says Schwartz. A month would not go by without a Polaris event: baseball, football, a deli spread in the office. "It seems insidious, but it works," states the former owner.

In his first five years of operation, Abe Schwartz never lost a single employee to the competition. "We paid no better, but it was like Mary Kay or McDonald's. We were the best known for what we were doing." They had an "internal stock exchange," in which they valued the company and sold shares in it. Over 65% of the employees—75 in all—ended up buying treasury shares from the company. In the biweekly newspaper, announcing everything from baby births to parties, shares would be offered. They issued the shares at $8 each; within a month, they were at $11; nine months later, when Schwartz sold Polaris to Crowntek, they were $20 each.

The story behind the selling is fascinating. Schwartz had run into Datacrown Inc., a subsidiary of Crown Life Insurance, an $80 million company, which provided hardware services and time sharing. The company had gotten caught in the hardware squeeze as the prices of computers fell, and they were late in diversifying. He saw they were losing $4 million a year but informed them that they had "an interesting firm" on their hands. "Acquire companies to fill out your portfolio!" he told them. "You've got a great base here!" Schwartz was asked to work on a strategic plan to identify a company they could take over, and they ended up buying 10% of Polaris for $500,000.

Schwartz then recommended that the firm purchase Computer Corporation of America, out of Cambridge. One of the best-known R & D companies in the States, it had no idea of how to market its computers, and "they were mainly research; you had to beg to buy their products." He had previously sold over $1 million of their computers to the Ontario government, Becker's, and Eaton's, which had given them credibility. While Schwartz was negotiating for the American firm, Crown Life offered to purchase Polaris for $10 million, which Schwartz saw "as a good deal, and a good opportunity to get involved with a major firm," soon called Crowntek. He was offered the presidency of the international division of Crowntek, but he spent the next 12 months on planes between Toronto, Boston, New York, and Washington (since he had to get C.I.A. and Department of Defense approval for that takeover; CCA had done a lot of top-secret work. One general told Schwartz that "the Computer Corporation of America is a national asset, and we're not happy to allow a foreign country—albeit a friendly NATO ally—to buy it." Wait till the prime minister reads about this).

On May 23, 1984, Schwartz closed the purchase for $40 million, having gotten the price down from $42½ million in the final week of negotiations.

"People thought that I was crazy to turn down the jobs offered to me by Crowntek," says Schwartz, who now does special assignments for the biggie that bought him out. But he wanted to work on a Computer Museum, named Exploracom. But what need did he have for jobs with compensation plans of $250,000? Here was immortality. "When I negotiated with the Americans, it grew on me that we were better in Canada than we'd been given credit for; we didn't sell ourselves enough." (Sounds familiar.) "The museum is a brilliant concept," he says, adding with a grin, *"he modestly said."*

It *was*, until the Ontario government pulled the plug, in early 1987. Schwartz put hundreds of thousands of dollars of his own money into the project, and he still hopes to build one, perhaps in the U.S.

Schwartz has been accused of being a workaholic, and "I deny it, which means that I am." When he started Polaris, he would often not go home when he finished at 2:00 A.M., but would just collapse on the couch at the office, to be ready for that 8:00 A.M. breakfast meeting. The free time he has now is spent fighting on behalf of the mentally retarded. When a group home was to be placed on his street in suburban Mississauga, 150 were against it and Schwartz was the only one for it. "I thought they'd burn a cross on my lawn!" He occasionally speaks on behalf of that group, when not visiting every theater he can.

"You've got to be blessed with some intelligence," says Abe Schwartz, formerly of McDonald's and Polaris. "You've got to be willing to work hard, to have an open mind, and be willing to learn. Willing to go upstream and against the flow. You've got to have the guts to be different. Yet I know people with all those attributes who are still working in pretty dreary environments. So you've got to be in the right place at the right time."

Schwartz denies that he has ever been money-motivated. "I'm money-*conscious*," he admits, since "that's what society keeps score on." He gave "a fair bit" of his $5 million windfall to members of his family, and put the rest away into safe investments, but "it hasn't changed my life-style that much." And the future certainly won't lie within the giant Crowntek firm which bought his own creation. "It's probable that I'll get involved in a new business sometime in 1987," he says. "It will be in the entrepreneurial vein. A lot of people know I get things done, and they have faith in what I do."

# SOME FINAL WORDS

We are taught:
Who is to be considered truly wealthy?
He who derives peace of mind from his wealth.
He who has a hundred vineyards, a hundred fields,
and a hundred workers working in them.

THE TALMUD

The above quotation often came to mind as I was interviewing these remarkable men and women across Canada over the past number of years. For isn't that precisely what the goals of business *should* be? To gain peace of mind for the businessperson, and, one hopes, to create jobs for many others. The 80 men and women profiled in the preceding pages have often, but not always, gained peace of mind. In many cases, it took years of hard work, risk, near-disaster, low pay, and often shaken confidence. But all of them have created employment for their fellow countrymen. Some, for as few as a half dozen; many, for hundreds; a handful, for a thousand and more. The fact that less than seven dozen souls could create over 10,000 jobs is, to me, one of the most admirable things about them, and—dare we write that often maligned word?—about capitalism.

You have read about the lives, ideas, careers, frustrations, hopes, and (often glorious) successes of 80 of your fellow citizens. They come from all ten provinces, from every walk of life, from educational backgrounds that range from grade school dropouts to M.B.A.'s and doctorates. But all of them had a certain spark that allowed them—no, even forced them—to create a business, even an empire.

One of the entrepreneurs in this book gave me an interesting analogy: "If I drove a Mercedes through the worst slum anywhere in the States," he told me, "the youth there would look at the car and say, 'Hey—*I* want to have a car like that!' And if I were to drive the same car through any part of Canada, the youth would say, 'Who does that bastard think he is?' "

Are we Canadians really that petty? Are we that envious that we cannot rejoice in the successes of the people around us? There is little question that the Giant to the South seems to ooze with Iacoccas and jump with Jobs. But then, a Scot named Bell came to Canada to work on his telephone, and if Edison's father—and Walt Disney's—had *not* chosen to move down to the United States, would not we Canadians be claiming the light bulb and Donald Duck as our own?

No, intelligence, tenacity, brightness, creative thinking, hardly have to stop abruptly at the 49th parallel, as though the frost would kill them. And, as I think this book clearly shows, those attributes have *not*.

When I was an academic and teacher, I never fully understood, much less appreciated, the kind of people who would choose to start their own businesses. After speaking with them and meeting with them over the past few years, I now fully realize just how driven and inspired they are. And, unlike writers like myself, *they* create jobs for others, allowing thousands of their fellow Canadians to share a bit of the dream of a decent life in this very decent country of ours. I trust that all of the entrepreneurial Canadians in this book derive as much peace of mind from *their* wealth, success, and job-creation as *I* have gained insight from studying their lives and businesses.

# INDEX

## About the Author

**ALLAN GOULD** is a frequent contributor to *The Financial Post*, *Successful Executive*, *Chatelaine*, *Toronto Life*, *Homemaker's*, *TV Guide*, *Canadian Living Magazine*, *en Route*, *CBC Radio Guide*, and other publications. Among his books are *The Toronto Book*, *The Top Secret Tory Handbook*, *The Unorthodox Book of Jewish Records and Lists*, *Air Fare*, and *Letters I've been Meaning to Write*.